WORLD® AIR POWER

JOURNAL

Aerospace Publishing Ltd

AIRtime Publishing Inc.

The *World Air Power Journal* web site can be found at:

http://www.airpower.co.uk

Published quarterly by
Aerospace Publishing Ltd
179 Dalling Road
London W6 0ES
UK

Copyright © Aerospace Publishing Ltd
Cutaway drawings copyright
© Mike Badrocke/Aviagraphica

ISSN 0959-7050
Aerospace ISBN   1-86184-035-7
                          (softback)
                          1-86184-036-5
                          (hardback)
Airtime ISBN   1-880588-07-2
                          (hardback)

Published under licence in USA and
Canada by AIRtime Publishing Inc.,
USA

Editorial Offices:
WORLD AIR POWER JOURNAL
Aerospace Publishing Ltd
3A Brackenbury Road
London   W6 0BE   UK
          E-mail: info@aerospacepbl.co.uk

Publisher: Stan Morse
Managing Editor: David Donald
          E-mail: dave@aerospacepbl.co.uk

Editor: Robert Hewson

Deputy Editor: Dave Willis
          E-mail: willis@aerospacepbl.co.uk

Sub Editor: Karen Leverington

Editorial Assistant: Tim Senior

Origination by Universal Graphics
Printed in Italy by Officine Grafiche
          de Agostini

Correspondents:
General military: Jon Lake
USA Washington: Robert F. Dorr
USA Southwest: Randy Jolly
Europe: John Fricker
Russia/CIS: Yefim Gordon
Asia: Pushpindar Singh
Canada: Jeff Rankin-Lowe
Argentina: Jorge Núñez Padin
Chile: Patrick Laureau

The author would like to note that this expanded account of
the F-22's history draws on two recently published sources:
'F-22 Design Evolution' by Eric Hehs, published in
Lockheed Martin's *Code One* magazine in April and October
1998; and *F-22 Raptor – Origins of the 21st Century Air
Dominance Fighter* by David C. Aronstein, Michael L.
Hirschberg and Albert C. Piccirillo (AIAA, 1999).
John Haire, Chief PAO, AFFTC.

For their help with the Golden State Guard feature the
author would like to thank MGENs Tandy Bozeman, Bob
Barrow, Bob Brandt, Colonels Alan Heers, Bob Nelan, Putt
Richards, Tommy Williams, Lt Cols Randy Ball, Ed Bellion,
Doug Hart, Chuck Manley, LTCs Jim Berdan, Kent During,
Brad Jones, Thomas Lasser, Majors Carl Allen, Paul Bryant,
Jamie Goodpaster, Gary Wentz, Captain Diane McKinzy,
CW4 Thierry Richards, TSGT Gary Howard, SGT Andy
Seybold, Airman Andrew Hughan, and the many other
Guard members who contributed

The author acknowledges the essential assistance of the
following in the Australian Air Power Analysis: Sgt
Bernadette Wheeler, Sgt Mark McIntyre, Deanna Ialacci,
HQ Air Command; Phil Smith, DPAO Brisbane; Sqn Ldr
Mark Quilligan, DPAO Canberra; Air Cdre Peter Growder,
Commander Strike & Reconnaissance Group; Group
Captain Geoff Shepherd OC 82 Wing; Flt Lt Dave Riddel,
6 Sqn; Captain Brendan Dwyer, 162 Sqn; Major Nick
Sanders, 1 Avn Regt; Capt Ed Smeaton, 2IC TASS, 5 Avn
Regt; Captain Brian Rowe, DNASPO; Commander Paul
Folkes, CO HS816; Lt Justin Hardiman, HS816; The Late
Lieutenant Huw Paffard, HS817; Mr Nick Mudge, Kaman
Aerospace Australia; Mr Ian White, Raytheon Australia;
Major Rob Barnes, Army PR Townsville; Sqn Ldr Lenn
Bayliss, 23 Sqn Amberley; Sqn Ldr Jo Elkington, Admin
Officer No.92 Wing; Wing Commander Murray Nielson,
CO 2 Sqn RNZAF and Group Captain Bill Spears,
Commander ARDU.

For their contributions to the CH-47 feature: Patrick Allen,
Yoshitomo Aoki, David F. Brown, Leo Burnett, Jon Chuck,
Steve Harding, Craig Kaston, Nigel Pittaway, Tom Ring,
David Shirlaw, Bill Upton, Robert S. Wadey. A special
thanks to Jack Satterfield at Boeing Helicopter in
Philadelphia.

**World Air Power Journal is a
registered trademark in the
United States of America of
AIRtime Publishing Inc.**

**World Air Power Journal is
published quarterly and is
available by subscription and
from many fine book and hobby
stores.**

**SUBSCRIPTION AND BACK
NUMBERS:**

**UK and World (except USA and
Canada) write to:**
Aerospace Publishing Ltd
FREEPOST
PO Box 2822
London
W6 0BR
UK

**(No stamp required if posted in
the UK)**

USA and Canada, write to:
AIRtime Publishing Inc.
**Subscription Dept
10 Bay Street
Westport
CT 06880, USA
(203) 838-7979
Toll-free order number in USA:
1 800 359-3003**

**Prevailing subscription rates are
as follows:
Softbound edition for 1 year:
          $59.95
Softbound edition for 2 years:
          $112.00
Softbound back numbers
(subject to availability) are
$16.00 each, plus shipping and
handling. All rates are for
delivery within mainland USA,
Alaska and Hawaii. Canadian
and overseas prices available
upon request. American Express,
Discover Card, MasterCard and
Visa accepted. When ordering
please include card number,
expiration date and signature.**

U.S. Publisher:
          Mel Williams
Subscriptions Director:
          Linda DeAngelis
**Charter Member Services
Manager:**
          Janie Munroe
Retail Sales Director: Jill Brooks
Shipping Manager: E. Rex Anku

WORLD AIR POWER ®

AIR POWER

J O U R N A L

CONTENTS

Volume 38   Autumn/Fall 1999

Military Aviation Review

Europe

AUSTRIA:

Draken replacement plans

To help extend the operating lives of the OeLk's 24 Saab 35Oe Draken fighters until their planned replacement from 2005, five Austrian pilots and four fighter-controllers are being sent to Sweden for 12 month's training with the SAF in the current year, followed by a second similar batch in 2000. The pilots will each fly 100 hours on the Saab JA 37 Viggen interceptors of F 21 from Lulea, to gain experience with advanced airborne weapons systems in a sophisticated air defence environment.

The Saab/BAe JAS 39 is one of five contenders for the OeLk requirement for at least 30 new combat aircraft to replace its Drakens, but Austria has stressed that the training arrangements in Sweden do not necessarily indicate any Gripen preference.

BELGIUM:

More F-16 upgrades

Deliveries will start in March 2002 of 18 more F-16A/B mid-life upgrade (MLU) kits costing $46 million, recently ordered from Lockheed Martin for a further increase in FAeB Fighting Falcon operating totals. Of the 133 Block 10/15 F-16s remaining from 160 it procured from European

licensed production, Belgium originally committed only 48 for upgrades in the initial five-nation $1.26 billion MLU programme launched in 1991. This programme also included 61 Danish, 136 Dutch and 56 F-16A/Bs receiving similar MLU upgrades to Block 20 standards.

Another 24 options were then taken up by Belgium, and its new order increased FAeB MLU commitments to 90 F-16s, including 18 as reserves, for completion by SABCA by June 2003. No. 349 Squadron is currently receiving its first dozen MLU F-16s at Kleine Brogel, and will begin operations with some of the 72 Raytheon AIM-120 AMRAAMs ordered in 1996, plus limited procurement of Raytheon AGM-65 Maverick ASMs. New short-range AAMs, and accompanying helmet-mounted sights, are also planned, with selection from the MATRA/BAeD ASRAAM, BGT Iris-T and Raytheon AIM-9X.

About 30 surplus FAeB F-16s, which have been in storage at Weelde for some time, are being offered for sale on the international market. Belgium's F-16s are planned for replacement from around 2013 with new multi-role combat aircraft, for which a budget of some BFr101 billion ($2.68 billion) must be allocated by 2020.

CROATIA:

MiG-21 upgrade contract

Contrary to earlier reports, the Croatian air force (Hrvatsko Ratno Zrakoplovstvo – HRZ) is apparently

planning a major upgrade for virtually all its 24 MiG-21bis fighters and four MiG-21UM two-seat combat trainers. Although a contract worth $100 million or more was signed on 15 February for this programme, with Elbit as prime contractor, this will be on a joint basis with the Lahav Division of Israel Aircraft Industries – its previous long-term rival in the 'Fishbed' upgrade market. Features of both IAI's MiG-21-2000 for Cambodia and Elbit's Romanian Lancer programmes are therefore expected to be combined for joint modernisation of the Croatian 'Fishbeds'. Among these are likely to be Elta EL/M-2032 fire-control radar, El-Op head-up and twin multi-function liquid-crystal colour cockpit displays, HOTAS, new computerised nav/attack systems, DASH helmet-mounted sight, integrated electronic warfare suite, and other NATO-compatible digital equipment, for use with Rafael Python 4 AAMs and precision-guided ground-attack weapons. Kit production for installation in Croatia by the ZTZ factory in Zagreb will follow prototype single- and two-seat modifications in Israel in the coming year.

DENMARK:

Defence economy plans

Major funding cuts in the proposed four-year defence plan, which will reduce annual military spending from DKr17.336 billion ($2.5 billion) in 2000 to DKr16.292 billion ($2.35 billion) by 2003, will impose substantial economies on the Danish armed forces. For the Royal Danish Air Force (KDF), the principal loss will be its enforced withdrawal as an informed customer in the US Joint Strike Fighter programme. Personnel totals would also drop from 14,800 to 11,600, plus some air base closures, and disbandment or amalgamation of several combat squadrons. Recent KDF procurement has included an unspecified number of LANTIRN systems ordered from Lockheed Martin Electronics & Missiles, to achieve a precision-guided munition delivery capability. This forms part of the RDAF's F-16 rotational mid-life upgrade programme, involving 61 GD F-16A/Bs currently being worked on at the Aalborg air base depot. Denmark is the 12th nation to order the LANTIRN system, which comprises discrete all-weather Pathfinder navigation and Sharpshooter targeting pods. Taiwan was another recent customer for 20 pairs, costing $106.2 million.

FRANCE:

Rafale production order

A go-ahead for full-scale Rafale multi-role fighter production was finally received by Dassault in January 1999, with long-discussed multi-year orders for 28 more costing FFr10.3 billion ($1.82 billion), plus options for another 20 for FFr5.5 billion. The new contract followed earlier orders for 13

Rafales, comprising three for the French air force (AA), and 10 for the Aéronavale and, according to Defence Minister Alain Richard, will include 14 AA two-seat Rafale Bs and seven single-seat Cs, plus seven naval single-seat Rafale Ms.

Having made its initial flight at Bordeaux-Merignac in November 1998, the first production Rafale B1 two-seater was transferred to the air force in early December. All 13 of the initial batch will be completed by October 2003. Follow-on deliveries will start in February 2004, with the 28th completed in January 2006. The 20 options comprise seven Rafale Bs and five Cs for the AA, plus eight naval Rafale Ms, for delivery by February 2007, increasing total orders to 61.

Hawkeye delivery begins

The Aéronavale was due to form Flottille 4F as its first AEW unit in January 1999, at Lann-Bihoué, following delivery on 18 December 1998 of the first of three Northrop Grumman E-2C Hawkeye carrierborne airborne early-warning aircraft ordered from a mid-1995 Fr5.9 billion ($1 billion) FMS contract. Equipped with Lockheed Martin's new AN/APS-145 surveillance radar, the first two French Group II E-2Cs will embark on the new 40,000-tonne carrier *Charles de Gaulle* when it enters service in 2000. Delivery of the Aéronavale's recently-funded third E-2C is not scheduled until 2003, and a fourth Hawkeye is still on option.

Circulatory problems with the cooling water of its nuclear powerplants curtailed initial sea trials of the *Charles de Gaulle* from Brest after only 48 hours in late January, without reaching its maximum design speed of 27 kt (50 km/h). These problems were not regarded as serious, but airfield tests of the first Aéronavale E-2C indicated that the new carrier's angled flight-deck required lengthening by about 4 m (13 ft) for Hawkeye operation. This was mainly a question of obtaining more deck-manoeuvring space rather than take-off or landing area requirements, involving no hull extension.

Army helicopter strength

Some 484 helicopters and 10 fixed-wing aircraft, manned by 7,000 personnel, are currently operated by French Army Aviation (Aviation Légère de l'Armée de Terre – ALAT), according to a recent Aérospatiale survey. They comprise 61 first-generation Sud Alouette II and III, 288 later SA 341/2 Gazelle, 96 SA 330 Puma, 17 AS 550 Fennec and 22 AS 532 Cougar helicopters. Three single-turboprop SOCATA TBM700s and five Pilatus PC-6/B2 Turbo Porters, plus two Cessna Caravan II light turboprop twins, comprise the fixed-wing inventory. ALAT's tri-service training centres at Cannes-des-Maures and Dax operate 117 of the service's helicopters.

Left: Four of Austria's SA 316B Alouette IIIs have received GPS, Nitesun searchlight and FLIR turret to facilitate border patrol missions. The quartet operates from a new helicopter facility at Punitz.

Below: All of Austria's OH-58Bs have received the taller 'bush' skids so that they can also carry FLIR and Nitesun. Three operate from another new site at Allentsteig. The AB 206As on strength retain standard-height skids.

GERMANY:

Helicopter upgrades

A $25 million German Federal Office for Defence Technology & Procurement Agency (BWB) order, announced by UK Marconi Avionics in February for 16 Seaspray 3000 360° surveillance pulse-compression radars, was part of a $132 million mid-1998 GKN Westland and Eurocopter contract to upgrade 17 German navy Sea Lynx Mk 88 ASW helicopters to Super Lynx Mk 88A standards. Other system modifications include Racal Doppler 91 navigation radar, Rockwell Collins GPS, and MATRA/BAeD Sea Skua anti-ship missile capability to match similar equipment in seven new-build Super Lynx Mk 88As ordered by Germany in late 1995, and due for delivery to Marineflieger Geschwader 3 (MFG 3) at Nordholz later in 1999. Following trial-installation modifications to a German Navy Lynx, GKN Westland is producing 16 Mk 88A upgrade kits, including new fuselages and reverse-direction tail rotors, for incorporation by Eurocopter Deutschland at its Donauworth facility in Bavaria.

This unit is also involved in upgrading 20 Sikorsky CH-53G medium-lift helicopters from 96 operated by German Army Aviation (Heeresflieger), with special equipment for participation in UN peacekeeping roles. Main changes include adding two 1,080-Imp gal (4910-litre) auxiliary fuel tanks on fuselage outriggers, for a 1797-km (970-nm) maximum range, NVG-compatible cockpit lighting, and a new electronics warfare suite with two threat-warning displays, plus an advanced digital chaff/flare dispensing system. DASA's Dornier division has also received a BWB order for 20 of its DKG 3 digital colour map displays for Germany's CH-53s operating with the UN SFOR units in Bosnia. Delivery of the first upgraded German CH-53GS is planned in June, with the last following by late 2001.

GREECE:

HAF selects Typhoon

First serious prospects for Eurofighter export sales emerged in February from plans announced by Greek Defence Minister Akis Tsochadzopoulos to buy 60-80 Typhoons for the HAF's next-generation fighter requirements. He said that the HAF would have to wait until 2005 for its first Typhoons, for which Greece is apparently seeking further industrial participation. Some 1,200 underwing fuel tanks are already being produced for Eurofighter from a DASA contract by Hellenic Aerospace Industries, which is seeking a wider role in Typhoon production.

Detailed negotiations through DASA for the proposed Greek Typhoon programme, which has an estimated value of some $3.5 billion, were expected to follow almost immediately. Procurement seems likely to involve at least two batches, however, since only $1.5 billion will apparently be available for initial contracts. Funding is also being sought to place orders for 15-20 each attrition replacement Dassault Mirage 2000EGs and Lockheed Martin Block 50 Plus F-16C/Ds in the coming year.

CL-415s delivered

As a long-term operator of 15 twin piston-engined Canadair CL-215 water-bombing and SAR amphibians, the Hellenic air force is now receiving 10 CL-415GR turboprop versions, with options for another five, from a recent $250 million Greek government order to Bombardier Aerospace. Powered by Pratt & Whitney Canada PW 123AF turboprops, the first CL-415s began arriving in Greece earlier in 1999, with deliveries due for completion in early 2001.

HUNGARY:

C-130K proposal

Negotiations were reported earlier in 1999 by the Hungarian government with Lockheed Martin to acquire up to six ex-RAF C-130K Hercules, taken back by the US company in part exchange for the 25 new C-130Js now being delivered. Although well-used, the former RAF C-130H-based Hercules have undergone previous upgrades, and have been maintained in pristine condition, as well as incorporating NATO-compliant avionics. Until late 1998, LMAS had a 50 per cent share in the joint-venture Aeroplex of Central Europe maintenance, repair and overhaul organisation, then sold back to the Malev state airline to facilitate Hungarian privatisation plans.

Belgian colours – the FAB/BLu is experimenting with a high-visibility red/white colour scheme for its SF.260M primary trainers (above), intended to replace the current three-tone camouflage. Meanwhile, the training aircraft of 1 Wing at Beauvechain are all receiving a wolf's head on the fin – the badge of the parent wing. It is seen below on an Alpha Jet of 11 Sm/Esc.

ITALY:

Growing JSF interest

Having received in late 1997 its 16th and final radar-equipped Boeing/MDC AV-8B Harrier II Plus from assembly by Alenia in Turin, and two TAV-8B two-seat combat trainers, with purchase of four more single-seaters planned, the Italian navy is already considering the question of their eventual replacement. This is not planned before about 2015, and will coincide with the estimated retirement date of Italy's reduced fleet of 96 AMXs, from 136 originally planned.

Italian naval requirements for up to 30 STOVL versions of the JSF, being developed for the US Marine Corps, plus possible AMX successors from the USAF's CTOL variant, could increase Italian needs to 120 or more new combat aircraft in the JSF category. Despite defence budget limitations, the Italian government is proposing additional funding to expand its Future Interested Customer status in the JSF programme, for which it paid $10 million to the US in April 1998, joining such countries as Australia and Canada in receiving data and information on the concept-definition stage.

LITHUANIA:

Jet aircraft expansion

Four Aero L-39C advanced jet trainers operated by the Lithuanian air force from Siauliai-Zokniai were supplemented late in 1998 by two refurbished L-39ZA versions, with provision for underwing and ventral-fuselage armament. Costing only $2 million, they were delivered by Aero

On 31 December 1998 the Statní Letecky Utvar (SLU – Czech government air unit) was disbanded, handing its aircraft over to the air force's 6. základna Dopravního Letectva (6.zDL) at Prague-Kbely. Aircraft consisted of one Tu-154M, one CL-601 Challenger (above), one Let 410-UVP-E and two Yak-40s (above). The aircraft have all received military serials in the process.

Military Aviation Review

Centre d'Essais en Vol

Renowned for its famous hangars, the CEV facility at Bretigny will close soon. Budgetary pressure, a slowing down of flying activity, crowded airspace and a growing urban neighbourhood have all contributed to the decision. As major programmes such as Mirage 2000D, Rafale, Tigre and NH 90 have matured, test requirements have fallen, with the result that CEV flying hours have dropped 30 per cent since 1996, to 5,100 hours in 1998. The overall CEV fleet is to drop from 64 to 54 aircraft, with the number of liaison aircraft slashed. Sixteen of Bretigny's aircraft will go to Cazaux, where fixed-wing, optronic and EW testing will take place, while 11 will go to Istres to join the rotary-wing and navigation systems fleet. **Frederic Lert**

Left: This Mystère 20 is used to test a new version of the Thomson-CSF Antilope radar which equips the Mirage 2000D and 2000N. The experimental version adds a synthetic aperture radar capability to enhance the penetration effectiveness of the Mirage. Shown above is the cockpit, with a replica of the 2000D cockpit in the right-hand seat.

Above: This Transall C-160 is at Bretigny to test the RAMSES radar on behalf of ONERA, the government agency for aerodynamic studies. RAMSES is a synthetic aperture radar which is said to be capable of 'seeing' between 10 to 20 m (33 to 66 ft) below ground level. The liaison fleet includes the Wassmer (CERVA) Ce.43 Guepard (below left) and Robin HR.100-250 (below right). Several of these aircraft will be retired upon the reduction of CEV aircraft numbers.

This Puma is fitted with the Thomson-CSF/GEC Marconi CLARA (Compact LAser RAdar) pod and an internal work station. The pod combines a LIDAR and video camera which provide a superimposed image for the detection of obstacles such as power lines. Other modes available include terrain profiling and the identification of targets according to their speed. The pod weighs 350 kg (770 lb).

Vodochody from the Czech Republic, and comprise the first combat equipment for No. 21 Fighter Squadron of the Lithuanian Military Air Forces (Karines Oro Pajegos – KOP).

MACEDONIA:

F-5 transfers expected

Turkish military assistance for the Macedonian army air element (Armija Republika Macedonija – ARM), which includes the transfer of 20 surplus THK Northrop F-5A/B fighter-bombers planned in the current year, has been extended to the provision of training facilities in Turkey. They include pilot training on THK Cessna T-37s and Northrop T-38s at Cigli-Izmir, since ARM equipment has hitherto been restricted to four Zlin 242 lightplanes and a half-dozen Mil Mi-8/17 general-purpose helicopters.

NETHERLANDS:

Air unit reductions

Military budget reductions of about $120-190 million per year from FY 1998 onwards, to DFl13.7 billion ($4.36 billion) in the current year, resulted in extensive restructuring plans

for the armed forces. Accompanying KLu cut-backs will include retirement of the 18 F-16A/Bs of No. 306 Squadron at Volkel, as a dedicated reconnaissance unit, and its disbandment, followed by distribution of its current roles.

Three of the navy's 13 Lockheed P-3C-II Orions will also be withdrawn and only seven of the remainder will be funded to participate in the planned Capability Upgrade Programme. Further maritime patrol economies will include retirement of both Fokker F27-200MPAs from No. 336 Squadron, and its disbandment. Scaled-down replacement is also planned at the turn of the century of the 27 MBB BO 105CBs and nine Alouette IIIs of Nos 299 and 300 Squadrons.

On the plus side, appropriations of up to $6 billion are being sought to fund replacement of 136 upgraded Block 20 F-16A/B MLUs (probably now reduced to 120), by a similar number of combat aircraft in the Joint Strike Fighter-class between 2010 and 2015.

NORWAY:

Combat aircraft urgency

Responses to requests for proposals issued by the Norwegian government

in early February to Eurofighter, via DASA, and Lockheed Martin for the Typhoon and Block 50N F-16C/D, as finalists for the RNoAF's $1.4 billion requirement for 20 new combat aircraft, plus options on 10 more, were due by 1 June. Some urgency is now attached to the RNoAF's new combat aircraft requirements, since its seven remaining F-5As and eight F-5Bs equipping No. 336 Squadron at Rygge are to be retired at an early date.

Planned new combat aircraft selection by the year-end, followed by contract signature in 2000, and delivery requirements between 2003-2006, may present problems for both contractors in Norway. Eurofighter production is still in its early stages, as is Block 50N F-16 development, while Norwegian requirements for 100 per cent industrial offsets from its contract represent a daunting prospect.

POLAND:

NATO-compatibility plans

While government funding to lease new Western combat aircraft is still being sought, Polish membership of NATO from March 1999, with the Czechs and Hungarians, accelerated requirements for its existing fighters to achieve alliance equipment compatibil-

ity standards. For the 22 PWL MiG-29 'Fulcrum' air defence fighters, these are being met by a contract placed with DaimlerChrysler Aerospace (DASA) in February. Initially for only four aircraft, the Polish 'Fulcrum' upgrade also involves Russia's VPK MiG MAPO through the joint MiG Aircraft Product Support (MAPS) group, and is expected to have an eventual value of up to $58 million.

Poland's MiG-29 communications, navigation and IFF equipment changes are expected to be similar to those made by MAPS to the 23 Luftwaffe 'Fulcrums', to reach NATO operating interface standards. Selected equipment, probably including locally-produced SC-10 Suprasi IFF systems, will be installed by year-end from MAPS kits at the WZL2 air force depot in Bydgoszcz, under DASA supervision. Similar upgrades and logistic support are also being offered by MAPS to other European MiG-29 operators.

RUSSIA:

New helicopter flight-development programmes

A successful first flight of the prototype 6.5-tonne Kamov Ka-60 Dauphin lookalike utility helicopter (s/n 601) was finally made from the group's

Lyubertsy factory airfield in Moscow on 24 December, after protracted development over some six years because of funding problems. Initially intended for Russian air force (VVS) use, the Ka-60 carries up to 16 passengers or 2 tonnes (4,409 lb) of cargo on two 970-kW (1,300-shp) RKBM/ Rybinsk RD-600 turboshafts.

Similarly long-awaited flight trials officially started on 4 March at Mil Moscow's Planki Helicopter Plant of Russia's upgraded Mil Mi-24M attack helicopter, which employs the new Mi-28's five-bladed composite main rotor and narrow X-type tail rotor. Under development since 1994, the Mi-24M also incorporates Mi-28 gearbox and transmission components, to cope with power increases from the Klimov TV3-117VR turboshafts emergency ratings of up to 2238 kW (3,000 shp).

SWITZERLAND:

Cougar follow-up order

A FFr1 billion ($177 million) Swiss Air Force and Anti-Aircraft Command (SAFAAC) order for 12 AS 532UL Cougar transport helicopters was confirmed with Eurocopter in December 1998, from funding first allocated in the 1998 defence budget. All but the first two Cougars will be co-produced by the Swiss Aeronautics & Systems Enterprise at Emmen, between mid-2000 and 2002. They will supplement three similar long-fuselage SAFAAC AS 332M1 Super Pumas delivered in mid-1987, and 12 more ordered in 1990, for a wide range of tactical and cargo transport, SAR and medical evacuation roles, with new digital avionics.

TURKEY:

First upgraded F-4E flies

Flight trials began on 11 February at IAI's Lahav facility of the first of two prototype MDC F-4Es upgraded by Israel Aircraft Industries to Phantom 2000 standards from a $632.5 million 1996 Turkish air force (THK) contract, followed by its formal acceptance on 1 March. Similar upgrades of a further 24 THK F-4s are being continued by IAI, in conjunction with Elbit, Elta and other Israeli companies, which are also supplying 28 kits for local installation in other Turkish Phantoms from 165 or so in current service.

Their incorporation is expected at the THK's First Air Maintenance Factory at Eskesehir air base, plus programmed depot maintenance (PDM) and a structural life extension programme (SLEP), to provide another 20 years of airframe life from initial deliveries in February 2000. New avionics include Elta EL/M 2032 multi-mode fire-control radar, El Op wide-angle head-up display, multi-function cockpit displays, INS/GPS, Astronautics air data computer, an Elisra SPS-1000 defensive EW suite, and other digital systems. Associated armament is planned to include 46 Rafael AGM-142 Popeye heavy air-to-surface missiles.

F-16 production extended

A follow-on THK contract for a further 32 Fighting Falcons was expected earlier in 1999, to extend production in Turkey by Tusas Aerospace Industries of 232 Block 30 and 40 Lockheed Martin F-16C/Ds. With an estimated package cost of around $750 million, the follow-on batch will be Block 50 F-16s, optimised for the SEAD role and integrated with Raytheon/TI AGM-88 HARMs.

More Black Hawks ordered

A $560 million Turkish government contract signed in February with Sikorsky for a further 50 US-built S-70s was a reversal of its earlier cancellation of planned orders for 45 Black Hawk transport and assault helicopters from local co-production. Earlier US Export-Import Bank programme funding was available to ensure immediate deliveries of the follow-on S-70s, for completion in 2001. Eight Sikorsky Seahawks are also awaited from 2000 by the Turkish navy, but Eurocopter was expected to receive a $100 million follow-up order for another eight locally-assembled AS 532 Cougar Mk 1s for the Jandarma.

Early selection is also expected to meet Turkey's $4 billion programme for 145 new attack helicopters, for which contestants effectively have been narrowed to the Bell Textron AH-1Z King Cobra, Boeing/MDH AH-64D Longbow Apache, and Kamov Ka-52 with Israeli mission system avionics.

In February, the Turkish army also invited proposals for its requirement for eight medium-lift helicopters, with payloads of up to 12.7 tonnes (28,000 lb), within a 23-tonne (50,706-lb) maximum take-off weight. Submissions were expected for the Boeing CH-47SD and Sikorsky CH-53E, as well as the Mil Mi-26, despite the Russian helicopter being over twice the required size.

AWACS decision expected

Greek selection in December 1998 of the EMB-145-based FSR890 Erieye AWACS has stimulated a parallel Turkish air force (THK) requirement for four airborne early-warning and control aircraft and ground-based equipment, for which short-listing of two candidates was expected by mid-1999 for which four US-led industrial teams have been competing. In addition to its AWACS 767, developed and recently delivered to Japan, Boeing is bidding an alternative option with similar radar and mission systems in a Boeing 737. Lockheed Martin is proposing a new version of its C-130J-30 transport with a dorsal radome installation and internal avionics based on the USN E-2C Hawkeye, which is

Above: On 5 March 1999 the KLu's 323 Squadron celebrated its 50th anniversary. The squadron's emblem – Diana the Huntress – was displayed in somewhat less than traditional style on the fin of J-248. 323 Squadron is the TACTESS (Tactical Training Evaluation and Standardisation Squadron).

Below: This F-16B of the Volkel Testgroep carries a Per Udsen MRP (Modular Reconnaissance Pod) under its belly.

also being offered to Turkey in a separate bid by Northrop Grumman.

Raytheon and Israel Aircraft Industries have also teamed together to propose Elta's Phalcon conformal electronically-scanned phased-array surveillance radar and associated avionics installed in an Airbus A310. Final selection is planned by the end of 1999, for initial deliveries from around 2003.

UNITED KINGDOM:

Eurofighter deployment

Coningsby will be the first and main RAF station to take delivery of the Eurofighter, with the planned establishment of an Operational Evaluation Unit, an Operational Conversion Unit, and two front-line squadrons from 2002. Revealing plans at Warton in March for the RAF's initial deployment of its 232 EF 2000s, including 40 two-seat combat trainer versions, scheduled for procurement, Air Commodore Rick Peacock-Edwards, director of the MoD's Eurofighter Programme Assurance Group, said that the first dozen pilots would train with BAe's Military Aircraft Division, to man the OEU and OCU at Coningsby.

Pilot conversion is due to begin there in 2004, and re-equipment is then expected of Nos 5 and 29 Squadrons from 12 Tornado F.Mk 3 air-defence fighters each at the same base from deliveries of up to 20 Eurofighters per year, to achieve initial operational capability by 2005. Tornado F.Mk 3 replacement is then scheduled between 2006-2008 in Nos 11 and 25 Squadrons at RAF Leeming, and in Nos 43 and 111 Squadrons, as the remaining F.Mk 3 air-defence units to receive up to 16 Eurofighters each, at Leuchars from 2008-2010.

Subsequent RAF Eurofighter deliveries will be of full multi-role versions, to re-equip Britain's strike and close-support force of Jaguars, Harriers and Tornados.

Nimrod MRA.Mk 4 cost and time-scale problems

In addition to a small cost increase, the planned service entry date of the RAF's upgraded BAe Nimrod MRA.Mk 4 maritime reconnaissance aircraft has slipped by nearly two years, according to Defence Under Secretary John Spellar. Answering a Parliamentary question in March, he said that the December 1996 contract placed with British Aerospace, as prime contractor, to rebuild 21 Nimrods specified an initial service date by April 2003. Resource and technical difficulties with the early phase of the programme at BAe meant that the company does not now estimate RAF service entry before early 2005, although the precise slippage was still being negotiated with the MoD.

Current MRA.Mk 4 procurement costs of £2.4 billion at September 1998 price levels, quoted by Spellar, were said to represent an increase of 0.5 per cent over original estimates for the Nimrod rebuild programme. Although Spellar gave no further details, BAe's successful Nimrod bid was based on retaining a major part of

On 1 May 1999 RAF Lossiemouth celebrated its 60th anniversary. Current residents are two front-line Tornado squadrons (Nos 12 and 617), the NTOCU Tornado training unit (No. 15(R) Squadron) and No. 16(R) Squadron, the Jaguar OCU. The latter is soon to move to Coltishall, making way for a fourth Tornado unit (No. 14 Squadron) which is to move from Brüggen.

the original airframes, but these now comprise more than 60 per cent of new-build components. Under the terms of its fixed-price contract, BAe has accepted liability to the MoD for liquidated damages, plus further similar penalties in the event of additional delays. Programme management changes now being formulated by BAe, however, are aimed at reducing the current forecast delay by up to 75 per cent.

Joint Force 2000 plans

As one of the main outcomes of 1998's radical Strategic Defence Review, the formation on 1 April 2000 of the new Joint Force 2000 HQ under Strike Command at High Wycombe, Bucks will combine Britain's V/STOL Harrier fighters previously operated independently by the RAF and the Royal Navy. JF 2000 will operate from two adjacent Midlands air bases under unified command, but its aircraft will also fly from the two new 40,000-ton light fleet aircraft-carriers each costing £740

million, which were another main feature of the SDR's recommendations.

At the moment, the Royal Navy operates some 28 of 45 Sea Harrier FA.Mk 2 radar-equipped carrierborne multi-role fighters, plus two T.Mk 4 and five new T.Mk 8 two-seat combat trainers, in two first-line squadrons from its long-term base at RNAS Yeovilton, in Somerset, when not at sea in one of Britain's three 'Invincible'-class V/STOL carriers. Around 58 of 85 Harrier GR.Mk 7 night/all-weather ground-attack fighters and 10 similarly-equipped T.Mk 10 trainers in the RAF inventory are available to equip three combat squadrons, each with 16 aircraft, and an Operational Conversion Unit in the UK and Germany.

RAF Merlin starts trials

Following its initial 55-minute flight from Yeovil on 24 December 1998, which included systems tests of the automatic flight-control, stabilisation and inertial navigation, ZJ117, the first production EH101 Merlin HC.Mk 3 of 22 on order for the RAF, completed further manufacturer's trials before initial service testing by the Defence Evaluation Research Agency at Boscombe Down. With fully integrated defensive aids suite, advanced navigation, avionics and electro-optical systems, and equipped for air-to-air refuelling, the Merlin HC.Mk 3 is due

Seen high over the North Sea in March 1999, this Tornado F.Mk 3 displays No. 111 Squadron's new toned-down markings.

to enter service with No. 28 Squadron at Benson in April 2000. Merlins will then join other RAF Boeing Chinook, Westland/Aérospatiale Puma and Westland Sea King support helicopters, plus the army's newly-formed 16 Air Assault Brigade Westland Lynx and WAH-64 Longbow Apaches and naval Westland Commando HC.Mk 4s, in the emergent tri-service Joint Helicopter Command. Due to form on 1 October 1999 at Wilton, in Wiltshire, the JHC will be under the initial command of the RAF's Air Vice-Marshal David Niven, with some 350 helicopters and 12,000 service personnel. The JHC is due to become operational by April 2000.

Grob grabs Bulldog replacement contract

Although the Grob G-115E was selected in preference to the Slingsby M260 Firefly for the RAF's long-planned BAe Bulldog primary trainer replacement requirement in mid-1998, differences between the MoD and the Department of Trade & Industry over the respective merits and national advantages of the two contenders were settled only in January. A 10-year

£100 million plus Private Finance Initiative contract was then agreed with Bombardier Services (UK), to re-equip and manage the RAF's 15 University Air Squadrons and 12 Air Experience Flights, involving annual flying requirements for up to 50,000 hours with about 100 Grob G-115s.

Five civil-registered G-115D2s with 160-bhp (120-kW) Lycoming engines have been operated since 1995 by Bombardier Services for Royal Navy pilot grading from Plymouth Airport. Known in the RAF as the Tutor, the G-115E is a new version of this glass-fibre composite two-seat trainer, with an uprated 180-bhp (135-kW) Lycoming O-360 engine, and revised instrumentation, and was selected after competitive evaluation against the Firefly, bid by FRA SER.Co.

A new operating site for UAS/AEF units will be RAF Wyton, Hunts, reopened in September 1999 for military aircraft operations after some four years. It will house Cambridge UAS and No. 5 AEF upon their transfer from Marshalls airfield in Cambridge. London University Air Squadron and No. 6 AEF are also moving to Wyton from RAF Benson, in Oxfordshire, for it to become a main support helicopter base.

Middle East

EGYPT:

More F-16s planned

New orders now emerging or in the pipeline are expected to result in further extension of F-16 production by Lockheed Martin, from 3,882 built by early February. A USAF decision to buy 30 new Block 50 F-16C/Ds, with requirements for at least 20 more, is being supplemented by another 24 Block 40 versions in a new $3 billion FMS arms package requested by Egypt. These would cost around $1.2 billion, equivalent to a year's US military aid grants to Egypt, and extend EAF Fighting Falcon procurement to 220 aircraft.

IRAN:

'New' helicopter flies

Iran's first indigenous helicopter design, the Shabaviz (Owl) 2-75, was ceremoniously unveiled in Tehran at the end of 1998 and bears an uncanny resemblance to the Bell 205 or

UH-1D, extending to the two-bladed twin bar-stabilised rotor, skid landing-gear, and the same capacity for a crew of two and 14 troops. Production by Aviation Industries of Iran, with 'imported engines', is claimed to have started in 1999 for both military and civil use.

IRAQ:

Air operations taper off

Intermittent provocation by Iraqi air force MiG-23 and MiG-29 fighters and ground air-defence systems against US and RAF aircraft patrolling the northern and southern 'No-Fly Zones' wound down by mid-March, with no losses to allied forces, at a cost of the claimed destruction of 20 per cent of Saddam Hussein's SAM capabilities. Between the end of Operation Desert Fox in mid-December and 1 March, coalition Boeing B-52s, Fairchild A-10s, Grumman F-14s, MDC F-15s, Lockheed Martin F-16CJs, MDC F/A-18s and Tornado GR.Mk 1s expended more than 200 air-to-surface

A recent 'acquisition' for the Royal Air Force is this AS 355 Twin Squirrel. Two aircraft are already supplied by McAlpine Helicopters to No. 32(TR) Sqn for staff transport, operated in full RAF colour scheme and serials (ZJ139 and ZJ140), but occasionally a third is required to meet demands. This aircraft has received serial ZH141 (from an earlier security block), although it retains its civilian colour scheme.

missiles and laser-guided bombs on Iraqi AAA, SAM, ground-radar and control sites, without loss.

By late February, US European Command reported that aircraft operating from Turkish air bases over the northern NFZ dropped five 907-kg (2,000-lb) GBU-10 and 74 277-kg (611-lb) GBU-12B Paveway II LGBs, plus 19 Raytheon Systems/Texas Instruments AGM-88 HARMs with 64-kg (140-lb) blast fragmentation warheads, and 10 1361-kg (3,000-lb) Boeing Autonetics & Missile Division AGM-130/GBU-15 glide-bombs with 907-kg (2,000-lb) Mk 84 HE or BLU-109/B penetrator warheads.

US Central Command claimed an even wider variety of over 100 missiles and bombs launched in 3,500 sorties by coalition aircraft over the southern 'No-Fly Zone' in the same period. In addition to GBU-10s, GBU-12s, AGM-88s and AGM-130s, these included 306-kg (675-lb) IIR-guided Hughes AGM-65G Mavericks, and B-52-launched 1429-kg (3,150-lb) Boeing AGM-86C CALCMs with 907-kg (2,000-lb) HE/steel-ball shrapnel warheads.

This marked the operational debut from F-15Es on 25 January of the first three Raytheon/Texas Instruments AGM-154A Joint Stand-off Weapons (JSOW), with 145 BLU-97/B Combined Effect Bomblet sub-munition warheads.

ISRAEL:

Fighter decision imminent

Earlier speculation that the IDF/AF would opt for split procurement to meet its requirement for up to 100 new multi-role combat aircraft, for which the field had effectively been narrowed to more Boeing/MDC F-15Is or Lockheed Martin F-16C/Ds, was countered in March at a press briefing by Israeli Defence Minister Moshe Arens. He forecast selection of a single type within a couple of months of final submissions then becoming due from Boeing and LMTAS, without specifying overall aircraft numbers or procurement costs.

YEMEN:

Procurement resumed

Having virtually ceased since the 1994 civil war, military procurement was resumed in February by the Republic of Yemen in the form of a contract

with Aero Vodochody in the Czech Republic for 12 L-39C jet trainers, plus personnel training, spares and technical support. Delivery is expected within the next few months from an Aero inventory of 29 unsold L-39s, to the originally Soviet-equipped Unified Yemeni air force. This has been effectively grounded for the past few years because of spares and funding problems.

Africa

ANGOLA:

Rebel SAM successes

Russian Strela 3 (SA-14 'Gremlin') and Igla 1-M (SA-16 'Gimlet') shoulder-launched IR-homing missiles fired by UNITA rebels have shot down several Angolan air force combat and support aircraft in renewed fighting with government troops in recent months. In addition to the destruction of two Lockheed C-130s on lease to the United Nations and an Antonov An-12 late in 1998 near Huambo,

confirmed losses have included three MiG-23MF 'Flogger-E' multi-role fighters during ground-attack operations in the Central Highlands area in January. Several Angolan Mil Mi-24s have also been claimed shot down.

ETHIOPIA:

Su-27 success

One of the eight surplus Sukhoi Su-27 'Flanker' advanced combat aircraft airlifted to Ethiopia from Russia late in 1998 was lost after its Russian pilot

ejected during a flight demonstration near Addis Ababa on 6 January. The others, including two Su-27UB two-seat combat trainers plus associated weapons and support equipment, were used with some success in cross-border conflicts with Eritrea. Two of Eritrea's 10 MiG-29s recently acquired from Moldova were claimed to have been shot down by Ethiopian Su-27s on 25 and 26 February before a peace agreement was negotiated by the Organisation of African Unity. An immediate replacement for the crashed Ethiopian Su-27 was promised by Russia.

Southern Asia

BANGLADESH:

Air force expansion

In addition to recent procurement by the Bangladesh Defence Force Air Wing of new aircraft from both China and Russia, negotiations have been reported for further purchases of combat and support types. Delivery of four more Guizhou GAIC FT-7B two-seat combat trainers between 1997 and

2000 will double BDFAW equipment of this type, to supplement 16 single-seat Chengdu F-7MBs received in 1989 for air defence roles. Fifteen uprated Mil Mi-17 armed transport helicopters have also recently been delivered from Russia's Kazan Helicopter Plant, to replace the BDFAW time-expired Mil Mi-8s.

Negotiations have been reported with MIG-MAPO and the Rosvoorouzhenie state arms export

Israeli 707 miscellany – above and right is one the IDF/AF's shadowy RC-707 Sigint aircraft landing at Ben Gurion, while below is a VC-707 seen bringing in the first batch of Kosovar refugees on 22 April 1999. Below right is the new VC-707 recently outfitted for VIP transport. The transport 707s are believed to be on the strength of 122 Squadron, while the Sigint operator has been reported as 134 Squadron.

C-47TP Turbo-Dakota serial 82 has received numerous aerials and **FLIR** turret for the maritime reconnaissance role. It is seen here at Ysterplaat being prepared for service, presumably with No. 35 Squadron.

A new type in South African service is the Pilatus **PC-12**, operated from Waterkloof by No. 41 Squadron in a VVIP role. The five **HS** 125 Mercurius VIP aircraft operated by No. 21 Squadron have been retired.

agency for the possible purchase of eight MiG-29SE 'Fulcrum' multi-role fighters, with associated standard IR-homing Molniya R-60 (AA-8 'Aphid') and R-73E (AA-11 'Archer') close-combat AAMs, plus R-27R/Ts (AA-10 'Alamo-A/B') or Vympel R-77Ms (AA-12 'Adder') for medium-range air-to-air engagements, and precision-guided air-to-surface missiles.

INDIA:

Naval carrier procurement plans

Replacement of the Indian navy's venerable 24,000-ton light fleet carrier INS *Viraat* (ex-HMS *Hermes*), which exercised with its V/STOL Sea Harrier Mk 51s and Sea King Mk 42s in the Arabian Gulf in March and is due for retirement in about 2006, is planned by a new air-defence carrier of similar displacement, recently approved by the Defence and Finance Ministries in Delhi. Funding approval for the new $360 million carrier was still awaited earlier in 1999 by Cabinet committees; construction is to start in 2000 at Cochin Shipyard, from late 1980s layouts which originated in France, with modifications by the Indian Naval Design Institute.

A bow ski-ramp is planned for operation of 10 navalised HAL Light Combat Aircraft (LCAs), which will also have long-stroke undercarriages and arrester hooks for deck landings. Current carrierborne ASW roles undertaken by IN Sea Kings will be taken over by five naval versions of HAL's Advanced Light Helicopter.

Since the prototype GE F404-powered LCA has not yet flown, some three years after roll-out, and earliest commissioning date for the new carrier has been quoted as around 2009-10, India is pursuing negotiations with Russia for the acquisition of its surplus 45,200-ton aircraft-carrier *Admiral Gorshkov*. A decision in principle has been taken by the Indian government to go ahead with a $700 million package which would not only include purchase, refurbishment, re-equipment and modifications of the *Gorshkov*, but also a squadron of navalised MiG-29Ks, developed but not so far procured for the Russian navy, plus supporting Kamov Ka-28 ASW and Ka-31 AEW helicopters. The Russian carrier package is hoped to be available

to replace INS *Viraat* on its retirement, and fill the gap before LCA service entry, as well as providing a back-up for the new carrier in future refit cycles.

'Hind' upgrade contract

A $20 million Indian Defence Ministry contract awarded earlier in 1999 to the Tamam Division of Israel Aircraft Industries for the mission system upgrades of some 25 IAF Mil Mi-24 'Hind' attack helicopters will involve installation of Tamam's 30-kg (65-lb) multi-mission digital optronic stabilised payload (HMOSP) package. This achieves all-weather acquisition and weapon targeting from variable field-of-view LLLTV and FLIR sensors, with automatic target-tracking. A helmet-mounted sighting and display system, revised tandem cockpit layouts with a digital map, new mission data management equipment and an integrated defensive aids suite are also included in the HMOSP package. More than 1,500 Mi-24s are estimated to remain in worldwide operation, for which IAI is proposing further upgrade options, in conjunction with Mil and Rosvoorouzhenie in Russia.

Su-30 follow-up order

Earlier reports of IAF requirements for a follow-up batch of 10 Su-30 advanced multi-role fighters were confirmed by a new contract with Sukhoi in late 1998. These will increase IAF procurement to 50 Su-30MKIs, of which only eight (ex-Su-30PUs), equipped to earlier Su-30K air superiority standards, have so far been delivered. Su-30MK development is still continuing, with new NIIP N011M phased-array multi-mode radar, digital Sextant Avionique Totem liquid-crystal cockpit displays, INS/GPS, VEH3000 head-up display, and an Indian mission computer. Proposed Israeli electronic warfare systems have been vetoed, however.

New avionics in the next eight IAF Su-30MKs will be supplemented from 2000 in the following 12 by integrated canard foreplane control systems. Subsequent IAF examples will further integrate thrust-vectored Lyul'ka Saturn AL-31FP turbofans to full Su-30MKI specifications.

PAKISTAN:

US repays F-16 funding

Funding of $463.7 million is being returned by the US to the Islamabad government following the RNZAF's lease agreement for the 28 GD F-16A/B Block 15OCU fighters bought by Pakistan for $658 million, subsequently vetoed by the State Department. In addition to $324.6 million in cash, Pakistan is receiving $140 million more in goods and commodities. A further $157 million had previously been recovered through payments for three Lockheed P-3C Orion maritime patrol aircraft and AIM-9L Sidewinders released to the PAF. Budget allocations are now expected for PAF procurement of up to 50 upgraded Chengdu F-7MG developments of the MiG-21, featuring a cranked delta wing, with leading- and trailing-edge manoeuvre flaps, improved avionics including Marconi Super Skyranger pulse-Doppler radar, and an uprated LMC WP13F turbojet, to replace its remaining two squadrons of Shenyang F-6 fighters. Joint development and procurement are also planned of the Klimov RD-93-engined Chengdu FC-1 or Super 7.

Far East

CAMBODIA:

MiG-21 upgrade problems

Delivery of four completed 'Fishbeds' from nine Cambodian air force MiG-21bis fighters and four MiG-21UM two-seat combat trainers being upgraded by Israel Aircraft Industries was reportedly suspended earlier in 1999 because of payment problems. According to some sources, Cambodia paid for and received its first two upgraded prototype MiG-21s, including a 'Fishbed-B' trainer, in January 1997, and negotiations were continuing for completion of the contract.

CHINA:

First Shenyang Su-27 flies

Initial flight tests in December 1998 of the first two Sukhoi Su-27SK 'Flankers' from 200 scheduled for assembly by the Shenyang Aircraft Industry Group was a major milestone

Mirage deliveries delayed

Deliveries of 34 ex-French air force Dassault Mirage 5F fighter-bombers and six Mirage IIIBE two-seat combat-trainers, bought by the Pakistan air force from the French government for $116 million in 1996, have reportedly fallen well behind schedule. All 40 aircraft were originally due for delivery by the end of 1998, after refurbishment in France by SAGEM and installation of a new HUD, nav/attack system and HOTAS controls.

SRI LANKA:

C-130s expected

Overhaul and refurbishment of three ex-RAF Lockheed C-130K Hercules C.Mk 1K former tankers, plus removal of their air-refuelling equipment, was under way earlier in 1999 by Marshalls of Cambridge prior to their planned delivery to the Sri Lankan air force. Heavy operational losses of SLAF transport aircraft, including three of five Antonov An-32s and two of three Shaanxi Y-8Ds, from Tamil action or accidents over the past two or three years, have accelerated requirements for additional replacements.

in a licensed production programme which will build up slowly over the next few years. Output is expected to remain at only six or seven aircraft per year until about 2002, when it is planned to double. It does not include production of the Su-27's Lyul'ka AL-31F turbofans, although negotiations are continuing to establish a facility for their local repair and overhaul.

JAPAN:

Tri-service procurement

FY99 military budget allocations of 4,939 billion yen ($37.43 million), approved in January, represented a decrease of some 0.16 per cent over the previous year. Defence Agency approval for tri-service Self-Defence Forces' procurement plans was received for 51 new aircraft costing over $2 billion, following earlier requests for 56. JASDF requests for 680 million yen ($5.15 million) for the first two of 50 upgraded Fuji T-7

Seen on a test flight from BAe Warton, this Hawk Mk 209 is destined for the Indonesian air force. The carriage of Mavericks is notable, although BAe occasionally uses aircraft drawn from the production line to undertake weapon tests unconnected with the eventual recipient of the aircraft.

turboprop trainers required were also withdrawn when allegations of corruption were made against Fuji Heavy Industries' management. These were in connection with Fuji's participation in the JMSDF programme for an upgraded ShinMaywa US-1A Kai flying-boat with Allison 4,500-shp (3357-kW) Allison AE2100J turboprops, and new digital avionics. Fuji's T-7 contract was then deferred for a year, and the JASDF's T-X basic trainer requirement was reopened for a new bid from Pilatus for its originally-proposed PC-7 Mk 2, as the short-listed contender.

Revised FY 1999 JSDF procurement approval comprised, with original requests in parentheses, comprise: Air SDF: Mitsubishi (MHI) F-2A/B combat aircraft, 8 (8); Kawasaki (KHI) T-4 advanced trainer, 10 (12); Raytheon Hawker/BAe U-125A SAR aircraft, 2 (2); KHI/Boeing CH-47J medium airlift helicopter, 2 (2); Sikorsky/MHI UH-60J SAR helicopter, 2 (2). Maritime SDF: ShinMaywa US-1A SAR amphibian, 1 (1); SH-60J ASW helicopter, 9 (10); Beech TC-90 King Air 90 instrument trainer, 3 (3). Ground SDF: UH-60JA utility helicopter, 3 (3); KHI OH-1 scout helicopter, 3 (4); FHI/Bell UH-1J utility helicopter, 5 (5); KHI/Boeing CH-47J airlift helicopter, 2 (2); Beech LR-2 King Air 350 liaison aircraft, 1 (2).

AWACS enter service

Delivery of the second pair of Boeing 767 AWACS aircraft ordered and developed for the JASDF, as initial customer, from 1993, was completed ahead of schedule late in 1998. First delivered in March 1998, the four aircraft recently completed a 12-month test and trials programme from Hamamatsu air base, near Nagoya, before entering operational JASDF service. The JASDF is also considering a considerably cheaper tanker/transport version of the $449 million Boeing 767 AWACS for its $700 million four-

aircraft air-refuelling requirement, in competition with the Airbus A300/A310 MRTT, Boeing C-17 and Lockheed Martin C-130J.

SOUTH KOREA:

F-16 production extended

An extension of Samsung's licensed production programme for 80 Block 52 F-16Cs and 40 similar two-seat F-16Ds by another 20 aircraft is expected in a new 26,700 billion won ($21.83 billion) 2000-2004 defence plan, made possible by the recovery in the RoK's economy over the past year. This would be in addition to the 5,000 billion won ($4 billion) F-X new twin-turbofan combat aircraft programme, for which the Boeing F-15K, Dassault Rafale, Eurofighter and Sukhoi Su-35/37 are competing. Other major procurement funding in this programme includes 2,000 million won for new attack helicopters, for which the Boeing/MDH AH-64D Apache and Eurocopter Tiger are major contestants.

SINGAPORE:

AH-64D procurement

A $620 million FMS arms package was agreed in early March with the US Army for the long-discussed Foreign Military Sales purchase of eight Boeing/MDH AH-64D Apache attack helicopters, with options on 12 more.

Also included were 216 Boeing/Rockwell AGM-114K Hellfire 2 laser-guided ATMs, Hydra 70 unguided rockets, other weapons and associated equipment. State Department export approval to Singapore for the AH-64D's Lockheed Martin/Northrop Grumman AN/APG-78 Longbow millimetric mast-mounted radar was its first release to a Pacific Rim country. Rolls-Royce/Turbomeca is proposing installation of its RTM322 turboshafts in RepSAF Apaches, as in the UK's WAH-64s, to improve their 'hot-and-high' performance.

THAILAND:

More F-16s sought

RTAF procurement of between 12 and 24 refurbished surplus USAF F-16A/B fighters costing up to $100 million was being discussed by the Thai government earlier in 1999 with the Pentagon, to replace the eight new Boeing/MDC F-18C/Ds costing $392 million which were cancelled before delivery because of economic problems. The F-16s would supplement the 36 similar aircraft.

South America

BRAZIL:

Carrier requirements

Having received government clearance to operate fixed-wing aircraft, Brazilian naval aviation (FAMB) acquired 20 surplus ex-KAF McDonnell Douglas A-4KU (A-4N) and three TA-4KU Skyhawks in 1998 from long-term storage in Kuwait for operation from its light fleet carrier *Minas Gerais*. They are now being refurbished, and proposals are also under consideration for a carrierborne airborne early-warning aircraft to operate in support of the Skyhawks, for which EMBRAER has teamed with Marsh Aviation for an S-2F3T turboprop conversion of the Grumman Tracker, with 1,760-shp (1313-kW) AlliedSignal TPE331-14GR engines.

COLOMBIA:

US donates more Huey IIs

Earlier deliveries from the US of eight upgraded Bell Huey II utility helicopters to the Colombian air force were followed in March by the first two of another 10 UH-1Ps, for the Colombian National Police. Donated by the US State Department for drug interdiction roles as part of $234 million FY1999 military aid to Colombia, the Huey IIs are being upgraded from Bell UH-1H Iroquois

through a $1.3 million package which includes a Textron Lycoming T53-L-703 turboshaft uprated from 1,400 to 1,800 shp (1044 to 1343 kW), and Bell 212/412-type main and tail rotors, lift-beam, tail-boom and transmission. They provide a 290-kg (642-lb) increase in useful load, plus improvements of up to 275 per cent in 'hot-and-high' performance, 40 per cent lower operating costs, and extended component overhaul lives.

PANAMA:

Taiwan donates UH-1s

Five surplus Bell UH-1H Iroquois utility helicopters supplied under US military aid programmes were transferred by the Taiwanese government late in 1998 to the Panamanian National Police. This now operates at least a dozen helicopters in paramilitary roles, supplementing a similar number operated by the Fuerza Aérea Panamena.

SURINAM:

Transport reinforcement

Latest military customer for the CASA Aviocar light twin-turboprop transport is the Surinam air force, which took delivery of two C.212-400s from late 1998. They are undertaking general transport and utility roles, supplement-

On 7 March 1999 the Indian Air Force conducted a major firepower demonstration at the Pokhran ranges in the Rajasthan desert. In addition to an impressive amount of live firing, an equipment display was staged, including this MiG-23BN of No. 31 Squadron 'Lions'.

Vinson's Air Wing

Having supported *Enterprise* during the US/UK Operation Desert Fox against Iraq, the 'Starship Vinson' set course for the southern oceans for exercises with Australian units.

Right: VFA-22's CAG-bird displays two mission marks for an LGB and AGM-154 JSOW strike. The latter is believed to have been made after Desert Fox.

Left: Marked 'XO', a VF-22 'Fighting Redcocks' F/A-18C prepares for launch. Note that the pilot's hands are held away from the controls.

Above: Vinson's Tomcat squadron is VF-213 'Black Lions', flying the F-14D. The squadron insignia has reverted to the single-tailed lion.

Above: VFA-97 'Warhawks' operates the F/A-18A, including this ex-NSAWC adversary aircraft.

Left: The 'Mighty Shrikes' of VFA-94 are CVW-11's third Hornet squadron. Here one of the unit's aircraft taxis behind the departing VFA-22 aircraft to position for launch. The Hornet carries the AAS-38 NITE Hawk targeting FLIR pod on the port fuselage station, a sensor usually carried in conjunction with the ASQ-173 LST/SCAM pod on the starboard position.

---

ing two PBN BN.2B Defender light twins delivered to the SAF in late 1993.

URUGUAY:

Jetstreams delivered

Continued procurement of surplus British military support aircraft, following recent acquisition of six ex-RAF Westland Wessex HC.Mk 2s, have included two BAe Jetstream T.Mk 2s twin-Astazou turboprop trainers, formerly operated by the Royal Navy. They were delivered from RNAS Culdrose to the Uruguayan navy in January 1999.

North America

CANADA:

CF-18 upgrade plans

From original \$C5.2 billion procurement of 98 CF-18As and 40 CF-18B two-seat combat trainers between FY81 and FY86, the Canadian Armed Forces were awaiting government approval earlier in 1999 to begin a rolling upgrade programme for about 100 of their 122 remaining Hornets over an eight-year period. Planned replacement of more than a dozen systems, plus structural reinforcement and replacements required to maintain 87 CF-18s in operational service until at least 2020, would eventually cost up to \$C1.2 billion (\$786 million), if the necessary funding can be found.

Some \$C68 million (\$44.5 million) is initially being sought in the first phase of the programme for a new GD Information Systems XN10 mission computer and operational flight programme software from the USN. Funding of \$C14 million is also required for Have Quick II secure radios and Link 16 data transfer systems, plus major expenditure of about \$C500 million to replace the current APG-65 fire-control radars with the Hughes AN/APG-73 unit installed in the F-18E/F.

Also required are advanced colour flat-panel cockpit displays, a new stores management system, GPS and defensive EW upgrades. A helmet-mounted sight and associated advanced fifth-generation close-combat air-to-air missile, plus more Lockheed Martin AAS-38B NITE Hawk FLIR targeting pods, are planned at a later stage.

NATO training expansion

An order from Bombardier Inc. for two more BAe Hawk 115 lead-in fighter trainers, increasing its overall total to 20, followed a UK Ministry of Defence announcement in March of an RAF decision to participate in Canada's NATO Flying Training (NFTC) programme. From 2001, up to 20 RAF student pilots will undertake the NFTC course utilising the latest digital cockpit instrumentation, technologies and techniques over the next 10 years.

UNITED STATES:

No. 2 Global Hawk crashes

The second Teledyne Ryan RQ-4A Global Hawk, serial 95-2002, crashed at NAWS China Lake, California on 29 March 1999. The unmanned aerial vehicle was lost on China Lake's Echo Range approximately 20 minutes after taking off from Edwards AFB. The Global Hawk was flying at 41,000 ft (12500 m) when it pitched nose down and entered a right-hand roll. The USAF has begun an investigation into accident.

The Global Hawk is planned to visit Australia in spring 2001 to participate in a series of joint US/Australian exercises. Australia is planning to purchase a wide-area surveillance system and the exercise will enable an evaluation to be undertaken. The visit will be the first overseas deployment for the Global Hawk.

Additional C-37s

Gulfstream received an order on 6 April 1999 for two additional C-37A (Gulfstream V) aircraft, bringing the total order to six. The latest two will be primarily used for counter-terrorism and disaster response missions, providing a flexible, worldwide capability for federal agents tasked to respond to emergencies. All six will be operated by the 89th Airlift Wing at Andrews AFB, Maryland.

New F-15Es begin testing

The first of 17 additional Boeing F-15E Eagles made its inaugural flight at St Louis, Missouri, on 1 April 1999. The aircraft was 96-0200, which is the first of six ordered in FY 1996. A further six were funded in FY 1997, followed by five more in FY 1998.

USAF on alert in WestPac

The US Air Force has assumed alert duties in the Western Pacific in place of the US Navy carrier battle group normally tasked with this mission. The war in the Balkans and the ongoing need to enforce the air exclusion zones above areas of Iraq have seen the US Navy's Pacific Fleet resources stretched. USS *Kitty Hawk* (CV-63), which is the only carrier permanently assigned to WestPac, has sailed to the Gulf region, enabling USS *Theodore Roosevelt* (CVN-71) to join Operation Allied Force in the Adriatic. To enable a credible alert to be maintained in the region, combat squadrons of the USAF's Pacific Air Forces have been brought to a higher state of readiness. These include F-15s of the 18th Wing at Kadena AB, Okinawa, as well as the F-16s of the 8th FW at Kunsan AB and 51st FW at Osan AB in South Korea, and the F-16s of the 35th FW at Misawa AB, Japan. The situation was expected to remain stable until autumn 1999, when USS *Constellation* (CV-64) was scheduled to arrive in the Western Pacific.

E-6B conversion contract

Raytheon has been awarded a \$31.5 million US Navy contract to convert a further two E-6As to E-6B configuration. The conversion involves the removal of communications equipment from retired USAF EC-135Cs, including Airborne Launch Control systems, UHF radios and Digital Airborne Intercommunications Switching systems. Additionally, the aircraft will receive structural modifications to house the equipment, including a large dorsal fairing located aft of the flight deck containing the Milstars satellite communications system. To date, Raytheon have modified eight aircraft to E-6B standard which are operated by VQ-3 as part of Sea Control Wing One at Tinker AFB, Oklahoma. The final eight will serve with VQ-4.

VXE-6 disestablished

The US Navy's Antarctic Development Squadron Six 'Ice Pirates' was disestablished on 31 March 1999 after 44 years of Antarctic resupply operations. The squadron was formed in January 1955 as VX-6 at NAS Patuxent River, Maryland, and has conducted resupply flights across the Antarctic landmass during the austral summer months of October to February under Operation Deep Freeze, undertaken on behalf of the National Science Foundation. A variety of ski-equipped fixed-wing aircraft, plus helicopters, has been operated, including P2V Neptune, UC-1 Otter, R4D Skytrain, R5D Skymaster and C-121 Constellation. The LC-130F arrived in 1961, followed by the LC-130R.

LC-130Rs to USAF

Two former US Navy ski-equipped LC-130Rs of VXE-6 are to be modified to LC-130H standard prior to being reassigned to the US Air Force, joining the 109th Airlift Squadron (New York ANG) based at Schenectady Airport. Raytheon is modifying the aircraft under a $17.8 million contract at its Waco, Texas, facility. The modification involves fitting new avionics, navigation and communications systems, and displays in the cockpit. The first LC-130H will be delivered in July 2000 and the second four months later. An option exists on a third aircraft.

USAF structure changes

On 5 March 1999 the USAF announced a series of force structure changes designed to enable the implementation of the expeditionary aero-space force concept to proceed as planned with effect from 1 January 2000. Most of the changes involve manpower levels, although the strategic bomber force will see some alterations. At Dyess AFB, Texas, the 7th Bomb Wing will see the activation of the 13th Bomb Squadron with six B-1Bs as a second training unit. The 77th BS of the 28th BW at Ellsworth AFB, South Dakota, will add six B-1Bs which will primarily be budgeted for the aircrew proficiency and training role, although they could be restructured for combat operations if required. The active-duty air force has 77 B-1Bs while the Air National Guard has a further 17, although the 184th BW, Kansas ANG, is to reduce its strength by two aircraft. However, only half of the active-duty fleet is funded as mission-capable for combat operations at any one time, with the remainder classified for test and training, or undergoing maintenance. Others are held as back-up and attrition replacement.

The B-52H fleet is also split between those aircraft classified as mission-capable and a number maintained for other purposes. The active-duty fleet is budgeted for 49 mission-ready B-52s at present, with a further 36 available. Air Force Reserve Command operates nine.

Under the force restructuring, 18 attrition reserve B-52Hs are to be removed from Minot AFB, North Dakota, and probably placed in storage at AMARC.

Within Air Mobility Command the C-141B is gradually being phased out of active-duty service. The 437th Airlift Wing at Charleston AFB, South Carolina, will lose 12 StarLifters, while the 305th Air Mobility Wing at McGuire AFB, New Jersey, will retire 10. However, the latter unit is due to receive around 12 when the Special Operations Low Level II (SOLL II) versions are transferred from Charleston in late 1999. At McChord AFB, Washington, the 62nd AW will retire 10 C-141Bs in exchange for nine C-17As. The 375th AW at Scott AFB, Illinois, will transfer one C-9A to the 374th AW at Yokota AB, Japan.

The fighter community will see a few changes, including the 354th FS/355th Wing at Davis-Monthan AFB, Arizona, which will gain six additional A/OA-10As. The 524th FS/27th FW at Cannon AFB, New Mexico, will retain 24 Block 40 F-16CG/DG instead of switching to Block 30 aircraft. Three more F-15Es are due to be delivered to the 333rd FS/4th FW at Seymour Johnson AFB, North Carolina, probably from the current production. At Moody AFB, Georgia, the 347th Wing will inactivate the 68th and 69th FSs, with their 36 F-16CG/DGs being relocated. The fate of the 70th FS and its A/OA-10As has not been announced. The 347th will be redesignated as a Rescue Wing operating the HC-130P and HH-60G. The 54th FS/3rd Wing at Elmendorf AFB, Alaska, will gain six F-15C/Ds, probably from the 1st FW at Langley AFB, Virginia, which has acquired several additional Eagles following the inactivation of the 53rd FS at Spangdahlem AB, Germany.

Air Education and Training Command will also experience a number of alterations. At Columbus AFB, Mississippi, the 14th FTW will activate the 41st FTS as a second T-37B unit. The 43rd FTS will expand its operations as part of the Air Force Reserve Command associate programme. The 58th SOW at Kirtland AFB, New Mexico, will gain additional assets, including four HH-60Gs for the 512th SOS and two HC-130Ps for the 550th SOS. At Laughlin AFB, Texas, the 47th FTW will activate the 84th FTS as an addtional T-37B unit. Likewise, at Vance AFB, Oklahoma, the 71st FTW will add the 33rd FTS as a second T-37B unit.

The situation within Air Force Special Operations Command is confusing, as the 5th SOS is due to relocate with its MC-130Ps from Duke Field, Florida, to nearby Eglin AFB. In its place the 8th SOS will move from Hurlburt Field to Duke Field with its MC-130Es, although the squadron is to lose four aircraft. The 5th SOS is part of AFRC, while the 8th SOS is an AFSOC unit. Duke Field is an AFRC installation, but would appear to be gaining importance by becoming the main facility to house both active-duty and reserve MC-130Es. Likewise, the active-duty and reserve MC-130Ps will be centralised at Eglin.

Within AFRC the 94th AW at Dobbins AFB, Georgia, will assume the training role with its eight C-130Hs. The Air National Guard is largely unaffected by the changes, although the 111th FS (Ellington Field, Texas), 119th FS (Atlantic City, New Jersey), 162nd FS (Springfield, Ohio), 178th FS (Hector, North Dakota), 179th FS (Duluth, Minnesota) and 182nd FS (Kelly AFB, Texas) all switch from air defence to a general-purpose ground attack mission. At Moffett Field, California, the 129th RQS will convert its four HC-130Ps to MC-130P configuration.

USAFE to train in Slovakia

The Republic of Slovakia has agreed to permit USAF Europe fighter and attack aircraft to utilise Malacky Air Base for training purposes. Squadrons flying the A-10, F-15 and F-16 will deploy on two-week weapons firing

Military Aviation Review

The V-22 Osprey is well on its way to service entry. In January 1999 this aircraft was aboard Saipan for a series of shipborne trials.

exercises, utilising the Kuchyna live bombing range. The first visits were planned for mid-1999, but these were delayed due to ongoing operations over the Balkans.

Lead Expeditionary Wings

The US Air Force has announced the 10 units which have been identified as Aerospace Expeditionary Lead Wings (Combat) to form the core of the new concept designed to enable forces to be deployed on a global basis. The Expeditionary Aerospace Force system has been formulated to allow theatre commanders to combine the capabilities of various units to form an effective fighting force. The 10 units are:

1st Fighter Wing	F-15C/D
2nd Bomb Wing	B-52H
3rd Wing	F-15C/D/E
7th Bomb Wing	B-1B
20th Fighter Wing	F-16CJ/DJ
27th Fighter Wing	F-16CG/DG
28th Bomb Wing	B-1B
48th Fighter Wing	F-15C/D/E
355th Wing	A-10/EC-130
388th Wing	F-16CG/DG

These units will act as the core element, with other squadrons assigned for the duration of their overseas deployment. The 10 wings will hold an alert status for three months at a time, before being relieved of this duty and handing responsibility to the next core unit. During this three-month period the core unit and its attached squadrons can be deployed on a worldwide basis. The USAF hopes to relieve the burdens of rotations falling upon personnel from the same units, while attempting to implement the strategy of no more than 120 days deployed away within each year.

Five Air Mobility Command units have been identified as Aerospace Expeditionary Force Lead Wings (Mobility) for operations such as humanitarian relief. These consist of units operating the KC-135 and/or KC-10, as well as the C-5 and C-130. These mobility AEFs have been established following the devastation caused

by Hurricane Mitch in central America. Their airlift duties are considerably different from those of the Combat AEFs, although both will draw their assets and personnel from other wings. The five mobility AEFs are:

22nd Air Refueling Wing	KC-135
92nd Air Refueling Wing	KC-135
319th Air Refueling Wing	KC-135
43rd Airlift Wing	C-130E
60th Air Mobility Wing	C-5, KC-10

The new structure has also included a pair of On-Call Aerospace Expeditionary Wings which are designed to be available to deploy at very short notice to conduct combat operations. These are the 366th Wing at Mountain Home AFB, Idaho, and the 4th Fighter Wing at Seymour Johnson AFB, North Carolina. The 366th Wing is unique as it is almost self-sufficient, operating a mix of B-1Bs, F-15C/Ds, F-15Es, F-16s and KC-135Rs, whereas the 4th FW is equipped solely with the F-15E.

F-16C Fighting Falcon

On 26 March 1999, Lockheed Martin delivered the 3,035th F-16 Fighting Falcon to be assembled at its Fort Worth, Texas facility, setting a record for aircraft of a single type at that location. The fighter was an F-16C Block 50C (96-5081) for the US Air Force and the ceremony took place two days after F-16s began flying combat sorties in Operation Allied Force.

The Fort Worth plant, which has been operated by Consolidated, Convair General Dynamics, Lockheed, and now Lockheed Martin, turned out 3,034 B-24 Liberator bombers (of a total of 19,256 of all variants built at five factories), culminating in a Consolidated B-24J-105-CF Liberator (44-44501) which made its maiden flight in 1944 bearing the signatures of all who helped build it. No such honor was bestowed on the drab, grey F-16.

F-16 production at the plant has now lasted 29 years and reached a peak rate of 33 aircraft in one month in October 1981. The Fort Worth Liberators, in contrast, were built in just 33 months between April 1942 and December 1944, with a peak rate of a remarkable 230 bombers in January 1944, or seven per day. The plant's

3,035th Fighting Falcon was the 2,202nd for the US Air Force (which currently has 1,847 in inventory, a figure which includes some examples in storage) and the 3,900th altogether, when including production or final assembly in Belgium, Korea, Netherlands and Turkey. The last two countries are still turning out F-16s, while Japan is producing the Mitsubishi F-2, based in part on the Fighting Falcon design.

The USAF's air staff in the Pentagon, influenced by the war with Yugoslavia, has decided to recommend purchasing more F-16C/D block 50 fighters and is considering a new powerplant competition between Pratt & Whitney and the manufacturer of the block 50 powerplant, General Electric.

The F-16 decision is expected to be followed by a decision to significantly slow the USAF's schedule for the JSF (Joint Strike Fighter), possibly with the result that the Marine Corps version of JSF will be developed before the USAF model.

In May 1999, Greece announced that it would purchase 50 F-16C/D Block 50+ (50-plus) Fighting Falcons as well as 15 Dassault Mirage 2000. The decision came as something of a surprise, since the Hellenic air arm had been expected to re-equip with an export version of the F-15E Strike Eagle. In contrast, South Korea is said to be digging in its heels against purchase of additional F-16C/Ds, fearing this would jeopardise its air force's interest in an F-15E-type fighter. Samsung's Sachon, Korea plant has delivered about 90 of the 120 F-16C/D Block 52 aircraft on the current order but officials are baulking at a recommendation by the Ministry of Commerce, Industry and Energy for 20 to 40 more Fighting Falcons.

C-130J for US Air Force

Lockheed Martin delivered the first USAF C-130J to a US Air Force Reserve unit at Keesler Air Force Base, Mississippi on 31 March 1999. Named *Spirit of Biloxi* (after the city adjacent to Keesler), the transport C-130J will be one of two aircraft assigned for training to the 815th Airlift Squadron, 403rd Airlift Wing, although initial training will actually be the responsibility of the Detachment 2 of the 33rd Test Squadron.

On 1 May 1999 the Maryland Air National Guard named its first Lockheed C-130J Pride of Baltimore II. The dedication ceremony took place at the 135th Airlift Squadron's home base of Glenn L. Martin State Airport.

Keesler's two C-130J training ships will be followed later in 1999 with the start of deliveries of nine WC-130J weather reconnaissance aircraft, commonly known as 'Hurricane Hunters'. The manufacturer halted production of earlier C-130 variants several years ago (the final C-130H model being delivered to Japan in 1997) and has pegged the future of the Hercules to the C-130J model, which has new engines and propellers, and dispenses with navigator and flight engineer positions, being crewed by two pilots and a loadmaster. The reduced crew size has created problems for the reserve component, a term which encompasses the Air Force Reserve and Air National Guard, because the elimination of jobs is a domestic issue at the state level. The USAF takes the official position that it did not want the C-130J, which costs almost twice as much as a C-130H, but that the aircraft were foisted on it by Congress. Led by Senate Majority Leader Trent Lott, Capitol Hill legislators have added Hercules aircraft to budget appropriations year after year and have dictated where the aircraft will be stationed. Lott represents Mississippi.

Controversy surrounding the aircraft is not limited to the circumstances under which it was funded. 'Hurricane Hunter' crews claim that the performance of the C-130J will require them to penetrate a storm front at lower altitude than the 'Super E' model they now employ. At another unit, referring to the deletion of the two crew positions, one pilot says, "Yes, practically every pilot I know wants at least a flight engineer to stay on the plane, and the vast majority still want a navigator, too. Maybe it sounds stupid, but if we're in combat and the 'Golden BB' takes out my cosmic navigation system, we're up the creek without a paddle and half a boat.."

Second unit to take delivery of a C-130J transport was the Maryland Air National Guard's 315th Airlift Squadron, 175th Wing, at Martin State Airport in Baltimore, Maryland, on 1 May 1999. The Maryland unit, which now uses some of the oldest C-130E aircraft in service, planned a nine-month breaking-in period after which it would declare itself operational in the C-130J.

C-130J Hercules were also scheduled for delivery in 1999 to the Pennsylvania Air National Guard's 193rd Special Operations Squadron, 193rd

On 8 May 1999 Lockheed Martin achieved a major milestone in its JSF programme by completing the assembly of major structures of the first of two X-35 technology demonstrators. The first aircraft should fly in the spring of 2000, and is being assembled inside the Skunk Works at Palmdale, California.

Special Operatons Wing, located at the former Olmstead Air Force Base, Harrisburg, Pennsylvania. Acceptance of the J model is a particular problem in Harrrisburg, where one officer says, "Unfortunately, the tactically sound C-130 is no longer the best airplane for the job. With our C-130E fleet of Commando Solo aircraft, we got to the point that we were adding so much weight and drag to the airplane to do its mission that were compromising its mission effectiveness. The last mod, for example, took the unrefuelled on-orbit time from 5.5 hours to under 5.0. The problem was that the C-130 was designed to land on short runways, hence a stocky, beefed-up gear configuration and a low door sill height for austere locations. Result: no room for antennas under the fuselage – everything would have to be hung under the wing. The Rivet Rider modification placed an external pod that hung down within 5 ft of the ground – so much for the advantages of a high wing aircraft for landing on austere runways!

The PSYOP MAP [Psychological Operations Mission Area Plan] recommended buying used airline widebody aircraft and modifying them (a used DC-10-30 would be much cheaper than the C-130J). The high door sill height made it possible to put the antennas aerodynamically under the fuselage. The lower lobe made it possible to eliminate external pods. The range, cruise ceiling, speed, on-orbit time, electrical generating power from the engines, and every other employment factor and flight characteristic was superior for the mission. The large main deck was big enough for a real-time television studio. Higher altitudes and more powerful generators gave the airplane a further broadcast range and better stand-off capability. The giant C-130 Hercules, Hero of the Skies, Workhorse of the Nation, was no longer the right aircraft to be our country's only airborne broadcast platform."

Lockheed Martin says it may have to close the assembly line for the C-130J in 2000 unless the US Air Force finds about $2 billion to speed up its purchases of the aircraft. A shutdown would mean millions of dollars in lost revenue to the world's top defence contractor, and it is deemed more likely that the Pentagon and Congress will work out something to keep the line open. Lockheed Martin has produced 40 of 83 transports ordered by the United Kingdom, Australia, Italy, and the US Air Force. It will complete production of the rest the government-owned Marietta, Georgia, plant by late 2000. Despite its official position against the C-130J, the USAF has

a requirement for as many as 150 more aircraft beyond the 35 already authorized, starting with eight in 2004 and 10 in 2005. That could leave a four-year gap in the production line with no customer currently on tap to fill it.

C-5 Galaxy upgrade

The USAF's primary heavyweight airlifter, the C-5 Galaxy, is set to undergo an upgrade to extend its operational career well into the next century. The first contract, valued at $450 million, was placed with Lockheed Martin Aeronautical Systems on 22 January 1999 for the modernisation of the avionics. Principal sub-contractor Honeywell Defense Avionics Systems will install its digital versatile integrated avionics package, which is FAA certified and is identical to that fitted to the majority of US commercial airliners. The new system integrates an advanced flight control and navigation/communications system with collision and terrain avoidance systems.

The second stage of the upgrade, to be funded later, will involve the replacement of the General Electric TF39 turbofans (of 41,000 lb/182.45 kN thrust) with General Electric CF6-80C2 powerplants, capable of 60,000 lb (267 kN) thrust but derated by 17 per cent. The new engines will significantly improve take-off and climb performance, as well as raising cruise ceiling by 25 per cent. It is estimated that the C-5 has utilised only 20 per cent of its planned airframe life. The Galaxy has the highest operating cost of any USAF aircraft, and the upgrade programme is designed to reduce these costs significantly.

Last Block 20 B-2 leaves Whiteman

The last B-2A from Block 20 production, serial 93-1085 *Spirit of Oklahoma*, left Whiteman AFB, Missouri, at the beginning of 1999, heading for Palmdale, California, to be upgraded to Block 30 standard. All operational B-2As have been given an official name which is displayed on the main undercarriage doors. These have been allocated to aircraft seven through 21 (known as Air Vehicles 7 to 21 by the manufacturer), with the names being applied during ceremonies performed soon after delivery to Whiteman. In addition, the first six aircraft (Air Vehi-

cles 1 to 6), which were all initially assigned to the test and evaluation role, have begun to be upgraded to operational configuration and delivered to Whiteman. These, too, have been allocated an official name, although is some confusion. However, according to the 509th Bomb Wing, AV-5/82-1070 was named *Spirit of Ohio* on 15 June 1997, followed by AV-3/82-1068 as *Spirit of New York* on 10 October 1997, AV-2/82-1067 as *Spirit of Arizona* on 20 March 1998 and AV-6/82-1071 as *Spirit of Mississippi* on 23 May 1998. The 325th Bomb Squadron was activated on 8 January 1999 as the second operational B-2 unit under the 509th Operations Group, and is expected to gain two operational Block 30 aircraft and a single T-38A fro pilot proficiency.

Navy vacates Miramar

After more than four decades of naval fighter operations at Miramar, the Commander Airborne Early Warning Wing Pacific finally vacated the southern California base during November 1998. The last unit to leave was VAW-117 which departed on 18 November to join the USS *Carl Vinson* as part of Carrier Air Wing 11. The E-2 squadrons have relocated to NAWS Point Mugu. In October 1997 Miramar was redesignated as an MCAS when control was transferred to the Marine Corps. The Naval Fighter Weapons School 'Topgun' moved to NAS Fallon, Nevada, while the F-14 Tomcat squadrons of Commander Fighter Wing Pacific relocated to NAS Oceana, Virginia. However, Tomcat units regularly deploy back to Miramar for exercises with the Marine Corps F/A-18 units which are now Miramar's principal inhabitants, and to NAS El Centro, California, for weapons training.

C-27 Spartan news

The US Air Force has retired from service the 10 Alenia C-27A Spartans formerly based at Howard AFB, Panama, with the 310th Airlift Squadron, 24th Wing. Three were flown to Davis-Monthan AFB, Arizona, for storage with AMARC during September 1998, followed by four more which left Howard in January 1999. The final three left Howard the next day, and all were at AMARC by 15 January. The USAF was due to have vacated Howard by May 1999. Should Air Mobility Command not have a future use for the C-27s, they will be disposed of, probably on the export market.

Meanwhile, in Italy, the prototype Alenia G222 conversion to become the C-27J was taking shape. The prototype aircraft is Italian air force aircraft MM62127, and is fitted with Allison AE2100D3 engines similar to those installed in the C-130J. The project is a joint venture by Alenia and Lockheed Martin.

Additional C-17 offer

Boeing has offered the USAF an additional 60 C-17As at a substantially reduced cost per aircraft. Currently, the USAF is paying $198 million per aircraft, but this could be reduced to $149 million under the new offer. The aircraft would incorporate extra centre-section fuel tankage adding 67,000 lb (30391 kg) of fuel, resulting in a 15 per cent range increase. This modification can also be applied to the existing C-17 order from the 71st aircraft. Scheduled for delivery in June 1999 is the first C-17A for the 62nd Airlift Wing at McChord AFB, Washington. This is the 51st aircraft (98-0051), which incorporates a new, lighter tail assembly.

Apology

World Air Power Journal would like to apologise to the author, Mr Bill Sweetman, and those concerned with the proposed RAF F-16 purchase for editorial alterations made to the text on p. 96 of *World Air Power Journal* Volume 36. The additional remarks were not Mr Sweetman's, and may have caused some confusion concerning the motives of those proposing the deal. There was no editorial intention to suggest any ulterior motives on the part of these advisors, and we acknowledge that they were acting only in the best interests of the Royal Air Force.

Operation
Allied Force

The First 30 Days

By late March, President Slobodan Milosevic of Serbia had failed to act upon NATO's ultimatum to withdraw troops and special police from Kosovo. NATO's response came from the air.

Above: This Dutch F-16AM is marked with a MiG-29 silhouette for the aircraft it shot down on the first night of the air war. The kill was scored using AIM-120, as were the two MiGs downed by USAF F-15s that night.

Left: A Canadian CF-18 taxis out at Aviano clutching a GBU-12 laser-guided bomb. A pair of EA-6B Prowlers departs in the background.

Wednesday 24 March – Day 1

■ Eleven nations participate in the first wave of air strikes – Belgium, Canada, Denmark, France, Italy, Germany, Norway, Turkey, Spain, the UK and the USA. In the words of General Clark, "we're going to systematically and progressively attack, disrupt, degrade, devastate and, ultimately, unless President Milosevic complies with the demands of the international community, we're going to destroy his forces and their facilities."

■ Six B-52Hs launch from RAF Fairford at 10.42 local time, initiating the first wave of NATO airstrikes against the former Republic of Yugoslavia. B-52Hs proceed directly to tanker rendezvous over Atlantic. They do not reach their launch boxes until much later that evening, when darkness is falling over the target area.

■ Two B-2As of the 509th Bomb Wing launch on the first combat mission for the 'Stealth Bomber' from their home base at Whiteman AFB, Missouri. B-2s each drop 16 2,000-lb 'GPS-guided weapons' (either JDAMs or GAM-84s) against unspecified targets, believed to include airfield and facilities at Podgorica airport, Montenegro. Each mission involves two 15-hour legs, with two refuellings each way. *Sky News* reports a Yak-42 airliner arrived at the airport only minutes before the bombs began to fall.

■ Four Armée de l'Air Mirage 2000Ds participate in NATO action for the first time, dropping 1000-kg BGLs against targets in Serb Republic.

■ Six RAF Harrier GR.Mk 7s launched to attack an ammunition storage facility but failed to hit their target. The attacking aircraft dropped a single 1,000-lb Paveway II, which fell short and missed the target. The mission was then aborted. Smoke was blamed for breaking the lock of the Harrier's TIALD system, and with no clear target designation available the mission was scrubbed.

■ Royal Navy attack submarine HMS *Splendid* fires an unspecified number of Tomahawk cruise missiles, believed to be only one, marking the first use of such a weapon by British forces. *Splendid*'s target is understood to be the same as the RAF Harriers and its attack may have contributed to the smoke over the target which blocked the aircraft.

■ Majority of strikes aimed at air bases and air defence network in Serbia, Kosovo and Montenegro, but also included power stations and power grid, arms factories, military and police barracks and command and control centres. Explosions were reported at Batajnica air force base and the VJ's Kosovski Junaci barracks, Pristina. Targets hit in Montenegro between 21.40 and 21.00 local include Golubovci airport, munitions stores at Danilovgrad plus military sites at Radovac, Sipcanik and Ulcinj. Military targets in northern Belgrade and elsewhere in Serbia also hit. Yugoslav accounts of the attack said that five airports, five barracks and command and control positions had been hit.

■ Cruise missiles fired from USS *Gonzales* and USS *Philippine Sea* at 20.35 GMT. *Gonzales* fires 18 Tomahawks that night, including two misfires. An unknown number of Tomahawks also fired from total of three US vessels in the Adriatic. A total of 65 aircraft is recorded departing Aviano AFB.

Stealth technology has played its part in the war over Kosovo as both the F-117 (above) and B-2 (right) have been heavily involved. The F-117 made the news early in the war when one was shot down by a Serb SA-3. B-2s have been flown on non-stop missions from Whiteman, using JDAM weapons against infrastructure targets, some within Belgrade city limits.

■ Russia announces it is considering the deployment of tactical nuclear weapons to Belarus, in response to the NATO bombings, which it claims violate international law and called "illegal military action" in UN session.
■ Serb media report the shoot-down of a NATO aircraft in the mountains northwest of Pristina. All NATO aircraft return to base.

Thursday 25 March – Day 2

■ NATO fighters record three air-to-air kills against JRV aircraft during operations on the night of 24/25 March. All are claimed as MiG-29s. The MiG-killers include two Cervia-based F-15Cs of the 493rd FS, 48 TFW and a KLu F-16A MLU (J-063, 322 Squadron) – making the first Dutch air force air-to-air kill since World War II. A MiG-29 kill marking was quickly applied. One of the USAF MiG killers is Cesar 'Rico' Rodriguez, who, as a captain during Operation Desert Storm in 1991, was credited with two kills.
■ Another JRV MiG-21 loss is reported, but not as a direct kill. Aircraft may have crashed after

running out of fuel or flown into the ground.
■ MiG-29 pilot Major Nebojsa Nikolic later appeared on Serbian TV to say that he had been shot down in a dogfight with 24 NATO aircraft. As he put it during the interview, "I received the signal to take off very quickly and without thinking I took the aircraft up and flew towards the odious enemy. I knew that I was going towards those who had appeared in great numbers in our skies, but I went to defend them anyway, not thinking about their strength." Nikolic recalled how he avoided three air-to-air missiles but was hit by a fourth and had to eject. "The enemy vultures circled over me, trying to spot me. They also fired at me," he said.
■ An F-15C makes a precautionary

landing at Sarajevo, having "suffered damage" according to a NATO spokesman. Unofficial sources later suggest that this aircraft may have been the victim of 'blue-on-blue' cannon fire from its wingman.
■ Serbian forces fire across the Kosovan border at the Albanian town of Dobruna for several hours.
■ Second wave of NATO air attacks launched at 18.30 GMT, by US, UK, German and Turkish forces – in an assault described as 'significantly heavier' than the first night. Targets struck include barracks at Urosevac and Prizren (Kosovo); airports in Nis (southern Serbia) and Golubovci (Podgorica, Montenegro); military facilities in Trstenik, Danilovgrad and elsewhere in Montenegro. Strikes were conducted in the Logovac-Srbica, Kosovska Mitrovica, Bajgora,

Mt Cicavica and Podujevo areas.
■ Greek Prime Minister Konstantinos Simitris opposes air strikes, saying "military operations will not bring any solution" at the EU summit in Berlin. Demonstrations against the NATO action break down into riots in Athens, and also in Skopje, Macedonia. Italian government threatened by withdrawal of support from left-wing and Church-aligned coalition partners. Italian aircraft not involved in direct combat missions but are flying CAP sorties.
■ Increased looting and fighting reported across Kosovo province.
■ Russian press reports that a German two-seat aircraft has been shot down are repeated in the Serbian press. No NATO aircraft were lost.

Friday 26 March – Day 3

■ Three B-52Hs launched from RAF Fairford, at 13.30 GMT. USS *Philippine Sea* makes cruise missile launch at 13.20 GMT. The first NATO aircraft launch from Aviano at 16.15 local – E-3 followed by large strike package, including F-117s. At 22.00 GMT Pentagon spokesman confirms third wave of strikes are underway. Targets attacked in Belgrade, Mali Mokri Lug, Avala,

Bearing the brunt of the air defence mission over Serbia have been the F-15C Eagles of the 493rd Expeditionary Fighter Squadron, detached from RAF Lakenheath to Cervia in Italy. 493rd crew have been augmented by those from Alaska.

Left: Harrier GR.Mk 7s began the war using TIALD pods and Paveway II LGBs, but were soon toting more traditional weaponry such as the BL755 cluster bomb, seen here.

Below: Portuguese F-16As have operated from Aviano. Optimised for air defence, the aircraft have been mainly used on defensive CAPs.

Vozdovac and Topcider areas. Serbian forces making widespread use of smokepots to obscure targets from LGBs. NATO also admits that it is unable to locate the expected number of Serbian mobile SAM batteries.

■ Forty per cent of targets hit on day three were inside Kosovo, compared to 20 per cent on the first two days. Air Commodore David Wilby says that NATO flew 249 sorties on day three.

■ The first ethnic Albanian refugees begin to cross the border from Kosovo into Albania as reports mount of killings and destruction of homes and villages by Serbian forces. Sustained fighting between KLA and Serbian forces.

■ Russia cuts off all contact with NATO agencies and expels NATO representatives from Moscow. NATO accused of conducting "undisguised genocide" against the Yugoslav population. Greece again calls for an end to NATO air strikes, against a background of mounting disquiet in Italy. Italian Prime Minister, Massimo D'Alema, later clearly reaffirms Italy's backing for the NATO campaign.

■ OSCE monitors, having been withdrawn from Kosovo, are now pulled out of Macedonia. Bosnian Serbs attack offices of British, French, German and US representatives in Banja Luka. Yugoslav state TV reports the shoot-down of another NATO aircraft on the night of 25/26 March. Tanjug News Agency reports two more NATO aircraft and 15 cruise missiles downed. All NATO aircraft return to base safely.

■ Carrier battle group led by USS *Theodore Roosevelt* prepares to depart Norfolk on scheduled deployment to 'the Mediterranean and Persian Gulf'.

■ General Clark announces the next wave of strikes will be aimed at Serbian forces in Kosovo. NATO reports 50 targets have been hit, over the course of 400 sorties, since the air campaign was launched. The overall effectiveness of these missions remains in doubt, though food and fuel supplies in Belgrade are reported to be restricted.

Saturday 27 March – Day 4

■ Two B-52Hs depart RAF Fairford at 21.30 GMT. NATO attacks continue into the early hours of the morning. US National Security Advisor states that as of 04.00 GMT NATO air attacks were ongoing. NATO states that day four had begun with a cruise missile strike against a 'target of opportunity'. This is believed to be a MiG-29 hit by a Tomahawk on the runway at Batajnica, using near real-time imaging information from a U-2S.

■ Two JRV MiG-29s shot down five miles inside the Bosnian/Serbian border, near Bijelina, by two F-15Cs of the 493rd FS, 48th TFW. The MiG-29s were part of a three-ship formation but the third aircraft escaped. The F-15 pair fired three AIM-120 AMRAAMs to down the two MiGs. Both Serbian pilots were widely reported as captured by SFOR troops but later reports were modified to say SFOR units were still searching for them. Sources close to SFOR later stated that the two pilots were 'captured' by Russian SFOR troops who allowed JRV helicopters to illegally cross the border into Bosnia and recover their two pilots.

The MiG-29s were armed with R-60 (AA-8) and R-73 (AA-10) missiles – the best information indicates that they were attempting to shoot down a NATO E-3 or E-8 J-STARS. The crash site of one aircraft revealed English stencilling on the wreckage, leading to – clearly false – Yugoslav claims that the aircraft could thus not be a JRV aircraft. Second crash site later identified in a minefield 15 miles southwest of Biejeljina, in the Bosnian Federation side of the zone of separation between Bosnia and the Serb Republic. Bosnia ambassador to UN request emergency meeting of Security council saying that the aircraft had "the intention of committing military strikes against our country".

■ NATO launches 'Phase Two' of Operation Allied Force, directed at VJ and MUP forces on the ground in Kosovo – but there is little immediate evidence that the character of operations has changed greatly from 'Phase One'. Phase Two will focus on areas below the 44th Parallel to stop the ethnic cleansing tactics of the Serbian forces which are moving ahead at an increasing pace. The deployment of more USAF A-10s is announced but not elaborated on. More B-52s will be deployed to Fairford. The RAF announces it will deploy four additional Harrier GR.Mk 7s.

■ General Wesley Clarke acknowledges that air power alone cannot stop Serb attacks on Kosovo villages, but NATO still denies that it has any intention of sending in ground troops. Reports suggest that Serbian forces have been rounding up Kosovo Albanian men in door-to-door searches.

■ Serbian cinemas now reportedly showing only World War II films (with Western films banned – apart from a national TV screening of *Wag The Dog*.)

■ Serbian TV announces that a NATO warplane was shot down at 17.15 GMT and shows film of burning wreckage. The aircraft is clearly an F-117A, but NATO initially refuses to confirm the loss. By the following morning Serbian sources claim they have shot down five other aircraft and have captured one German crew of a 'phantom' jet. This appears to be a confused report originating from the 'Stealth fighter' shoot-down. No Luftwaffe Phantoms are deployed over Kosovo and no other aircraft have been lost. The F-117 pilot ejected safely 70 miles from the Bosnian border and Serbian forces are reported to be searching for him. The unnamed pilot is rescued by a NATO C-SAR team in an operation shrouded in secrecy. No details of the unit involved are released.

The loss of the F-117 is blamed variously on mechanical failure, an air-to-air kill and shoot-down by Serbian SA-3 or SA-6 SAMs. Fears are expressed that Yugoslavia and Iraq have been co-operating closely on their ADA strategies and technology. High-level visits by Yugoslavian personnel to Baghdad in February 1999 are reported. Iraqi experience may have given Serbian technicians vital clues and information to help them track F-117s and defeat US tactics. On 2 April the Yugoslav government announces that it will hand pieces of the F-117 to the Russian authorities.

When **Roosevelt** arrived in the Adriatic it brought with it a large air wing ready to carry out precision strikes. Here a VF-14 Tomcat returns to the carrier with LGB and LANTIRN pod.

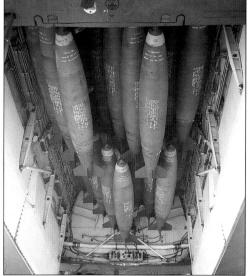

'Buffs' and 'Bones'

The deployment by 2nd Bomb Wing B-52Hs to RAF Fairford in October 1998 was intended to send Belgrade a clear affirmation of NATO's resolve to use military force. While the six bombers returned to Louisiana the following month, all eight of the Stratofortresses which subsequently returned to the Gloucestershire base on 21 and 22 February participated in the first wave of Allied Force air strikes on 24 March. With two bombers acting as an unarmed decoy and an air spare, respectively, the remaining six Stratofortresses launched AGM-86C Conventional Air-Launched Cruise Missiles (CALCMs) from stand-off positions. These and subsequent attacks have reportedly involved both the 2,000-lb (907-kg) blast fragmentation (Block 0) and the 3,150-lb (1429-kg) (Block 1) warheads. The 20th EBS was designated the lead unit and drew aircraft from all four regular B-52H squadrons – the Barksdale-based 11th BS and 96th BS plus the 23rd BS from Minot AFB, ND. Over the course of the next few weeks a shortage of CALCMs, which reportedly fell to just 70 missiles including those in deep maintenance, saw the number of aircraft deployed fall to three.

On the third day of the war, ground crew cheer off a B-52H, one of three which launched AGM-86C CALCMs that day. All CALCM carriage is internal, a maximum of eight being carried.

The 2nd AEG expanded on 1 April with the arrival of four B-1Bs from the 77th EBS, 28th BW at Ellsworth AFB, SD accompanied by a single example from the co-located 37th BS to be used as an emergency spares source. Each of the Lancers deployed had received the latest Defensive System Upgrade Program (DSUP) or Block D upgrade which was hurriedly tested and approved by the 53rd Wg at Eglin less than a week before the deployment. By mid-May only Mk 82s had been dropped by the B-1Bs, principally in two-ship missions aimed against area targets. **Dylan Eklund**

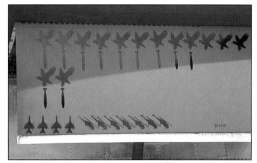

Above, far left: An AGM-86C is seen prior to loading on a 2nd AEG B-52H.

Above, centre: Mission marks are seen on a B-1B nosewheel door.

Above: Internal carriage of 500-lb (227-kg) Mk 82 bombs in a B-1B.

Left: A 77th BS B-1B displays the revised tailcone which houses the ALE-50 Advanced Airborne Expendable Decoy system. This is part of the Block D upgrade.

Sunday 28 March – Day 5

■ NATO air attacks during night of 28/29 March claim one MiG-21, one SOKO Galeb and "some" MUP helicopters destroyed on the ground (at Podgorica). A total of 66 aircraft hit 17 targets, including 11 in Belgrade and six at other locations. Two waves of attacks involved 253 sorties. Tanjug News Agency reports explosions south of Pristina at 21.00 local (19.00 GMT).

■ First reports surface of SAS deployment to Kosovo to ground designate targets. SAS teams are likely to have been in-country prior to the breakout of hostilities.

■ Refugee crisis in Albania deepens and thousands of refugees are arriving at the Albanian border each day.

■ Serbia claims that five NATO aircraft plus a helicopter were shot down on the night of 28/29 March. No NATO losses occur.

■ Russian peace negotiators arrive in Belgrade. They are later denounced as "scum and trash" by the Serbian media following a meeting with Deputy Prime Minister Vuk Draskovich. Indian Prime Minister Atal Behari Vajpayee announces that India is considering an alliance with China and Russia following the NATO attacks (Vajpayee's right-wing nationalist government collapses after a no-confidence vote just three weeks later).

Monday 29 March – Day 6

■ NATO announces that air attacks will now be conducted around the clock. Imagery of attack on SA-3 site ('Low Blow' guidance radar destroyed) and Special Police headquarters building in Pristina (totally destroyed) site shown at daily NATO briefing. Serbian forces attacked in the field include 243rd combat group of VJ, based at Donja Semanja.

■ First strike package of approximately 50 aircraft departs Aviano at 18.16 GMT. RAF Harriers come under 'heavy fire' but succeed in hitting their targets. OSCE reports that 60,000 Kosovar refugees have arrived in Albania since Saturday, with 4,000 refugees per hour now crossing the border from Kosovo into Albania. Another 10,000-14,000 have crossed into Macedonia and others into Montenegro. Estimated 500,000 Kosovo Albanians have fled their homes due to Serbian 'ethnic cleansing' tactics, with 150,000 now trying to escape into Albania. Serbian forces confiscating all identity and official papers from those fleeing Kosovo in an obvious attempt to render them 'non-citizens' should they wish to return. NATO reports that Serbian forces are also grouping civilians around troop formations. Pec, Kosovo's second city, is reported to be "fully ethnically cleansed and in flames".

■ US DoD estimates that 40,000 Serbian troops with 300 tanks, 400 artillery guns and 100 other IFVs are in the Kosovo region.

■ UK announces plans to deploy four additional Harrier GR.Mk 1s and eight Tornado GR.Mk 1s. The Tornados will operate from their base in Germany, RAF Brüggen. US DoD announces an additional four B-52s and five B-1Bs armed with Sensor-Fused Weapons will be deployed to Europe (to replace some B-52s). Other new deployments announced include five EA-6Bs and 10 additional tankers.

■ Albania announces that its airspace is at the complete disposal of NATO forces and air bases are available for contingency use. German envoy in Bosnia, Hans Koschnick, refuses to rule out deployment of NATO troops in Kosovo, saying, "We want to protect the population of Kosovo. If that cannot be done with air strikes then we must think again."

■ Russian Defence Minister Igor Sergeyev claims that over 1,000 Serbian civilians have been killed since the launch of the offensive. Russia agrees vital $4.5 million credit with IMF and a new economic plan to pay off its debts to Western banks. The IMF later denies that any firm settlement has been reached yet.

BOOMER's kill

On 26 March, two F-15C Eagles shot down two MiG-29 'Fulcrums' over Bosnia. A 27-year-old USAF captain of the 493rd Fighter Squadron based at RAF Lakenheath, with tactical callsign BOOMER, claimed the first one. He had taken off from Cervia air base, Italy at 14.00 in F-15C 84-014 (tailcode 'LN') to set up a typical two-ship CAP over Bosnia. He was wingman to CLAW, also a captain from the 493rd, who flew in 86-0156.

BOOMER's Eagle was a distinguished one. It was decorated with an Iraqi flag painted under the canopy after Captain Danesky of the 53rd Tactical Fighter Squadron had downed an Iraqi Sukhoi Su-22 on 20 March 1991. Soon, it would be a one-of-a-kind Eagle sporting both Iraqi and Serbian flags.

BOOMER and CLAW were tasked with the protection of NATO troops (Stabilisation Forces, SFOR) in Bosnia-Herzegovina, known as Operation Deliberate Force. Being the flight leader of this mission, CLAW was the mission commander and the tactical brain; BOOMER was the primary targeter and had to watch his leader's six o'clock, a common Eagle tactic. Both pilots were seasoned veterans from actions over Bosnia and Iraq. BOOMER had three tours in Turkey under his belt, but had never encountered enemy aircraft before. Although they were at war, it seemed they were flying in a peaceful environment and, apart from some low clouds, the sky was clear. In Bosnia the surface-to-air threat was much lower than over Kosovo, Montenegro or Serbia, but it was not to be ignored. They did not observe any ground fire, not even smoke or explosions on the far horizon during the flight. This all changed suddenly, about halfway through their sortie.

"We got a group on our radar displays heading from Serbia towards Bosnia," BOOMER said days later at Cervia. "Our onboard identification system identified it as a MiG-29. CLAW turned us cold, which means he directed us into a better position for the engagement. In this particular case, it also meant staying clear of Serbian territory and possible ground-based air defences. It lasted about three minutes before we got in the position CLAW wanted us."

In the meantime, AWACS had confirmed the contact, and the coming engagement gained momentum after the MiG was verified and met the five rules of engagement.

"After CLAW turned us flight hot I requested to be engaged," said BOOMER. "CLAW responded by saying 'press', indicating I was authorised to shoot. Not much later I fired one beyond-visual-range missile from my port wing pylon in a head-on engagement. At nearly the same moment, AWACS informed us the contact was not one but two planes." CLAW, being in a better position now, spiked the second contact. Fifteen seconds after BOOMER's missile had streaked off its rail, CLAW shot two missiles in rapid succession.

"Meanwhile, I continued monitoring the missile guidance. I did not get any spikes from the bogies. I remember looking over my shoulder to see the two contrails from the two missiles CLAW had fired towards the second MiG. They made a trio with the missile I had fired. It was an awesome sight. I did not see any explosions as I was just too occupied scanning the skies for potential dangers. CLAW did see two fireballs at approximately the moment the computer had calculated the missiles would impact."

Above: 84-0015, an F-15C of the 493rd EFS, sports a single kill mark beneath the cockpit.

Left: 84-014 wears kill marks for both the MiG-29 shot down by BOOMER and an Su-22 'Fitter' while flying with the 36th TFW in the aftermath of Desert Storm.

Neither BOOMER nor CLAW saw any chutes. According to the Pentagon, the two MiGs came down some 5 miles (8 km) from the Serbian border, one in a mine field. NATO initially confirmed the two pilots had been captured, but denied that five hours later. At least one pilot came down in the Russian sector. The story goes that he and his colleague had been taken by the Russians and returned to Serbia by an Mi-8/17 a couple of hours later.

After the kills, the two Eagles pressed on towards their prey which were now tumbling down in burning debris. They had to 'sanitise' the skies behind the shoot-down site to verify if other contacts were around. Press reports afterwards indicated other MiGs might have managed to escape, but CLAW and BOOMER saw nothing. They returned to their CAP station. "We still had three hours of CAP time to go, which was rather hard. We were much more vigilant about the presence of other MiGs but, after our adrenaline had drained away, it took a lot more effort to stay focused on the mission."

They did their victory rolls en route to Cervia and landed after dark. "Our arrival was very rewarding. All the people from maintenance, armament and whatever else welcomed us with lots of cheering and applauding. Of course, there was a celebration – though small, because the war was going on – and I had to fly again the next day."

Looking back at the event BOOMER was impressed by the short time the whole engagement lasted. "It took between three to five minutes," he said. "I was glad to be in an F-15C and come out the winner. Our great training really helps us to stay on top."

Flying time and type of missiles, as well as the altitude, heading and speed of both the Eagle and MiG flight remains classified. BOOMER also did not want to disclose the callsign the flight used; remaining anonymous is an unofficial NATO policy for all military personnel involved, except for detachment commanders, spokesmen and personnel who have no objection to having their names revealed.

Cervia is an Italian Air Force air base located close to the Adriatic Sea in the northeast of Italy. It is home of the 5º Stormo, whose 23º Gruppo flies the venerable F-104ASA-M Starfighter in the air defence role. The Starfighters are tasked with being on 24-hour quick reaction alert to protect Italy when Yugoslavian aircraft manage to penetrate the various layers of NATO combat air patrols. Until the end of April, Yugoslavia did not attempt this, as the Yugoslavian air force probably realised it would be extremely difficult to succeed.

The 493rd arrived at Cervia on 21 February with 10 Eagles. Some weeks later, when it became clear that war operations against Yugoslavia would be inevitable, more arrived from Incirlik, Turkey, where they had been enforcing the 'No-Fly Zone' over northern Iraq in support of Operation Northern Watch. They formed the 48th Expeditionary Operations Group and began Allied Force on the evening of 24 March with escorting NATO strikes. That night, two F-15Cs on two different missions shot down two MiGs. One probable kill of a still-undetermined type was claimed on that night. One hour after the much-publicised shoot-down of an F-117, four Eagles were airborne for rescue combat air patrol, guarding the rescue helicopters and support aircraft. They flew the northern CAP in a six-hour mission.

At the start of the operation the 48th had about 30 pilots from the 493rd FS and one staff officer from Mildenhall, a major assigned to 3rd Air Force headquarters and fully qualified on the Eagle who took the chance to fly a real fighter instead of desk. In the middle of April the 493rd was strengthened with a handful of pilots of the 3rd Wing stationed at Elmendorf AB, Alaska. They had taken six F-15Cs to Lakenheath, which would eventually rotate with Eagles from Cervia. **Gert Kromhout**

Fully armed F-15Cs of the 493rd EFS are seen on the flight line at Cervia AB. The 48th EOG has been tasked with a variety of missions, including CAPs over Bosnia to prevent Serb aircraft hitting SFOR forces.

Armée de l'Air attack aircraft, spearheaded by the Mirage 2000Ds of EC 3/3, have been very active from their base at Istrana. These 2000Ds carry the PDLCT FLIR/laser designation pod.

F-117 shoot-down

On 27 March the Serbs gained their first (and so far only) major success of the air war by downing an F-117A using an SA-3 missile. The pilot was rescued soon after, but the wreckage was taken away for analysis by Serb authorities and offered to the Russians. The aircraft came down in flat terrain near a Yugoslav military range. The shoot-down appears to have been a lucky shot against an aircraft that had flown a similar flightpath four nights running, and whose SEAD support may for some reason have been less than effective.

Above: At the start of the war the first deployment of F-117s operated from Aviano, but moved back to Spangdahlem in Germany, where they joined a second batch of aircraft sent to bolster the force. The 52nd AEF stood up on 14 April at the German base, to which the F-117 unit (49th EOG) reports.

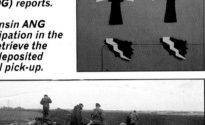

Right: This KC-135 of the Wisconsin ANG wears a mission mark for participation in the large CSAR effort mounted to retrieve the F-117 pilot. MH-53Js may have deposited 'dune-buggies' to make the final pick-up.

Right: Serb troops examine the wreckage of the F-117 the next morning. Sizeable segments of the aircraft remained relatively intact, including the rear fuselage. The cockpit canopy also survived its fall to earth after the pilot ejected.

Tuesday 30 March – Day 7

■ Missions over Kosovo are affected by poor weather, but Air Commodore David Wilby announces that NATO is stepping up the air war, saying, "More offensive assets specifically suited for this role are entering our order of battle, and the weather is set to improve." He also noted that there was "a well orchestrated and dynamic tactical air defence campaign against us." The French Defence Minister, Alain Richard, says that NATO strikes have knocked out 50 per cent of Yugoslavia's air defence and air combat capability. The French Army Chief of Staff Jean-Pierre Cowlick said, "There is no longer any co-ordinated and sophisticated capacity of Serb air forces to oppose Alliance air forces."

■ Pentagon spokesman Ken Bacon says that NATO has a "degree" of air superiority over Kosovo, but admits that NATO has not succeeded in delivering a "knock-out punch" to Serbian ground forces in Kosovo. He also states that the US has no plans to deploy AH-64A Apaches to support troops in any possible ground attack. The US supply of cruise missiles is also running out, according to Bacon: "We have a supply right now, but it won't last for ever. But we certainly have enough to strike important targets."

■ Between six and eight A-10As are redeployed to Aviano on the instruction of NATO Commander General Wesley Clark. A-10s have not been used in combat to date. B-52s at Fairford reinforced by three additional aircraft from Minot.

■ Albania's President, Rexhep Mejdani, calls on NATO to halt the killing of Kosovars by Serbia. Russia's Foreign Minister, Igor Ivanov, accuses NATO of committing "unconcealed genocide against the people of Yugoslavia". A Saudi delegation led by Foreign Minister Prince Saud al-Faisal visits Moscow, asking the Russians to change their stance on the Kosovo issue. Russia President Yeltsin later announces, "Russia has made its choice. We will not be drawn into a military conflict." UN Secretary-General Kofi Annan declares his profound outrage at Serbian atrocities in Kosovo.

■ Following a meeting with Germany's Chancellor Gerhard Schroeder, Russian Prime Minister Yevgeny Primakov meets President Slobodan Milosevic in Belgrade. US State Department reveals information that Serbia may be planning a coup to overthrow the government in Montenegro, which is following an abstentionist line and is opposed to the Belgrade leadership.

Wednesday 31 March – Day 8

■ NATO confirms all intended targets have been hit during 30/31 March, despite bad weather. NATO operations have not yet reached their full potential; instead, NATO is increasing its operational "range and tempo", according to spokesman Jamie Shea. There will be no pause in operations over Easter, following a Greek proposal for a truce from 4 to 11 April.

■ It is estimated that the USAF has only (approximately) 100 AGM-86C CALCMs left in its inventory. The US Navy's supply of AGM-84 Tomahawks is much larger, at approximately 2,000, but they are being used at an even faster rate.

■ At 05.00 GMT the Yugoslav embassy in Washington and the ambassador's residence are seized by the US State Department.

■ Allegations that Russian military transport aircraft have overflown Romania *en route* to Yugoslavia are firmly denied by the Romanian Ministry of Defence.

■ A signals intelligence ship of Russia's Black Sea fleet will be deployed to monitor operations in Kosovo – to be followed by a flotilla of seven ships departing Sevastopol on

Right: Armed with LGB and Magic II missile, a French Jaguar is prepared for a mission from Istrana.

Below: Quite apart from the 15,000 hours commemorative artwork on the fuel tank, this 2000D carries five mission marks on the nose for successful LGB sorties. Note the PDLCT pod used for nocturnal designation.

allege that a damaged F-117 had to make an emergency landing in Zagreb, Croatia after operations on the night of 9/10 April.
■ There is increasing unease that attacks on empty barracks and other facilities are not affecting Serbian forces now well dispersed in the field.
■ One-third of the Kosovo Albanian population has been forced out of the province.
■ President Milosevic asks Russia for military aid.

Saturday 3 April – Day 11

■ US Secretary of Defense William S. Cohen issues a directive for the USS *Theodore Roosevelt* battle group to remain in the Mediterranean and support Operation Allied Force. *Roosevelt*'s battle group includes the guided missile cruisers USS *Leyte Gulf* and USS *Vella Gulf*, the guided missile destroyer USS *Ross*, the guided missile frigate USS *Halyburton*, the fast combat support ship USS *Arctic*, and the attack submarine USS *Albuquerque*.

The *Roosevelt*, which arrived in the Mediterranean on 3 April, was originally slated to deploy directly to the Persian Gulf to relieve the USS *Enterprise* battle group. *Enterprise* was due to return to CONUS in May 1999 for scheduled maintenance. Instead, the USS *Kitty Hawk*, home-ported in Yokosuka, Japan, will be deployed to the Gulf to support operations over Iraq. The controversial deployment of *Kitty Hawk* will leave the US without an available operational carrier in the Pacific for the first time since the end of World War II. To cover the short-fall, the USS *Constellation* will be deployed but will not be available until autumn. By then the *John F. Kennedy* would also be available for a scheduled Mediterranean cruise.
■ The US dispatches the first C-17 loaded with relief supplies to Albania.

2 April. Russia's Armed Forces Chief of Staff General Anatoly Kvashnin tells the Interfax news agency that if Russia's security is threatened, "if the choice is between life or death for Russia, then whatever the armed forces have, in particular nuclear weapons, should be used."
■ German Defence Minsiter Rudolf Scharping reports evidence of Serbian concentration camps in Kosovo. Italy's Prime Minister D'Alema says the "inhuman violence" and "genocide" taking place in Kosovo must be stopped and acknowledges that a diplomatic solution is no longer likely.

Thursday 1 April – Day 9

■ The largest number of aircraft so far, approximately 100, launches from Aviano and air raid sirens begin sounding in Belgrade at 19.00 GMT. NATO begins 'Phase Three' attacks against basic infrastructure targets in Serbia. These include the Petrovaradin bridge on the Danube at Novi Sad, a bridge on the Magura-Belacevac

railway, the main water supply to Novi Sad and targets near Pec, Zatric, Decane, Dragodan, Vranjevac, Bajin Basta and Pristina Airport. No targets in Belgrade are attacked.
■ General Clark admits, "Air power alone cannot stop paramilitary murder on the ground, and that's what's going on down there." The US has only generated an average of 48 combat sorties per day in the first week of operations.
■ Three US soldiers of the ARRC patrolling the Macedonian border are captured by Serbian forces – perhaps having crossed the border in error – and exhibited battered and bruised on Yugoslavian TV, in contravention of the Geneva Convention.
■ Five B-1B Lancers, supported by two C-5Bs, are deployed to RAF Fairford. More EA-6Bs are to be transferred from Incirlik, Turkey, to Italy. Operations in the 'No-Fly Zone' over Northern Iraq have been scaled back.
■ NATO Secretary General Javier Solana admits in a Spanish radio inter-

view that sending in ground troops will be a difficult decision, but if necessary it will happen.
■ Russia announces that NATO 'spy flights' over the Baltic, in the sensitive Kaliningrad area, have increased three-fold and air defence troops are now on 24-hour alert. The possible airlift of advanced SAM systems to Yugoslavia is also mooted. Yugoslavia's Deputy Prime Minster Vuk Draskovic is reported as saying that if NATO air attacks continue, Russia will not be able to hold back the outrage of its people and will be forced to declare war on NATO.

Friday 2 April – Day 10

■ Air strikes again hindered by bad weather but Tomahawks are launched against targets in 'downtown' Belgrade – including the Serbian Interior Ministry. The first strikes are flown by B-1Bs. Two aircraft attacked unidentified targets. Serbian media report attacks on the Pancevo oil refinery.
■ Croatian and Yugoslavian sources

Left: With the constant demand for SEAD, the EA-6B Prowler force has been stretched to the limit. Here an AGM-88 HARM is prepared for loading aboard a Marine Prowler.

Above: The Aviano residents of the 31st FW have been in the thick of the fighting, employing Block 40 F-16CGs with LANTIRN and various LGBs (GBU-12 illustrated).

Dutch/Belgian Allied Force

The mid-life updated F-16s, designated F-16AM, of the Dutch/Belgian Air Force detachment at Amendola AB, Italy were among the most heavily-tasked NATO aircraft in the first weeks of Allied Force. The detachment, called Deployable Task Force (DATF), started with eight Dutch F-16AMs, eight Dutch F-16A OCUs (Operational Capability Upgrade) and eight Belgian F-16As. DATF immediately started round-the-clock combat operations.

"The CAOC tasks our F-16AMs twice as much as the unmodified F-16s," says Lieutenant Colonel Jon Abma, who until 21 April (when Lieutenant Colonel Frank de Winne of the Belgian AF assumed command of DATF) was the Dutch commander of the Dutch/Belgian F-16 detachment at Amendola and squadron commander of the first Dutch F-16AM squadron. "They regard the unmodified Fighting Falcons as second choice. On average, an F-16AM flies two missions a day, the F-16A only one. … We have a shortage of F-16AMs. Because the combat missions last two to 5½ hours, the aircraft need maintenance much earlier than in peacetime operations."

In the first weekend of Allied Force two F-16As were exchanged for two F-16AMs. On 8 April the effectiveness of the Dutch/Belgian F-16 detachment was further enhanced when the Belgian Air Force exchanged three unmodified F-16s for an equal number of normal F-16As, bringing the total of MLU F-16s to thirteen. They were much needed.

Meanwhile, NATO requested an additional 300 warplanes for the effort. The RNlAF responded by sending an additional four F-16AMs from Twenthe AB on 21 April, bringing the total to 14. The Belgian Air Force also offered four additional F-16s but NATO accepted two F-16AMs on 26 April to bring the Belgian total to 12. At that time, Twenthe was in the process of relieving Leeuwarden at Amendola.

The core Twenthe unit is 315 Sqn, which had reached initial operational capability with the MLU in February 1999. The 'Lions' were augmented by F-16A-equipped 313 Sqn, the operational training squadron also based at Twenthe, together with the few Volkel reconnaissance pilots who undertook normal air defence missions during the first weeks when tactical reconnaissance was not necessary. They started reconnaissance operations on 30 April using the MARS (Medium Altitude Reconnaissance System) and Orpheus recce pods.

Although targeting pod deliveries were scheduled to begin in 2000, the RNlAF started operations on the night of 28/29 April with two LANTIRN AAQ-14 targeting pods borrowed from the USAF. They destroyed five helicopters and two Super Galebs at Podgorica AB. In early May the air force stepped up LGB operations when it received three pods of a batch of 10. The Improved Datalink (IDM), also called intra-flight datalink, has become a popular system. "With this excellent asset we do not have to give our positions by voice over the radio. We use it all the time. A few days ago we linked up with F-16CJ defence suppression F-16s for the first time. During a night mission we normally do not exactly know were they are because we do not use night vision goggles, but with the IDM we clearly saw their positions and when we saw a bright flash we knew they had fired a HARM." The F-16CJ normally uses the IDM for the exchange of data about ground radar targets. Despite the value of the system, Abma said that it does not always work 100 per cent and is sometimes "somewhat jammed".

By 10 May the Dutch F-16s had flown 644 Allied Force missions, the Belgians 418.

Transport ops

The Dutch No. 334 transport squadron at Eindhoven Air Base became involved in the operation from day one. The two KDC-10 tanker/transports were heavily committed to refuelling in the first three weeks.

A typical daylight flight in support of Allied Force was made on 21 April 1999. Take-off time was 09.00, to arrive in one the tanker tracks around the theatre of operations some two hours later. The KDC-10 relieved

Above: F-16AMs with AMRAAMs and Mavericks await their next mission at Amendola. The aircraft routinely carry ALQ-131 ECM pods on the centreline pylon.

Right: KDC-10 tankers have been flying missions from their home base at Eindhoven.

another tanker which had left 10 minutes earlier. Scheduled 'customers' were four F-15Cs and two Turkish F-16Cs. "It is always possible that other receivers will show up," said the boom operator. "It is war, so everything is possible."

His words were proved true as the first two Eagles appeared. In peacetime, normal procedure for all fighters is that they arrive at the starboard wing first before advancing to the receiver position under the boom. The Eagles, however, did not waste any time: they approached from the port wing and the wingman entered the hold position on the port wingtip, the leader immediately entering the receiver position.

"For us, this war mission is not significantly different than a training mission in peacetime," said one major. "Basically, our missions are never training missions. The only difference about this flight is the remote possibility a hostile fighter might appear."

"Then, we perform an immediate breakaway procedure to get the hell out of here," added the boomer. It has happened at least once during the first weeks of Allied Force.

The F-15Cs and F-16s were refuelled twice. They flew high-value CAP missions between the tanker(s) and the theatre of operations. After being on-station for roughly two hours, the crew initiated the return flight to Eindhoven, to be replaced by another tanker 10 minutes later.

The tankers, the four Fokker 60s and two C-130H-30s also became heavily involved in refugee relief operations and transportation of military personnel and equipment to Albania, Macedonia and the air base of Amendola, Italy. The two KDC-10 tankers flew day and night refuelling operations from Eindhoven. The Dutch tankers differ from the USAF KC-10 in that they do not have the rear fuselage boom operator compartment where the boomer is in visual contact with the receivers; instead, he relies on a three-dimensional video system and is located immediately aft of the flight deck. Operational employment does not differ very much from the KC-10.

When the humanitarian relief operation started, the KDC-10s as well as the two C-130H-30s and the four Fokker 60s became involved in flying supplies to Albania and bringing refugees back. By 10 May the tankers had flown 85 refuelling missions and the transports more than 25 relief missions. The Belgian air transport wing (15 Wing) at Brussels Melsbroek also put a lot of effort into the relief operations. The C-130 Hercules fleet and the Airbus A310s flew many missions to Macedonia and Albania, in addition to regular supply missions to Amendola.

Helicopters

Dutch CH-47D heavy transport helicopters of 298 Sqn were already in Macedonia when Allied Force began, having left their home base of Soesterberg on 14 January for Petrovac to support the Extraction Force. Shortly after the refugee exodus began, the Chinooks

became heavily involved in humanitarian operations in support of regular military transport flights. The Chinooks are equipped with MAG 7.62-mm guns in the port and starboard doors, enlarged flare ejectors and protective Kevlar matting in the cockpit. The Chinooks have relocated to Farke near Tirana, Albania and had flown 302 flights by 10 May.

Orions

The navy started flying reconnaissance missions over Kosovo (Operation Eagle Eye) with a P-3 Orion from NAS Sigonella, Italy in mid-January. Three P-3s have been modified to carry a FLIR camera and self-defence systems, at a cost of DGL10 million. The Orions are involved in patrol duties from Sigonella.

First kill

A Dutch pilot claimed one MiG-29 kill on the first night of the operation, marking the first Dutch air-to-air victory since the war in Netherlands New Guinea in the early 1960s when a P2V7-B Neptune shot down an Indonesian plane. The F-16 pilot is not allowed to speak to the press and his name remains classified, but Lieutenant Colonel Abma indicated that he was on a SEAD escort mission into Serbia with three colleagues in two pairs. The four F-16AMs had taken off from Amendola at 19.30, and sometime later AWACS told them three MiG-29s had taken off from Batajnica air base, home of the MiG-29 unit near Belgrade. The NATO package was over Kosovo, moving from south to north towards Serbia, when they got radar contact. The forward pair could not get close enough because of package routing and mission tasking. The second pair had better changes.

The MiG was orbiting at low altitude at a long distance, so the Dutch pilot had to calculate carefully when his target was in his missile's range. The declassified HUD tape started on 20:29 when the F-16, serialled J-063, was at an altitude of 34,000 ft (10360 m) in a slight descent, heading 018. At 20:52 the F-16 pilot turned towards the target, which he had kept at his 11 o'clock. Now flying in an exact opposite heading to the MiG, though not precisely boresighted, he fired one AMRAAM from his port underwing station at 20.30.08 at a distance of 18 km (11 miles). Five seconds later he sharply broke away on a different heading, while looking over his shoulder to see his missile detonate 30 seconds after launch. The kill was immediately confirmed by the fighter controller in the AWACS who had seen his radar contact disappear. The engagement took approximately five minutes.

Gert Kromhout

Right: Two unmodified Belgian F-16As taxi for a CAP mission. MLU aircraft are used for the more dangerous attack sorties.

Left: Some DATF missions have involved the delivery of CBU-87 cluster weapons. The AIM-120 is routinely carried for self-defence.

Providing a welcome augmentation to the **USAF SEAD** effort are the ... aboard *Roosevelt*. Complete with AGM-88s, this is VFA-87's brightly coloured CAG-bird.

Most lethal **SEAD** missions have ... their air defence systems around.

... in addition to missions directly ... of other former Yugoslav republics.

Sunday 4 April (Easter) – Day 12

Bad weather continues to hamper ...

NATO states ...

Monday 5 April – Day 13

Targets hit on the night of 4/5 ...

Tuesday 6 April – Day 14

Wednesday 7 April – Day 15

An SFOR UH-60 Black Hawk ...

NATO names nine Yugoslav unit ...

Thursday 8 April – Day 16

Brüggen's Tornados

The RAF's initial contribution to Allied Force consisted of Harrier GR.Mk 7s flying from Gioia del Colle, but on 4 April began to involve Tornado GR.Mk 1s flying from Brüggen in Germany, supported by VC10 tankers. Further missions were launched on 5, 6, 13, 15, 17, 19, 26, 28, 29 and 30 April, and continued into May. Missions usually consisted of six Tornados (eight have been offered to NATO) accompanied by three (later two) VC10s. The force usually routed south across France and out into the Mediterranean, before swinging east across southern Italy for the run-in to Serbia. Three hours after take-off the Tornados refuel, off the coast of Italy, receiving a top-up some 30 minutes later. They then push for their mission, returning to the shepherding tankers after around 40 minutes. During this interlude the VC10s receive fuel themselves, either from another VC10 or the No. 216 Squadron TriStars based at Ancona. This refuelling typically takes about 20 minutes. When the Tornados return from their attack, they join up with the VC10 for the long journey home and a third refuelling. They land first, followed by the VC10s, after a mission flight time of about seven hours. In late May, RAF Tornados were dispatched to Corsica to increase the RAF's commitment. **David Donald**

Right: Three VC10s await a mission at Brüggen. The tankers are detached from No. 101 Squadron at Brize Norton.

Below: Armourers prepare a 1,000-lb (454-kg) CPU-123 Paveway II bomb in a HAS at Brüggen.

Friday 9 April – Day 17

The US DoD admits that B-2s again flew combat missions against Serbia overnight.

According to USAF General Charles Wald, "NATO is starting to take the fight to the VJ and the MUP in Kosovo." On the night of 8/9 April targets in Istok, Decani, Dakovica, Podujica, Pristina and Urosevac were hit and, in all, 22 targets had been attacked in southwest Kosovo. Serb units had sustained "significant casualties", with equipment and facilities destroyed also.

Despite bad weather, US F-16s and A-10s, Dutch F-16s and UK Harriers attacked Serbian troops and vehicles on the ground in Kosovo – missions were flown against "five major target sets and troop concentrations".

The US announces its intention to deploy six additional F-15Es from Aviano next week, followed by 12 more aircraft.

Russia's President Yeltsin says he cannot allow the Western alliance to "seize" Yugoslavia and states that Russia will not be drawn into the Balkans. As pointed out by the Americans, the Speaker of the Russian Parliament, General Seleznov, has said that Yeltsin's order to retarget Russian strategic missiles away from the US was more for the benefit of the communist MPs in the Parliament than an actual command. The commander of Russia's strategic forces says no such order has been issued.

KFOR observers report gun, mortar and shell fire around several Albanian villages near the Kosovan border.

A Macedonian border guard is killed by a group of armed Serbian personnel.

The UNHCR cannot establish the fate of up to 200,000 Kosovar refugees who have been prevented from crossing into Macedonia and Albania by closed borders.

On Sunday 11 April the indicted Serbian war criminal Zeljko Raznatovic, "Arkan", announces to reporters that an F-117 was shot down on Friday 9 April and the pilot captured near Batajnica air base. No NATO aircraft are lost.

Saturday 10 April – Day 18

NATO spokesman Jamie Shea says NATO aircraft have hit 130 targets in the past 17 days of bombing, and have now destroyed 50 per cent of Yugoslavia's fuel supplies.

General Clark calls for more aircraft, specifically EA-6Bs and F-16CJs, to be deployed to the region. The US DoD announces 82 additional aircraft to be deployed.

United Arab Emirates Air Force AS 332 Super Pumas are airlifted to Tirana to join the refugee relief efforts.

Yugoslavia reopens its border with Albania, allowing refugees to cross over again.

Right: Sizeable fleets of helicopters were assembled in Albania and Macedonia to provide mobility for relief forces. Few machines saw use in their intended roles. Supporting the relief effort was this Chinook HC.Mk 2 of the RAF's 28 Squadron. HD is from the RLU's 230 Squadron.

Below: A vital part of the electronic warfare surveillance effort was the RC-135 Rivet Joint. Operating from RAF Mildenhall, No fewer than three RC-135Ws were seen at the UK base at the start of May.

Sunday 11 April – Day 19

Air attacks on the night of 10/11 April faced increased SAM fire, with several SA-6s and shoulder-launched missiles being fired. At least one SA-3 site was attacked and destroyed.

NATO aircraft drop leaflets over Yugoslavia during Saturday and Sunday telling the Serbian people that the bombing will stop if President Milosevic accepts an international peace force and allows Kosovar Albanians to return to their homes.

Fifteen A-10s are redeployed from Aviano to Gioia del Colle to make room for other aircraft.

Britain announces that the aircraft carrier HMS Invincible will be deployed to the Adriatic to support NATO air strikes. What remains unclear, however, is that the air defence-orientated air wing aboard the ship will be unable to participate in any attack missions.

The United States begins to suggest that acceptance of the Rambouillet Accord may no longer be sufficient on the part of the Belgrade leadership.

Monday 12 April – Day 20

Targets attacked on the night of 11/12 April include an oil refinery at Pancevo and targets around Batajnica (both near Belgrade), the Zastava car factory near Kragujevac, the Zastava assembly plant, the "14 Oktober" assembly plant

Above: Based at Skopje in Macedonia, the Armée de l'Air put a pair of EH 1/67 Pumas in place for RESCO (combat SAR) duties.

Below: Part of the multinational helicopter force assembled in Albania are AS 332 Super Pumas from the United Arab Emirates.

In addition to Mk 82 bombs and AGM-65 Mavericks, CF-18s have been flying from Aviano armed with 2,000-lb (907-kg) GBU-10 laser-guided bombs. AIM-7Ms and AIM-9Ms provide a fighter capability.

Canadian contribution

The Canadian Armed Forces detachment of CF-18s is known as Task Force Aviano, and at the end of March it was manned by people and jets from CFB Bagotville. Four flew in the first Allied Force mission and dropped laser-guided bombs on military facilities in southern Serbia. The multi-functional Canadian Hornet is capable of air-to-air and air-to-ground warfare 24 hours a day, having received Night Hawk B laser targeting and FLIR pods in 1997. The armament available in the first days comprised the AIM-7 Sparrow and AIM-9 Sidewinder for air defence, and Mk 82 gravity bombs and GBU-10/12 LGBs for air-to-ground missions.

Soon after the operation began, 4 Wing from CFB Cold Lake took over Task Force Aviano responsibilities. The first two CF-18s of this wing arrived at the end of March to relieve two others which needed maintenance; an additional six from Bagotville were redeployed from Leeuwarden AB, the Netherlands to Aviano on 1 April. They had arrived to participate in exercise Brilliant Foil, which was to have lasted until 3 May but was later cancelled because of Allied Force. Another eight Hornets from Cold Lake and Bagotville arrived at Aviano on 3 May, two as replacements for Hornets that needed maintenance in Canada. Numbering 18 PGM-capable Hornets, the detachment also started operations with the newly acquired GBU-10 1000-kg LGBs which had reached Aviano in early May. Because the space in the Canadian area was tight, and the Hornets were already parked with wings folded, the additional six aircraft started operations from the other side of the air base. After four months as commander of the Canadian Task Force Aviano, Colonel Dwight Davies transferred command to Colonel Andr Viens on 11 May.

Under Operation Mikaido, CC-130 Hercules and CC-150 Polaris transports became involved in humanitarian relief operations to the Balkans. They returned to Canada loaded with refugees who received shelter in Canada under Operation Parasol.

In mid-May eight CH-146 Griffon helicopters of 408 Sqn, CFB Edmonton, arrived in Macedonia to take part in the NATO-led peace implementation force. They are part of an 800-member Canadian armoured contingent from Edmonton. The eight CH-146 Griffon crews are tasked with airborne surveillance, transport and medical evacuation missions. They will be rigged with speciality equipment to carry out night and day surveillance. **Gert Kromhout**

and city heating plant (all Kragujevac area); Stalina airport, Pristina-Urosevac and Pristina-Lipljan roads, Mirovac village and other targets in the Pristina region; a SAM storage and production site (Novi Sad); two industrial complexes (Krusevac). Strikes were conducted in the early morning and late evening.
■ The Pentagon announces that all Yugoslavia's oil refineries have been destroyed, but that some fuel is still in storage.
■ NATO Secretary General Javier Solana makes the first public statement indicating that NATO troops may be deployed in Kosovo with the express permission of the Yugoslav government, but in a "permissive" environment.
■ The Yugoslav parliament unanimously approves a motion to join a union with Russia and Belarus, next year.
■ A passenger train crossing the Grdelica Gorge near Lescovac is accidentally hit by an AGM-130 aimed at the bridge over the gorge. At least nine civillain passengers are killed and 16 injured.
■ UN Secretary Kofi Annan launches a peace initiative.

Tuesday 13 April – Day 21

■ United States officially designates Kosovo region as a war zone.

EXECUTIVE ORDER

DESIGNATION OF FEDERAL REPUBLIC OF YUGOSLAVIA (SERBIA/MONTENEGRO), ALBANIA, THE AIRSPACE ABOVE, AND ADJACENT WATERS AS A COMBAT ZONE

Pursuant to the authority vested in me as President by the Constitution and laws of the United States of America, including section 112 of the Internal Revenue Code of 1986 (26 U.S.C. 112), I designate, for the purposes of that section, the following locations, including the airspace above such locations, as an area in which Armed Forces of the United States are and have been engaged in combat:
The Federal Republic of Yugoslavia (Serbia/Montenegro)
Albania
The Adriatic Sea
The Ionian Sea north of the 39th parallel
For the purposes of this order, I designate March 24, 1999, as the date of the

commencement of combatant activities in such zone.

William J. Clinton
The White House
April 13, 1999.

■ As a result, all US servicemen now entitled to 'danger' pay and tax exemptions. No such benefits are available to British personnel.
■ Targets attacked during 12 April include oil refineries and POL facilities at Novi Sad, Pancevo, Pristina, Sombor; the Sloboda appliance factory at Cacak; Ladjevci airport and the Mt Kopanik area (Kraljevo); army barracks in Pristina and Belgrade.
■ Russia threatens to withdraw its SFOR troops from Bosnia. Macedonia expresses its interest in rapidly joining NATO.
■ The British Chief of the Defence Staff Sir Charles Guthrie says that British special forces on the ground in Kosovo are designating targets from the ground, allowing more accurate attacks, through cloud, by the Harrier GR.Mk 7s. This serves as another pointer to the failure of the TIALD airborne designation system as fitted to the GR.Mk 7.
■ Serb forces cross the border into Albania to occupy the village of Kremica, which had been under shell fire for two days. They withdraw later the same day.
■ General Clark confirms he has requested "300" additional aircraft from the US and NATO countries. This is in addition to the 80+ announced by the Pentagon on 10 April. The new request is understood to include approximately 100 tankers and 200 strike aircraft. A Pentagon official says, "He'll get whatever we can provide. There are limits to our inventory."
■ The Montenegran authorities protest that Yugoslavian naval vessels anchored in the port of Bar have fired on NATO aircraft, making the town a potential target.
■ Britain, France and Italy announce that they will deploy more troops to Albania in support of Operation Allied Harbour.

Wednesday 14 April – Day 22

■ Targets attacked on the night of 13/14 April include a railway bridge linking Belgrade to Montenegro, and the nearby Bistrica hydro-electric power plant; the Krusik factory in Valjevo; several targets across the Pristina region and Slatina airport; the Belacevac coal mine, one of two major coal mines in Kosovo.
■ The United States Navy announces the scheduled dispatch of the *Kearsarge* ARG (Amphibious Readiness Group), consisting of the USS *Kearsarge* (LHD 3), USS *Ponce* (LPD 15) and USS *Gunston Hall* (LSD 44). The *Kearsarge* ARG and the embarked 26th MEU (SOC) will ultimately replace the USS *Nassau* and its ARG on station in the Adriatic (see 7 April). *Nassau* ordered to remain on station for at least two weeks to aid refugee relief efforts. The *Kearsarge* ARG will deploy for six months.
■ It is announced that Tirana airport has been upgraded to handle two C-17s simultaneously. Two US Army logistics vessels also *en route* to deploy heavy material handling equipment (MHE) to support Task Force Hawk, in Albania. Both capabilities would be essential to support a ground invasion of Kosovo.
■ Pentagon warns that call-up of reserve forces is likely to be required.
■ Germany proposes a three-phase peace plan – a 24-hour NATO bombing halt, withdrawal of Serbian forces from Kosovo and a ceasefire until the arrival of an international peace force (to include Russian troops led by UN forces already in Macedonia). A transitional administration would then be established, under UN supervision. The US says there will be not halt in air strikes until Belgrade accepts all existing NATO demands.
■ Reports begin to emerge of an air attack on Kosovar Albania refugee columns, travelling between Prizen and Pec. Serbian Ministry of Information says at least 64 have been killed by NATO aircraft near the town of Djakovica. NATO confirms

that its aircraft may have been involved in an attack but that JRV aircraft have also been attacking refugees. NATO later claims that refugees have been attacked by Serb forces in retaliation for NATO attacks on them.
■ German Defence Minister confirms that a second CL-289 reconnaissance drone has been shot down.
■ The first AH-64As depart Germany for Albania.

Thursday 15 April – Day 23

■ Very heavy bombing reported over Belgrade. Targets hit on night of 14/15 April include Strazevica Hill, Rakovoca, in the Belgrade area; '14 Oktober' factory, Krusevac (for the second time); targets in and around Kraljevo, Nis and Valjevo towns; a bridge at Pepeljevac; TV transmitters at Mt Zlatibor, Uzice and Mt Ovcar, Cack; communications relays on Mt Ovcar, near Krupani.
■ NATO aircraft strike targets in Montenegro for the first time in a week. Targets include military facilities at airfield 10 km southwest of capital Podgorica, facilities in the Uicinj mountains, the harbour at Bar and a railway bridge connecting Prikepolje (Serbia) and Priboj (Montenegro). Montenegro maintains an abstentionist (loosely pro-NATO) stance and Serbian authorities begin to crack down on media and local government. Yugoslav naval vessels again accused by Montenegran authorities of firing at NATO aircraft in an attempt to inflame conflict. VJ's Second Army already deployed in Podgorica is reinforced and a hard-line commander installed. Fears of a Serbian-inspired coup are raised.
■ NATO changes its statement on the convoy attack. Charges that the Serbs attacked the convoy are withdrawn and the Pentagon says that NATO aircraft aborted their attack on a suspected military convoy when it was identified as civilian. NATO later admits that two columns appear to have been attacked by its aircraft. A statement by an unidentified F-16 pilot is released, saying that he believed Serbian forces who had been burning and destroying nearby villages were in the column.
■ Twenty-four F-16s and four A-10s arrive in Italy. France pledges thousands more troops if an invasion is called for. Denmark announces it will deploy additional F-16s.
■ After the loss of a third CL-289 in a week, Germany suspends reconnaissance overflights. Eighteen drones remain available.

Friday 16 April – Day 24

■ During the night of 15/16 April NATO also records attacks on Pancevo oil depot/refinery, a fertiliser factory and other petro-chemical complex; the oil refinery at Novi Sad; the completed destruction of the

Smederevo-Kovin Bridge; targets around Mrsac, Samaila, Drakcici, Vrdila; Mali Radanovac near the Hungarian border; in Kosovo – many targets around Pristina; and in Montenegro – Danilovgrad (underground military facilities) and Podgorica (military facilities around the capital).
■ NATO still fails to clarify its involvement in the Djakovica refugee incident, admitting involvement in one mistaken attack, but no others. At one point accusations of four attacks are being levelled against NATO, but there seems to be clear evidence for two incidents north and south of the town. NATO says F-16s were involved in one aborted LGB attack, but damage shown on Serbian TV is not consistent with such weapons. NATO restates there is no indication that it had any involvement in any attacks other than the one to which it has made (incomplete) reference.
■ Six EA-6Bs arrive in Italy. USS Inchon MCM vessel is deployed to Adriatic to deal with potential Yugoslavian mine threat. NATO now stopping and searching all ships inbound to Yugoslavian ports.
■ Germany's CL-289s return to service as causes of losses cannot be determined accurately.
■ In a vote of 326-46 the Russian Duma votes to accept Yugoslavia into

the Union of Russian and Belarus. Ukraine formally opposes the move, as threatening European stability.
■ The UNHCR states that 12,000 refugees have escaped from Kosovo in the last 24 hours and that it expects the Serbian forces to have ejected the remaining 400,000 ethnic Albanians in the coming days or weeks.
■ The Washington Post reports that Yugoslavia possesses nuclear material which could be used in some form of radiological weapon. While of insufficient quality to build a nuclear weapon, such material could be dropped or scattered by a conventional explosive, seriously contaminating a wide area. The material is reported to be stored at the Vinca Institute of Nuclear Sciences, Belgrade.
■ Foreign reporters taken to Kosovo by the Serbian authorities see Serbian tanks hidden in civilian buildings and military units moving freely in civilian vehicles.
■ The Yugoslav air force claims two kills against NATO aircraft. None is lost.

Saturday 17 April – Day 25

■ Vice Admiral Sir Ian Garnett says that bad weather forced RAF Harriers to carry out only two of their 22 planned missions.

■ General Clark goes on record to say unless President Milosevic meets NATO demands, NATO will "destroy everything (he) values".
■ NATO launches Operation Allied Harbour in Albania, ferrying relief supplies from Tirana airport to the 335,000 Kosovar refugees in camps along the border.
■ Romania announces that it will not let Russian aircraft cross its airspace on relief missions to Belgrade, as they may be carrying arms. All Russian truck relief convoys will be allowed through, but searched.

Sunday 18 April – Day 26

■ Canada announces it will deploy six additional CF-188s to Aviano.
■ The deployment of Apaches to Albania is delayed yet further and aircraft will not now arrive until next week. Heavy rain at Tirana's airport has reportedly made the ground largely unusable. Albanian military sources report the arrival of several AH-64As in Lezha, northern Albania.
■ Much confusion still surrounds the Djakovica refugee attacks. NATO says the pilot's statement issued previously was not from a pilot involved, but merely illustrated the difficulties facing pilots in the region. NATO has still not given a comprehensive account of its involvement in the attacks.
■ Voice of Russia radio reports NATO has lost over 40 aircraft and 90

'We own the night' – the widespread use of infra-red/laser systems by aircraft such as the F-15E (above) and F-117 (left) characterises modern aerial warfare, but bad weather over the warzone has highlighted the 'Achilles heel' of the system.

Tuesday 20 April – Day 28

■ According to the daily briefing, NATO air attacks on the night of 19/20 April hit "a number of targets in Yugoslavia, ammunition depots, an ammunition plant near Belgrade, and ammunition storage facilities across the country. NATO hit a number of tactical targets in Kosovo, including tanks, trucks, a FROG missile support site and a high level command post".

■ Five successful strike packages were flown in the last 24 hours against fielded forces in Kosovo. Initial assess= ments indicate the destruction of six tanks, seven military vehicles in an assembly area and a command post. A number of 'strategic' targets were also struck, including an army facility, the DIN tobacco factory, the Ogrev Invest and Kopaonik buildings at Nis; an ammunition plant and the Krusik holding company complex at Valjevo; a bridge southwest of Nova Varos on the Belgrade=Podgorica road; Slatina airport and the Belacevac strip mine.

■ Many of the commercial buildings attacked were owned by the Milosevic family or close colleagues of the President.

■ Video imagery is shown of attacks on a petrol storage facility, Ponikve airfield, an ammunition storage building at Pristina, and the headquar= ters of the 549th Mechanised Brigade in Prizen.

■ Greece announces it would put its infrastructure at NATO's disposal, to support a ground invasion, should such a request be made. The essential port of Thessaloniki is mentioned by name.

■ NATO also noted that "the troops of President Milosevic on the ground in Kosovo continue their clean and sweep operations, particularly around Kosovska, Metrovica and Pudujevu in northern Kosovo where clearly the resistance of the Kosovo Liberation Army continues. They have also continued to conduct operations against Kosovo Liberation Army elements between Prizren and Djakovica and there is a continuing build-up of artillery in the western part of Kosovo and shelling across the border with Albania."

■ With little fanfare, the B-2 force has flown its first missions.

■ Defense Secretary Cohen allocates additional Apaches and infantry units to support the Task Force Hawk deployment in Albania. The Apaches will be drawn from 229 Aviation Brigade, which has two Apache battalions (1-229 and 3-229 Aviation).

■ The Apaches previously deployed from Germany still have not arrived in Albania. They are now expected on 21/22 April.

---

airmen between 24 March and 15 April. Actual losses comprise one aircraft and no personnel.

airmen between 24 March and 15 April. Actual losses comprise one aircraft and no personnel.

■ NATO still maintains that no deci= sion on ground troops has been made, or is planned.

Monday 19 April – Day 27

Monday 19 April – Day 27

■ The Serbian BEONET web site uploads an audio file claiming to be recorded communications of a NATO aircraft shot down that day over Yugoslavia. The 'tape' is clearly real, but in fact records the shoot-down of a Royal Navy Sea Harrier FRS.Mk 1 during operations over Gorazde, on 16 April 1994. The shoot-down of

VIXEN 23 is relayed through his wingman VIXEN 24 to the on-scene ABCCC, and two A-10s already in the area are dispatched to act as RESCAP. TPC map co-ordinates and verbal position reports heard on the recording all place the incident at "Gorazde". As an attempt at disinfor= mation and propaganda it is a poor one, but complete mystery surrounds the source of what is an excellent piece of Comint. NATO later referred to it as a doctored hoax.

■ USAF Brigadier General Daniel Leaf tells reporters at a special NATO briefing that NATO did attack two convoys near Djakovica on 14 April, separated by distance and time. It is

possible that civilians were "injured" in both attacks. One convoy was northwest of Djakovica. It was a mili= tary target and was attacked first. Serbian claims of civilian casualties could not be explained. The second attack was southeast of the town and was on a mixed military/civil column. This is the attack NATO referred to on 15 April. After a "number of bombs" had been dropped this attack was called off. UK press reports that RAF Harriers had already identified this column as civilians and warned off the US aircraft, were not commented on. General Leaf went on to say, "This is a very complicated scenario and we will never be able to establish all the details."

■ A Danish F-16 makes an emergency landing at Sarajevo, Bosnia in the early hours of the morning. This is blamed on "critical engine problems", but not combat damage.

■ Brigadier General Giuseppe Marani, holding the daily NATO briefing at Brussels, admits that Serbian military aircraft are making short flights over Kosovo and that "every time we see them we try to hit them". NATO reports it has destroyed 70 per cent of Yugoslavia's oil supply and that this is now hurting Serbian forces in the field.

■ France places two reconnaissance drones and the HORIZON Puma battlefield surveillance system, already in Macedonia, at NATO's disposal.

■ NATO produces evidence of 43 mass grave sites in Kosovo and says Kosovar Albanians are being forced to work as "grave-digging chain gangs".

■ The Yugoslav navy seizes control of six Montenegrin ports.

■ The Czech Republic grants NATO forces right of passage and the use of airfields for tanker aircraft.

■ Norway and the Netherlands announce from End. 'H. United will increase their deployed total by four, increase their deployed total by four,

With Mavericks hanging from its wings, a Belgian F-16 leaves on its latest mission. Between them the Amnuniation... the aircraft... Fighterbombers... 'have been busy with some of the... which... were... fielded... discerned milly... NATO forces operating in Kosovo, by both day and night.

Although many individual successes were achieved in the first month of Allied Force – notably in the air-to-air arena, where aircraft such as this F-15C were highly successful at keeping the Serbian air force on the ground – it was becoming increasingly obvious as the campaign developed that the Serbian nut was a lot tougher to crack than had been initially imagined.

■ Approximately 70,000 refugees have left Kosovo over the past weekend, compared to 50,000 who left between 6-15 April. Around 600,000 refugees have departed Kosovo in the last month alone. The United Nations High Commission for Refugees expects 100,000 more refugees to try to leave Kosovo over the next few days.

■ NATO reports that in the last 24 hours the Yugoslav Army in Montenegro has begun 'ethnic cleansing' of villages not only along the border between Montenegro and Kosovo, but also in Montenegro itself.

■ Bulgaria and Romania give permission to allow NATO combat missions to use their airspace.

Wednesday 21 April – Day 28

■ NATO attacks the headquarters of Slobodan Milosevic's Socialist Party (Usce) in central Belgrade at 03.15 local (01.15 GMT). The building also houses Pink TV, BK TV and Kosava radio broadcast facilities, run by President Milosevic's wife. Four cruise missiles hit the building, destroying the 12th through 17th floors.

■ Zezel bridge, the last remaining bridge over the Danube at Novi Sad, is destroyed at 00.40 GMT (two other bridges had earlier been destroyed on 1 and 3 April). An oil refinery at Novi Sad is also attacked. Serbian TV transmitters at Iriski Venac are destroyed along with targets around Mrsac and Samalia villages. The Krusik facory is attacked again.

■ Already overstretched, the Pentagon is considering sending a second carrier to the Adriatic – the USS *Enterprise* – in order to boost the number of aircraft now required. The *Enterprise* arrived in the Mediterranean on 20 April after its six-month Persian Gulf deployment was extended. The Pentagon is also examining basing options in Turkey and Hungary.

■ At approximately 16.00 GMT the first group of six AH-64As arrives at Tirana-Rinas airport. 24 Apaches, all carrying AGM-114 Hellfires, have reportedly departed Pisa, in Italy, where they have been standing-by for six days. Support helicopters include two CH-47s and six UH-60s.

■ Boeing is awarded a fixed-price contract for $41,310,00 to convert 95 'excess' AGM-86B ALCMs into the Block 1 AGM-86C CALCM variant. Expected completion date is 30 November 1999.

■ The Slovak government announces that NATO can transport military equipment on its railway system to Hungary, transforming the latter into a possible stepping-off point for any future invasion.

■ Both Washington and London say that NATO leaders will soon examine the "ground forces option".

■ President Clinton requests $5.458 billion in additional funding from Congress to cover the situation in Kosovo – $3.6 billion to cover air operations from 24 March to the end of FY99; $698 million for additional cruise missiles and PGMs; and $335 million for refugee relief.

Thursday 22 April – Day 29

■ NATO air attacks on the night of 21/22 April include President Slobodan Milosevic's residence at 15 Uzicka Street, Dedinje, Belgrade, at 02.00 GMT. Other targets include Batajnica airfield, the Krusik industrial facility at Valjevo and targets around Pristina. Over 30 targets were hit in all, including bridges at Barri, Beska, Dunnes, Malasevo and Mure. Imagery is shown of recent strikes against the Rakovina bridge, Pristina airport, Urosevac garrison, base of the 243rd Mechanised Brigade and an underground oil storage facility neat Novi Sad.

■ NATO says that it is now striking twice the number of targets it was hitting each night, two weeks ago.

■ According to the UPI agency, the USAF has fewer than 70 CALCMs available. The inventory stood at 238 in December 1998, but 90 were fired during the Operation Desert Fox strikes against Iraq. As of 7 April, 62 had been fired at Yugoslavia. Stocks of 'all-weather' PGMs (Tomahawk, JDAM, etc.) are also running very low.

■ Germany's Chancellor Schroeder indicates his willingness to deploy German ground troops to Kosovo.

Nordic efforts

The Royal Norwegian and Danish Air Forces deployed to Grazzanise AB in autumn 1998. The Danish contingent is manned by personnel from different units but the squadron designation is always 730 (Skrydstrup AB) as this is the Immediate Reaction Squadron of the Danish AF. The detachment started with six F-16As but was later enlarged to eight, plus one spare, when three F-16 MLUs were added. According to Lt Col Frits Rasmussen, Danish detachment commander in the first weeks of the operations, said that the unmodified F-16s does not play a significant role in the air operations. Rasmussen said that his pilots fly second-line defensive counter air missions solely during daylight hours: "In general we fly long boring missions with nothing happening". The F-16As flew with a mix of AIM-120s and AIM-9s, and an internal electronic warfare system.

A Danish F-16 made an emergency landing at Sarajevo airport on 19 April because of engine problems. A C-130H flew in the same day from Aalborg with a new engine and a maintenance crew. The Danish MoD also assigned a C-130H of Esk. 721 at Vaerløse to the humanitarian operation in Macedonia and Albania.

The initial force of six Danish F-16s deployed to Grazzanise comprised non-MLU aircraft, although these can carry AIM-120s. Combat air patrols are the main mission.

The Norwegian Air Force had initially planned to end the 338 Skv detachment on 30 April as this squadron was to commence conversion to MLU around this time. However, the outbreak of Allied Force interfered with this plan. The Norwegian detachment is comprised of six F-16As which were initially armed with AIM-9 Sidewinders. AMRAAMs were added in late April. On their way to Grazzanise the Norwegians had a brief work-up period at Volkel AB, the Netherlands, learning to master the ALQ-131 ECM pod. When they left for Italy they took the Dutch pods with them. 338 Skv is the Immediate Reaction Force squadron of the RNoAF. Like the Danish detachment, the Norwegians at Grazzanise maintain the same squadron designation no matter how long the operation lasts, although it is manned by personnel from several units. The Danish and Norwegian detachments are located in the same area but are not integrated like the Dutch and Belgians at Amendola, and therefore have two detachment commanders.   **Gert Kromhout**

Wearing the markings of 334 Skvadron, this F-16A carries an ALQ-131 ECM pod on the centreline. These pods are borrowed from the Dutch air force. The missile fit of four AIM-120s and two AIM-9s is standard.

■ The first NATO train with 32 cars crosses through Slovakia to Hungary as the US indicates if "ground troops become necessary it will support their deployment".

■ Romania and the IMF agree on a $500 million loan.

Friday 23 April – Day 30

■ Italian TV reports over 50 aircraft departing Aviano AFB at 05.00.

■ Serbia's state news agency Tanjug reports that NATO has again hit a bridge at Novi Sad.

■ The Pentagon announces that the USS *Enterprise* will return to its home port at Norfolk, Va., in early May, as scheduled.

■ Dispute grows over the composition of any future peacekeeping force in Kosovo. Russia's envoy Viktor Chernomyrdin says that Serbia will accept a UN presence, but with no NATO troops. NATO says this is unacceptable. Germany's Foreign Minister warns Russia against adopting too-close ties to Serbia.

■ NATO Secretary General Javier Solana confirms planning is underway for a ground invasion.

■ The European Union and NATO impose an oil embargo on Serbia.   **Robert Hewson**

Desert Fox

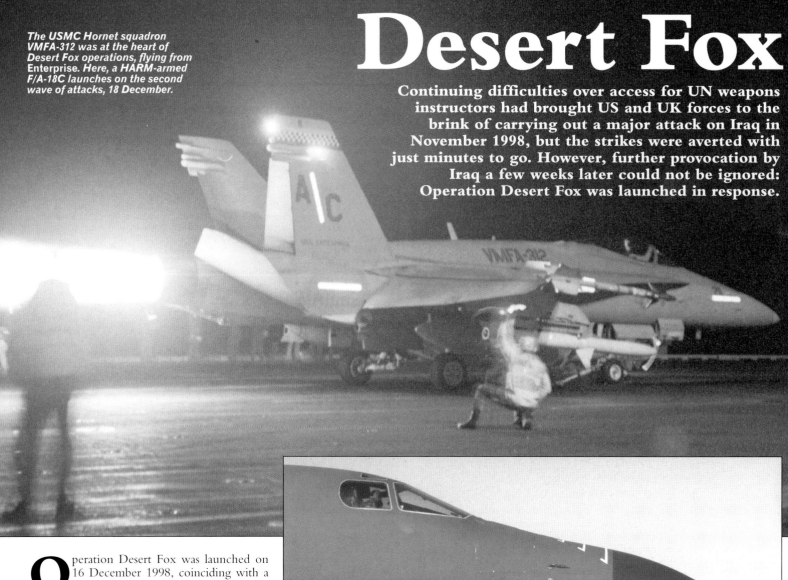

The USMC Hornet squadron VMFA-312 was at the heart of Desert Fox operations, flying from Enterprise. Here, a HARM-armed F/A-18C launches on the second wave of attacks, 18 December.

Continuing difficulties over access for UN weapons instructors had brought US and UK forces to the brink of carrying out a major attack on Iraq in November 1998, but the strikes were averted with just minutes to go. However, further provocation by Iraq a few weeks later could not be ignored: Operation Desert Fox was launched in response.

Operation Desert Fox was launched on 16 December 1998, coinciding with a coup attempt against Saddam Hussein from within the Iraqi Army's 3rd Corps. The air attacks by American and British warplanes and cruise missiles were briefly in the world's spotlight, while the internal situation within Iraq remained in shadow. Within months, the four-day Desert Fox effort has been eclipsed by Operation Allied Force, the larger, sustained air campaign against Yugoslavia – but, during its quick moment, Desert Fox introduced new weapons and tactics, and returned to action an array of familiar combat aircraft.

The campaign saw the combat debut of the LANTIRN-equipped F-14B 'Bombcat', the B-1B Lancer bomber and (just after the campaign) the AGM-130 air-to-ground missile. It brought innovative and successful tactics by F-15E Strike Eagles, Tornados and other warplanes that were no strangers to the Iraqi desert. Supposedly aimed at Iraq's ability to produce WMD (weapons of mass destruction), Desert Fox in fact had an entirely different purpose – the decapitation of Iraq's leadership. It would have disappointed no one in the allied chain of command if the attacks with precision weapons had got Saddam himself.

In the US, the timing and execution of Desert Fox drew criticism. Combat sorties began at 5:00 p.m. Washington time (midnight in Baghdad) on 16 December, with few hints that they were coming – and, entirely coincidentally, some 15 hours before the House of Representatives was scheduled to debate and

Desert Fox marked the delayed baptism of fire for the B-1B. Two aircraft flew a long dumb bombing mission (with Mk 82s) against a Special Republican Guard barracks. Here, two aircraft from the 28th Bomb Wing are seen at their temporary base in Oman.

vote on a committee recommendation to impeach President Bill Clinton. One critic of Clinton dubbed it Operation Desert Rat, while another correspondent called the military operation by American and British forces "the Vampire War" because it took place at night – in keeping with US doctrine and tactics that call for striking during the nocturnal hours. Secretary of Defense William Cohen insisted that the timing of strikes against Iraq was dictated solely by military considerations, but it was also launched during the approach of Ramadan,

For the first two days of strikes, USS Enterprise (CVN-65) shouldered the burden of providing carrierborne attack forces. Here, the carrier is seen on the morning after the first wave of strikes. On the third night it was joined by the USS Carl Vinson (CVN-70). Both carriers deployed F/A-18s and F-14 'Bombcats'.

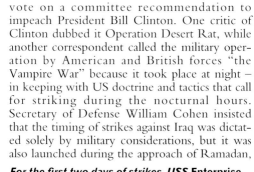

The flight deck of Enterprise *comes alive as the carrier launches the first wave of aircraft on 17 December. The first night's attacks did not involve any aircraft land-based in Kuwait, in order to maintain the element of surprise.*

An 'Arleigh Burke'-class destroyer launches a TLAM-C on 19 December, the third day of the campaign. TLAMs launched from a variety of ships and one submarine, together with CALCMs fired from B-52s, paving the way for attacks by conventional aircraft.

a hallowed season in the Islamic world when many observers thought it inappropriate to fight.

The military campaign capped off a period of frustration for members of the US armed forces. In October, US bombers had deployed overseas for action in Kosovo that came to the brink but never happened (though it was to occur months later). In November, US warplanes were actually in the air en route to Iraqi targets – in what would have been called Operation Desert Viper, a vastly more ambitious undertaking than the subsequent Desert Fox – when a stand-down was ordered at the last minute. According to one source, US jets were 20 minutes from 'the fence' – the line between friendly and hostile territory – when Desert Viper was called off. US and British leaders warned, then, that if Saddam Hussein's belated promise of co-operation with arms inspectors was not kept, strikes would take place with little notice.

Carrier war

From the standpoint of the Royal Air Force and the US Air Force, there was no action in the first 24 hours of Desert Fox. "We are still waiting for the 'execute' order," a USAF officer said on the dawn of the second day. The campaign – by naval forces – began with hundreds of attacks in Baghdad, Basra and against Republican Guard installations by BGM-109 Tomahawk (T-LAM) cruise missiles. F-14B Tomcat fighters from squadron VF-32 'Swordsmen' on the carrier USS *Enterprise* (CVN-65) struck air defence installations around the fringes of hostile territory using laser-guided GBU-12 and GBU-24 bombs. It was the first time the air-to-ground 'Bombcat' version of the F-14 had been used in combat. *Enterprise*'s F/A-18 Hornets also carried GBU-24s with their 2,000-lb warheads, to targets in Iraq. On the third day, USS *Vinson* (CVN-70) arrived to join the fray, bringing F-14D 'Bombcats' and more Hornets.

As usual, the US Navy's fleet of EA-6B Prowler jamming aircraft was seriously over-taxed, having to accompany most of the strike packages most of the way to their targets. Unpowered ADM-141 TALDs (Tactical Air-Launched Decoys) were dropped by Navy and Marine Corps F/A-18C Hornets and S-3B Vikings to confuse and confound Iraqi defences

– and to prompt Baghdad to claim, inaccurately, that it shot down over 100 cruise missiles.

Warships that fired Tomahawks included the 'Ticonderoga'-class cruiser USS *Gettysburg* (CG-64), the 'Arleigh Burke'-class destroyers USS *Stout* (DDG-55), USS *Paul Hamilton* (DDG-60), and USS *Hopper* (DDG-70) and the 'Spruance'-class destroyers USS *Nicholson* (DDG-982), USS *Fletcher* (DDG-992) and USS *Hayler* (DDG-997). The 'Los Angeles'-class submarine USS *Miami* (SSN-755) fired submarine-launched UGM-109 Tomahawk T-LAMs.

As in any war, the flow of adrenaline was furious for the aircrews caught up in the combat. A Tomcat strike leader, not previously trained for LANTIRN (Low-Altitude Navigation and Targeting Infra-Red for Night) or for NVD (Night-Vision Devices) described his experience. "Here I am flying the first night, first strike. I'm sitting in the jet, aft of the island, waiting to get the 11th-hour abort that doesn't come. Suddenly, off the port, I see about 10 T-LAMS get launched from one of the small boys in our battle group. What a sight!

"The first night was all Navy, NO Air Force (not even their tankers) or Brits. It was designed for single cycle ... surprise. We're [Tomcats] loaded with two GBU-16s [1,000-lb/454-kg bombs] and our target is within city limits. Tomcats were given most of the hard targets because of the LANTIRN. So ours has possibility of collateral damage (unacceptable, except to us who don't care). We find our targets and schwack 'em. Remember, this is me flying Night Vision Devices and LANTIRN for the first time. The learning curve was steep ... at least for me, my RIO may think different. To watch those buildings go away was impressive. We met AAA and ballistic-launched SAMs.

One of several important 'firsts' for Desert Fox was the participation of female aircrew in combat operations. Lt Carol Watts from VFA-37 'Raging Bulls' discusses her first mission into Iraq on 17 December.

"On night two, the first strike is mine. It's a double cycle with AF tanking and Tornado GR.1s from the UK. We're heading farther north to make the Republican Guards' life miserable. Targets are headquarters and barracks. I have three Tomcats carrying two GBU-10s [2,000-lb/907-kg bombs] each, eight Hornets with either GBU-16s or GBU-10s, HARM shooter, and of course the Brits – who are always on their own programme, it seems. Now this is my FAM-2 [second familiarisation] on NVD and LANTIRN. Two-thousand pounders are incredible to watch go off. My weapon of choice. You may have seen it on CNN. There wasn't a building standing when we finished. Again, there was AAA and ballistic SAMs."

Mixed force

Eventual participants included RAF Tornado GR.Mk 1s and B-52H Stratofortresses with AGM-86C Block 1 CALCMs (conventional air-launched cruise missiles). A-10 'Warthog' attack aircraft dropped leaflets telling some Iraqi troops that they were not being targeted and should stay still. The B-1B Lancer bomber made its combat debut on the second day when two B-1Bs (callsigns SLAM 01 and 02), flying from Oman, bombed a target near Baghdad. B-1Bs dropped 500-lb (227-kg) Mk 82 general-purpose gravity bombs – 'dumb' bombs, in contrast to the precision munitions used elsewhere – on the SRG (Special Republican Guard) Al Kut Barracks northwest of Baghdad. The first aircraft (86-0096) was piloted by Lieutenant Colonel Steve Wolborsky,

Throughout Desert Fox and subsequent operations, the EA-6B Prowler fleet has been hard-pressed to meet all the EW needs of the assembled strike forces. This VAQ-130 EA-6B takes off from Enterprise.

*Weapons are prepared aboard **Enterprise** for the third wave of attacks on 18 December. For the most part, Navy aircraft fired **AGM-88 HARMs** or dropped Paveway II/III laser-guided bombs. It is believed that **AGM-154 JSOW** was employed by F/A-18 Hornets for the first time during the campaign.*

*A few days after **Desert Fox** the USAF employed the **AGM-130 EO**-guided missile for the first time, fired by F-15Es. An Eagle of the 48th Fighter Wing (above) receives a weapons check prior to a January 1999 Northern Watch mission from Incirlik AB, Turkey. An F-15E (left) returns to the base on 14 January, after having flown a strike against an Iraqi SAM site.*

Enterprise deck crew launch aircraft on Desert Fox's fourth wave, on 19 December. The Hornet about to line up on the catapult is carrying laser-guided bombs.

with real-time, moving target information. The mixed-unit B-1B force of about half a dozen 'Bones' included aircraft from the 9th and 28th Bomb Squadrons, 7th Bomb Wing, from Dyess AFB, Texas.

Defense Secretary William Cohen and Joint Chiefs' Chairman General Henry 'Hugh' Shelton announced an end to Desert Fox, hours into the celebration of Ramadan. Desert Fox involved 656 sorties, used more than 200 cruise missiles (more than in the 1991 Gulf War), and struck about 100 targets associated with Iraq's development of missiles and chemical, biological, and nuclear weapons. Saddam Hussein announced 'victory' when the action ended after four days, even though his forces had made almost no attempt to mount a defence.

The United Nations' Richard Butler had reported Iraqi failure to co-operate with weapons site inspections. This was one of several developments which convinced the Pentagon that the pledge of co-operation in November – which headed off military action at the time – had been bogus. After Operation Desert Fox, all parties were saying that UN inspection of Iraqi arms sites was probably history now, and that the West would need to find some new way to cope with Saddam Hussein's mis-steps.

After the shooting started, one key allied target was a batch of Czech Aero L-29 Delfin fighters at Al-Sahra, north of Baghdad, which US officials claimed had been modified into drone anthrax carriers.

An analysis of target sets compels the conclusion that the real purpose of Desert Fox was to attack the Iraqi leadership. Among early targets were Saddam Hussein's sleeping quarters on the outskirts of Baghdad in the Radwaniyah complex adjacent to the now-vacant Saddam International Airport. Other targets including buildings that house secret units of the SSO (Special Security Organisation) and the SRG (Special Republican Guards) were locations where Iraqi leaders were expected to be; they were known to allied commanders with a degree of specificity that was not available during Operation Desert Storm in 1991.

commander of the 37th Bomb Squadron 'Tigers', 28th Bomb Wing, from Ellsworth AFB, South Dakota. The USAF quietly pointed out that thanks to surveillance by E-8C Joint STARS (Surveillance Target Attack Radar System), B-1Bs in the theatre were provided

There is also ground to believe that Americans and British intelligence supported an attempt to topple Saddam Hussein, possibly an inept one, while bombing him. On 18 December, while Iraqi troops mopped up what was clearly a coup attempt, the vice chairman of Iraq's ruling Revolution Command Council, General Izzat Ibrahim, reportedly sent a letter to Saddam Hussein noting that "we have instructed the armed forces to restrict their mission to the protection of the borders of the homeland". The letter, broadcast on Iraqi radio, noted that all internal security had been arranged for using "other armed bodies". In other words, the coup was finished and Iraq was, at least internally, secure.

In the wake of Desert Fox (and even after the start of the war with Yugoslavia on 24 March 1999), sporadic operations against Iraq have

'Before and after' reconnaissance images show the Iraqi military intelligence headquarters, graphically illustrating the extent of damage inflicted by Desert Fox.

An important target set for Desert Fox was Iraq's WMD facilities. Al Sahra airfield was suspected of housing aircraft modified for the aerial spraying of chemical/biological warfare agents, and received attention from laser-guided bombs. Each hangar has been hit by two bombs, which would have destroyed any aircraft housed within. Parked around the airfield are agricultural aircraft, mainly PZL Dromaders, which may have been capable of CW/BW delivery.

continued, beginning on 28 December 1998 when F-16CJ Fighting Falcons and F-15E Strike Eagles from Incirlik attacked air defence targets in the southern 'No-Fly Zone'. In early January 1999, US warplanes tried to root out Iraqi air defences in an hours-long operation during which they swept the northern zone. In the week of 8 January, an F-16CJ fired an AGM-88B HARM against a mobile Bar Lock early-warning radar; Iraq has more than 100 of these, but in the past they were not regarded as targets. On 14 January 1999 an F-16CJ fired a HARM at an anti-aircraft battery co-located with an SA-6 battery, the first time recently that a gun emplacement was attacked.

On 5 January 1999, in two separate incidents, American combat aircraft engaged Iraqi MiG-25 'Foxbat' fighters in the southern 'No-Fly Zone' and scored 0-for-6 in missile shoots from beyond visual range. After being illuminated by the tracking radar of the MiG-25s (at 2:15 a.m. EST), two US Air Force F-15 Eagle fighters (from Saudi Arabia, according to *Navy Times*) fired three AIM-120A AMRAAM and one AIM-7M Sparrow missiles at the Iraqis, who retreated across the 33rd Parallel. Some 15 minutes later and 80 miles (128 km) south, two US Navy F-14D Tomcats of VF-213 'Black Lions' from USS *Carl Vinson* (CVN-70) – unaware of the earlier engagement – fired two AIM-54C Phoenix missiles at a second group of MiG-25s. The Iraqis did not fire at the American aircraft. As to why the US missiles did not hit the mark, Pentagon spokesman Ken Bacon said that "air-to-air attacks look easy in the movies, but it's not that easy in real life". The Pentagon also reported that a MiG-23 'Flogger' crashed while landing at an Iraqi base. The air-to-air altercation was the first in Iraq since 27 December 1992, when a US F-16 shot down an Iraqi MiG-25.

USAF Colonel David Deptula waxed eloquent about one of the post-Desert Fox air

B-52Hs of the 2nd BW operated from the British Indian Ocean Territory of Diego Garcia, launching AGM-86C CALCMs. The aircraft below is returning to the base after a post-Desert Fox operation, while above an aircraft is marshalled at Diego Garcia after a successful CALCM launch on the first night of the campaign.

The F-16CJ Block 50 has played an important part in ongoing operations against Iraq. This HARM-carrying aircraft from the 23rd FS, 52nd FW (above) is seen in January 1999 while on Northern Watch patrol. At right is a similar aircraft from the 78th FS, 20th FW on Southern Watch.

Left: Carrying a mix of weapons, a VFA-94 Hornet patrols the Gulf during Southern Watch operations. During Desert Fox F/A-18s were employed as HARM shooters, laser bombers and launch platforms for ADM-141 TALD decoys.

actions that became routine in the months to follow: "I had the privilege of authorising and directing an attack [against] an Iraqi SA-3 site that launched three SA-3s at our Northern Watch aircraft. The aircrews involved did a magnificent job, and exercised absolutely superb judgement.

"We had a well thought-out plan that gradually moved us from north to south over the period of several hours. We operate up here differently than in the south, and work as complete composite force packages – this was our largest to date. After two hours working north of the known SAM sites we put our foot in the water and sent a bunch of F-16CJs through the northern fringes of the known SAM sites. About the time they were exiting, three of our F-15Es got uncorrelated SAM launch indications, and one an SA-3 launch warning – two missiles were observed passing above the aircraft and exploding.

"About a minute later one of our F-16s saw a third missile launch and at the same time one of the F-15Es happened to be observing a known SA-3 site through his LANTIRN pod from 37 miles away, and saw the launch! The mission commander called back to the CAOC [Combined Air Operations Center] and requested approval for a DEAD – that is, a 'destruction of enemy air defence' attack. We normally practise these in the AOR [area of responsibility] on a daily basis, and my JFACC

[joint forces air component commander] normally mulls for a couple of minutes over the decision to recommend approval or not to me ... not this time. To me, it was a issue of self-defence ... yours truly was up in the CAOC overseeing all this, and the JFACC didn't have a chance. It was the fastest approval ever made, seconds from receipt of the request to approval. You might say I had sort of thought this one over in advance.

"The attack was perfect ... first a couple of F-16s launched pre-emptive HARMs at two other SAM sites in the immediate vicinity of the SA-3 site that launched, to keep their heads down while a four-ship of F-15Es rolled in on the launching SA-3 site. Three out of four F-15Es dropped two GBU-12 500-lb PGMs each, for a total of six ... all 'shacks' on either the radar and optical tracking unit or the command and control van. The guy who didn't drop couldn't get a positive target i.d. – the kind of super judgement displayed throughout the entire mission. You should see the video on CNN.

"The most rewarding moment of my career to date was when the roll call was complete after the attack and everyone responded. I met each aircraft after it landed and I can't describe how elated everyone was with the outcome of the mission. To borrow a phrase from a good friend, 'It's a good day for bombing!'"

Further operations against Iraq were still

ongoing when this report was written. Having brought an end to the era of weapons inspections within Iraq, Desert Fox seemed to have opened a new era of frequent, persistent skirmishes against Iraqi air defences and other forces.

The post-Desert Fox actions had marked the combat debut of the AGM-130, a rocket-powered, air-to-ground missile that has been under development since 1984 and is carried by the F-15E Strike Eagle. The missile carries a 2,000-lb (907-kg) explosive warhead and is equipped with a guidance 'package' that enables the Strike Eagle crew to watch the missile's path on a television monitor and steer it to its target.
Robert F. Dorr

Desert Fox Tornados

The RAF Tornado force has supported Southern Watch operations (known as Operation Jural to the RAF) since the end of the Gulf War, but assembled a new force of 12 Tornados in Kuwait for Operation Bolton. Manned by No. 12 Squadron, the Tornado detachment flew alongside US forces during Desert Fox, employing its new GBU-24 Paveway IIIs for the first time.

Denied the use of the Operation Jural Tornados based in Saudi Arabia, the RAF contribution to Desert Fox came from the 12 Tornados based at Ali Al Salem AB, Kuwait. Using the GEC-Marconi TIALD Srs 400 laser designation pod, the Tornados employed the 1,000-lb (454-kg) Paveway II and 2,000-lb (907-kg) Paveway III laser-guided bombs. The Tornados were protected by a Sky Shadow ECM pod and BOZ-107 chaff/flare dispenser. A pair of AIM-9L Sidewinders was also carried.

Eleven of the 12 Tornados completed their first night attacks on air defence and command and control sites, airfields with a defensive potential, and Republican Guard infrastructure buildings, despite heavy Iraqi AAA fire. TIALD video films of the RAF attacks, shown at the daily MoD press briefings held by Defence Secretary George Robertson and the Chief of the Defence Staff, General Sir Charles Guthrie, included one showing a direct hit on a hardened aircraft shelter at Tallil airfield, believed to contain up to a dozen pilotless aircraft (UAVs) with the capability of delivering chemical and biological weapons.

Defence Secretary Robertson subsequently revealed that the UAVs were in fact adaptations of some of Iraq's remaining elderly Aero L-29 Delfin basic jet-trainers, developed from a 1990 Saddam edict ordering the production of unmanned aircraft to spray CW/BW agents from the air. Initial tests, he added, were unsuccessful, but in 1995 a new programme was launched using the converted L-29s, and is continuing.

"Each aircraft has two underwing stores, carrying 300 litres [66 Imp gal] of anthrax or other nerve agents," said Robertson, "which if sprayed over a built-up area could kill millions of people." With its two underwing pylons unavailable for drop tanks, the L-29 has a maximum range on internal fuel of 400 miles (640 km). Whether or not the L-29 drones were actually in the hangar could not be confirmed, but it was effectively destroyed. More IrAF L-29s parked in the open at Al Sahra air base were also attacked by US aircraft.

Thirty-two Tornado sorties were planned, of which 28 were completed. Weapons dropped consisted of 48 Paveway IIs and four Paveway IIIs. A success rate of 75 per cent was claimed for these bombs. On the final

night, a flight of four Tornados was recalled when they were at the hold-point, waiting for their push time. The campaign had ended.

Here, two Tornado crew-members recount their personal experiences. "In November we had got very close to the real thing [Desert Viper] until Kofi Annan managed to broker a deal. We were fairly tense before that one, and we were only about an hour away from the bombs dropping before it was called off. Having gone through all that once, it was easier a few weeks later when Desert Fox started. We were well prepared. We had already been to the brink twice.

"The night before the boss called all the aircrew together and said, 'We're going'. After that the operation went very smoothly. The first night was a US Navy and Air Force show, so our first missions were on the second night. We went to Tallil airfield and it was a bit nerve-wracking, although the AAA defences didn't appear to be effectively co-ordinated. We had two targets, and everything went well.

"On the second night we went to a Republican Guard barracks, which was further north, and we

Wearing No. 617 Squadron marks, a Tornado GR.Mk 1B taxis from its shelter. In the background is a hardened shelter that was attacked during Desert Storm. The Tornado is carrying the Vinten GP1 medium-altitude reconnaissance pod for post-strike reconnaissance.

Below: A No. 14 Squadron jet is marked with four mission symbols. It carries a TIALD pod on its port fuselage pylon. During Desert Fox Tornados worked in pairs, with one pod and three or four bombs between the two aircraft.

A Tornado GR.Mk 1A launches from Ali al Salem carrying a pair of GBU-24 Paveway III bombs on its fuselage pylons. Aircraft with various squadron markings (here No. II Sqn) were used during Desert Fox, but all were flown by No. 12 Squadron personnel who were manning the Operation Bolton detachment at the time. This aircraft displays combines elements of all four camouflage schemes in use across the RAF Tornado fleet: the basic aircraft is in the original grey/green camouflage, the port wing pylon Sky Shadow ECM pod is in the new medium grey GR.Mk 1 scheme, the port fuel tank is air defence grey while the starboard tank has 'desert pink' ARTF applied. As the Tornados attacked at night during Desert Fox, camouflage was not an issue.

encountered heavy AAA. The Americans were first in and as soon as their bombs hit the whole earth erupted below us with AAA fire. It was very impressive, as well as terrifying. There were different colours [of tracer] which merged as they followed differing arcs across the night sky.

"It was a surreal feeling, sitting in your warm, isolated cockpit. One thing that struck us was that you couldn't hear it. You had to concentrate on your task, but you were acutely aware of the dangers. Despite the distractions it was a good attack – a very satisfying experience from a professional point of view.

"On one raid we took out an ammo dump on an airfield. My navigator guided our bomb directly into a HAS, but we could see little damage as we left the area. After a few minutes there was an enormous explosion – we could clearly see it from 30 miles away.

"Perhaps the biggest concern was screwing up – letting your crew mate and the squadron down. The success is down to training, which overrides other distractions as soon as you get going. It was a godsend having some Granby veterans with us, who were like 'elder brother' types. They knew what to expect, knew we would get frightened, so they kept everything simple. What was tried and tested worked again.

"The missions were unrefuelled, and lasted about 1½ hours. Our support came from the US Navy, who were very impressive. The intelligence back-up was also excellent. There was a mix of co-operative and self-designated bombing. The Paveway IIIs we dropped proved to be much more accurate and effective than the older weapons. In all, the entire operation was very professionally conducted, and operating alongside the USAF and US Navy over Iraq is an experience I will never forget.' **David Donald**

35

Kawasaki OH-1
Japan's own military helicopter

Kawasaki's OH-1 scout/reconnaissance helicopter is a prime example of how the Japanese aerospace industry has bided its time and gained experience – through licence-production – before striking out and developing its own aircraft, closely tailored to national needs. The OH-1 is a sophisticated and elegant design, albeit an expensive one, and may yet be a stepping stone to Japan's first indigenous armed combat helicopter.

The sleek and compact OH-X/OH-1 was a major step forward for the Japanese aerospace industry – and a challenge for Kawasaki and its partners. Slowly, but surely, the aircraft has progressed through its flight test programme and now operational service with the JGSDF beckons. The camouflaged fourth prototype (above), carrying dummy AAM launchers, looks even more the part than the brightly-painted first prototype (below).

Before embarking on the OH-X/OH-1 project, Kawasaki had been building helicopters since 1954, all under licence, and chiefly from US manufacturers. The company built aircraft for the three branches of the Japanese Defence Forces and this experience allowed it to bid confidently to build Japan's first indigenously-developed military helicopter, the OH-1. The OH-1 will replace an ageing fleet of OH-6 scout/reconnaissance helicopters and may yet find itself with a wider combat role, unforeseen when the original OH-X requirement was drawn up in the early 1990s. The roots of the OH-X programme lie in the expansion of Japan's helicopter force in the 1970s and 1980s and the development of the first true military helicopter to be built in Japan.

In 1966, Rikujo-Jieitai (the Japan Ground Self-Defence Force, JGSDF) selected the Hughes OH-6J as a replacement for its Bell H-13 helicopters and Cessna L-19 lightplanes in the observation role. The J model of the OH-6 was a licence-production version of the basic US Army OH-6A, built by Kawasaki Heavy Industries (KHI). Because of production problems and rising costs in the USA, preparations for the Japanese production line were delayed by several months. KHI finally started work in 1968 and the first 11 OH-6Js were delivered to the JGSDF in March 1969.

These 11 OH-6Js were built from knocked-down kits, and full local production began with the 12th aircraft. The JGSDF procured 117 OH-6Js, which served not only in the observation

Above: Kawasaki's OH-X designers did not settle on a mast-mounted sight design, but neither did they constrain their aircraft with a nose-mounted sight system. Instead, a 'mid-set' solution was applied, positioning the laser and optical system as high above the cockpit as possible.

Right: The second prototype, seen here wearing TRDI markings, appeared in a revised black and white colour scheme.

role but also as basic training helicopters. In FY1978, production switched to the OH-6D which has an uprated engine, five-bladed main rotor and a T-tail. The OH-6D largely replaced existing OH-6Js in the same roles. In all, a total of 117 OH-6Js and 193 OH-6Ds was purchased by the JGSDF. KHI finished production only in March 1997, and the final JGSDF OH-6D was delivered on 12 March 1997, along with the last OH-6D for the JMSDF.

As an observation helicopter, the OH-6J/ OH-6D equipped every squadron controlled directly by each of the regional Army Divisions. In March 1986, the first JGSDF Anti-Tank Helicopter (ATH) squadron was formed at Obihiro Army Air Base (AAB), with AH-1S Cobras. OH-6Ds were also delivered to this unit for scout and reconnaissance tasks, operating in the traditional (US Army derived) scout/gun combination. Four OH-6Ds were allocated to each ATH squadron, five of which were ultimately established within the JGSDF.

The OH-6Ds which were delivered to ATH squadrons were different to standard OH-6Ds. They had armour protection around the crew seats and engine bay and also carried a UHF radio for communications with their accompanying AH-1Ss. An NVG-compatible cockpit and exterior lighting were later developed and fitted to many, but not all, aircraft. A new

night/bad weather sensor system comprising a FLIR, TV and optical systems was also developed and tested, but never actually fitted to the ATH-dedicated OH-6Ds. While the OH-6D just about fulfilled the requirements for a 1980's observation helicopter, it was clearly not suitable for the coming century.

A new approach

For this reason, the JGSDF began to define its requirement for a new scout/observation helicopter to replace the OH-6D, which would also have dedicated mission sensor/weapons systems that represented late 1980's technology. This requirement later became known as the OH-X programme. From the outset, the JGSDF's firm intention was to develop the OH-X as an entirely indigenous Japanese aircraft; however, the Japanese government began to come under US pressure to involve outside contractors, primarily US contractors. At the Japan-US Security Arrangement conference, held between 31 October and 1 November 1991 in Washington, D.C., the United States formally requested that US-built equipment and components be used in the OH-X. US moves to become involved in the OH-X programme may have been motivated by a lack of openness and competition in the Japanese market, but there is little doubt that the US also feared a successful

Japanese design appearing on the international market (even though Japanese political sensibilities made exports unlikely). Following negative publicity surrounding the early days of the FS-X programme, which in many ways was being led by US industry, the US Department of Commerce announced that it did not wish to see a similar level of 'co-operation' by American helicopter manufacturers with the OH-X programme. Yet US concerns about the alternative – a successful Japanese helicopter industry – were reflected by comments from the United States Trade Representative for Japan to the effect that "the United States was concerned that Japan might enter the international market with a commercial version of the OH-X."

Both Boei-cho (the Japan Defence Agency, JDA) and the Japanese aerospace industry were also reluctant to follow the example of the FS-X programme and suffer what they saw as similar 'interference' from the US government in this OH-X programme. Japanese officials involved with the OH-X stated that they did not want a pre-arranged 'co-development' with US manufacturers and the selection of equipment and components had to be open to fair competition – a novel concept for the Japanese system. Finally, the US gave up its political moves to gain a major role in the OH-X and the programme reverted to outright Japanese leadership.

Above: When the first XOH-1 was rolled out in March 1996 at Kawasaki Heavy Industries' main Gifu plant, it was little different to the original models (inset), thanks to KHI's exhaustive mock-up and design refinement procedures.

Left and below: The XOH-1 prototype, 32001, made its maiden flight on 6 August 1996. During the initial trials phase, this aircraft – and 32002 – was fitted with an instrumentation boom to monitor angle of attack and sideslip. Other temporary test equipment fitted to the development aircraft included load-measuring gauges on the gear and a main rotor tracking system in the windscreen of the front cockpit. Additional antennas were also fitted to relay flight test telemetry to the dedicated measurement and analysis facility at Akeno AAB. From the outset, the XOH-1 prototypes also carried dummy missile launchers and laser/FLIR turrets.

On 17 April 1992, the JGSDF issued a request for proposal (RFP) for the OH-X to three Japanese companies: Fuji Heavy Industries (FHI), Kawasaki Heavy Industries (KHI) and Mitsubishi Heavy Industries (MHI). The details of this RFP have never been released but, ideally, the OH-X had to incorporate two main new technologies. One was a new composite-material rotor system, which had to be resistant to a direct hit from a 20-mm round. The other was the development of an advanced sensor suite (FLIR, colour TV and laser range-finder) fully integrated with a digital cockpit.

The three companies submitted their proposals on 26 May 1992. The JDA examined them and then held a hearing with each company and examined their factories, as part of a thorough review process. The selection of KHI as OH-X prime contractor was announced on 18 September 1992, and FHI and MHI were named as 'co-operation companies', in a classic piece of Japanese political/industrial manoeuvring. A new design and development

team, named OHCET (Observation Helicopter Engineering Team), was set up on 1 October 1992 at KHI's Gifu factory. Members of OHCET came from all three companies and 83 members of staff were attached at the outset. More than 150 staff joined OHCET during its peak activity period. It was then decided to build four flying prototype aircraft and two static test airframes (one for structural tests and the other as a 'whirl rig' for tied-down dynamic systems testing).

KHI had already drawn up the basic design of the OH-X when it submitted its proposal. In its earliest days, KHI's design used a four-bladed offset tail rotor (similar to that of the AH-64), but this was soon changed to a ducted-fan 'fenestron' system, like the RAH-66's.

Configuration and design features

The OH-1 is the first truly Japanese helicopter – its airframe, engine and systems are all developed by Japanese companies – and the first to be specifically developed for the JGSDF. The commander of Hiko Kaihatsu Jikken-tai, Colonel Minoru Kohno, has said that this first experience of testing an all-new helicopter has taught them many lessons, forcing all the test personnel to work harder and change their approach from that of simply dealing with licensed production equipment.

The OH-X is a two-seat tandem configuration helicopter in which the pilot sits forward and observation officer sits in the rear seat. In the cockpit, two colour LCD MFDs, supplied by Yokogawa Electric, are located on each instrument panel. All systems are routed through a MIL-STD 1553B databus. The MFDs in the front

The silver tape on the cowling of XOH-1 32002 was applied as a quick means of detecting any flexing of the composite material evidenced during flight testing. Note also the full compression of the landing gear.

cockpit are mounted side-by-side and vertically in the rear. Some sources involved in the OH-1 development said that this configuration was inspired by the Eurocopter Tiger – though there is little space in the rear cockpit to put the MFDs side-by-side because the sensor control panel is located in the main instrument panel. The MFDs display sensor information, systems and weapons status, navigation information, flight information etc. A Shimadzu HUD is mounted above the main panel in the front seat and displays all required flight information and weapons symbology. Full dual HOCAS (Hands On Collective And Stick) flight controls are fitted to each cockpit. Those who have flown the aircraft agree that there are very good fields-of-view through the flat plate transparencies from both seats, especially to the side. The side windows are bulged outwards slightly to improve downward vision. The starboard side

The first XOH-1 flew with a pair of initial standard XTS1-10 turboshafts, soon upgraded to QT standard. These new and more efficient engines are closer to the desired standard of the final production powerplants.

windows hinge upwards for crew access.

The main rotor has four blades built of GFRP composite material. Blade chord is constant at 0.38 m, with a tapered tip. The main rotor hub is also built from GFRP composites. The bearingless and hingeless hub allows excellent control response and eases the helicopter's maintenance requirement. The hub and transmission are designed to be resistant to a 20-mm shell hit. The tail rotor has eight blades. This system eliminates the potential danger inherent in normal tail rotor systems, and is very suitable for NOE flight. The blades are set at different angles – 35° and 55° – to the hub, resulting in lower fan noise.

OH-1 in detail

Specification
Kawasaki XOH-1
Powerplant: Mitsubishi TS1-10, 663 kW (888 hp)
Main rotor diameter: 11.6 m (38.06 ft)
Fuselage length: 12.0 m (39.37 ft)
Tail plane width: 3.0 m (9.8 ft)
Fuselage width: 1.0 m (3.28 ft)
Height, overall: top of tail fin, 3.8 m (12.46 ft)/ top of main rotor mast, 3.4 m (11.15 ft)
Main rotor disc area: 105.7 m² (1,138 sq ft)
Empty weight: 2450 kg (5,401 lb)
Maximum weapon load: 132 kg (291 lb)
Design gross weight: 3550 kg (7,825 lb)
Maximum gross weight: 4000 kg (8,820 lb)
Maximum level speed: 150 kt (172.5 mph; 277 km/h), approx

Above and right: The cockpits of the OH-1 are dominated by the two side-by-side liquid-crystal colour multi-function displays. The screens are arranged vertically in the rear (observer/sensor operator's) cockpit, which also lacks the pilot's HUD.

The primary armament of the Kawasaki OH-1 is the (modified) Type 91 IR-homing AAM, carried in twin box launchers (above). For self-defence the OH-1 will be fitted with an IRCM system in the class of the ALQ-144 (right). Note also the heat-resistant panelling that has been added to the tail boom below the engine exhausts. The OH-1's ducted-fan anti-torque system (far right) uses eight blades in an asymmetric arrangement.

The engine for the OH-1, which was selected in 1994, is the Mitsubishi TS1-10, or XTS1-10 for the prototypes. Take-off power is rated at 663 kW (888 hp). Two versions of the XTS1-10 currently exist. The initial type fitted to all XOH-1s had adequate performance for the early test stages, but fuel consumption was higher than expected. A second version, dubbed the QT engine, has improved this and it more closely resembles the production powerplant. The first two QT engines were reinstalled in the first XOH-1 and flew on 30 March 1998. The engines are fitted with a full authority digital engine control (FADEC) system.

One of the most important features of the OH-1 is its integrated sight system, which is roof-mounted in front of the main rotor mast

fairing. A Fujitsu FLIR is fitted in the right side of the electrically operated ball turret, while an NEC colour TV camera and laser designator/ range-finder are fitted in the left side. The turret has a 110° field of regard and can look through 40° in elevation. These sensors allow day/night reconnaissance and observation and are connected to an onboard video recorder. They can also be used for weapons aiming from the rear seat. The OH-1 was not built with a mast-mounted sight (MMS). An MMS solution was undoubtedly considered, as it allows the aircraft to operate almost completely masked by terrain, increasing its survivability; on the other hand, an MMS brings with it higher drag and reduced overall performance. Nose-mounted sensors limit reconnaissance and observation capabilities

by fully exposing the aircraft to hostile fire. As a result, the OH-1 was designed with a roof-mounted sight.

The high-mounted stub wings have four hardpoints in total. Current authorised external equipment includes fuel tanks and air-to-air missiles (AAMs). Each tank has a capacity of 235 litres (52 Imp gal) and it is understood that two tanks extend mission endurance by one hour. The selected AAM is modified from the Toshiba Type 91 portable SAM. The IR-guided Type 91 SAM is largely similar to the FIM-92 Stinger. Two missiles are contained in one box launcher. Basic configuration for the OH-1 is one AAM 'box' on each outer stub wing hardpoint, with the inner hardpoint left free. The OH-1 has no gun or additional arma-

Acquisition and targeting systems
The electrically-operated turret above the OH-1's cockpit houses a FLIR and daylight colour TV optical system, along with a laser rangefinder/designator.

A robust and survivable airframe
The design *g* limits for the OH-1 are +3.5/-1 *g*. The composite materials used in the main rotor are ballistically tolerant (and even reduce radar cross section to a degree). If damaged, the main gearbox can continue to operate 'dry' for up to 30 minutes.

Rotor technology
The OH-1's rotor system is a novel design that has created something of a stir in aerodynamic circles. The composite hub (made from unidirectional glass-fibre and epoxy resin) is a bearingless design that prevents structural coupling between flapping and feathering motions. It also damps any lead-lag motion very efficiently, using very compact elastomeric bearings. As a result, KHI's design is reported to have the least aerodynamic drag of any comparable bearingless hub design.

Ground test tasks
In addition to the flying prototype, KHI built two static test airframes. These were used for stress, load and fatigue-life testing, but also for preliminary trials of airframe systems such as the hydraulics, anti-ice, transmission and gearboxes. By early 1999 all these associated systems had been confirmed and cleared for full-rate production.

Composite materials
About 15 per cent of the OH-1's airframe weight comes from advanced composite materials, but this rises to 37 per cent when the innovative new rotor design is included, as all four blades and the hub are composite.

Award-winning success
In an acknowledgement of the great progress made by TRDI and KHI in the XOH-1 development programme, the American Helicopter Society presented them with the prestigious Howard Hughes Award on 21 May 1998. The Hughes Award was created in 1977 to reward outstanding achievement in fundamental helicopter technology.

Kawasaki XOH-1 Hiko Kaihatsu Jikkenn-tai (Air Development and Test Squadron) Akeno AAB

This is the the third XOH-1 prototype, 32003, which first flew on 9 January 1997 and was delivered to the Technical Research and Development Institute (TRDI) of the Japan Defense Agency (JDA) in June of that year. When this aircraft passed into JGSDF control during 1998 it was given a new serial, 32603/JG2603. The four-ship XOH-1 test fleet is based at Akeno AAB, alongside the army's Aviation School.

Heat stress
One problem that cropped up during flight testing was heat damage to the tail boom from the engine exhausts. Additional protective plating was fixed to the boom as a result. KHI is also considering changing the exhaust pipe shape entirely as the efflux may interfere with the IR jammer, which is mounted between the engines, behind the main rotor mast.

'Fantail' features
The OH-1's ducted tail rotor, which uses eight carbon-composite blades, reduces the noise signature of the helicopter considerably and also makes it more responsive and controllable in flight, especially at low level.

obtained in FY95. A full scale mock-up was built and shown to the media, as the Kogata Kansoku (new small observation helicopter) on 2 September 1994.

The first prototype of OH-X (32001) was rolled out on 15 March 1996 at KHI's Gifu factory and made its first flight on 6 August 1996. After a series of over 40 test flights in company hands, this aircraft was delivered to the JDA on 26 May 1997. At this stage, the OH-X was allocated its official designation of OH-1, with the prototype becoming an XOH-1. The No. 2 prototype (32002) first flew on 12 November 1996 and was delivered on 6 June 1997. The No. 3 (32003) aircraft first flew on 9 January 1997 and was delivered on 24 June 1997. The No. 4 prototype (32004) first flew on 12 February 1997 and was delivered on 29 August 1997.

Two ground test airframes, 0-1 and 0-2, were delivered in 1996. They will undertake all airframe and component fatigue life testing, durability and vibration testing, limited and ultimate load testing, main landing gear drop testing and crash testing.

Test phase begins

In Japan, development test activity for equipment ordered by the JDA is normally handled by two bodies. The Technologies Test phase is conducted by a component unit of the JDA, Gijutsu Kenkyu Honbu (the Technical Research and Development Institute, TRDI). The subsequent Operational Test phase is conducted by a test unit of each Defence Force. The TRDI has responsibility for equipment for all three Defence Forces. Notionally, Technologies testing is followed by Operational testing, but the two areas often overlap and these tests are frequently undertaken almost simultaneously.

Towards the end of March 1997, the TRDI and the JGSDF formed a new dual unit at Akeno AAB for development testing of the XOH-1. The TRDI element was named Gijutsu Shiken-tai (Technology Test Unit), while the JGSDF element is Hiko Kaihatsu Jikken-tai (Flight Development Test Squadron), under the control of the Headquarters, Koku

ment options. To date, the aircraft has been firmly denied any kind of offensive role – despite being superior in performance, and in the all-important sensor systems, to the JGSDF's AH-1s. This may change, but under current plans the OH-1 will remain a scout helicopter with defensive (air-to-air) armament only.

Manufacturing share of the production aircraft is divided as follows. KHI, front fuselage (including landing gear), major dynamic components (main rotor, main transmission, tail fan, tail drive shaft and tail gearbox), final assembly and flight test; workshare is approximately 66 per cent. MHI, centre-fuselage and engine; workshare is approximately 17 per cent. FHI,

tail assembly, engine cowlings, canopy and stub wings; workshare is approximately 17 per cent. The landing gears for all four XOH-1 prototypes were produced by MHI but this will change to KHI for production models.

A development budget was allocated to the OH-X for the first time in FY 1992, with JYE2.5 billion reserved for design and components production of the prototype and test aircraft. This was followed in FY93 by JYE10.2 billion. In the FY94 budget, the construction of two flying prototypes and two static test airframes was funded and the budget allocation jumped to JYE50.1 billion. Funding for another two flying prototypes, JYE23.3 billion, was

Right: Flying alongside the XOH-1 test aircraft at Akeno AAB are two Fuji UH-1Js, also operated by the Hiko Kaihatsu Jikken-tai. The UH-1Js wear small 'SX' codes on the cabin door, signifying their role as part of the Experimental School.

Below right: The third prototype is seen here carrying two auxiliary fuel tanks. The additional fuel extends the aircraft's overall flying time by about one hour.

Gakko (Aviation School). There are no pilots in the TRDI, so all flying activities were undertaken by pilots from Hiko Kaihatsu Jikken-tai. The four XOH-1s are officially assigned to TRDI until Technologies Test has finished completely, and carry 'TRDI' titles on their tailfins.

Hiko Kaihatsu Jikken-tai consists of a head-quarters body, a flying unit, a maintenance unit and a test evaluation and recording unit. Hiko Kaihatsu Jikken-tai also operates two UH-1Js for chase missions and telemetry relay. They use the unit code 'SX' for 'School Experimental'.

Flight test programme

Flight tests with the XOH-1 started in June 1997 and are due to be completed in September 1999. The test programme consists of four phases: Phase 1, expansion of flight envelope (from June to October 1997); Phase 2, confirmation of basic configuration (from September 1997 to October 1998); Phase 3, confirmation of special external equipment configurations (from March to October 1998); Phase 4, final confirmation (from September 1998 to September 1999). Actual firing of air-to-air missiles and tactical nap-of-earth (NOE) flight evaluation was scheduled for the Phase 4 period, and successful weapons (AAM) firing trials were conducted and completed in early 1999 .

Flight test duties have been distributed among the four prototypes as follows. No. 1 aircraft, flight performance and handling, engine/airframe validation; about 275 flights in total are planned. No. 2 aircraft, flight loads and vibration testing, performance and handling; about 275

flights in total are planned. No. 3 aircraft, equipment and electric system testing, sight system functions, air-to-air missile system functions, engine/airframe validation and mission adaptability; about 230 flights in total are planned. No. 4 aircraft, mission adaptability, sight system functionality, air-to-air missile system functionality; about 200 flights in total are planned.

Analysis and evaluation of flight data is handled at the Measurement and Analysis Control Room, to which staff from both Gijutsu Siken-tai and Hiko Kaihatsu Jikken-tai are assigned. It comprises a control room and a data-processing room. The control room can simultaneously handle real-time digital coded flight data telemetry from two flying XOH-1s. Telemetry is broadcast on both UHF and VHF

Kawasaki history

Kawasaki Heavy Industries is the one of oldest Japanese aircraft companies. Its aviation activities started in 1916 when staff were sent to France to inspect the aviation industry there. In July 1918, an aviation section was established by KHI and it obtained the production rights for the Salmson 2A-2 reconnaissance aircraft and Salmson AZ-9 piston engine. The first two KHI-built 2A-2 prototypes were completed in November 1922 and Japan's Imperial Army acquired the type as the Otsu-1 reconnaissance aircraft.

KHI's manufacturing capabilities were established before World War II and it built many types of aircraft. One of the most famous wartime Japanese fighters was the Kawasaki Ki-61 Type 3 fighter Hien ('Tony'). Kawasaki developed an even higher-performance interceptor, the Ki-100-1 Type 5. This could intercept the high-flying B-29, but a third of the 99 built were destroyed when the factory was bombed. Only limited numbers were delivered before the end of the war, but they still managed to undertake some intercepts.

KHI was authorised to resume

aircraft manufacturing when it proposed a small light aircraft, the KAL-1, in July 1952. Later that year it began to produce parts for Bell 47D. In February 1953, the government authorised production of the Bell 47D under licence, and the first KHI-built Bell 47D was completed in January 1954. By 1956, KHI had started to refine the Bell 47 design with its own technical input, leading to the development and manufacture of the Kawasaki-Bell 47G3B-KH4 – a four-seat version of the three-seat Bell 47G3B which was completed in August 1957. The type served with the JGSDF, as the Kawasaki H-13-KH.

The next step was the Vertol V-107 programme. KHI started talks with Vertol to build a developed version of the V-107(H-46), the KV-107 II, in November 1959, and authorisation from the government was given on 6 December 1960. The first KV-107 II flew in April 1962, and the initial nine were built from kits. In 1965, KHI obtained world-wide sales rights for the KV-107 II.

The KV-107 II was operated by all three Japanese Defence Forces: as a

large transport helicopter by the JGSDF; as a mine-sweeping helicopter by the JMSDF; and as a search and rescue helicopter by JASDF. The type was exported to several countries, including Sweden where it is still in service. The last KV-107 II was delivered to the JASDF in FY89. KHI's large helicopter production continued with licence-production of the CH-47J Chinook, from 1984.

In the small helicopter field, KHI began licence-manufacture of the OH-6A in August 1966. This lengthy experience in helicopter technology led

The Kawasaki-built OH-6 is the aircraft the OH-1 will replace in JGSDF service. The experience that KHI gathered from the OH-6 became the cornerstone of its OH-X development.

to the development of an all-new light twin-engined helicopter, named KH7. MBB of West Germany (now Eurocopter Germany) was also developing a similar class of helicopter, and a joint development agreement was signed between two on 25 February 1977. This brought about the birth of the BK117 twin-engined utility helicopter. The first BK117 underwent final assembly with MBB and made its first flight on 13 June 1979. The second flying prototype, P3, was assembled in KHI's Gifu factory and made its maiden flight on 10 August 1979.

Left: All of the OH-1's key electronic systems – such as the cockpit displays, pilot's **HUD**, monitoring and warning systems – are routed through a dual redundant **MIL-STD 1553B** databus. Note the provision for **RWR** antennas on the otherwise clean nose.

Below left: This view of **XOH-1** 32003 clearly shows the blade tracker, main gear load-measuring equipment and white telemetry antenna fitted to the prototypes. Anything painted orange on an **XOH-1** is test equipment or a trial configuration, and subject to change.

32003 became 32603/JG2603 and 32004 became 32604/JG2604.

Procurement of the production-standard OH-1 by the JGSDF commenced in FY97. Three aircraft were authorised and two others followed in the FY98 budget. Individual aircraft cost was JYE1.924 billion ($13.7 million) in FY97 and JYE2.018 billion ($14.4 million) in FY98 (calculated with $1.00=JYE140). In FY99 three additional aircraft were authorised, for delivery in FY2001, and at a cost of JYE2.229 million.

Delivery schedule

The first three OH-1s will be delivered in FY99 and deployed to Koku Gakko (Aviation School) at Akeno AAB, the first arriving in January 2000 (the Japanese fiscal year ends on 31 March 1999, therefore FY99 ends in March 2000). The OH-1s will be used to train instructor pilots and to establish the flight training syllabus for the type. The two OH-1s ordered in FY98 will be delivered in FY 2000. One will be assigned to Akeno AAB and the other to Kasumigaura AAB. Pilot training will start at Akeno AAB and maintenance crew training at Kasumigaura AAB from FY00, by when six OH-1s will be based at Akeno AAB, as two of the XOH-1s (Nos 3 and 4) will be modified to production configuration and used for training, along with with four production OH-1s.

Under current plans, the JGSDF will replace all its OH-6Ds with OH-1s in the scout/reconnaissance, observation and training roles. This will require the acquisition of approximately 150 OH-1s. KHI is now studying the development the true attack helicopter derived from the basic OH-1, which will utilise the latter's airframe, rotor/dynamic system and basic avionics as much as possible. New capabilities may include expanded armament to give the aircraft anti-tank and AFV killing capability; new fire control and guidance systems; improved deployment capability; improved survivability; and a C³I (command, control, communications and intelligence) function.

Future developments

KHI is also examining increasing the aircraft's maximum gross weight (from 4000 to 5000 kg/ 8,820 to 11,025 lb), increasing main rotor diameter (from 11.6 to 12.4 m/38.06 to 40.68 ft), and uprating the transmission capability (from 1050 to 1200 kW/1,410 to 1,610 hp). Required engine power for any new combat version will be approximately 788 kW (1,055 hp), representing an increase of 20 per over the OH-1. It is possible that the aircraft will be re-engined with a developed version of the MHI TS1, LHTEC T800 or RR/Turbomeca/MTU MTR390 – all potential candidates. Modification to the airframe will include a lengthening of the

wavebands and printed out by plotter after decoding. The normal radio coverage of the flight test area extends to a 50-km (31-mile) radius from Akeno AAB. When flying outside this area, or at low level where signals are masked by terrain, the UH-1Js are used for telemetry relay. More detailed and classified flight data is stored on an onboard recorder.

As of early 1999, the four XOH-1s had made about 450 hours of flight tests and had proven most of the basic flight envelope, in clean configuration. V_{ne} speed tests and side-slip limit flight testing had been completed. Maximum attained altitude was 16,000 ft (4880 m). Basic flight tests with external fuel tanks and add-on skis had also

been undertaken. Trials are continuing at a rate of approximately eight or nine flights per week. The final test analyses and examinations will be made between October 1999 and March 2000. After this work, development tests will be complete and both Gijutsu Shiken-tai and Hiko Kaihatsu Jikkenn-tai will be disbanded.

By mid-1999 trials were still ongoing at Akeno AAB in the hands of the Hiko Kaihatsu Jikkenn-tai. However, responsibility for the test programme has been transferred from the TRDI to the JGSDF. As a result, the four OH-1 development aircraft have all been reserialled, to conform with JGSDF standards. 32001 became 32601/JG2601, 32002 became 32602/JG2602,

Above and right: In JGSDF service the OH-1 will enter service as a scout and, initially, will operate alongside the AH-1S Cobra. A set of closely defined national requirements imposes limits on the OH-X design, which was only ever intended to operate 'in country', in Japan. For example, the helicopter has an operational radius of just 124 miles (200 km). However, the AHX competition is likely to spur improved and more capable versions of the basic, very sound, design.

fuselage, redesign of the tailboom, increase of the stub wing span and the addition of avionics housings on both sides of front fuselage (in the style of the AH-64D). A 20-mm cannon will be installed beneath its nose.

This attack version of the OH-1 is still only an in-house study at KHI and no official authorisation has been given to this programme. The development of any overtly military equipment is a highly sensitive political issue in Japan, and developing a combat helicopter from an unarmed scout helicopter will be seen as controversial by some groups.

The JGSDF does have a formal requirement for a combat helicopter to replace its AH-1Ss, the AH-X. During the 1998 Farnborough air show in September, it emerged that the acquisition timetable for the AH-X was being accelerated and that the JDA is currently seeking RFPs from interested competitors. This seemed to be an attempt to secure funding for the aircraft before the economic situation in Japan deteriorated even more. The AH-X programme was not expected to receive the official go-ahead until sometime in FY 2000, with a procurement decision in FY 2001/02; now, a procurement decision is expected as early as July 1999. The AH-X RFP outlines a need for 100 aircraft, with 300 engines. At the moment it is uncertain whether KHI will put forward its 'combat OH-1' or not, but the preliminary design work has not been undertaken lightly. The JGSDF is widely believed to favour the Boeing AH-64D Longbow Apache, though rival bids are likely to come from the Eurocopter Tiger and Bell AH-1Z. The current weakness of the Yen and deepening recession in Japan may yet prove to be Kawasaki's greatest ally, as continued OH-1 procurement will ensure that valuable hard currency does not leave Japan and an important industrial base is preserved. Furthermore, the advent of an expanded OH-1 programme, with fully-developed combat and scout variants – spurred on by the need for exports and with costs reduced by increased production at home – will spread great unease among the international helicopter manufacturers. The OH-1 may yet become more than just a scout helicopter for Japan. **Yoshitomo Aoki**

Future AHX

This OH-1-derived design study is one of those under consideration by KHI for the JGSDF's AHX future combat helicopter requirement. Though no official proposal has been made, and this design remains provisional, it would incorporate several major changes over the basic OH-1. The most obvious of these is the addition of a new undernose 20-mm cannon with a new helmet-mounted display and sighting system for the crew. The front fuselage has been expanded to house additional avionics, in the same way as the Boeing AH-64D. Other external changes include longer-span stub wings to carry heavier loads (such as ATGMs) and an increased-diameter main rotor. Under the skin, an uprated engine and transmission would be fitted along with an improved Automatic Flight Control System and Stability Augmentation System. The cockpit would also benefit from a new mission avionics package and integrated GPS navigation system. If the legal bars on the export of Japanese military equipment are ever put to one side, the OH-1/AH-X combination could become a winning one on the international market.

CEAM

The French Test Team

With a large industrial defence base, and an active military, France's need for operational trials and testing of new aircraft and systems is extensive. For the Armée de l'Air, these essential tasks are handled by the Centre d'Expériences Aériennes Militaires (CEAM) – which also manages development programmes for the naval and army air arms.

The Centre d'Expériences Aériennes Militaires of France's Armée de l'Air (AA), headquartered at Mont-de-Marsan Air Base, is the main operational trials centre for the Armée de l'Air, and to a lesser degree for the air arms of the army and navy. The trials it conducts concern not only new aircraft, weapons and related systems but also equipment for personnel, medics, C[4], radar and much more.

Operational trials are the last hurdle before an aircraft or system enters full front-line service and involve a thorough shake-down with a 'real-world' evaluation. The aim is for the operational manual produced through these trials to contain as much information for the user as it possibly can. This testing process demands precise execution by experienced people, hence the pilots, weapon system operators, and other officers and non-commissioned personnel involved are among the very best in the French military. In the case of the CEAM they are captains, commandants and majors who have had the privilege of joining the unit after several tours with operational squadrons. They bring years of operational experience on specific aircraft types, systems or other specialities. For aviators, it is a good assignment – instead of being sent to headquarters to fly a desk, they can continue to fly real aircraft.

The majority of CEAM activities are concentrated at Mont-de-Marsan but it also has numerous smaller units and detachments spread out over France. Only two of the units actually operate aircraft (both at Mont-de-Marsan): Escadron de Chasse 5/330 'Côte d'Argent' which deals with all fighter programmes, and Escadron

Above: Included in the CEAM's recent workload has been the trials of the Transall C.160 Rénové avionics and systems upgrade. This adds a new navigation, radio and flight management fit, in a redesigned EFIS cockpit, along with a HUD. It also adds a new self-defence system with integrated RWR, MAWS and chaff/flare dispensers. Upgrade work began in 1988 and the prototype was delivered for evaluation in April 1993. The final upgraded Transall will be redelivered in 1999.

Right: Helicopter trials and testing is the responsibility of EET 6/330 – though it currently has no AS 555 Fennecs (as seen here) on charge.

d'Expérimentation Transport 6/330 'Albret' for all transport aircraft and helicopters. Its operational expertise means that the CEAM has an important advisory role from the very beginning of any procurement process. From the moment the DGA starts testing, the CEAM is involved. It undertakes operational and technical experimentation and trains the first operational crews. For example, the CEAM already has a programme office for the Future Large Aircraft at the Airbus offices in Toulouse.

The road from requirement to service entry is a long one. It starts with the operational requirement when the headquarters of the AA, the EMAA (Etat-Major de l'Armée de l'Air), issues an initial requirement followed by the technical specifications drafted by the Direction Générale pour l'Armement (DGA, the government arms procurement agency). The DGA, to which the Centre d'Essais en Vol (CEV, aerospace research establishment) also belongs, fixes the design. It undertakes initial flight testing, largely through the CEV, and then the new aircraft is handed over to the CEAM. The aviators of the CEAM learn how the systems cope with operational demands, produce the operational manuals and procedures, develop tactics, set up maintenance directives, and more. The CEAM closely monitors new systems after their service. In event of emergencies, or real operational needs, the test and trials process can be greatly accelerated. Recent examples of this have been driven largely by the conflict in the former Yugoslavia and include internal reconnaissance capability for the Mirage F1CT fighter-bomber, chaff dispensers for the Puma and protective jackets for aviators. When a foreign country procures French aircraft, the CEAM usually trains its first pilots and evalu-

ates the aircraft; for example, during the work-up and training of the Taiwanese Mirage 2000 pilots, the CEAM established an Escadron Transformation Temporaire to handle these tasks.

Mont-de-Marsan activities

The structure of EC 5/330 'Côte d'Azur' is built around three main departments, Operations, Technical Services Chief and the Centre d'Entrainement au Combat (CEC, air combat training centre). The Operations cell manages all flying operations and has a separate experimenta-

tion arm. The Technical Services Chief has main sections dedicated to the Mirage 2000, Mirage F1, Alpha Jet and Joint Services. In early 1999 this department had programme management teams for the Mirage 2000D and 2000-5F, RECOTAC (tactical reconnaissance), SLPRM (Système Locale de Préparation et Restitution de Mission, mission planning system), MICA missile, and APACHE cruise missile. Finally, the CEC has a simulation and air training section.

A management team is comprised of technicians and aircrew. The 2000D team, for

The Mirage 2000-5F multi-role upgrade is one of the most important ongoing fast jet programmes in today's Armée de l'Air. The CEAM has a central role to play in developing the operational procedure for this almost new aircraft.

Above: Much of the ongoing test effort at Mont-de-Marsan is devoted to the Mirage F1 fleet and the introduction of a follow-on reconnaissance system for the Mirage F1CR. However, the CEAM also developed a 'quick fix' camera fit for the Mirage F1CT (as seen here) during 1997. This is based around two small 'off the shelf' CCDs squeezed into the forward fuselage.

Right: The Mirage F1CR is the AA's dedicated tactical reconnaissance platform and can carry a number of podded optical and electronic systems. This aircraft is carrying a centreline ASTAC Elint pod.

example, has two pilots and two WSOs, one maintenance officer and six to 10 technicians. The number of aircraft operating from Mont-de-Marsan varies. Normally, EC 5/330 has between 20 and 30 fighters on the line, comprising Mirage 2000B/C/D/N and -5F, Mirage F1C/CR and CT, along with some Alpha Jets. Other aircraft may be detached from the operational squadrons for the duration of the trials.

The second flying squadron is EET 6/330 'Albret'. Its operations department has cells for operations, trials and liaison transport. The Technical Services department has a daily maintenance section and a checking and repairing section. Currently, the only active programme management team is for the Cougar RESCO (Recherche et Sauvetage de Combat, combat SAR). Until the first production-standard Cougar RESCO arrived in April 1999, EET 6/330 had just two permanently assigned TBM700s and two DHC-6 Twin Otters. Its single MS.760 Paris was retired during 1998.

Squadrons which do not operate any aircraft include the Escadron d'Expérimentations et de Soutien Technique (EEST, technical and experimentation squadron) 3/330 (which has departments for engines, avionics and photo/printing) and the Escadron Electronique, EE 4/330 (Electronic Squadron 4/330), which is dedicated to software studies/proving, communications and electronic warfare instruction/programming. The medical and physiological studies laboratory (Laboratoire d'Etudes Médico-Physiologiques, LEMP 16/330) is also part of the CEAM. This lab is part of the Institute de Medicine Aérospatiale du Service de Santé des Armes at Brétigny. LEMP 16/330 is the operational department. It is responsible for the aeromedical training courses for all pilot and WSO students in the air force and also has special departments for NBC and flight equipment.

The Operational Survival and Trials Parachutists Squadron (ESOPE) based at Mont-de-Marsan is another part of the CEAM. Combat aviators learn escape and evasion techniques to survive behind enemy lines.

New recce systems for the F1CR

One of the most important ongoing CEAM tasks is the expansion and upgrading of the Armée de l'Air's reconnaissance capabilities. The air force is pursuing a reconnaissance capability for every fighter-bomber type in its inventory. The dedicated platform is the Mirage F1CR, one of the most versatile tactical reconnaissance platforms in the world. Additionally, the Jaguar, Mirage F1C and F1CT have a limited capability, and future reconnaissance solutions for the Mirage 2000D and Rafale are under development. A new medium-altitude reconnaissance pod will be delivered to the CEAM in mid-1999 for operational trials, while a new medium-altitude digital pod for the Mirage F1CR, and later also for the Mirage 2000D and Rafale, is on the drawing board. Called PRESTO (Pod de Reconnaissance

Stand-Off) and developed by Thomson-CSF Optronique, it is the successor to the old RP35P wet film pod system originally designed for Mirage F1C operations in Africa. The RP35P was later rapidly reconfigured for F1CR operations over Bosnia. It has two 600-mm cameras housed in a converted Jaguar external fuel tank. This system had its drawbacks: for example, the pilot had to locate the target and fly a precise predetermined pattern because the fixed camera system did not slave to the target's co-ordinates.

When the PRESTO programme started, a decision had to be made whether to continue using wet film technology or to embrace the emerging electro-optical (EO) technology. As EO systems were not fully matured, the Armée d l'Air decided to build an EO demonstrator pod alongside the development of PRESTO with a wet film camera which would later be refitted with a CCD sensor, data recorder and datalink. From June to September 1997 the CEAM tested this demonstrator pod called DESIREE (Demonstrateur Simplifié de Recce EO), which had an MDS 610 (Medium Distance Sensor,

*Above: **CEAM** trials are not confined solely to national customers. This Mirage **F1EQ4-200** is fitted with the sizeable **Harold LOROP** pod – note the open cover over the main optical element.*

*Right and below right: During 1997 this Mirage **F1CR**, borrowed from **ER** 2/33, conducted the initial trials of the new **DESIREE EO**-backed camera pod. DESIREE is an interim solution leading to the AA's more advanced future podded system, **PRESTO**. A mock-up of the **PRESTO** pod is seen here (below right).*

610-mm) digital camera system and a Schlumberger DV 6410 data recorder. The camera is articulated, allowing the pilot to programme the target co-ordinates in flight, greatly improving operational flexibility.

Four different parameters (distance, speed, field of view and angle) are input on the ground via a laptop computer. Maintaining the right speed is very important, as the system records images using lines (linescan) which have to mesh into a single 'photo'. Flying slower or faster than programmed causes the lines (set at 10,000 pixels per line, 12 cm wide) to partly overlap or lay too far from each other, thereby losing essential parts of the target imagery. The digital recorder can hold 20 to 30 minutes worth of images. The MDS 610 has an 8X zoom and several modes (for example, 'push broom' and panoramic). DESIREE was used alongside a Mirage F1CR with an RP36P pod which took pictures of the same target, at the same time, in order to compare the results. The result with the new system was pictures of a similar or slightly better quality. From October to early December 1997 the AA took the system on missions over Iraq.

PRESTO at the CEAM

PRESTO will arrive at the CEAM in mid-1999, and the front-line reconnaissance squadrons are scheduled to receive it in early 2000. The system retains the MDS 610 camera – and still uses wet film – but now works in automatic and manual modes. All the pilot has to do is tell the system the target co-ordinates. The speed, altitude and angular limits of DESIREE no longer apply as rigidly. The computer autonomously processes the speed, distance to target and angle, and adjusts the recording system accordingly. This allows the pilot to approach the target from a completely different direction than planned in case of bad weather or an undiscovered threat *en route*. The camera has several photography modes including area search, line search and pinpoint reconnaissance.

Within a few years it is planned to refit the PRESTO pod with an EO sensor and digital data recorder (databank), and a datalink. Integration should be straightforward, as the datalink is the same as the Rafale's SLAR pod – and has also been in use with the F1CR for years. Much more attention is being paid to how the recorder and CCD camera/sensor are integrated. PRESTO weighs 480 kg (1,058 lb) and is 4.6 m (15 ft 1 in) long, and the camera has a 10° field of view. The system can be used at altitudes below 50,000 ft (15240 m), speeds below Mach 1.4 (600 kt; 690 mph; 1110 km/h) and between 2.4 and 6 *g*.

With PRESTO, the Armée de l'Air also conceives a future reconnaissance role for the Mirage 2000D. CEAM will start working on this combination shortly after PRESTO becomes operational on the F1CR. Adjustments will be made to the ground-based mission planning system, and the aircraft cockpit will have a few extra switches fitted. Seven PRESTO pods will be acquired for the two F1CR squadrons, to be able to use two pods in two theatres simultaneously, while keeping three pods in reserve and for training. Additional pods may be acquired later if the Mirage 2000D plans come to fruition.

The CEAM is also involved in the development of the Pod de Reco Nouvelle Génération (new generation reconnaissance pod) for use by the Mirage 2000D and Rafale. The requirements for this all-new system were given to industry in 1998. It will be capable of undertaking low- and medium-altitude reconnaissance, by day and night, and will incorporate an infra-red line scanner and a digital video system. The pod should be operational between 2005 and 2008.

F1CT recce 'quick fix'

The Mirage F1CT fighter-bombers based at Colmar now have a limited reconnaissance capability, developed in a crash programme whose aim was to provide an 'out-of-area' reconnaissance capability without the need to deploy the Mirage F1CR. The F1CT project was launched in 1995 and during 1997 some operational F1CTs were fitted with two Sony Colibri CCD cameras. It was not easy to find space for them in the compact F1; they were first fitted in the cockpit but it was soon found that they would impede the pilot in the event of an ejection, and finally two places were found in the fuselage. The cameras are mounted laterally and face forward. Depending on the desired altitude over the target, a 12-mm, 35-mm, 50-mm or 75-mm lens can be mounted by the cameras. The reconnaissance system is coupled with the HUD recorder to fix the position of the target. Initially, to aim the cameras F1CT pilots simply drew a crayon square on the canopy; now they have a glass visor attached to the canopy. This new reconnaissance solution was very cheap, the modifications and systems costing less than FF15,000 (roughly US$2,500) per aircraft.

Dassault is still delivering Mirage 2000Ds to the Armée de l'Air, but a new standard called R2 is already being developed. The R2 has improvements to the navigation/attack system (through the further integration of GPS), essential new software for the MATRA/BAe APACHE, an improvement to the Thomson-CSF PDLCT (Pod de Désignation Laser et Caméra Thermique) FLIR/laser designator and an improved chaff/flare capacity. All Mirage 2000D-R1s will return to Dassault for R2 modification, and the first is expected to arrive at Mont-de-Marsan in the summer of 2000. The changes to the laser designator pod have affected several of its components, including the thermal imager, which is new. The modified pod is called PDLCT-S (S for *synergie*). The AA has received a total of 14 PDLCT pods.

In addition to these expensive systems, the air force redirected 10 ATLIS 2 daylight-only EO/laser designator pods to the three Mirage 2000D squadrons at Nancy. The CEAM was central to the ATLIS 2/Mirage 2000D integration process, with was an uncomplicated one. Modifications were restricted to a few adjustments to the pod itself, and CEAM finished its integration trials during the summer of 1998. 'Spare' ATLIS 2 pods have now come from the sharply decreased Jaguar community. Despite its age, ATLIS 2 still has a better daylight performance than PDLCT. The TV camera is more powerful – with twice the magnification of the PDLCT system – so the WSO can find and identify the target easier and earlier, allowing the pilot to remain farther from the target, while the WSO has more time to set up the attack run.

APACHE

The MATRA/BAe APACHE (Arme Propulsé A Charges Ejectables, powered dispenser weapon) is a French-developed stand-off weapon intended for use on the Mirage 2000D and Rafale. Although it began life as a

Franco-German project, German industrial support was withdrawn in 1988. With the merger of MATRA and the missile and weapons division of British Aerospace, APACHE was further developed into the longer-ranged SCALP/Storm Shadow stand-off weapon that will arm the RAF's Tornado GR.Mk 4s and Eurofighters. The Mirage 2000D can carry the heavy APACHE only on the centreline station, but Rafale can carry one under each wing. APACHE has now reached the end of its development, with only the completion of the mission planning system and mission-aircraft integration remaining. The new SAGEM Système Locale de Préparation et Restitution de Mission (SLPRM) mission planning system is well advanced and will be the future common planning system for all Armée de l'Air types which now use different systems. The crew programmes the flight path of the missile on the SLPRM, takes it via a data cartridge to the aircraft and loads it via the onboard computer into the computer of the missile. SLPRM will be operational at the end of 1999.

Live fire testing has been undertaken at the RFN Vidsel range in northern Sweden. Film of these tests, taken from a Saab Lansen chase plane, shows the missile flying low over woods towards its target of flat concrete, simulating a runway. Above the target, the main body of the missile released 10 sub-munitions which descended vertically under quick-deploying parachutes. The rocket engines in the sub-munitions fired to penetrate the concrete at a very high velocity, followed by an explosion deep underground, leaving large craters in the once-smooth surface. Because APACHE has room for only 10 sub-munitions, more than one is needed to damage a runway sufficiently. CEAM attention is now turning to the development of the SCALP-EG, a derivative intended for use against hardened targets. A problem will

Above and right: The major changes made to the multi-role Mirage 2000-5F are largely under the skin and there are few external clues to the French fighter's new-found combat power. The -5F does have additional fuselage hardpoints, but the most obvious visual clue is the removal of the pitot tube from the nose when compared to its predecessor, the baseline Mirage 2000C.

be finding a suitable test area, for Sweden has restrictions concerning the use of terrain and the dimensions and nature of targets.

Mirage 2000C mid-life update

In November 1998 the CEAM welcomed the first group of pilots and technicians from EC 2/2, one of two Mirage 2000C units at Dijon, for conversion to the Mirage 2000-5F. The Armée de l'Air is converting 37 Mirage 2000Cs to this updated multi-role version, the main changes being the improved RDY radar, MATRA/BAe MICA missile, four additional pylons under the fuselage and a 'glass' cockpit. The updates meant much work for EC 5/330, which conducted all the tests necessary to verify whether the fighter performed according to specifications, and also developed new tactics and transferred all its knowledge to the first front-line squadron.

With the -5F the pilot can track 24 targets at ranges up to 120 miles (193 km) and track eight of them simultaneously within 80 miles (128 km). With MICA missiles he can engage four of them simultaneously (the 2000-5F can carry four MICAs and two Magic 2s). The four new fuselage stations free the inner wing pylons for fuel tanks. The old 2000C can only carry two of the older, larger and less effective MATRA Super 530D semi-active radar-guided missiles. The standard warload of the 2000C is therefore limited to only four missiles and a single centreline fuel tank. With the increased fuel load, the -5F can be on station three times longer, with two more missiles.

To convert to the -5F a new pilot uses the simulator and is briefed on the new systems and tactics. In total he flies 25 missions. The second group from EC 2/2 arrived in December 1998 and the final group followed in January 1999. They left in April to become fully operational early in the summer of 1999.

EC 5/330 has far-reaching plans for the Combat Training Centre. The current Armée de l'Air CTC has three simulation domes fitted for the Mirage 2000C and F1, allowing two-on-two dogfights to be conducted. Additionally, the CTC has four Mirage 2000-5 cockpit trainers to teach new pilots 'switchology' and to familiarise them with the improved weapons systems. The

existing dome simulators are now far from state-of-the-art, especially in display technology. This will change in the summer of 2000, when three new domes and software are installed. All the stations, including the 2000-5 terminals, will be connected to allow 10-ship formations to fight up to 33 simulated targets. The six domes can be configured for the Mirage 2000C, -5, D and N, including the WSO cockpits with all air-to-ground and air-to-air weapon systems.

The objective is to train for essential tasks which are difficult to undertake regularly during peacetime – such as EW and missile firing – and to prepare pilots for TLP, Red Flag or real war. A mission rehearsal capability may be incorporated with realistic ground simulations. This would allow strike and fighter squadrons to 'deploy' to the CTC at the same time, for joint training. Various foreign air forces which fly the Mirage F1 and Mirage 2000 fighters also use the CTC for training. For the time being the new facility will only be accessible to French personnel, but others may be allowed to use it in the future.

RESCO Cougar

The major programme currently concerning the Commandement de Force Aérienne de Projection (CFAP), the main 'customer' of EET 6/330, is the AS 532AL Cougar Mk 2 as used for

combat search and rescue (CSAR) – known in France as RESCO (Recherche et Sauvetage de Combat). In April 1999 the CEAM acquired the first of this new breed, a heavily modified version of the regular Mk 2 for which the AA has placed an initial order for four to be delivered by 2000. The dedicated CSAR squadron, EH 1/67 'Pyrénées' at Cazaux AB, will be operational with four aircraft in 2002, to replace the ageing Puma. The CEAM needs the intervening years to test and evaluate the new helicopter.

The air force required a helicopter with a three-man cockpit, capable of carrying five in the cabin – one hoist operator, one rescue swimmer and three commandos. It had to be a safe, precise and autonomous helicopter capable of flying at night in all weather conditions over long ranges. The operational requirement called for a helicopter capable of flying more than 250 nm (287 miles; 462 km) behind enemy lines, at night, in tactical conditions after transiting 30 nm (35 miles; 55 km) through a friendly area, then perform 30 minutes of hoist operations, and return to base – with 20 minutes of fuel remaining.

The resulting helicopter has an immense internal fuel load of 4000 litres (880 Imp gal). It gained a large 320-litre (70-Imp gal) tank in the rear of the cabin, which is jettisonable if necessary. The big sponsons accommodate not only the

Above: This Puma testbed has been used to trial several of the systems now being fitted to the AA's RESCO Cougars – France's dedicated combat SAR helicopter. Note the FLIR ball under the cabin, the revised antenna fit under the nose and the air data sensors above the nose. The CEAM also undertook all the self-defence systems trials for the RESCO.

Left: Testing of the CN.235M tactical transport was a lengthy process and at one time all of the AA's initial batch of six aircraft were in service with EET 6/330.

main gear but also more fuel tanks. To lift the additional weight, the two Makila 1A2s (with FADEC) have each been uprated to a maximum continuous power of 1,656 hp (1253 kW); take-off power is 1,844 hp (1376 kW); an engine can deliver 1,956 hp (1459 kW) MCP under one engine inoperative (OEI) emergency conditions and 2,108 hp (1572 kW) during take-off for two minutes. All fuel tanks are self-sealing and crash-worthy. The Armée de l'Air has not opted for external jettisonable fuel tanks or the inflight-refuelling probe which were offered by Eurocopter, but they may be added in the future. The RESCO Cougar has a Eurocopter Aircraft Recording and Monitoring System (EURARMS), an improved version of the Health Usage Monitoring System (HUMS) used in the Dutch Cougars Mk 2s. EURARM monitors and controls all airframe and rotor vibration and significantly improves helicopter reliability.

Apart from full NVG compatibility in both cockpits and cabin, the RESCO Cougar has other night-flying aids. Low-level tactical flying at night requires skill and training, but even the most experienced pilot can lose sight of his wingman. The RESCO Cougar has a low-intensity beacon which is not visible from the ground and can only be seen with NVGs. It is also equipped with infra-red formation lights. Another useful aid for night operations is the infra-red landing light that allows the crew to find a good landing spot without using visible 'white' light.

The helicopter had to have defensive armament, an integrated self-defence system and dedicated CSAR equipment like FLIR, hoist, personal locator system (PLS) and radios. The Armée de l'Air has not yet decided on the final self-defence fit. A choice has to be made between the ELIPS system fitted to the Dutch Cougars or the MATRA Saphir system also carried by the

Cougars of the French army. The Missile Warning Receiver (MWS) would be either the Damian (as on French Pumas), or the MILDS which is fitted to the Eurocopter Tigre and NH 90. The RESCO Cougar will also get a radar warning receiver and perhaps a laser warning receiver.

The Cougar has two 7.62-mm machine-guns firing through the front cabin sliding windows. Unlike the Dutch Cougars, the French version has double sliding doors on each side which do not interfere with the guns. The seats and doors for the pilot and co-pilot, as well as the main servo-control and autopilot hydraulic unit (which is in engineering development), are all armoured. The Cougar has a wide variety of frequency hopping and secure radios, a single Identification Friend or Foe (IFF) Mode 4, and an improved Chlio FLIR. The gyro-stabilised Chlio can perform as a FLIR or as an observation camera

To support the many CEAM detachments around the country, the CEAM maintains its own dedicated transport fleet, ferrying personnel and materiel to wherever they are needed. These aircraft are flown by EET 6/330 and include the DHC-6 Twin Otter (below left) and the TBM700 (below). The faster, pressurised and quiet TBM is definitely the passenger's preference.

Above: EC 5/330 'Côte d'Argent' is an active NATO Tiger Squadron and regularly decorates aircraft that take part in Tiger Meets and other special occasions.

Right: The Mirage F1C still has a place in the CEAM test fleet, although no two-seat Mirage F1Bs are in service any longer. This aircraft is carrying an unusual load of a centreline Thomson-CSF Raphaël/SLAR 2000 pod.

for navigation and reconnaissance. The NADIR Mk 2 610 navigation set is comprised of an inertial navigation system, global positioning system and Doppler radar with a back-up navigation set. The automated flight control system has a variety of automated search and rescue modes such as auto-hover and auto-descend in specific profiles. The variable-speed winch can lift 272 kg (600 lb) from a maximum length of 70 m (230 ft); a second electrical winch with 40 m (131 ft) of cable and a 138-kg (304-lb) weight limitation acts as a back-up. A special infra-red winch light helps the winch operator during night operations. The French variant does not have a search radar, only a weather radar with maritime functions.

The second and third Cougars are expected later in 1999. The CEAM will use the second one to test the self-defence systems and the third for de-icing tests. Before EH 1/67 becomes fully operational with the RESCO Cougar in 2002, a number of crews will go to Mont-de-Marsan for training. The target is 14 operational Cougars after 2002, but there will probably be a second batch of just three.

Detachments

The CEAM has several detachments throughout France. The air-to-ground weapon testing and training department has its hub at nearby Cazaux AB, where almost all armament-related trials are conducted – Cazaux is the main air-to-ground trials base for French aviation. It is situated near the huge Centre d'Essais Landes test area on the Gulf of Biscay. Additionally, within the perimeter (south side) of the air base, the CEV maintains the large Calamar test range that once belonged to the air force. Like the CEL ranges, it is fully instrumented for trials purposes. The CEV has its air-to-ground department at Cazaux and companies such as Dassault and MATRA maintain offices

there. This CEAM detachment does not have any aircraft of its own and, instead, aircraft are assigned from Mont-de-Marsan for the duration of trials. 00/331 has a test section, an instruction and a technical section and programme management teams for the APACHE and air-to-ground weapons in general.

Brétigny-sur-Orge south of Paris is also an important outpost (det 00/332), although this will change when the CEV abandons this historic home within the next five years. Its aviation assets are to be moved to Istres and Cazaux in 1999. Brétigny accommodates the programme offices of various communications and C^2 systems, the SARIGUE Nouvelle Génération (upgraded DC-8 Elint platform) and an element of the Rafale programme office. The Armée de l'Air will finally receive its sole long-awaited (and hugely expensive) DC-8 SARIGUE NG electronic and communications intelligence gathering platform at the end of 1999.

The CEAM's main Rafale office is located at Istres (det 00/333), near Marseilles. In November 1998 Dassault flew the first production Rafale B from the line at Bordeaux-Mérignac to Istres for trials with the CEV. The first Rafale, however, will not arrive at Mont-de-Marsan until after the first Navy flottille becomes carrier-qualified. This flottille will then transfer to the CEAM for operational work-ups. This unusual process has come

about because the navy's highest priority is getting the Rafale cleared for embarkation – once the Crusader is phased out at the end of 1999, French aircraft-carriers will have dedicated fighters for fleet defence or strike escort.

The CEAM is also present at Avord Air Base (det 00/336), home to EDCA 36 with its four Boeing E-3F AEW&C platforms. The activities of the CEAM here are focused on air surveillance and datalink systems development. Metz AB (det 00/336) accommodates the programme offices for electronic intelligence, Elint research and protection measures. Metz is the home base for the C-160G Gabriel tactical Elint/Comint Transalls of Escadron Electronique 54.

Future programmes

Within a few years CEAM activity will be dominated by the Rafale and (hopefully) the Future Large Aircraft programmes. The first Armée de l'Air Rafale was delivered to Istres Air Base for permanent duty as a testbed for the CEV. In 1999 two more Rafale Ms will be produced for the Marine Nationale: one will go to the CEV, the second directly to the Marine Nationale. The priority for the Marine Nationale is to get its first Rafale M squadron carrier qualified by 2001. Then the squadron will proceed to Mont-de-Marsan to learn to fly the aircraft operationally, from the CEAM. **Gert Kromhout**

Lockheed Martin
F-22 Raptor

Lockheed Martin's F-22 promises to be the single most effective air superiority aircraft of the modern era. With an unparalleled design and development effort behind it, the F-22 should combine speed and stealth in an agile airframe that uses the most advanced weapons and systems to find and kill its targets without warning. Like all the current crop of next-generation fighters, the F-22 is far from being an operational aircraft and far from backing up such words with deeds. Today the F-22 is still stepping, steadily, through its flight test programme. Among the test team confidence in the aircraft is high, but the greatest threat to the F-22's future is financial. With a shrinking budget, the US is struggling to pay its defence bills and the F-22 is just one of three current 'high-ticket' fighter programmes – to say nothing of other systems – looking for funds.

Lockheed Martin F-22

Lockheed Martin's F-22 Raptor is a great deal more lethal than it looks. Smooth, grey, broad-bodied, apparently unarmed and deceptively conventional, it arguably represents the greatest single advance in fighter design since the advent of the jet. The F-22 features stealth, supercruise and integrated avionics. All three are essential to the way the F-22 flies and fights and, in the minds of many, the F-22's combination of these assets is unbeatable.

The F-22's stealth has two main purposes. By protecting the aircraft against detection and attack from airborne or ground-based weapons, it endows the fighter with much greater freedom of operation. It also gives the pilot a greater chance of achieving surprise in the attack and allows missiles to be launched at closer range.

Supersonic cruise – the F-22 should be capable of cruising 50 per cent faster than any fighter today, without using full military power – also has defensive and offensive value. Combined with stealth, it reduces the fighter's susceptibility to SAMs and other weapons. By the time a SAM radar detects an approaching F-22, the fighter may overfly it before a missile can reach its altitude, turning the engagement into a tail-chase in which the missile quickly runs out of energy. A supercruising fighter is less likely to be surprised by an attacker approaching from its rear quadrant, and more likely to surprise a slower adversary. Higher speeds give the F-22's missiles more energy at launch and, consequently, in the endgame.

Integrated avionics allow the pilot to tactically exploit stealth and supercruise. The F-22's avionics system fuses the inputs from onboard and offboard sensors, giving the pilot the situational awareness necessary to handle an air combat scenario that unrolls 50 per cent faster than it does for the pilot of a subsonic aircraft. The sensors are managed automatically, to maximise the use of offboard and passive systems and to minimise the chance that the F-22's emissions will be detected. This capability has not been developed overnight: when the F-22 enters service in 2005, more than 20 years will have passed since the USAF started committing serious money to the project.

Origins of the ATF

Today, 10 years after the collapse of the Berlin Wall, it is sometimes hard to remember just how unstable the world looked 10 years before that event. In the late 1970s, the Soviet Union was rearming at an awe-inspiring pace. The low-performing tactical fighters of the 1960s were being rapidly replaced by MiG-23/27s, Su-22M3/M4s and Su-24s, carrying an increasing range of guided weapons. A complete new generation of surface-to-air missiles (SAMs) was being developed. New cruiser and destroyer classes appeared yearly, designed to engage NATO navies while Soviet submarines targeted the Atlantic convoys which

were critical to NATO's plans for the defence of Europe. Factories were turning out tanks by the thousand. At the same time, intermediate and strategic nuclear forces were being improved, while research institutes explored radical new technologies that promised military breakthroughs.

Yet this glittering armour concealed the truth. The bloody stalemate in Afghanistan, the bottomless pit of inefficiency that was Soviet industry, the lack of funds for the country's basic mechanical infrastructure – roads, railways and heavy industry – and the fundamental failure to adequately feed its people, all combined to leave the USSR in a dangerously unbalanced state. Discontent bubbled in the Warsaw Pact states, and not even the Kremlin's hardliners believed that the Soviet Union could invade and subdue all its 'loyal' allies at the same time.

This contrast between short-term military strength and long-term weakness was apparent to Western observers. Many military planners believed – though the subject was seldom discussed in public – that the Soviet leadership might conclude that the road to peace and prosperity led across the West German border; that they might gamble on war as a way of eliminating NATO and gaining access to Europe's industrial technology on favourable terms. Western military planning, in all its aspects, thus gained an increasing sense of urgency.

In the late 1970s, as the F-15, F-16 and A-10 made their first flights, went into production and entered service with the US Air Force, the service's fighter arm – Tactical Air Command (TAC) – was already looking beyond them. In a 1969-70 study called TAC-85, the USAF examined the targets and threats that would face its next new fighter. This led TAC to devise a Concept of Operations in 1971 for an Advanced Tactical Fighter (ATF) – the first time this term was used in an official context. The ATF became the focus for a number of small-scale studies in the 1970s. In early 1975, USAF Systems Command even developed a plan to build and fly two pairs of ATF prototypes in 1977-81, but funds were not available.

LO technology emerges

The threat from the Soviet air defence system soon became the overriding design consideration, and at first attempts to defeat it centred around speed alone. By 1976, the USAF was sponsoring studies which looked at another means of achieving survivability – low observables (LO), or stealth. At this time, LO was very much a black art. Few people knew that Lockheed and Northrop had demonstrated, with tests of large-scale radar cross-section (RCS) models, that it was possible to achieve RCS levels so low that published references did not even include them on their charts, or that one of the two would be chosen in March that year to build a stealth prototype. On the other hand, the basic physics of the problem were no secret, and the Rockwell B-1 and SR-71 showed how reduced RCS could be used to make life safer for combat aircraft.

Through the remainder of the 1970s, studies continued at a low level. The major fighter producers (not including Lockheed) participated in the Air-to-Surface Technology Evaluation and Integration (ASTEI) study in 1976, reaffirming the value of supersonic cruise. In 1978, the USAF defined a two-phase approach to a new strike system: a near-term Enhanced Tactical Fighter (ETF), followed by an Advanced Tactical Attack System (ATAS) which would incorporate new weapons and other advanced technologies.

ATF development was spurred by startling advances in the Soviet air threat. Look-down/shoot-down fighter radars and a multitude of SAMs threatened targets at all altitudes. The Soviet Union was also developing the new Beriev A-50 'Mainstay' AEW&C aircraft to complement its new fighters, the MiG-29 and Su-27. The USAF conducted a 'quick-look' assessment in 1982, to see whether the F-117A could be armed with air-to-air missiles to attack the 'Mainstay', but found it would not be effective. However, a high-performance, air-to-air ATF could defeat advanced Soviet fighters and threaten the 'Mainstay'. In so doing, it would restore the low-altitude sanctuary, allowing the strike aircraft to enter hostile airspace below and between the interlocking SAM zones. This would extend the effective lifetime of existing strike aircraft and any F-15/F-16 derivative.

Lockheed Martin F-22

Inset, right: By 1986 some perhaps deliberately confusing artwork was released by Lockheed and the DoD to illustrate the lines that an ATF design might be taking. While the configuration of this proposed ATF adheres to some of the actual thinking of the time, its size and proportions are almost laughable.

Right: 'Raptor 01' (temporarily christened Spirit of America) was rolled out at Marietta on 9 April 1997 and made its first flight on 7 September. The maiden voyage had been expected as early as 29 May but fuel leaks, an APU fault and software gremlins conspired to delay it. In its final form the F-22A looked very different from the YF-22 and nothing like the horde of initial ATF concepts.

Most of the 1970s studies focused on the air-to-ground mission, with the aim of replacing the F-4 and F-111. TAC was concerned that its strike aircraft would not be able to penetrate the dense and interlinked Soviet air defence system. Survivability, therefore, became a dominant consideration. The stillborn ATF prototype effort of 1975 was intended to demonstrate supersonic cruise technology as a way to defeat SAMs. Lockheed's A-12 and SR-71 had already blown through North Vietnamese and Egyptian air defences with ease. As a result, even before the ATF competition, Lockheed produced designs such as the CL-1980 – a large aircraft configured for very high speeds at high altitude, with vectored thrust and pop-out canards.

The emphasis on the air-to-surface mission reflected the assumption that the new F-15 and F-16 would be able to handle the air-to-air threat into the 1990s. As the F-15 became operational in 1978, however, alarming evidence suggested that the new fighter's superiority might be transitory. Western analysts were shocked by the speed with which the Soviet Union had been able to modernise its fighter force in the 1970s, building as many as 500 new MiG-23/27s each year. If this pattern repeated itself, the MiG-29 would enter service as a one-for-one replacement for the MiG-21, with the Su-27 replacing the MiG-23. Moreover, the Soviet Union was developing the MiG-31 long-range interceptor from the Mach 2.8 MiG-25: exploiting the same 'high, fast sanctuary' that the USAF hoped to use for the ATF, it could track and engage low-flying NATO aircraft over a wide area. The prospect was described by one analyst as "a high/low mix, with their 'low' equivalent to our 'high'."

Consequently, the USAF redirected its advanced-fighter planning, starting in late 1979, to consider air-to-air and air-to-surface developments in parallel. In April 1980, the ETF work was suspended and ATAS became, once more, the Advanced Tactical Fighter. Under the ATF programme, the USAF would look at both air-to-air and air-to-surface requirements and technology. The ATF study would determine whether a single aircraft could cover all the missions, and, if not, which mission should be addressed first.

One significant pair of supporting studies was ATAS Mission Analysis (ATASMA) and Advanced Counterair Engagement Mission Analysis (ACEMA). ATASMA noted the likely effects of anti-airfield attacks on TAC operations, and explored the value of short take-off and landing (STOL) performance: STOL would make it easier to repair enough runway to resume operations. ATASMA and ACEMA both looked at the value of greater range, particularly in the Korean and Middle Eastern theatres of operations.

Money was a serious limitation on the ATF studies. In the final mark-ups of both the Fiscal Year 1981 and FY 1982 budgets, Congress excised ATF funding, preventing the USAF from doing all the work needed to support a formal ATF programme. Consequently, in May 1981, the USAF's Aeronautical Systems Division issued a request for information (RFI) for the ATF to nine companies: Boeing, Fairchild, General Dynamics, Grumman, Lockheed, McDonnell Douglas, Northrop, Rockwell and Vought. (An RFI for the engine was issued in the following month.) Described by one participant as "a way to get industry to pay for our studies", the ATF RFI was wide-ranging. It included information from the ACEMA and ATASMA, and asked industry to look at air-to-air and air-to-surface designs. Industry could propose identical aircraft, related variants or entirely different aircraft for the two mission areas.

The first ATF studies

In November 1981, the USAF received Pentagon approval to go ahead with development of the new fighter (although there was still no money for it) and seven companies presented their initial responses to the RFI. (Fairchild and Vought did not respond.) The responses were remarkably diverse. Northrop offered a 'co-operative fighter' with a gross weight of 17,700 lb (8030 kg). Lockheed's design was seven times bigger – clearly related to the SR-71, it had a take-off weight of 116,400 lb (52800 kg) and a cruising speed of Mach 2.8. Dubbed a 'battlecruiser' by one retired USAF general, it would have been a dual-role aircraft carrying different weapons for air-to-air and air-to-surface missions. Between these two lay a spread of configurations including swept-back, swept-forward and unswept wings and blended deltas. Some contractors proposed designs which could perform both air-to-ground and air-to-air missions; others offered different designs.

Lockheed and Northrop were the two dissenters from what was otherwise a consensus view: that the ATF should

Left: Another Lockheed artist's impression from October 1986 shows an ATF design much more in keeping with the final 50,000-lb (22680-kg) aircraft that emerged. The accompanying caption mentions the ATF's highly manoeuvrable airframe and low-observable technology credentials. As early as 1983, stealth had become an all-important design consideration for the ATF competitors and any discussion of its application, at least in public, quickly became impossible.

Above: At one time it had been planned to fly aircraft 4001 from its Marietta birthplace to Edwards AFB where the flight test programme proper would be conducted. In the event, after some structural testing, 'Raptor 01' was disassembled and flown by C-5 to Edwards on 5 February 1998. The aircraft did not fly again until 17 May, when Lt Col Steve Rainey became the first USAF pilot to fly the F-22A. On 9 July Chuck Killberg made his first flight. On 26 August Steve Rainey flew aircraft 4002 non-stop from Marietta to join its sistership at Edwards.

avoid being either a simple and relatively limited aircraft (which might have trouble achieving the range required for operations outside Europe) or a very large and expensive design (which could not be acquired and operated in sufficient numbers to deal with all the threats). Apart from the Lockheed and Northrop designs, most of the RFI responses were relatively close in size to the F-15 or F-14.

One other design was evaluated in parallel: an in-house USAF study for a subsonic, low-observable strike fighter. This was a surrogate for a highly classified design from General Dynamics, which was a precursor to the GD/McDonnell Douglas A-12.

The USAF selected four concepts for more detailed study of how they would fare in view of likely budgets, force structures and threats: the stealth aircraft, a Northrop-like low-cost fighter, Lockheed's 50-ton monster, and a supersonic cruise and manoeuvre (SCM) fighter which fell

into the middle of the pack for weight and performance, and would make some use of LO technology. The SCM did best in the air-to-air mission. Cruising above 50,000 ft (15240 m) at speeds of Mach 1.4-1.5, it could evade many SAMs; it was more manoeuvrable than the big Lockheed aircraft, and weighed half as much.

ATF for air superiority

1982 was a critical year for the ATF. The USAF, as noted above, found a favoured balance in terms of size, supercruise and manoeuvrability early in the year. The final RFI reports were delivered in May. Meanwhile, a number of factors were pushing the USAF towards an ATF optimised for the air-superiority mission.

First, the requirement for a new strike aircraft began to seem less urgent, for several reasons. In 1980-82, McDonnell Douglas and General Dynamics flew modified versions of

The Dem/Val (demonstration/validation) phase of the ATF competition, which came in late 1985, called for four selected candidates to set out the detailed technological goals of their baseline ATF designs. Of the four, little is known about the Grumman Dem/Val proposal, but the other three ATF designs shown here illustrate the varying approaches taken during this once highly-classified period.

BOEING ATF Dem/Val design *(ranked fourth overall)*
Featuring a twin-tailed, trapezoidal wing layout, Boeing's ATF design was larger than its rivals. It also had an unusual split single inlet that fed both engines. The aircraft was optimised for high speed, but the driving factor in its design was its three internal weapons bays; two side bays for short-range AAMs and one centre bay for BVR missiles. Larger air-to-ground weapons would be carried conformally. Boeing made provision for three nose-mounted radars and two IRSTs.

GENERAL DYNAMICS ATF Dem/Val design *(ranked second overall)*
General Dynamics poured immense development effort into its ATF proposal and was widely seen as a front-runner in the competition. Three distinct families of design approach – the so-called conventional, all-wing and semi-tailless configurations – coalesced into the final T-330 design. This had a single vertical tail (with no tailplanes), an unusual ATF feature which was a compromise between stealthiness and overall controllability. Another unique feature was the position of the two radar arrays – behind the cockpit, over the engine intakes. Each radar was steerable over an arc of 60° and augmented by an IRST placed on the nose.

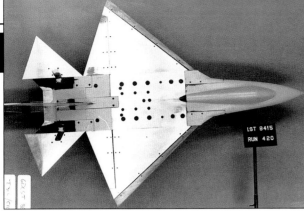

Above: General Dynamic's 'Conventional' studies did follow largely conventional lines, using single and twin vertical tails, with tailplanes, and recognisably normal wing layouts.

Above and below: GD's radical 'All-Wing' designs were another design approach that ultimately did not bear fruit. They were certainly in keeping with the more exotic ideas of ATF design that appeared in notional artist's impressions.

GD's 'Tailless' design approach won out. Several widely spaced wingtip-/tailboom-mounted fin configurations were first tested (above). Stealthier inward-canted fins were tried out just before the Dem/Val deadline (below).

LOCKHEED ATF Dem/Val design (ranked first overall)

Lockheed almost completely reinvented its final ATF proposal, drawing on F-117 experience but making the airframe smoother and rounder. The F-117 heritage in Lockheed's 1985 submittal – known as Configuration 090P – is clear, with its swept trapezoidal wings, twin canted fins and tailplanes. From the front the aircraft had some of the visual cues of the YF-22 design that finally emerged, but Lockheed actually won the $700 million Dem/Val contract (along with Northrop) with a design that looked nothing like the aircraft it would build. When Lockheed teamed up with Boeing and General Dynamics, their experience and input was folded into the design process and this had a major effect on the YF-22 design that emerged.

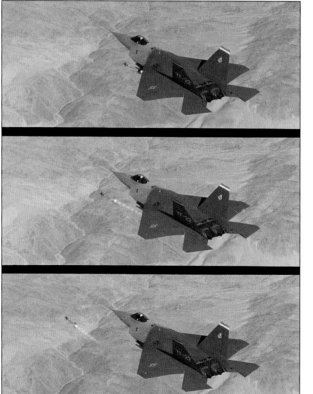

Above: The YF-22 design was always heavily influenced by F-117 stealth technology and, when it was unveiled in August 1991, some observers pointed to its resemblance to an inverted F-117. More advanced modelling and testing techniques allowed the YF-22 to avoid the hard faceted edges of the 'Stealth Fighter'. The Dem/Val YF-22 would be quite different to the EMD F-22A configuration, however. For example, the tail fins on the YF-22 were huge – Lockheed wanted to avoid the control problems they had experienced on the the F-117's early flights because its tail surfaces were too small. The fins on the YF-22 were overkill, and would be reduced by 30 per cent on the EMD aircraft.

One of the areas where Lockheed stole a march on Northrop during Dem/Val testing was weapons firing – which was never a USAF requirement for that stage in the programme. Lockheed forged ahead using the second YF-22 (the aircraft that unfortunately crashed in April 1992 after an FCS failure) to undertake inert AIM-9 Sidewinder firings (above right) and AIM-120 AMRAAM firings (right). A temporary fixed spoiler was fitted in front of the weapons bay. The aircraft later wore little missile firing symbols on the engine inlet.

the F-15 and F-16, dedicated to the strike mission. By 1982, the USAF was formally evaluating these aircraft as an interim solution to its need for a precision bomber capable of operating at night or in bad weather. Studies had shown that the F-111, with some upgrades, would continue to be effective into the late 1990s. Moreover, the F-117A 'Stealth Fighter' had flown, and the USAF had decided to buy three squadrons. In a European war, the F-117As would destroy key air defence sites, making other attack aircraft more effective.

Tactical Air Command, for its part, was opposed to a dual-role ATF, arguing that a true air-superiority fighter would not carry enough weapons to do the interdiction mission, while an aircraft with an adequate weapon load would be oversized for air combat. TAC also argued against a solution which leaned to one or another extreme in terms of technology. High-speed, high-altitude aircraft and slow LO aircraft could not be adequately offensive, TAC argued: "The ATF cannot avoid the conflict but must go where the targets are and beat the enemy where he is found."

In October 1982, representatives from most of the fighter manufacturers, together with planners and requirements specialists from the USAF, met at an aerospace engineering conference in Anaheim, California, for a half-day session on the ATF. (It was the last unclassified meeting on ATF for many years.) The outlines of today's fighter began to emerge: a supersonic-cruise aircraft, with a combat radius of 600–800 nm (1110-1480 km) – a 20 to 60 per cent increase over the F-15. It would be able to take off and land on a 2,000-ft (610-m) runway, and it would be easier to maintain

in the field than the F-15. The USAF's planners had concluded that range and supersonic persistence set a lower bound to the fighter's size, and price set a top limit. The requirements balanced at a normal take-off weight of about 80,000 lb (36200 kg) for an interdiction/strike aircraft, and 60,000 lb (27215 kg) for an air superiority fighter.

Although the fact was not disclosed at the time, the USAF had officially set air superiority as the primary goal for the new fighter, in a programme management directive issued in August. This was reflected in a draft request for proposals (RFP) for the concept definition investigation (CDI) stage of the ATF programme, issued in late 1982. By this time, ATF was a real programme with money behind it. The USAF's fighter 'roadmap' called for the service to buy a strike version of the F-15 or F-16 first (McDonnell Douglas won this contest with the F-15E), and follow that with a fleet of 750 ATFs to replace the F-15, starting in the mid-1990s.

Stealth in the shadows

The final RFP for the CDI phase was issued in May 1983 – and amended significantly eight days later, because of the black art of stealth. The USAF had expected that the ATF would use stealth technology, but security firewalls separated most participants in the ATF programme from the highly classified projects under which very low observable (VLO) aircraft such as the F-117, Northrop Tacit Blue and B-2 were being designed and developed. The leaders of TAC and USAF Systems Command were aware of these programmes, and decided to establish a conduit between the Directorate of Low Observables, buried in Wright-Patterson AFB's locked vaults, and the 'white' world of ATF. Then-Major Claude Bolton, leader of the ATF concept development team, has recalled that "someone grabbed us by the shoulder as we walked down the hall and said, 'We need to talk to you.'"

Bolton and his colleagues learned that the F-117 and Tacit Blue had demonstrated minuscule RCS numbers, and that designers were developing techniques and materials which promised dramatic RCS reductions without a sharp increase in weight and drag. The ATF RFP was amended, calling for more LO data.

In 1983, an ATF System Program Office (SPO) was formed at Wright-Patterson AFB. Headed by Colonel Albert C. Piccirillo – a fighter pilot with F-4 experience in Vietnam and time in F-15s – its task was produce a specification which met all the users' essential requirements and as many of their desires as practical. The traps to avoid were

requirements of marginal value and disproportionately high cost. Every pound of equipment added to the aircraft meant a five-pound increase in gross weight to meet the same performance requirements. "Early in this stage," Piccirillo remarked in an interview, "we found four or five significant drivers" – these were specific requirements which added a great deal to the fighter's weight – "and making just one of them cost us 10,000 pounds [in weight]." In other cases, Piccirillo said, "backing off by half a per cent was important."

In September 1983, concept definition contracts were issued to all the companies which responded to the RFP – Boeing, GD, Grumman, Lockheed, McDonnell Douglas, Northrop and Rockwell. The final reports would be presented in May 1984. This would allow the USAF to tighten the requirement and hold a competition for the next phase of the programme.

Above: Of the two YF-22s built, the first prototype (N22YF) was powered by General Electric YF120 variable-cycle engines, while the second (N22YX) used the winning Pratt & Whitney YF119s. The first prototype is seen here fitted with a spin recovery parachute for use during handling and high-Alpha trials. When Lockheed won the Dem/Val competition in 1991, N22YF did not fly again. The second YF-22 returned to flight duty in October 1991, this time wearing its USAF serial (87-701). Supporting development work for the EMD phase, the YF-22 flew 39 times – more than it had during the Dem/Val stage. Its contribution was limited by the major changes between it and the final F-22A design. After the April 1992 crash – when the YF-22 entered a series of oscillations during a low, slow pass along the Edwards runway, then crashed, slid 8,000 ft and burned – the surface of the airframe was repaired. The YF-22 was then used to test antenna designs for the F-22A on a pedestal at the Rome Air Development Center, Griffiss AFB.

Above left: Seen overhead one of the runways at Rogers Dry Lake, Edwards AFB, this view of YF-22 N22YF clearly shows its rotating IFR receptacle (similar to the F-22As) located to port. Inflight refuelling was carried out as a matter of routine by the YF-22 test fleet.

Northrop YF-23: The greatest fighter never built?

The Northrop ATF design was widely acknowledged as the most innovative and sophisticated of the two and was widely tipped as a winner, even by the closest observers of the ATF competition. Lockheed's triumph was greeted with surprise, yet the YF-22 had scored on several important points. Not only had Lockheed pushed the YF-22's flight test envelope further than Northrop felt necessary, it also convinced the USAF that it would be better able to integrate and manage all the work required to meet the ATF specification in full.

The Northrop/McDonnell Douglas YF-23 is one of the most radical and interesting fighter designs of the modern era. It remains mysterious in many ways. Much less information on the design, its development and test programme has been released than on the YF-22 programme. Paul Metz, who was Northrop's chief test pilot on the YF-23 before moving to Lockheed to lead the F-22 flight-test programme, also flatly refuses to compare the two aircraft.

The YF-23 evolved from two strands of development in Northrop design: fighters and stealth aircraft. Northrop had been a pioneer of agile, smaller fighters, building the YF-17 prototype for evaluation against the YF-16. Although the Northrop design was later selected for development as a Navy fighter, the customer insisted on a 'Navy house' as prime contractor. When the F/A-18 was built, Northrop was relegated to a sub-contractor on its own design, and the company failed in its efforts to sell a land-based version of the F/A-18 for export. By the early 1980s, Northrop was looking to the next generation: the ND-102, proposed to Germany as a joint venture with Dornier, had a clipped delta wing, no horizontal tail and vectored thrust.

Meanwhile, Northrop had demonstrated its ability to design stealthy aircraft with curved surfaces. By the time the USAF had defined the ATF as an air-to-air, supersonic-cruise fighter, Northrop's Tacit Blue radar surveillance aircraft had flown and the company had won the contest to develop the B-2.

Lockheed and Northrop had both run simulated combats and operational analyses and had come to different conclusions. Northrop believed that an ultra-stealthy fighter could force a decision in the air battle before the hostile force could close to visual range. A few 'leakers' would survive, but they would be outnumbered and disorganised. Consequently, stealth and speed were the priorities.

From the aerodynamic viewpoint, the design which emerged resembled the ND-102, except that the nozzles were designed for stealth, and did not feature vectoring. Instead, pitch control was provided by large, shallow-angle V-tails.

The LO approach resembled the B-2 and Tacit Blue in that every component of the aircraft, including the inlets and exhausts, was located inside a continuous perimeter. Every line of that perimeter followed one of two alignments, and no two surfaces overlapped. The perimeter, in fact, was created by the junction of the upper and lower surfaces, each of which was made up of two continuous curves.

The wing was diamond-shaped, with the same sweep angles on the leading and trailing edges. The aerodynamic sweep was moderate, and the body was area-ruled to avoid excessive wave drag: the long forebody, which accommodated the cockpit, electronics and weapons, tapered off towards the mid-chord point, and the engine nacelles grew towards the rear of the wing.

Designed to operate at high altitude, the Northrop fighter had its exhausts located above a broad afterbody, and masked from the side by the V-tails. The single expansion-ramp nozzle (SERN) exhausts were located in trenches, fitted with air-cooled liners developed by Allison. The inlets were below the wing, close behind the leading edge. The wing itself formed the first compression ramp for the inlet system.

The flight control layout was unique. The immense V-tails were primarily used for pitch and roll control. The wing carried large two-section flaperons, which were used not only for lift augmentation and roll control but also as airbrakes and for yaw control: deflecting the outer sections upward, and the inner sections down, created drag without any other moments, and operating the surfaces on one side only produced a yawing force. The YF-23 featured an optically signalled 'fly-by-light' flight control system.

The YF-23, Northrop later claimed, looked almost exactly like the design that it proposed for Dem/Val. It did not go above 25° Alpha in its tests; Northrop claimed that conventional and spin-tunnel tests showed that the aircraft could perform tailslides and had no Alpha limits. Neither did it fire weapons. The fighter supercruised at Mach 1.6 with the GE YF120 engines, and 7.2 hours in the total 65 hours of flying were performed at supersonic speeds.

Lockheed won the EMD competition on the basis of a strong development plan. At the time, too, McDonnell Douglas had just gone through the failure of the A-12, and Northrop was having trouble meeting RCS specifications on the B-2.

Another lesson from Northrop's defeat is that what the customer asks for is not necessarily what the customer wants. The Dem/Val RFP and statements from the ATF SPO stressed the importance of stealth and supercruise, which the YF-23 delivered. Lockheed managers said later, however, that their contacts with the user community (TAC and, later, ACC) consistently persuaded them that the fighter pilots and commanders were wary of total reliance on stealth, and that a successful ATF must balance stealth and agility.

The YF-22 and YF-23 were photographed together on just one sortie, when they met on a tanker when their test periods at Edwards overlapped. This historic moment was reportedly set up on the spur of the moment by the two test pilots just the night before. When Northrop lost the ATF competition, its Chief Test Pilot was immediately signed up by Lockheed and he is now the F-22 Chief Test Pilot for Lockheed Martin. Metz is thus the only man to have flown both ATF contenders – but he remains tight-lipped on comparing the two types. Even more intriguing is his official test pilot's 'bio' as released in the 1997 F-22 Media Guide, produced by the F-22/F119 Integrated Product Teams and the USAF. Metz is credited with a flight test career spanning more than 6,200 hours on 73 different aircraft types. However, the exact 'types' and 'hours flown' log that follows lists only 6,080 hours on 70 types. It may be that Metz, as the former CTP of Northrop during the height of its black project research, may have more than just YF-23 flight time under his belt.

When the USAF launched development of the F-15, the new F100 engine was kicked off at the same time – and it turned out to be a constant source of problems. For ATF, the service was determined to start the engine early. The USAF had a good idea of the ATF's approximate size and speed, and, consequently, how big its engines should be. The request for proposals for the ATF engine, then known as the Joint Advanced Fighter Engine (JAFE), was issued in May 1983, and General Electric and Pratt & Whitney were awarded contracts in September. Unlike the ATF contracts issued at the same time, these were not paper studies: the companies would build and test prototype engines.

The companies showed their CDI designs to the USAF in early 1984, most of which resembled the manufacturers' responses to the RFI that the USAF had issued in 1982. Lockheed, however, had made a substantial change. Instead of a high-supersonic battlecruiser, the company proposed a very stealthy ATF based on F-117 technology.

Lockheed gets into gear

Lockheed had not initially regarded ATF as a major opportunity, because it had little recent fighter experience. However, Northrop had defeated Lockheed in the competition to build the B-2; Lockheed then turned to Navy requirements, but dropped out of the Navy's competition for an Advanced Tactical Aircraft in 1984, when it became clear that the Navy was going to insist on a fixed-price contract and that the leading Navy suppliers, Grumman and McDonnell Douglas, were going to team with other companies. This drove Lockheed to pay more attention to ATF. However, its CDI design was clumsy, overweight and inefficient. Bart Osborne, the company's chief ATF engineer at the time, describes it as "a real dog", and it placed last in the USAF's evaluation.

With the CDI designs in hand, the USAF began to write an RFP for the next stage of the ATF programme. This would be the first of two competitions in the ATF programme. The USAF did not want to pick a winner on

the basis of a paper proposal, but was not sure that it wanted a full-scale fly-off competition – among other things, this would restrict the number of competitors. Instead, the USAF would conduct a new kind of competition: a demonstration and validation (Dem/Val) programme in which the riskiest technologies would be tested at large scale. After the Dem/Val programme, the USAF would pick a winner – expected to enter service in 1995.

The first draft of the Dem/Val RFP was issued in October 1984, calling for ATF to have an operational radius of about 700 nm (1300 km), enough to allow it to cover the entire central region of Europe from bases in central England. ATF would be able to cruise at Mach 1.4-1.5 throughout that segment of its mission that crossed hostile territory (up to 250 nm/460 km in and out) and it would be able to manoeuvre at supersonic speed. It would be able to operate from fewer than 2,000 ft (610 m) of runway. The target for normal take-off weight was 50,000 lb (22700 kg), about the same as an F-15C with its centreline fuel tank and eight AAMs – although, Piccirillo would say much later, the SPO fully expected a 60,000-lb (27215-kg) aircraft to emerge.

Above: In terms of futuristic looks the YF-23 had the YF-22 beaten hands down. Its diamond-shaped wings and deeply recessed (non-vectoring) engine nozzles indicated that the aircraft was optimised for all-aspect stealth – unlike the YF-22. After the EMD decision, NASA looked at the idea of using the YF-23s as high-speed research aircraft, but could not find the funds. The engines were returned to the manufacturers for experimental use, and the prototypes were placed in open storage at Edwards AFB. One is still there, and the other is now exhibited at the Western Museum of Flight in Los Angeles.

The F-22A uses a highly blended design and one-third of its total span lies between the wing attachment fittings. The inlets are widely separated and the ducts snake upwards and inwards, concealing the engine face from radar. The inlets are fixed geometry – one of the ways the USAF's decision to forego a high-Mach capability (seldom used operationally on the F-15) saved time, weight and money. Boundary layer turbulence is controlled by drawing air through pores in the duct wall which is then dumped via exhaust grills and a bleed door. The nose probe, Alpha sensors and blade antennas on the first EMD F-22A are for flight test purposes only. The F-22A will have over 30 antennas for communications, navigation and identification (CNI) and electronic warfare (EW) systems. All are flush with the surface of the aircraft – with major arrays in the wing leading edges. The EW system uses azimuth and elevation antennas to provide a three-dimensional air picture.

It took a year to get from the draft RFP to a final version, as the USAF, senior Pentagon leaders and Congress argued over the fighter's cost. Finally, senior Pentagon leaders prevailed and established an average flyaway cost goal of $35 million, in FY 1985 dollars, based on a production rate of 72 aircraft per year.

Into the Dem/Val phase

The Dem/Val RFP was released in October 1985, and all seven design teams responded. The logical favourites were McDonnell Douglas and GD, the two companies which had built all the fighters the USAF had bought for its own use since the early 1960s. Grumman worked almost exclusively for the Navy. Rockwell had not flown a new fighter since 1956 and was extremely busy with the B-1. Lockheed had built only one operational supersonic fighter, the F-104, and the USAF had not liked it very much. Northrop was totally committed to the B-2, and was known for small, light fighters of the kind the USAF detested. Boeing had never built a jet fighter or a manned supersonic aircraft.

The conventional wisdom was wrong, because the conventional wisdom did not incorporate details of the bizarre aircraft being tested at the USAF's secret flight test centre at Groom Lake, Nevada.

The Dem/Val RFP called for the ATF to have a radar cross-section in the VLO class in the frontal sector only. However, a debate continued over the costs and value of all-aspect stealth – as featured by the F-117 and B-2. Lockheed and Northrop's internal studies were beginning to show that an agile, supersonic fighter could be as stealthy as these subsonic aircraft. Since the CDI phase, Lockheed's stealth experts had developed ways to model and predict the RCS characteristics of curved surfaces and rounded edges. When these techniques were not mature, the company reverted to making models and testing them on its RCS range. Lockheed's ATF design still resembled the F-117, but lacked most of its sharp edges and its heavy coat of radar-absorbent material (RAM).

Northrop, meanwhile, was evolving an extraordinary design which somewhat resembled a stretched, sleeker version of the Tacit Blue radar surveillance aircraft.

Stealth would change the nature of air combat. The pilot of a stealth fighter could acquire, identify and select targets before his own aircraft had been detected, and fire missiles well outside visual range, and the target would have no idea that his chance of survival was down to about 10 per cent. Colonel Piccirillo compared the new fighter's use of stealth to the emergence of the U-boat in World War I; the objective is "to kill without being seen, disengage and disappear," he said in late 1985. "The last thing you do is surface and use the deck gun. Close-in combat is something you try to avoid." The longer a one-versus-one engagement lasts, the greater the chance that a third party will cruise into the arena and casually dispatch one of the contenders with a single shot. "There's a big luck factor in a dogfight," observed Piccirillo. "Ninety per cent of people who get shot down, and come back, never saw who shot them down."

As had happened in the CDI stage, the RFP for Dem/Val was amended just after it was released, in November 1985, with tighter stealth requirements. The response deadline was set for March 1986.

The magnificent seven

All seven competitors produced very different designs. Boeing defined a V-tail, diamond-wing design. The single shark-mouthed inlet fed both engines – a unique and not necessarily desirable feature in a fighter, because of the risk that an engine failure or stall in one engine would affect the airflow into another.

General Dynamics proposed a tailless delta design that reflected the success of the arrow-winged F-16XL. To meet the tougher all-aspect LO requirements, GD modified its design with a serrated trailing edge that had the same alignments as the leading edge of the wing. GD proposed to put dual radar arrays in the leading-edge root extensions, above the inlets, and an infra-red sensor in the nose. The company's biggest problem was that it could not come up

F-22 Armament

The USAF is counting on the F-22A's stealthy performance and the active-radar AIM-120C's proven credentials as a lethal air-to-air missile to dominate the future air battle. AMRAAM's 30-mile (48-km) range is sufficient for now, but air forces around the world are increasingly looking to the future, and engagements at ranges of up to 100 km (62 miles). The RAF, for example, will field a ramjet-powered missile with advanced seeker technology on Eurofighter, with a 100-km range. F-22 will rely on stealth to get closer to its target and its Mach 1.5 supercruise capability to give extra push to its missiles. Eurofighter, though, supercruises (routinely) at Mach 1.3 so can impart the same launch velocity to a weapon with twice the range of AMRAAM.

Armament was one of the controversial issues in the early part of the ATF programme. A stealth aircraft needs internal weapons, but the standard USAF weapon, the Raytheon AIM-120 Advanced Medium-Range Air-to-Air Missile (AMRAAM), was not designed for internal carriage. In 1984-85, following a Hughes feasibility study of a folding-fin AMRAAM variant, the SPO selected a 'compressed carriage' solution: an AMRAAM with clipped wings and tails. The ATF could carry six of these weapons in a space that would accommodate four standard missiles.

The compressed-carriage AIM-120C was introduced as the standard USAF production version in 1996. Its performance is virtually identical to earlier AMRAAMs, and it can be carried internally or externally. By the time the F-22 enters service, the standard production version will be the AIM-120C-5. The main improvements in this new version are a new warhead and a repackaged control section, which makes it possible to lengthen the motor by 5 in (127 mm), increasing missile performance without changing its overall length. Three missiles are carried in each of the F-22's ventral bays, which are covered by thermoplastic-composite doors. The AIM-120s will be propelled from the bays by pneumatic/hydraulic AMRAAM Vertical Ejector Launcher (AVEL) units. The USAF is not yet interested in a ramjet-powered missile of the kind proposed for the Eurofighter. With launch energy provided by the F-22's speed, the AIM-120C-5 should have ample energy in the endgame, and the F-22 uses its stealth to close to ranges where the missile's time of flight is short and its lethality is high.

The side bays will each hold one Raytheon AIM-9X Sidewinder, carried on the AIM-9 Trapeze Launcher (ATL), a mechanically extending rail incorporating an exhaust plume deflector. The AIM-9X is a radically modified version of the veteran AIM-9, retaining only its motor tube. It has thrust-vector control and an imaging infra-red seeker capable of locking on to targets 90° off the fighter's boresight. With small movable rear fins replacing the canards and large wings of the current AIM-9, its kinematic performance is greatly improved.

The ATL will be extended automatically as the F-22 nears the point of achieving launch parameters on the target, allowing the infra-red seeker to lock on before launch. Between them, the two ATLs locate the seekers where they can lock on to any target in the forward hemisphere.

Three AIM-120Cs fit into each of the two ventral bays, which are covered by bi-fold doors. A pneumatic-hydraulic launcher pushes each missile out with a force of 40g.

The AIM-9X, like other advanced infra-red AAMs, is a beyond-visual-range (BVR) missile, capable of locking on to targets before the pilot sees them. Both long-range and off-boresight engagements will be controlled by the pilot with the aid of the Joint Helmet-Mounted Cueing System (JHMCS), being developed for the USAF and Navy by Vision Systems International, an Elbit/Kaiser joint venture.

Although the number of gun kills in air combat has declined precipitously since new-generation missiles such as the AIM-9L Sidewinder entered service in the late 1970s, pilots argue that the gun is the only effective weapon against an adversary who has forced the fight inside the minimum range envelope of the missile. Also, the gun has been made more effective by improvements in ammunition, gun-aiming software and HUD symbology. The F-22's gun is probably the oldest part of the aircraft, dating back to a weapon first fired in the 1940s. The M61A2 20-mm six-barrelled cannon is a lighter version of the original M61, with slimmer, composite-wrapped barrels and a redesigned breech. It is mounted above the right wingroot, and the muzzle opens on to a shallow trench in the fuselage, covered by a side-hinged door. The F-22 carries 480 rounds of ammunition in a linear feed system, aft of the weapon bays.

In 1994 the USAF asked Lockheed to develop an air-to-surface capability for the F-22, and the lower weapon bays have been modified to accommodate the 1,000-lb (454-kg) Boeing GBU-32 Joint Direct

Lockheed Martin technicians make form and fit checks on an AIM-9M Sidewinder and LAU-141/A launcher in the F-22 sidebay. AIM-9M will be replaced by AIM-9X.

Attack Munition (JDAM). The F-22 can carry two JDAMs, two AMRAAMs and two AIM-9s. A synthetic aperture radar (SAR) mode is being added to the F-22's radar for air-to-surface operations.

Two 1,000-lb bombs may not seem much, but with SAR and JDAM the F-22 will be able to deliver weapons within 30 ft (9 m) of a target in almost any weather. The USAF plans to develop a low-cost programmable seeker for JDAM which will make it as accurate as a laser-guided bomb – but autonomous, and unaffected by most weather.

With the advent of the F-22 and the Joint Strike Fighter, any new-generation weapons under study are being designed for internal carriage. They include a follow-on for the AGM-88 HARM – a ramjet-powered, Mach 6 weapon with a 100-nm (185-km) range and a dual-mode seeker. Boeing is working on the Miniaturised Munition Technology Demonstration (MMTD), a small hard-target guided weapon weighing a mere 250 lb (110 kg) but able to punch through 6 ft (1.8 m) of concrete. The F-22 could carry up to eight such weapons.

When stealth is not critical, the F-22 can carry up to 5,000 lb (2270 kg) of external stores on each of four underwing pylons. For ferry flights, each can accommodate a 600-US gal (2270-litre) fuel tank and a pair of AMRAAMs, reducing the need for tanker and cargo support, or the F-22 can carry two tanks and two dual AMRAAM launchers for defensive missions after the enemy air force has been overwhelmed.

with a good location for twin, canted vertical tails, and therefore needed a single vertical tail, which detracted from the fighter's all-aspect stealth.

Grumman's design has never been described in much detail. The company's RFI responses had included a forward-swept wing (FSW) design, and its Dem/Val proposal may have shared this feature.

F-117 inspiration

Lockheed's original ATF design echoed the F-117, with an arrowhead planform and a leading-edge 'glove' which extended in a straight line to the nose. However, it featured more conventional trapezoidal wings, vectored thrust and a horizontal tail. The body cross-section resembled an inverted F-117, with the inlets beneath the wing. Serpentine, absorber-lined ducts shielded the compressors from radar – the F-117's gridded inlets would not work on a supersonic aircraft. Internally, it featured a single weapons bay in the mid-fuselage housing a rotary launcher. The launcher was loaded with missiles away from the aircraft, and the complete unit was then installed in the bay.

Some of McDonnell Douglas's senior executives were convinced that the SPO's emphasis on stealth was overrated, and listened instead to F-15 pilots and Tactical Air Command officers, who were sceptical about the new technology. McDonnell Douglas produced a disappointingly conservative design, with a wedge-shaped chin inlet and sharply swept wings. Northrop stuck to its radical diamond-wing design, with weapon bays in the long forward fuselage. Unlike most of its competitors, it did not use thrust vectoring.

Rockwell's design resembled its CDI concept which the company had described publicly in 1983-84: a near-flying-wing design with a large, highly blended delta wing. The Dem/Val design was modified to reduce its RCS.

ATF development plans changed again in early 1986. On the day the USAF received the technical proposals for Dem/Val, a commission headed by electronics industry pioneer David Packard, who had been asked to look at reforms in Pentagon practices, issued its report. It came down heavily in favour of building prototypes of complex weapons. After a short debate, the USAF announced in May 1986 that it would build and fly ATF prototypes, and issued a supplemental RFP to cover a prototype programme.

Around the same time, the USAF and Navy announced an agreement: the Navy's Advanced Tactical Aircraft (ATA) would be designated as a replacement for the F-111, and an ATF variant would replace the F-14. In theory, this added up to a joint requirement for well over 1,000 ATFs, but it was less important than it sounded. The services were acting to deflect Congressional pressure to develop a single, multi-role fighter, which all agreed was a sure-fire recipe for catastrophe. Neither service's commitment to the other's aircraft was guaranteed, and the requirements were far in the future. (The Navy, for instance, was developing the F-14D, and expected to use it until the early 2000s.)

Teaming to compete

By now, it was clear that USAF money alone would not support a winning Dem/Val effort, and the winning contractors would have to contribute their own money to the project. Five of the competitors formed teams to share the load: Boeing and Lockheed with GD, and Northrop with McDonnell Douglas. The Lockheed/Boeing/GD team was formed in July 1986, on the basis that the team would collaborate on whichever design was selected.

The teams had been formed along lines which coincided with the USAF's own evaluation of the competing designs. Overall, Piccirillo remarked later, "we had two excellent designs, three good designs, and two where the designers hadn't quite got the idea." In the final evaluation, Lockheed and Northrop led by a clear margin because they went

Lockheed Martin F-22 Cutaway

1 Composite radome
2 Northrop-Grumman/Texas Instruments AN/APG-77 multi-mode radar scanner
3 Canted radar-mounting bulkhead
4 Pitot head
5 Air-data sensor system receivers, four positions
6 Radar equipment bay
7 Missile launch detector (MLD) window
8 Canopy latch
9 Cockpit front pressure bulkhead
10 Integrated avionics racks (IAR), downward-hinging for access
11 Electro-luminescent formation lighting strip
12 Machined aluminium cockpit sidewall and composite chine skin panelling
13 Rudder pedals
14 Engine throttle levers, sidestick controller to starboard
15 Instrument console housing six full-colour multi-function touch-sensitive LCD display panels
16 GEC Marconi Avionics head-up display (HUD)
17 Upward-opening cockpit canopy
18 McDonnell Douglas ACES II (modified) ejection seat
19 Off-base boarding ladder stowage
20 Cockpit sloping rear pressure bulkhead
21 Electrical power system equipment bay
22 Battery
23 Landing and taxiing lights
24 Forward-retracting nosewheel, hydraulically steerable
25 Torque scissor links
26 Port engine air intake
27 Intake bleed air spill duct
28 Bleed air door/spoiler panel
29 Bleed door hydraulic actuator
30 Datalink support antenna, microwave landing system (MLS) antenna in ventral position
31 Boundary layer diverter spill duct
32 Onboard oxygen generating system (OBOGS)
33 No. 1 fuselage fuel tank
34 Canopy hinge point
35 Canopy actuator, electrically operated
36 Starboard intake

37 Intake spill and boundary layer bleed ducts
38 Lateral avionics equipment bay, vehicle management system
39 Datalink antenna
40 MLD window
41 Air-cooled flight critical (ACFC) cooling air exhaust ducts
42 L-band antenna
43 No. 2 fuselage fuel tank
44 S-shaped intake ducts
45 Ventral weapons bay housing four AIM-120 AMRAAMs or six in compressed stowage, or two JDAMs
46 Environmental control system equipment bay
47 Canopy emergency jettison control
48 Ventral missile bay doors
49 Ventral bay missile launch trapeze mechanism
50 Trapeze fast-acting hydraulic actuator

51 Lateral missile bay doors
52 Missile launch rail and hinged trapeze arm
53 Lateral missile rail hydraulic actuator
54 Port band 3 and 4 EW antenna
55 Leading-edge flap hydraulic drive unit
56 Port combined communications/navigation/identification (CNI) UHF antenna
57 Airborne auxiliary power unit (APU)
58 APU hinged intake door
59 APU exhaust
60 Airframe-mounted accessory equipment gearbox, shaft-driven from engines
61 Ventral transverse cannon ammunition magazine, 480 rounds
62 Intake overpressure spill ducts
63 Global positioning system (GPS) antenna
64 Illuminated flight-refuelling receptacle, open
65 Overpressure spill duct hinged flaps
66 M61A2 six-barrelled lightweight 20-mm rotary cannon
67 Cannon muzzle aperture beneath flip-up door
68 Starboard band 3 and 4 EW antenna
69 Starboard CNI UHF antenna
70 Leading-edge conformal CNI band 2 antenna
71 600-US gal external fuel tanks

72 AIM-9 Sidewinder missiles, two per wing pylon in transport/deployment configuration
73 Starboard leading-edge flap, lowered
74 Flap drive shaft and rotary actuators
75 Conformal ILS localiser antenna
76 Starboard navigation light, above and below
77 Wingtip band 3 and 4 EW antenna
78 Formation lighting strip
79 Starboard aileron
80 Airbrake function via differential movement of aileron and flaperon
81 Aileron hydraulic actuator
82 Starboard flaperon
83 Starboard wing integral fuel tank
84 Power system inverter, port and starboard
85 Starboard mainwheel, stowed position
86 Fuselage side-body integral fuel tank

87 Hydraulic reservoir and accumulator
88 No. 3 fuselage fuel tanks port and starboard
89 Fuel/air and fuel/oil heat exchangers
90 Fuel transfer piping
91 Onboard inert gas generating system (OBIGS), fuel tank venting and purging

92 Engine bleed air pre-cooler exhaust
93 Intake compressor face
94 Port hydraulic reservoir
95 Hydraulic accumulator
96 Port side-body fuel tank
97 Pratt & Whitney F119-PW-100 afterburning turbofan engine
98 Engine bay dividing firewall
99 Stored energy system (SPS), engine restart
100 Engine bay thermal lining
101 Fin-root attachment fittings
102 Multi-spar all-composite fin structure
103 Fin leading-edge CNI VHF antenna
104 Composite rudder
105 Airbrake function via differential rudder deflection
106 Starboard tailplane
107 Cats-eye control surface interface, all positions
108 Rear CNI VHF antenna
109 Rudder hydraulic actuator
110 Engine exhaust nozzle shroud plates

111 Two-dimensional convergent-divergent thrust-vectoring afterburner nozzles, maximum deflection +/- 20°
112 Rear CNI band 2 antenna
113 Runway emergency arrester hook stowage
114 Formation lighting strip

115 Port rudder
116 Tailplane pivot mounting
117 Port rear CNI band 2 antenna
118 Port all-moving tailplane
119 Tailplane all-composite structure with boron-fibre spar
120 Tailplane hydraulic actuator
121 Port all-composite flaperon lowered
122 Flaperon hydraulic actuator
123 Titanium rear spar
124 Multi-spar sine-wave carbon composite wing panel structure
125 Port aileron hydraulic actuator
126 Formation lighting strip
127 Port all-composite aileron
128 Port band 3 and 4 EW antenna
129 EW power supply modules
130 Port navigation light, above and below
131 Port all-composite leading-edge flap, lowered
132 ILS localiser antenna
133 Leading-edge flap-drive shaft and rotary actuators
134 Port outboard stores pylon

135 Titanium leading-edge spar
136 Pylon mounting hardpoints
137 Titanium pylon mounting ribs
138 Port wing panel integral fuel tank
139 Wing-root attachment fittings
140 Port mainwheel bay
141 Main undercarriage pivot mounting
142 Hydraulic retraction jack
143 Mainwheel leg shock absorber strut
144 Port leading edge CNI band 2 antenna
145 Port mainwheel
146 Inboard stores pylon
147 AIM-120 AMRAAM air-to-air missile
148 GBU-30 JDAM 1,000-lb Joint Direct Attack Munition
149 AIM-9M Sidewinder air-to-air missile
150 AIM-9X Advanced Sidewinder, for future integration

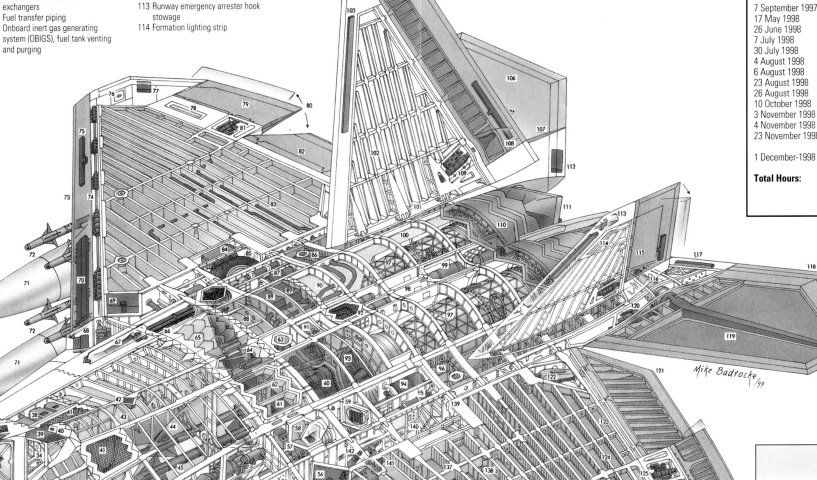

Mike Badrocke '99

F-22 Flight test milestones 1997-1998

Date	Flight	Aircraft	Pilot	Duration (hours)	Event
7 September 1997	1-1	4001	Metz	1.1	First flight
17 May 1998	1-3	4001	Rainey	1.2	First flight at Edwards
26 June 1998	2-1	4002	Metz	1.2	First flight 4002
7 July 1998	1-11	4001	Rainey	0.9	First flight above 30,000 ft
30 July 1998	1-21	4001	Rainey	2.6	First aerial refuelling
4 August 1998	1-24	4001	Rainey	1.4	E-0 and E-1 complete
6 August 1998	1-25	4001	Beesley	2.5	First flight in E-2
23 August 1998	2-9	4002	Rainey	4.6	Endurance mission
26 August 1998	2-10	4002	Rainey	4.5	Ferry to Edwards
10 October 1998	1-31	4001	Beesley	2.8	First supersonic
3 November 1998	2-29	4002	Beesley	1.8	First time at 26° AoA
4 November 1998	1-40	4001	Beesley	2.1	First main bay open
23 November 1998	2-41	4002	Nelson	3.1	183 Flight hour milestone
					(Program Milestone for 1998)
1 December-1998	1-47	4001	Moore	3.1	First flight at 50,000 ft

Total Hours: 4001 — 98.8 Hours
  4002 — 107.4 Hours
  206.2 Combined hours

Above: Boeing's 757 flying testbed began operations in April 1990, in its original (fairly conventional) AFL configuration. It was based at Boeing Field, Seattle where Boeing was tasked with various elements of F-22 avionics development.

The radically reconfigured 757 FTB will be fitted with working CNI antennas in its sensor wing during August 1999.

757 testbed

The prototype Boeing 757-200 (N757A) was modified by Boeing to act as the Avionics Flying Laboratory (AFL) during the Dem/Val stage of the ATF competition. Fitted out with actual avionics hardware, sensor systems and test instrumentation, it began operations in 1990, supporting the YF-22 flight test programme.

For the EMD test phase the aircraft was reactivated and put through a major modification programme, emerging as the F-22 Flying Test Bed (FTB) in 1998. A representative F-22 forward fuselage structure was grafted onto the 757's forward pressure bulkhead and a wing-like structure added above and behind the flight deck. The modifications added about 9 ft (2.74 m) to the 757's overall length and its unique new configuration quickly earned it the nickname 'Catfish'.

An EMD APG-77 radar is fitted in the nose, while the 26-ft (7.92-m) wide wing shape, known as the sensor wing, will house the F-22's flush-mounted EW and CNI antennas. The sensor wing has the same sweepback and orientation as the F-22's wing.

Inside the FTB a fully-functional F-22 cockpit mock-up has been installed and there is room for 30 software engineers and technicians.

The FTB made its first flight, with just the new nose fitted, in June 1997 (the radar was installed later that year). The sensor wing modification began in August 1998 and the fully-modified aircraft took to the air again on 11 March 1999. By August 1999 it is planned have validated the Block I avionics package, including radar function and mission software. 'Raptor 04' will be the first F-22 to fly with these integrated avionics installed.

The aim of the FTB is to cut flight test hours on the F-22 by up to 50 per cent. By fitting the radar and other sensors in the nose (above left) and antennas inside and upon the sensor wing (above) much of the avionics test work load can be shifted off the EMD F-22s.

Left: To address Congressional concerns about the slow pace of software development, the F-22 team took the FTB to Andrews AFB in April 1999. The FTB flew missions against ANG F-16s to demonstrate its advanced radar performance.

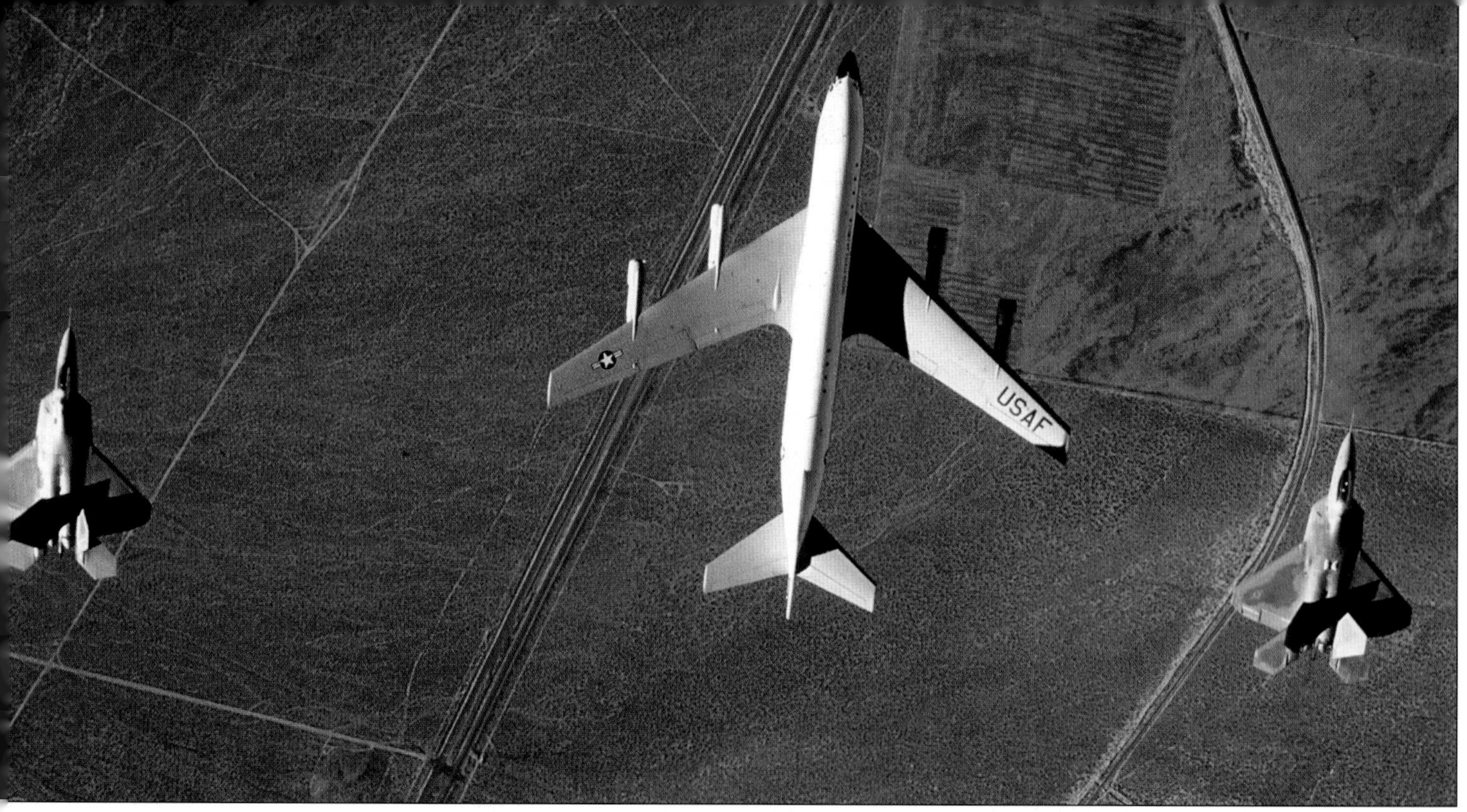

rther than their rivals in blending stealth with supersonic eed and agility. GD's delta placed third. Boeing came urth, unexpectedly pushing McDonnell Douglas into fifth ace. Grumman and Rockwell trailed the pack. Each team cluded one of the top two contenders; the three mid-pack ntestants earned a place in the Dem/Val programme, and e two last-place contenders were excluded.

Lockheed's YF-22 and Northrop's YF-23 were declared e winners on 31 October 1986. At the same time, P&W d GE were both awarded contracts to develop and build ght-test engines. At this stage, there was no engine mpetition; one of each pair of prototypes would be fitted ith the P&W YF119, and the other with the GE YF120.

The programme changed in many ways. It grew much gger. Dem/Val was the largest fighter competition in story, lasting more than four years and costing almost $2 llion – the $691 million contracts covered only part of the st. In addition to the two prototype aircraft, the winning ams had proposed to build complete avionics systems, hich would be tested in ground-based and flying laboraries. Full-scale RCS models would be built and tested on mpany ranges in California (Northrop's facility at Tejon ss, and Lockheed's Helendale range) which would be graded to perform the tests. Each design would undergo ousands of hours of wind-tunnel testing.

Security precautions became tighter. Although the ogramme was not 'black' in itself, many of its elements ere classified at the Secret/Special Access Required (SAR) vel. As well as the shapes of the prototype designs, and her stealth-related technologies, these included some of e advanced avionics features of the aircraft. Early in the ogramme's history, the SAR codename Senior Sky was ed to control access to the most sensitive areas, and is still use today.

The ATF SPO grew larger, and acquired a new director: igadier General James Fain, who had previously headed e LANTIRN programme. While Piccirillo had taken ins to keep the industry at large informed about ATF, eaking at technical conferences and granting interviews, in did not feel the need to build a public constituency hind the programme. While ATF did not go black, it rned a very dark shade of grey.

Behind the razor wire and multiple locked doors, Lockeed's team was dealing with major challenges. Lockheed's nning design clearly resembled the F-117, with a swept pezoidal wing and tails – but, as the alert reader will te, this description does not resemble the YF-22.

Starting late in the game, after spending the RFI phase in rsuit of the high-altitude option, Lockheed had concented on developing the tools and procedures that would allow it to conduct a successful Dem/Val programme, one that would result in a prototype that looked like an operational fighter. Less time was spent on a point design; Boeing and GD had spent more time designing the aircraft.

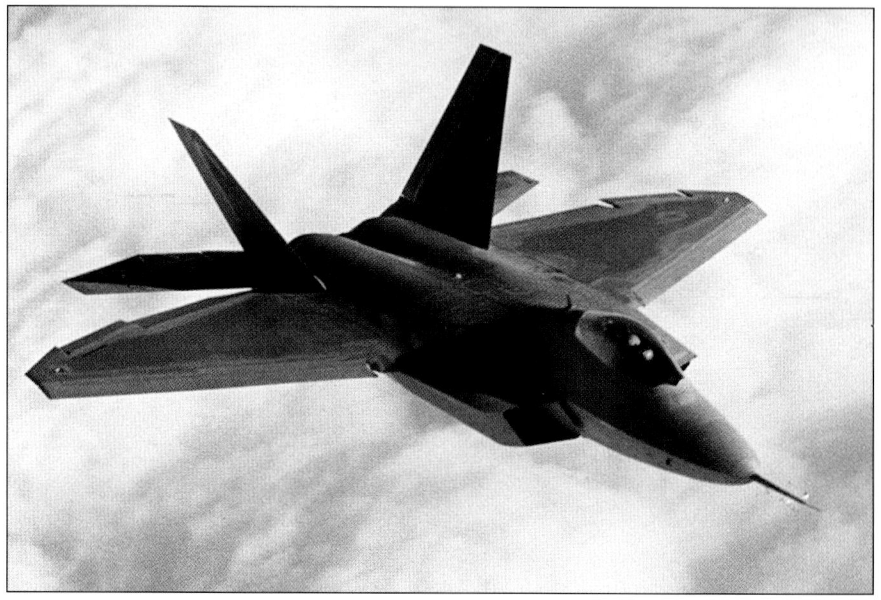

Above: With just the removal of the air data sensor from the nose, this is how an operational F-22 should look, even if going to war. The aircraft will not be hampered by drop tanks or weapons racks. Its smooth clean lines are fundamental to its design philosophy and essential to its mission.

Top: The two dart-shaped EMD F-22As formate on the tanker during a test sortie from Edwards. There are now three F-22s in existence. On 19 December 1998 Lockheed Martin installed aircraft 3999, a non-flying static test airframe, into the stress test rig at Marietta. 3999 will undertake all the F-22 fatigue testing.

Lockheed makes major changes

Immediately after the Dem/Val contracts were announced, Lockheed, Boeing and GD engineers met at the Lockheed Skunk Works' headquarters (then in Burbank). In a blizzard of presentations, the teams shared their work for the first time.

In the teaming agreement signed in July 1986, each company had outlined how the work would be divided if it won. Lockheed had claimed the forward fuselage, cockpit, core avionics and most of the specialised stealth work (RAM and antenna integration). Boeing's share comprised the aft fuselage and wings, the radar, the flying laboratory and leadership of the training system. GD would be responsible for the mid-body section and infra-red stealth technology, the flight controls and leadership on logistics.

Lockheed's design, known as Configuration 092, was the starting point for the team. Almost immediately, Lockheed and its partners initiated a process of analysis and critique which resulted in a complete redesign.

"We soon realised that the airplane would not fly," GD chief engineer Gerry Murff recalled in 1998. "The F-117-like design, with its long glove extending all the way to the nose, could not be controlled in pitch: the pitch-up generated by the glove overwhelmed the force that any reasonable tail surface could provide. The rotary weapon bay had its advantages, but had to be installed between the inlet ducts. This widened the fuselage and increased wave drag."

Not surprisingly, this was not music to the ears of Lockheed engineers. The job of keeping disagreement constructive and moving the programme forward fell to Lockheed programme manager Sherm Mullin. "I think I was reasonably fair with all," Mullin recalled later. "On an average week, I had at least as many Lockheed engineers upset with me as I did Boeing and GD engineers."

Searching for the final form

By February 1987, the design had been modified with a flat weapon bay and the 'glove' had been cut back. At the end of June, it became clear that the design would not make the desired weight or cost without trading off some performance and mission requirements. "After a bloody debate, we agreed to trash the current design and start over," says Mullin. Armed with then-new three-dimensional computer-aided design (CAD) software, the team set a 90-day deadline to reopen the configuration in search of a better answer.

The team started with nine basic designs with different permutations of key features: trapezoidal and diamond wings; dual or chin inlets; four-tail or V-tail; six or eight missiles. By August, the diamond wing, four-tail configuration had emerged as the best solution. The principal advantages were weight and internal efficiency. With its long root section, the diamond wing's loads were better distributed through the body, avoiding a concentration of loads and structure in the mid-section of the aircraft. What engineers called 'the great tail chase' continued into early 1988. The diamond-shaped vertical tails were adopted in February. Still, though, the design had too much supersonic drag to supercruise.

STOL is written out

Then, in May, the USAF announced a major change in the requirements. It had been understood from the outset that the only way to meet the 2,000-ft (610-m) STOL requirement was to use thrust reversal both on the ground and in flight, providing a direct control over speed and glideslope and permitting a very accurate touchdown. Under a USAF contract, Pratt & Whitney and McDonnell Douglas had modified an F-15 with canards and vectoring, reversing nozzles. The NF-15B STOL/Maneuver Technology Demonstrator (S/MTD) was completed in 1987, but the nozzles turned out to be complex, heavy and expensive. (The F-15 nozzle included 5 miles/8 km of welds.) To everyone's relief, the runway requirement was relaxed to 3,000 ft (915 m), eliminating the need for reversers.

F119 engine

The Pratt & Whitney F119-PW-100 engine was the only part of the F-22 developed ahead of the airframe, a measure of the challenge that it presented. It is the world's most powerful fighter engine: although its thrust is officially quoted as "in the 35,000 lb (155 kN) class", the actual figure may be as much as 39,000 lb (173 kN) with full augmentor, implying an intermediate (non-augmented) rating of 25,000-27,000 lb (111-120 kN).

Static thrust is only part of the story. P&W has said that at supersonic speed, on intermediate thrust, the F119 generates twice as much power as the F100-PW-200. This was the critical requirement from the start of the ATF programme. Today's fighter engines are efficient at subsonic speeds, but can propel aircraft supersonically only by burning extra fuel in the afterburner. This limits the use of maximum thrust to minutes between refuellings.

The only way to sustain supersonic speed was to do so on intermediate thrust, without the augmentor. Most earlier fighter engines could not run at full throttle at supersonic speed: above a programmed limit, the flow of fuel to the combustor was actually reduced with increasing speed, leaving the less efficient augmentor to produce more thrust. This is because the inlet compresses and heats the incoming air in proportion to the aircraft's speed; consequently, temperatures increase throughout the engine, attaining limit levels in the rear compressor stages, combustor and turbine.

It was clear from the outset that, compared with the F100, the ATF engine would have to run at higher temperatures and it would have a lower bypass ratio – that is, almost all the air would flow through the core, comprising the compressor, combustor and turbine. Even though the engine might not be much bigger than those of the F-15 and F-16, it would have a much larger and hotter core. This would present a challenge in terms of weight, because the core is the heaviest part of an engine.

The F119 was designed using new three-dimensional computational fluid dynamics (CFD) technology, which permitted engineers to design more complex, thicker and more twisted blade shapes. These blades carry higher loads, leading to a virtuous spiral of improvements. There are fewer blades on each stage; the blades are thicker, so the disk-to-blade junction is wider and stronger; the disk can spin faster without the risk of a failure and can do more work. Consequently, each stage can produce a larger pressure rise, so the engine needs fewer stages. The engine is shorter, lighter and stiffer, and has fewer parts. In the turbine, too, there are fewer stages and blades, reducing the need for cooling air.

The F119 is larger than the F100, with a total airflow around 335 lb (150 kg) per second. Its bypass ratio is around 0.2:1, versus 0.7:1 for the F100, so the compressor, combustor and turbine are at least 50 per cent bigger. It has a three-stage fan, a six-stage compressor and single-stage low- and high-pressure turbines. (The F100 has 10 compressor stages to achieve the same 25:1 pressure ratio.) The low-pressure and high-pressure shafts spin in opposite directions, which eliminates a stator, reducing engine length and cutting the requirement for cooling air.

All the stages except the first-stage fan are 'blisks' with blades and disks in one piece. The first stage of the fan has massive, wide-chord blades, made of hollow titanium, which are more efficient, lighter and more robust than the F100's blades. The fan blades are made separately and joined to the disk by linear friction welding, a technique in which the blade is rubbed so hard against the disk that it bonds to it.

New materials are the key to withstanding higher temperatures. The engine features 'dual heat treat' turbine disks: the centre of the disk, where stress loads are concentrated, has a fine-grain crystalline structure for maximum strength, while the rim has a coarser grain for better damage tolerance. The Floatwall combustor, with a 'shingled' design to reduce stress, is expected to last 10 times longer than the state-of-the-art rolled-ring design. Each of the high-pressure turbine blades, small enough to fit in the palm of a hand, extracts 1,000 hp from the gas stream.

The vectoring nozzles can divert the full augmented thrust 20° upwards or downwards in a second. The F119 nozzles represent a fifth-generation design for P&W and weigh 600 lb (272 kg) less than the nozzles on the YF-22. They are largely made of burn-resistant Alloy C titanium and incorporate a sophisticated internal cooling system.

F119 is designed so that all exterior maintenance can be performed with a small set of wrenches, ratchets and sockets, and only a few types of clips and fasteners – none attached with safety wires – are used. Virtually all the engine's plumbing is accessible without removing the engine itself, and all lines are colour-coded.

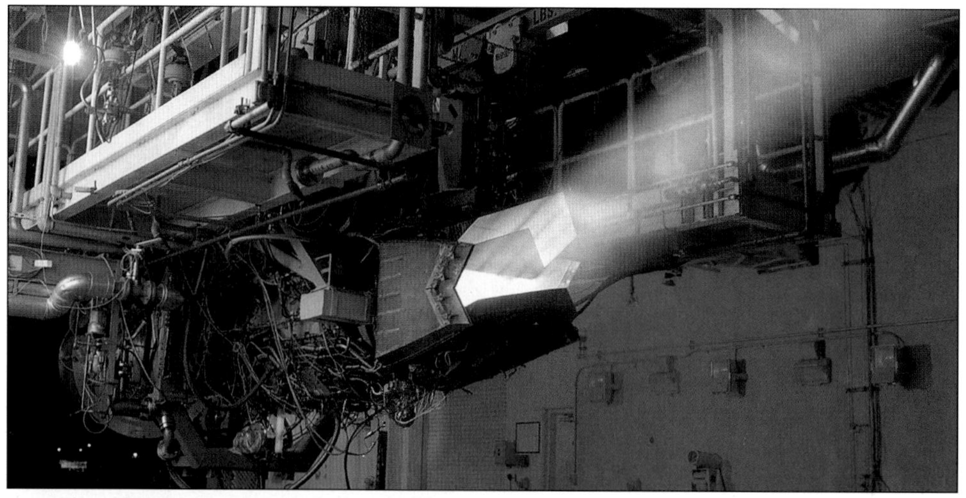

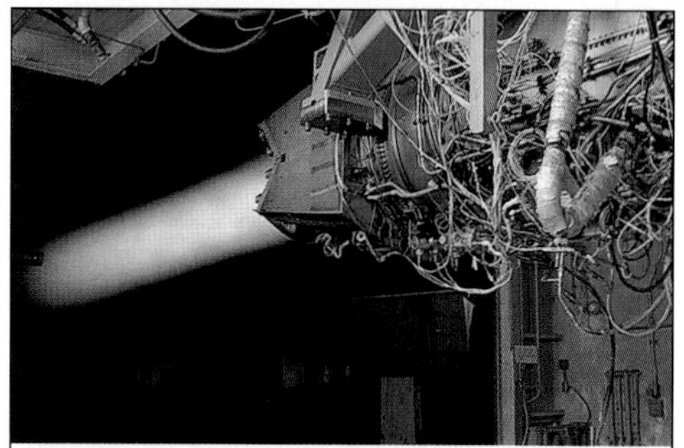

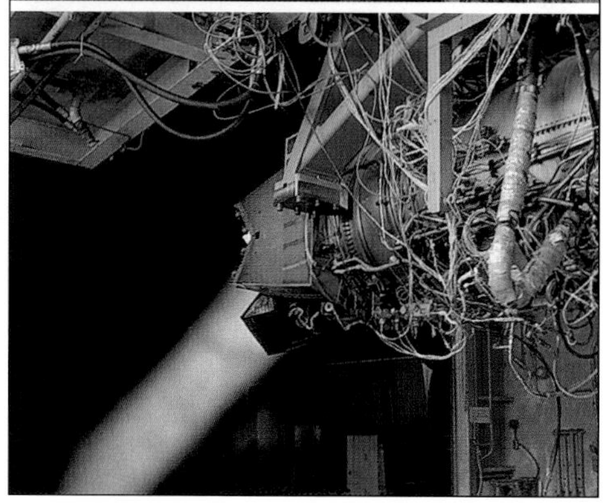

The thrust-vectoring nozzles of the F119 engine can divert the full augmented thrust over a 40° arc, moving from neutral to full deflection in less than a second. Two-dimensional nozzles are necessary for stealth. The edges of a 2-D nozzle flatten the exhaust plume and speed its mixing with cooler ambient air. The vectoring nozzles were available for use on the F-22A from the first flight onwards.

F-22's APG-77 active array radar is not the same ...g as the electronically-steered antennas used on ...ong others) the MiG-31 and Rafale – although ... types are confusingly identified as phased ...ys. An electronically-steered radar has a single ...smitter and receiver, and an antenna which ...prises hundreds of 'phase shifter' modules ...ch steer the beam. An active array consists of ...usands of more sophisticated modules, each of ...n a tiny radar transmitter or receiver.

Paying attention to the avionics

Conventional air-cycle environmental control systems (ECS), which cool the cockpit and the avionics, have two drawbacks for the F-22: they require cool incoming air, which may be hard to come by at Mach 1.5, and their exhausts are infra-red hot spots. The F-22 ECS uses air-cycle cooling only for flight-critical avionics and to feed the onboard oxygen generating system (OBOGS) which provides the pilot with oxygen. Mission avionics, which impose higher cooling loads, are liquid-cooled, and the coolant flows through coolant-to-fuel heat exchangers. The heat is either dumped overboard as fuel is burned, or removed through an air-cooled heat exchanger on top of the fuselage. The ECS and other systems are very important in achieving another F-22 goal, that of cutting both the cost of maintenance and the number of people and tonnage of equipment needed to support the fighter in the field. For example, the use of OBOGS simply eliminates liquid oxygen (LOX), a major element of the logistics chain.

New gear for the pilot

The F-22 is the first USAF fighter in many years to have a specially developed life support system (produced by Boeing), designed to reduce the risk of g-induced loss of consciousness (G-LOC). Unlike the familiar symptoms of 'blackout' at high g, G-LOC causes sudden and complete loss of consciousness, followed by a recovery that can take minutes. It emerged as a problem with the arrival of the F-16 and other high-performance aircraft, because it is associated with rapid increases in g loadings. The F-22 life support system reduces the risk of G-LOC in several ways. It includes a new anti-g garment that covers more area than earlier g-suits, so it can exert pressure on more of the body's blood supply and raise blood pressure in the head more effectively. The oxygen system can pump oxygen into the pilot's lungs under pressure, increasing the oxygen content in the blood. This requires a special oxygen mask and a counter-pressure vest which prevents the pilot's chest from emulating a pigeon. The g-suit and positive-pressure system are controlled by a breathing regulator and anti-g garment (BRAGG) 'smart valve' which reacts to the rate of g onset. The system also includes the HGU-86P helmet, developed by Helmets Integrated Systems of the UK, which is lighter than previous helmets and is designed to fit better.

Lockheed Martin F-22A EMD Aircraft No. 2, 91-4002 F-22 Combined Test Fleet Edwards AFB

'Raptor 02' was rolled out from the LMTAS production line on 17 April 1998 and made its first flight on 29 June, from Dobbins ARB, Marietta, with Paul Metz at the controls. By 26 August, 4002 had arrived at Edwards AFB and was immediately deployed on handling qualities trials. By late September, 4002 had already been flown to 24° AoA.

F-22 design philosophy

The philosophy behind the F-22 design is different to the norm. The classic process of aircraft design was serial. The aircraft was designed by one group of engineers. As they completed the design of each part, they passed it to manufacturing engineers, who would work out how to make and assemble the parts. When the aircraft reached the user, the maintainers would learn how to repair and service it. The result was usually something that worked, but which cost more than necessary. The initial design would prove expensive or difficult to make, and would have to be changed. Maintenance would be difficult because of design features that would be obvious to a maintainer on the ramp, but had been overlooked in the original design. Production difficulties would mean that parts would have to be removed from the line and reworked or modified to fit. The F-22 has been designed by integrated product teams (IPTs), each responsible for one part or aspect of the system. The IPT included design engineers, manufacturing specialists and maintainers, and no part could be released until all their requirements were met. At the same time, the IPT also generated all the documentation that would follow each part through production and service, describing the process for making and repairing it.

Cockpit canopy

The F-22 canopy, made by Sierracin, is made from two 9.5-mm (0.4-in) sheets of polycarbonate sandwiched between two sheets of optical glass. Both materials are fusion-bonded in an autoclave and drape-formed over a mould at 750° F (399° C). A metallic coating of indium-tin oxide is added to the canopy to reflect radar waves, giving it a gold tint.

Radar technology

The radome is a 'bandpass' or frequency-selective type, which reflects signals at all frequencies except the precise wavelengths used by the F-22 radar. It evolved from a design developed for the F-117, and tested experimentally in the F-117 full-scale development aircraft with an experimental Westinghouse radar.

Low-observable design approach

The F-22's stealth design, produced with the aid of refined computer analysis tools, evolved from that of the F-117, with a preponderance of flat, canted surfaces and a sharp chine line from the nose to the wingtips. A basic difference between the F-117 and the F-22 is that radar absorbent material (RAM) is not applied to the entire aircraft, but used selectively on edges, cavities and surface discontinuities: the new computational tools made it possible to model the effects of RAM much more accurately. Lockheed Martin builds all the edges of the aircraft, which probably consist of wide-band radar-absorbent structures with honeycomb or foam-type internal structures, doped with 'lossy' ingredients, which convert radar energy to heat. Heat-resistant ceramic-matrix RAM is likely to be used on the exhaust nozzles.

The march of time

Of the seven companies that bid on ATF in 1986, only three survive today. In March 1993, Lockheed acquired the Fort Worth division of General Dynamics, increasing its share of the programme from 35 per cent to 67.5 per cent. Two years later, Lockheed and Martin Marietta merged into Lockheed Martin; partly in response, Boeing and McDonnell Douglas merged in August 1997. Boeing's share of the F-22 programme is now part of its McDonnell Aircraft & Missile Systems business unit. Key avionics suppliers Texas Instruments (radar modules) and GM-Hughes (CIP) have been acquired by Raytheon. Radar integrator Westinghouse was acquired in 1995 by Northrop Grumman.

Canopy optics

The Sierracin canopy, too, is unique in that it is a one-piece bubble with no arch or bow. Most canopy specifications require near-perfect optics only in the forward field of view, but the F-22 will have a helmet-mounted sight and therefore needs 'zone 1 quality' throughout.

Helmet-mounted display

A helmet-mounted display (HMD) based on the Kaiser Electronics Agile Eye HMD is being developed for the F-22. A tiny CRT fitted to the back of the HGU-86/P helmet will project targeting, flight and navigation symbology onto the helmet visor – in conjunction with a magnetic head-tracking system that always knows where the pilot is looking. As a result the pilot will nearly always be able to remain 'heads up' in critical situations.

Construction approach

The F-22 is built in large sections. The rear fuselage and wings are built in Seattle, the mid-body and tails in Fort Worth. When they are delivered, all electrical, fuel and hydraulic lines are already installed, and simply need to be connected when the sections are mated. Invented in wartime Germany and rediscovered and refined in the 1970s by Airbus Industrie, this technique makes final assembly simpler and more efficient. The heart of the structure is the massive and complex mid-body section, built by Lockheed Martin Tactical Aircraft Systems in Fort Worth. It incorporates the four weapon bays, the main landing gears and the complex inlet ducts. Made of carbonfibre/epoxy, the ducts curve sharply upwards and inwards from the inlets to mask the engine faces from radar, changing section smoothly from rhomboid to circular. Their inner contours must be smooth and accurate to maintain their stealth characteristics. Attached to the mid-body are the forebody, accommodating the cockpit and avionics, which is built by Lockheed Martin in Marietta; and the wings, aft fuselage and engine bay, and the tailbooms, built by Boeing. The mid-body and rear fuselage include some unusual structural features. The forged and machined titanium bulkheads in the mid-body carry most of the flight loads, and the largest of them weighs more than three tons before machining. The inlet lip and the fittings that support the wing and rudder are hot isostatic process (HIP) castings, made from titanium alloy powder formed under very high pressure. HIP was originally developed for disks in engines, but is used to form highly loaded, rigid, complex-shaped components – the only other way to build them would be from many small parts. The tailbooms are titanium, welded by an electron beam in a vacuum chamber. The aft fuselage is 67 per cent titanium because of the high temperatures found there.

Wing material technology

Carbonfibre/bismaleimide (BMI) composite is the primary material in the F-22 wing. BMI resin replaced the thermoplastic-matrix composite used in the YF-22 because it was stronger and less expensive, and because tougher, more damage-tolerant BMI resins had become available during Dem/Val. Thermoplastics tolerate higher temperatures than BMI, so the change to BMI in the EMD aircraft meant a reduction in maximum Mach number, from 2.0 to 1.8. The multi-spar wings incorporate sine-wave spars – in which the web is an undulating curve – produced by a resin-transfer moulding (RTM) process developed by Boeing and Dow/United Technologies. In the RTM process, dry carbonfibre fabric is laid up in a mould and BMI resin is injected at high pressure. One in four of the spars is still made from titanium, a change made after live-fire damage-tolerance tests.

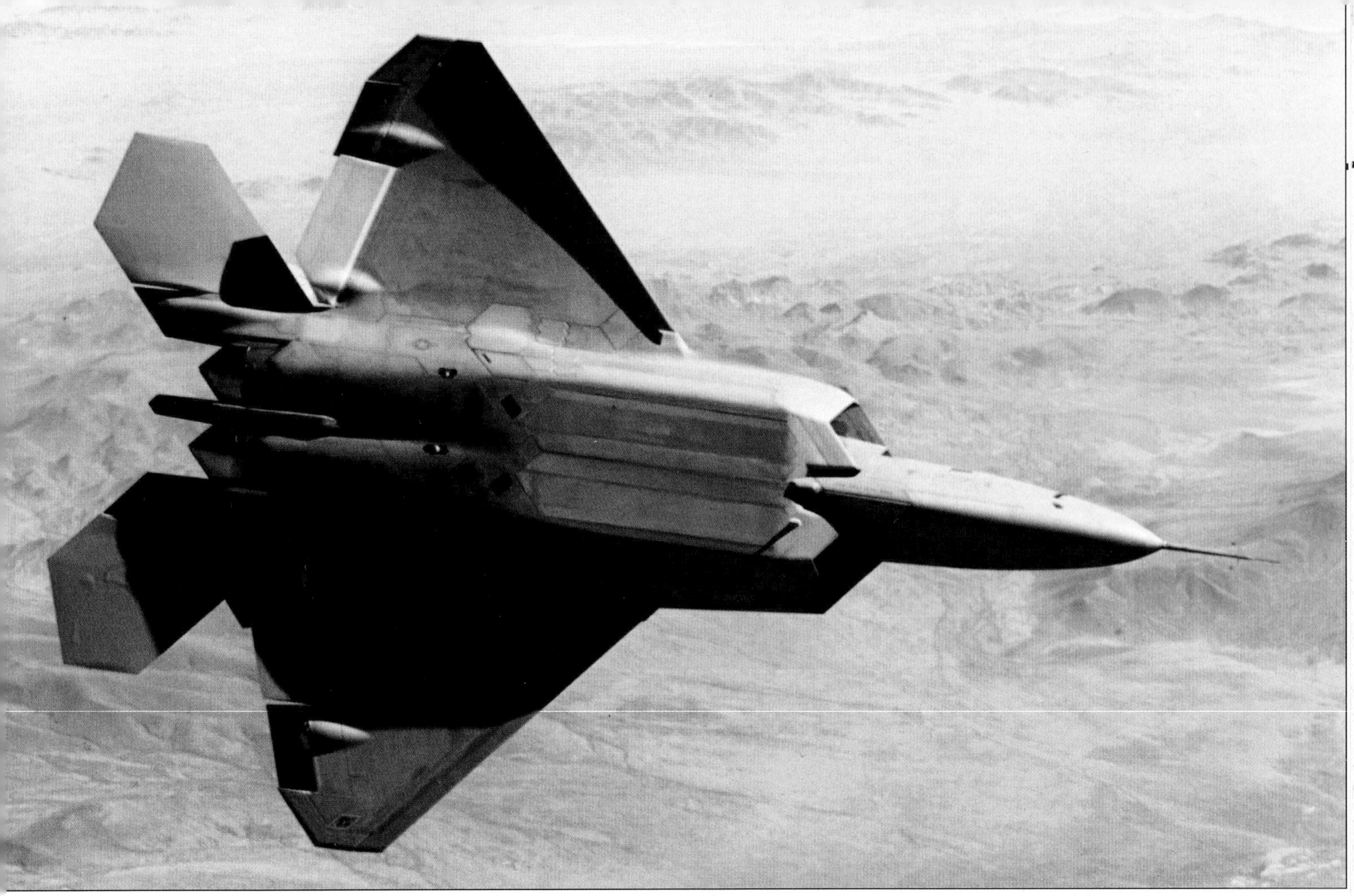

Ed Glasgow, the Skunk Works' chief flight sciences engineer, led a team effort to redesign the fighter's afterbody, which no longer had to accommodate the bulky reversers, and the forward fuselage. Glasgow's team managed to reduce wave drag to the point where the new Configuration 1132 could supercruise. In the new design, too, the horizontal tails mirrored the shape of the wing. In May 1988, the YF-22 design – which now looked only vaguely like Lockheed's original configuration – was frozen, and manufacture could begin. As well as building the two prototypes, the Lockheed team produced a full-scale RCS model and at least nine fully instrumented wind tunnel models, which underwent 18,000 hours of testing.

The shapes of the rival designs were not revealed until the summer of 1990, when they were almost ready to fly. The programme was running a few months behind schedule, partly as a result of Lockheed's redesign.

Dem/Val flight test

The flight-test programme was intended to be short and intense. The goal was to test a strictly limited number of key data points, identified by the contractors in their original Dem/Val proposals, as quickly as possible. This was not a fly-off programme in which the best-performing prototype would win; the winning ATF contractor would be selected on the basis of its proposed development and production programme, and the flight-test results were intended to validate the projected numbers in those proposals. As a further test of the contractors' ability to predict how their designs would work, the USAF required them to submit 'sealed envelope' estimates of various performance parameters before the test programme started. After the programme, these would be opened and compared with the actual numbers.

The prototypes were designed to match the production aircraft in the aspects that would affect their flight performance. The external shapes were representative; the weight of the airframe and engines, the internal fuel capacity and the structural lifetime did not need to match those of a production aircraft. Some RAM was installed, but only to evaluate its durability on a high-performance aircraft; RCS tests were carried out on the ground.

Northrop was first in the air, on 27 August 1990. The first YF-22, powered by the GE F120 engine, flew on 29 September piloted by Lockheed chief test pilot Dave Ferguson. An early snag in flight testing was that the landing gear refused to retract, a problem which Lockheed's flight-test manager, the late Dick Abrams, ascribed to 'fascist software' in the vehicle management system. Testing proceeded rapidly once a hard-wired switch was installed.

The first F-22 went supersonic on 25 October. The second, F119-powered aircraft flew on 30 October with Tom Morgenfeld at the controls. The two F-22s made 74 test flights in three months. In early November, the first YF-22 sustained Mach 1.58 without afterburner. With afterburner, it exceeded Mach 2. During December, it demonstrated its low-speed manoeuvrability, performing 360° rolls at a 60° Alpha (angle of attack). Unarmed AIM-120 and AIM-9 missiles were fired from the side and centre missile bays. The YF-22 flight-test programme was completed on 28 December.

The second YF-22 resumed flying in October 1991 to support flight qualities and performance work during the EMD programme. It performed 39 flights during this period, more than it had flown during Dem/Val. In April 1992, the aircraft entered a series of oscillations during a low, slow pass along the runway at Edwards, crashed, slid 8,000 ft (2440 m) along the runway and burned. The pilot survived, testimony to the prototype's overbuilt structure. The aircraft could not be economically restored to flying condition, but was repaired externally and moved to Rome Air Development Center at Griffiss AFB in New York, where it was mounted on a pedestal and used to test antenna designs for the F-22A. (The first YF-22, used as an engineering fixture during development, was restored in 1997 and is now on display at the USAF Museum.)

As flight testing continued, the competitors prepared their proposals for the engineering and manufacturing development (EMD) stage of the programme. This included designs for two production versions – for the USAF and Navy – and plans for development and production. Proposals were submitted on the last day of 1990.

A USAF team evaluated the proposals (Lockheed's ran to 21,000 pages) but it was up to USAF Secretary Donald Rice to make the final selection. The decision hinged not just on what the contractors promised, but on the customer's confidence in their ability to deliver. In early 1991, Northrop's partner, McDonnell Douglas, found itself

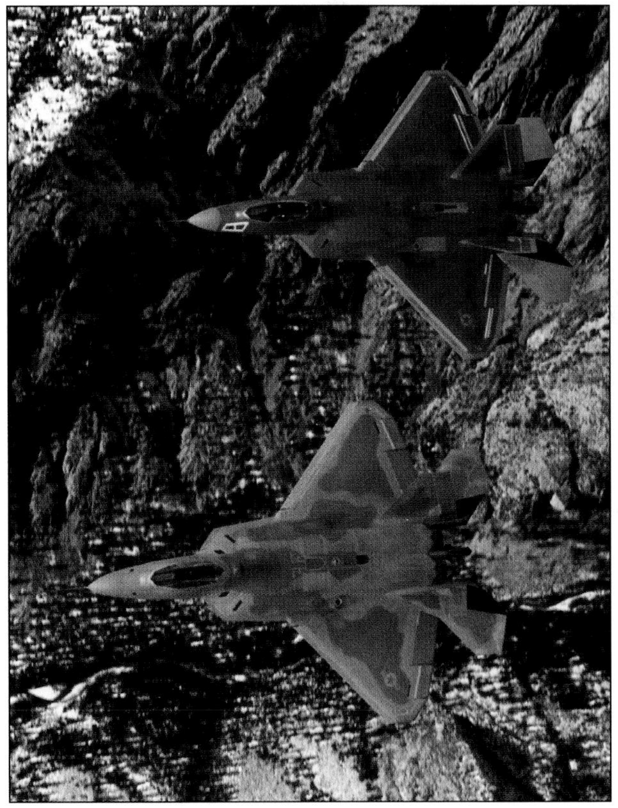

The most important achievement of the F-22 CTF in 1998 was reaching 183 flight hours, which was an 'all-or-nothing' target set by the US Congress to ensure smooth continued funding. The CTF had already been set a target by the US DoD's Defense Acquisition Board, as a prerequisite for Lot 1 low-rate initial production funding, but the Congressional target was higher. On 23 November USAF test pilot Dave Nelson flew a 3.1-hour sortie that took the F-22 past its 183-hour goal and removed a not-inconsequential shadow from the programme. The Combined Test Force now needs to keep the schedule for aircraft 4003 – provisionally planned to fly in late 1999 – on track to ensure Lot 2 funding. The important project events planned for mid-late 1999 include: Block I avionics testing and certification (using the Boeing FTB); delivery of the first configurable AIM-9 launcher; initiation of Block II avionics testing; first flight readiness for 4004; contract award for Lot 1 aircraft and engines; and long-lead funding allocation for Lot 2 production (10 aircraft and 25 engines).

Performance

Most F-22 performance figures are classified. However, enough has been released over the years to put together a broad picture of what the new aircraft will do.

Continuing flight tests should confirm that the F-22's conservative looks belie its performance. A chart published in 1991 shows that the F-22 is faster on intermediate power than an F-15C on full 'burner, when both aircraft have eight AAMs on board. (The speeds are probably around Mach 1.6-1.7.) "We expect that this will be one of the things that surprises the Air Force," says Lockheed Martin test pilot Paul Metz. "If you don't know what you're doing, you'll be supersonic." Unlike most fighters, too, the F-22 achieves its highest rate of climb at supersonic speed.

The F-22 is very nearly as fast with afterburner as without. The augmentors will be used mainly for acceleration and supersonic manoeuvring. Metz believes that the "afterburner will generally not be required", and that when it is used it will be in bursts of seconds and tens of seconds, at the outside.

The maximum speed – between Mach 1.8 and Mach 2.0 – is lower than the nominal maximum speed of the F-15. The F-15 can attain its top speed only with a minimal weapons load and no external fuel, however, and most pilots never see 2.5 on the Mach meter. The F-22 has plenty of thrust for Mach 2.5, but providing that performance would have demanded variable inlets and higher-temperature materials throughout the aircraft.

The principal breakthrough in terms of straight-line performance is supercruise. The USAF has stated that "about 30 minutes in a one-hour mission" can be flown at supersonic speed, three to six times the supersonic endurance of any fighter using augmentors. On a typical mission, the F-22 can sustain supersonic speed for most of the time it is over hostile territory – 30 minutes at Mach 1.5 is equivalent to more than 220 nm (400 km) each way. Supersonic endurance varies with speed: a supercruising F-22 may vary its speed between Mach 1.1-1.2 to Mach 1.5-plus according to the tactical situation.

Supercruise goes along with high altitude. USAF fighters are normally limited to a maximum altitude of 50,000 ft because, if power and cockpit pressure are lost, the pilot will lose consciousness before the aircraft descends into thicker air. The F-22 life-support ensemble has been chamber-tested to 66,000 ft and its emergency oxygen system will function long enough for the pilot to reach lower altitudes.

Cruising higher and faster than other aircraft, the F-22 will give its pilot control of the engagement, and it is more likely to surprise its targets from the rear.

The future of visual-range air combat has been a controversial issue throughout the F-22 programme. As pilots put it – if you have a rifle with a telescopic sight, and you're trying to kill a midget armed with a knife in a phone booth, the last thing to do is get into the phone booth with the midget.

The argument has been sharpened by the spectacular low-airspeed, high-Alpha manoeuvres demonstrated by Russian fighters, culminating in the vectored-thrust Sukhoi Su-37. Some critics suggest that the F-22 represents a move in the wrong direction and that it is the Russian design which points to the future of air combat. Other observers point out that dumping speed and yanking the nose around makes it possible to take a fast shot at an adversary – but at the same time, it makes you a big, slow target for anyone else in the sky. You have killed your energy, you are not going fast and for the next few, long seconds the only direction you are going is forward and down. "It's a neat trick, but it's [deleted]-all use in air combat," is the assessment of one US fighter commander.

Whichever way the argument goes, the F-22 should be able to match the agility of any other aircraft in service or under development. Its flight envelope is very large: Alphas as high as 60° were demonstrated in the YF-22 programme, and some roll manoeuvrability was retained at that extreme pitch angle. At Alphas of 15° and above, the F-22 rolls at least twice as fast as the F-15, and the gap widens until the F-15 hits its roll limit of 30° Alpha.

The F-22 will be able to get around its envelope quickly. Maximum pitch rates, boosted by vectored thrust, are up to twice as fast as the F-16. In fact, the F-22's pitch rate is so fast that it is inhibited by a soft stop in the aft movement of the sidestick. Pulling the stick through the stop overrides a limit in pitch acceleration. The stop is there to remind the pilot that the F-22 is about to respond very quickly and that the smart anti-*g* valve will respond in turn. Lockheed Martin engineers and pilots have named the maximum pitch-rate regime 'Mongo mode' in tribute to the horse-punching heavy from the film *Blazing Saddles*.

The large flight envelope is usable in combat, because the systems have been fully tested to high Alpha (the fuel-system rig, for instance, goes to 60°) and because the FCS protects the aircraft against departure. Some air show manoeuvres in recent years could not be performed without disabling FCS limiters which normally constrain Alpha and pitch rate.

The F-22 pilot who decides that the tactical situation warrants high-Alpha, low-speed manoeuvring may be reassured by the fighter's controllability and thrust-to-weight ratio. The F-22 should be able to end a manoeuvre rapidly when required, and will accelerate quickly to a safer combat speed. The F-22 will be evaluated against "actual and simulated adversary aircraft" during its flight-test programme, Metz states.

The F-22 is claimed to have more than twice the range of the F-15C at subsonic speed, with a greater margin when the mission includes supersonic flight. Such numbers have to be treated with caution. In this case, the comparison is probably based on a full missile load and internal fuel only. The F-22's internal fuel load appears to be greater than that of an F-15C with three 600-US gal (2271-litre) tanks, and it has much less drag, so it should have a greater combat radius on a similar mission profile.

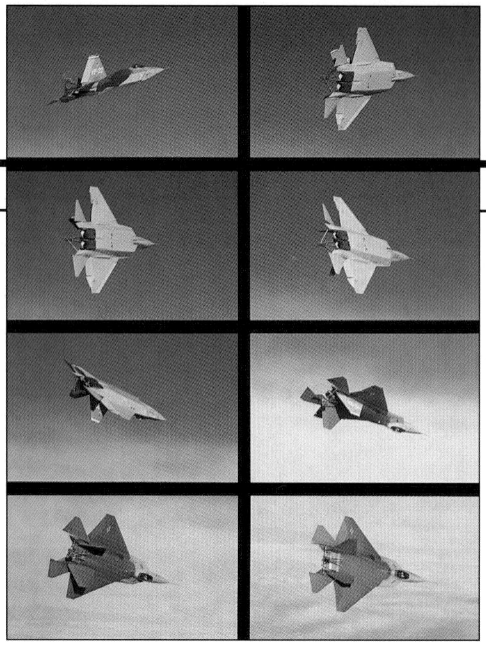

The YF-22 flight test programme gave many clues to the ultimate performance of the F-22A. Here, the second prototype indulges in a rapid 360° roll which will be augmented by thrust vectoring in the F-22A. This doubles the already impressive roll rate and makes the nose far more 'pointable'.

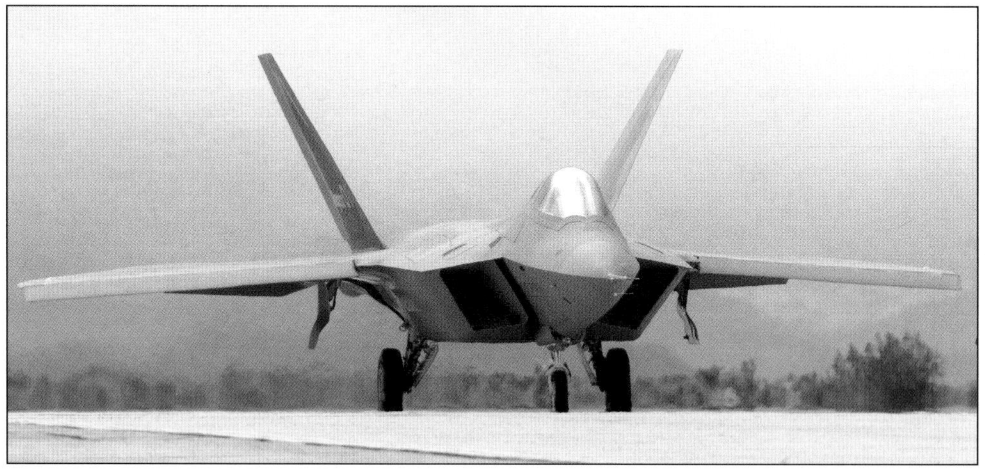

The F-22's wing-blending and complex wing camber are apparent in this view. With no centreline pylons, the gear stays short and the fuselage remains chest-high and therefore accessible to maintainers.

embroiled in the collapse of the A-12 programme; Northrop itself was in trouble on the TSSAM missile. "The A-12 helped us," remarked a Lockheed official at the time, "because nobody's buying promises any more."

Lockheed's F-117, meanwhile, became the hero of the Gulf War. As a Lockheed executive put it: "They chose us because they believed us. When we thought that you couldn't do something, or more importantly that you couldn't do something for the money, we said so."

In several key areas, Lockheed had gone further in its demonstration programme. The YF-22 had gone to high Alpha and had fired missiles, and it had flown with a proto-type advanced cockpit. The Lockheed team's avionics demonstration was more comprehensive.

Of the two proposed EMD designs, Lockheed's more closely resembled the craft that had flown in Dem/Val. The wing sweep was reduced and the span was increased, to improve low-speed and manoeuvring performance. The cockpit was moved forward, and the inlets aft, to improve the pilot's field of view over the nose and sides. The wingtip shape was changed to provide a better location for antennas. The vertical tails were shortened and the speed-brake was removed.

Influence of the NATF

It was a double irony that Lockheed, which had won the Dem/Val contract with a design different from the aircraft it built, scored points in the EMD selection for another design that would never see the light of day. Lockheed's Navy ATF (NATF) design "was an important factor," according to USAF Secretary Donald Rice.

The NATF was due to start EMD in late 1993, with the first aircraft flying in January 1997. It was a fighter/strike aircraft. Lockheed proposed to blend the F-22 engines, avionics and cockpit into a new swing-wing airframe. The Navy planned to buy 546 NATFs to replace F-14s, but after the A-12 was scrapped in January 1991, the Navy diverted NATF and A-12 money into the F/A-18E/F Super Hornet, followed by a new attack aircraft called AX.

Lockheed, Boeing and GD's team was declared the winner in April 1991. The formal EMD contract was awarded in August, after a final review of the entire programme. The contract called for the construction of 11 EMD aircraft, including two F-22B two-seaters. The first aircraft was due to fly in August 1995, and initial operating capability (IOC) was set for 2001.

IOC had slipped steadily since 1985. The decision to build prototypes meant that the Dem/Val programme was protracted. This, combined with a desire to reduce concur-rency in the programme, had moved IOC to 1999. Then, development and production plans had been revised again under the Pentagon's Major Aircraft Review (MAR), published in April 1990. Worried about its ability to afford

all the major aircraft programmes that would reach production in the 1990s, the Pentagon delayed ATF production by two years and cut the annual production rate of the USAF version from 72 to 48 aircraft. A year later, USAF Secretary Rice announced that total production would be cut from 750 to 648 aircraft, in an early post-Soviet-era budget cut.

Lockheed had announced before the EMD contract was awarded that, if it won, it would locate the new programme in Marietta, north of Atlanta, Georgia, where the forward fuselage would also be built. Marietta, where Lockheed operated a massive production facility, offered lower costs and a larger labour force than California.

The powerplant race

The engine competition was just as intense, and there was a fundamental difference between the two engines. General Electric's F120 was the first 'variable-cycle' engine. For maximum power, supersonic acceleration and supercruise,

Flying in tandem with a chase-pane F-15B of the 445th FLTS, 'Raptor 02' shows off the substantial size of the F-22. Structurally, the F-22 could be described as almost tailless. Very little of its mass lies behind the line of the trailing edge. The tailplanes are carried on booms projecting aft of the engine nozzles and their root leading edges fit into cut-outs on the flaperons. This unique layout keeps the root chord long (reducing wave drag) while maintaining a constant sweep angle for stealth.

Stealth

Two operational stealth aircraft are known to have been developed successfully: the F-117, which sacrifices performance and versatility to achieve stealth, and the very expensive B-2. Another stealth project, the A-12, failed spectacularly. Some critics have suggested that the F-22 will be far more expensive to acquire and operate than a less stealthy fighter, implying that the benefits of LO are outweighed by its costs. This case is overstated.

There are some costs directly associated with LO. A stealth aircraft's inlet and exhaust system tends to be heavier than a non-stealthy design. It also requires internal weapon bays and fuel, which tend to drive size and weight upwards. Specialised antennas are also expensive. On the other hand, the F-22 does not require an active EW system – which is not cheap to start with, and has to be continuously updated during development – and it is effective with stock AMRAAM missiles rather than needing new long-range weapons.

The cost and difficulty of maintaining stealth features on the B-2 might also cast doubt on the F-22 developers' assertion that the fighter will require less logistics support – in terms of spares, equipment and people – than the F-15. According to Lockheed Martin and USAF officials, the F-22's low-observable systems have been designed using the lessons learned on the F-117 and B-2.

The F-22's RCS is described as "in the birds and bees class" – that is, in the same order as the F-117 and B-2, and enough to reduce radar detection range by a factor of 10 compared with conventional aircraft.

Some F-22 critics have talked about 'radar stealth', implying that even if the F-22 evades tracking by radar it will still be detected by infra-red (IR) sensors. But the F-22 was designed according to a philosophy of 'balanced observables', which mandated that the F-22's IR signature be reduced so that IR and radar sensors would have a similar detection range. The most prominent source of IR radiation from an aircraft is its exhaust plume. On the F-22, plume radiation is reduced by minimal afterburner use, the mixing of the core and bypass flows, and by the two-dimensional nozzles, which create a flattened exhaust plume with a wider perimeter than a circular plume. This causes the plume to dissipate more quickly.

Much of the remaining IR signature comprises reflected solar IR radiation and emissions caused by skin friction heat. IR-absorbent paint, which reduces solar reflection, is analogous to normal paint except that it absorbs in the IR band. Friction heat cannot be absorbed, but coatings have been developed that change the emissivity of a surface, i.e., they make it less efficient at emitting IR. They may also be able to shift the wavelength of remaining IR energy into wavebands which attenuate most rapidly in the atmosphere and are therefore harder to detect.

A key difference between the F-22 and earlier VLO aircraft is that the F-22 has been designed with the emphasis on balancing LO with other essential attributes – including maintenance and support costs. The first step in reducing the amount of maintenance time spent on LO materials is to minimise the need to 'break the low-observable bubble' – that is, to minimise the number of maintenance actions that involve the removal and restorations of LO coatings or seals. The first step – logical, but not intuitive – is to work harder to ensure that components are reliable, so maintainers do not have to reach them as often.

In the YF-22 flight-test programme, Lockheed and the USAF instrumented the interior of the aircraft to characterise and understand the environment in the equipment bays and the thermal and vibration stresses that sub-systems would encounter. These components have already proved more reliable than they would have been if they had been designed to standard specifications, in the usual way.

The next step in an integrated approach to LO support is diagnostics – if the maintainer knows exactly what has broken, he knows which panel to take off. Like improved reliability, this reduces the support costs of the entire system, as well as LO-related costs.

Where components continue to require regular access, or where the technology to ensure long inspection intervals does not exist, the F-22 has 'frequent access' panels. Like weapon-bay and landing-gear doors, these have frames, latches and gaskets which ensure that they can be opened and closed without compromising the LO 'bubble'. Those systems that need frequent attention are arranged so that the smallest number of frequent-access doors cover all the systems that need routine inspection. For instance, the core avionics are grouped in two racks, one on each side of the forebody, and are covered by two frequent-access panels, and the dataport for the portable maintenance aid (a laptop computer which downloads diagnostic data) is located in one of the main landing-gear bays.

As the F-22 engineering and manufacturing development (EMD) programme continues, the number of frequent-access panels may change. If a sub-system is not as reliable as expected, the engineers have two choices: improve it, or make it more accessible by replacing a 'putty panel' with a self-sealing door.

Structurally, the F-22 is designed to place minimal demands on RAM or coatings. Major structural joints, such as the junction of the mid-body and forward fuselage, are serrated so that the joint lines are aligned with the wing leading edges; this avoids the use of putties and tapes. The use of computer-aided design and manufacturing – an off-the-shelf technology for the F-22, but one which the B-2's creators had to invent – has been a significant advance, improving the

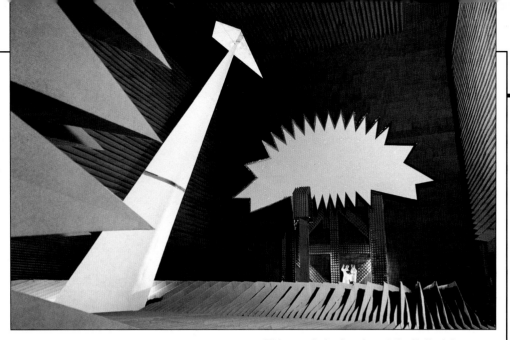

This anechoic chamber at the Kelly Johnson R&D Center, Santa Clarita, was one of those used to determine the emission signature of the YF-22's antennas. Reducing electronic emissions is almost as important as building in a low RCS in the first place. A whole new generation of compact flush antennas had to be designed for the F-22.

way that major assemblies fit together and reducing the size of steps and gaps.

There have been no revolutionary changes in RAM or other LO materials, but F-22 materials have to survive a harsher environment, including higher skin temperatures in sustained supersonic flight, and are intended to be more user-friendly than the materials used on earlier LO aircraft. One fundamental principle of the F-22's approach to LO materials was to minimise their number. In the F-117 or B-2 programmes, where LO goals were paramount, designers tended to select the material which was best suited to the different electromagnetic, thermal, vibration and structural requirements in any particular location – with the result that different types of material proliferated. On the F-22, the individual merits of each material type were balanced against a requirement to reduce the number of materials, with the result that the F-22 uses about one-third as many different LO materials as earlier LO aircraft. This reduces inventory, logistics and training costs and makes repair work easier.

There is still LO work to be completed. High-temperature RAM on the exhaust nozzles poses a challenge. The first F-22A EMD aircraft are not fully compliant in terms of LO, because maintaining their LO features would delay important early flight tests. As later, LO-equipped aircraft join the programme, the development of LO maintenance techniques will gather pace.

The objective is a fighter which has no extraordinary maintenance requirements and which rarely has to go to a hangar for LO restoration. Rarely does not mean never – there are some extreme conditions which will even drive an F-15 indoors – but it is clear that the F-22 has been carefully designed so that LO should not be the principal driver of its maintenance costs.

---

the engine was a pure turbojet, but at subsonic cruise the bypass ratio could be increased for greater efficiency. GE emerged from ground tests later than P&W. By that time, late in 1987, it was clear that the Dem/Val prototypes would weigh 60,000 lb (27220 kg) rather than 50,000 lb (22700 kg), so GE scaled up the YF120 to match. The GE-powered Dem/Val prototypes were faster, but the GE engine was not as mature as the P&W engine when Dem/Val ended. Pratt & Whitney argued that it could scale up the F119 to match GE's performance in a design which might be less complex and expensive, and which presented fewer technical risks, and that it had more experience with thrust vectoring, having been the contractor for the F-15 programme. The F119 was accordingly selected for the F-22.

Stealth was a complicating factor, at a fundamental level. In a stealth aircraft, everything is integrated and the external shape is sacrosanct. Excrescences such as bulges, antennas, ventral fins, fillets, vortex generators, notches and fences

often appear on conventional aircraft during development; on a stealth design, they are taboo. A deficiency in range on a conventional aircraft can be fixed with increased take-off weight and larger fuel tanks, but not a stealth aircraft. VLO incurs large penalties if you do not get it right first time.

F-22 features

The F-22's airframe and engine design has been driven by the often conflicting demands of stealth, supersonic cruise and agility. Stealth influences the shape and angle of all external surfaces. It requires that all weapons and fuel be carried internally, demanding an airframe of much greater volume than a non-stealthy design with the same speed and range. Supersonic cruise requires low supersonic drag, which in turn implies slenderness and thin wing and tail sections – neither of which is inherently compatible with large volume. Supersonic cruisers tend to be long and slender, militating against agility. Agility is achieved

through a large wing span and area and effective controls: this is hard to reconcile either with the need for a small, thin wing for supercruise, or with the fact that the best tail for a stealth aircraft is no tail at all.

The F-22 is about the same size as an F-15, but is heavier, tipping the scales at some 62,000 lb (28125 kg) in clean condition. In general layout, the F-22 is a moderately swept (42°) delta. The delta wing combines low thickness/chord ratio for supersonic drag with enough area to meet manoeuvrability requirements. It offers a useful amount of space for fuel, and its span is still short enough to fit inside standard NATO aircraft shelters. The wing and body are highly blended, providing more volume without driving wetted area and drag too high.

The Raptor is a fly-by-wire (FBW) aircraft. FBW, however, is not magic, and it can only perform within the limits set by the authority of the control system and the aircraft's physical responses. The designers' goals were ambitious, and would be achieved by a combination of the software in the FBW computers and effective aerodynamic control.

In-built agility

The F-22 was designed to be agile, reflecting a slightly more complex concept of manoeuvrability than the philosophy that lay behind earlier fighters. It would match or exceed them in basic parameters such as sustained turning or rolling rates, but it would also be able to move more quickly from one manoeuvre state to another – for instance, from a high-g turn to a straight-line acceleration. It would also be able to fly within a larger controlled envelope and would be able to reach high Alpha while remaining under full control. Another goal was to avoid stability and control deficiencies that would require the flight control system (FCS) to set limits on Alpha, or to restrict other manoeuvres (such as roll) at high Alpha.

The designers aimed for 'carefree abandon' handling, allowing the pilot to exploit a very large Alpha/airspeed envelope without overstressing the aircraft or causing it to depart from controlled flight. The F-22 is designed to be immune to deep stalls – stalls from which the aircraft cannot recover with normal control inputs – and to recover from high-Alpha, post-stall conditions with both engines flamed out. Lockheed chose a four-tail configuration

because it provided stability and linear control response in pitch, roll and yaw over a wide speed and Alpha range. The horizontal tails are in plane with the wing, masking them from radar from most aspects.

The F-22 is the first fighter to be designed from the outset to use vectored thrust for control. Thrust vectoring is not currently used to expand the flight envelope, because the USAF insists that the F-22 must be able to recover from all points in the envelope without it. Rather, thrust vectoring gets the F-22 from one manoeuvre state to another more quickly.

The flight control system operates the horizontal tails, the rudders, the vectoring nozzles, the wing surfaces (flappers, ailerons and leading-edge flaps) and even the brakes and nosewheel steering. There are no speedbrakes: for inflight deceleration, the flaperons go down, the ailerons deflect up and the rudders move outwards. On the ground, the entire trailing edge deflects up to spoil the wing lift. Flight and propulsion control are fully integrated.

The first F-22A flew with a set of FCS laws that will address the full flight envelope and all configurations, according to Lockheed Martin. Although testing will be incremental, YF-22 and wind-tunnel experience suggests that no major changes will be necessary.

The F-22 bucks the trend towards the use of composite materials. Only 35 per cent of the bare airframe is composite, although the designers had expected to use more than 40 per cent. The main reason was that the specialised composites needed to withstand high temperatures caused by skin friction at high speeds were expensive and hard to work with. The designers nevertheless reached their weight goal – 25 per cent lighter than an all-aluminium airframe – by using a lot of titanium, which makes up 41 per cent of the airframe weight. Composites are mainly found in the skins, and in the wings and tails where their stiffness is valuable.

Power and performance

The other principal contributor to the F-22's flight performance is sheer power. Particularly at high speeds, the F-22 has a higher thrust/weight ratio than earlier aircraft. This explains its high cruising speed and rapid acceleration, which otherwise is hard to reconcile with its bulky shape.

The first two F-22As fly in formation during a test flight from Edwards, highlighting the difference in finish between them. The US Air Force is eagerly awaiting the arrival in service of the F-22, and it has already had to make some considerable sacrifices in other programme areas to get the aircraft this far.

Lockheed Martin F-22

Aerodynamics, stealth and propulsion have been the obvious challenges to the development team. However, the F-22 is radical in another less obvious way: the systems by which it gathers and processes information.

Speed alone makes this task more challenging, while stealth gives the pilot a new dimension to consider. Like a submarine commander, the F-22 pilot must constantly weigh offence against concealment. Moreover, different radar systems can detect the F-22 at different distances, and radar can see it better from the side or the tail than head-on. Paradoxically, turning away from a radar can compromise the F-22's stealth.

Lockheed Martin chief test pilot Paul Metz takes this view. "Very few fighter pilots are effective," he says. In the 1939-45 war, only 21 per cent of fighter pilots made kills and about one in six of these (3.6 per cent of the total) became aces. In Korea, the 4.8 per cent of pilots who became aces made 38 per cent of the total kills. "What if we can increase the ratio of pilots who make kills from one in five to one in two, or even one in three?" wondered Metz. The implications in terms of force effectiveness are clear.

Two aspects of the F-22's aerodynamic and systems design help accomplish that goal, by making the task of flying the aircraft as simple as possible. The FCS and care-free-abandon characteristics mean that the pilot does not have to watch *g* loading and Alpha limits. In the systems,

automation and self-test are the rule. The F-22 features an Integrated Vehicle Systems Controller (IVSC), divided into six elements, which controls the landing gear, hydraulics, electrical power and flight control systems. Many operations which normally require a manual sequence of operations are executed automatically by the IVSC. Launching the F-22 is a matter of inserting a data transfer cartridge – which sets up the displays according to the pilot's preferences – switching the battery on, holding the auxiliary power switch in the on/start position and setting the throttles to idle. The engines start automatically and the avionics run through their diagnostic routines, and within a classified but extremely short time the fighter is ready to go.

It is the F-22's sensors and displays which play the greatest part in making the pilot effective, which means resolving a fundamental conflict: automation is essential, because no pilot can absorb all the data flowing into the system, but the pilot must be left in control of tactical decisions which only the human mind can make. The intention in the F-22 cockpit design, and the key to keeping the pilot in the loop without overloading the mind, is to maximise information and minimise data.

Basic concepts behind the avionics design include sensor fusion, combining data from all different sensors to display one target on the screen and relieving the pilot of the need to monitor and compare different displays. Sensor management means that, in normal operation, the pilot does not control the radar, the passive electronic warfare system or the datalinks. This is done automatically according to the tactical situation, so that the pilot can act as a tactician, not a sensor operator. Emission control (EMCON) is a task of the sensor management system, keeping tell-tale electronic emissions at the lowest possible level.

Until the enemy is within visual range, the pilot deals with this system through three full-colour liquid-crystal displays which dominate the instrument panel. The central, 8 x 8-in (20 x 20-cm) tactical situation display depicts the world around and in front of the F-22. The left and right 6 x 6-in (15 x 15-cm) displays are assigned to defence sub-systems and attack information.

Unlike some cockpit displays, all three displays are in the same orientation – 'God's eye view', with the F-22's track pointed straight up the middle of the screen – and use identical symbols. (A fourth display is used for systems information.) "These [on the attack display] are the guys I want to kill," explains a Lockheed pilot, "and these are the guys who are trying to kill me."

The symbols differ in shape and colour. Blue circles mark other members of the formation. Green circles mark friendlies,

and hostiles are triangles. The different shapes make the targets distinguishable if the pilot is wearing an anti-laser visor, which blocks certain colours.

One basic principle, borrowed from commercial aircraft, is the 'dark cockpit'; the absence of a light or a symbol means that everything is going smoothly. The displays are free from irrelevant data: the only ground-related symbol is a dashed line showing the forward edge of the battle area.

Datalinks and sensor fusion

The F-22s exchange their own positions via a secure intra-flight datalink (IFDL) which also harmonises the displays in the four cockpits, so that each pilot sees exactly the same situation. The IFDL operates at low power and in an RF band which attenuates rapidly in the atmosphere, so it is difficult for an adversary to detect or track.

The side displays show detail which could not be added to the central display without making it cluttered. For example, surface-to-air missile (SAM) sites are identified by pentagons. On the defence display, the pentagons will become solid when the radars are operating, and a circle around each site shows its detection range against the F-22.

The sensor management and EMCON functions define a sphere in the airspace around the F-22, divided into onion-like layers. In the outermost ring, targets are not yet close enough to be attacked. When a target enters the middle ring, the F-22 pilot can initiate an attack but the target cannot. In the innermost zone, the two aircraft are committed to passing within range of each other.

For example, AWACS or another source may report the presence of targets in the outer zone. The radar can identify them, but they are not close enough to present an immediate threat, so the computers inhibit the use of the radar.

Sensor fusion fills the gap. The F-22 has three primary sensors. In addition to the radar, it has an electronic warfare (EW) system which detects signals from other targets, and a datalink which imports information from AWACS and other aircraft. Today's fighters have all these sensors, but the F-22's passive, non-emitting devices – the EW system and datalink – are much more important.

Sensor fusion – blending the inputs from different sensors so that the pilot sees one target – is made possible by the F-22's revolutionary systems architecture. The radar, EW, and communications, navigation and identification (CNI) systems are not stand-alone devices, but peripherals serving the Raytheon Common Integrated Processor (CIP). This CIP comprises two banks of 32-bit computer modules housed in the forward fuselage. The square, book-sized modules plug into two racks in the fuselage, automatically connecting to the power supply, the databus and a liquid cooling circuit. Every function is backed up; if a module performing a critical function fails, its software will be loaded on to either a spare module or one which is doing a less important task.

On today's fighters, each sensor has its own display and it is up to the pilot to blend them into a single tactical picture. The F-22's computers sort the sensor data into 'track files'. For example, if an intercepted radar signal comes from the same location as a target tracked by AWACS it will go into the same track file. Next, the computer picks the best data from the file: AWACS will have measured the target's range and speed, but the F-22's EW provides a more accurate bearing and can identify it. Lockheed engineers stress that sensor fusion is hard to do on any other aircraft, where each system has its own different computer.

On the F-22, the design philosophy is that sensor fusion is transparent. Cockpit displays do not identify the sensor or sensors that have detected a target or a threat. That information would be unnecessary, says programme manager Brigadier General Mike Mushala: "We manage the sensors to answer the question, 'What's out there?' There are always several sensors looking – the aircraft is a sensor farm."

The 'apertures' themselves are very powerful. Datalinks may be the secret weapon in future air-to-air combats. "It's remarkable how much less you talk when the datalink is there," remarks a Lockheed pilot. "The first thing you learn is that the amount of information you share is tremendous." Even if only one F-22 is tracking an adversary on radar, the other three pilots can see it on their displays. "So if my

'Raptor 01' has received a unique camouflage scheme, using an overall grey with soft-edged darker areas on the wings, body and tail. The base colour is intended to match the luminance of the sky at typical combat altitudes and extreme visual range. The darker patches send mixed signals to the eye, and should serve to confuse an electro-optical missile seeker using an edge recognition algorithm. The F-22's wing is structurally efficient and stiff. At high g loadings, the ailerons deflect upwards to off-load the thinner inner sections. The wing design is more subtle than it looks: large leading-edge flaps and complex camber make it more efficient at low speeds and high-Alpha than earlier deltas. The twin fins are located well forward, so that even at high Alpha they are not blanketed by vortices from the forebody. Stability and full rudder effectiveness are retained as a result.

Lockheed Martin F-22

Top: Under current plans the F-22 flight test programme will encompass nine aircraft with a requirement to make approximately 2,400 flights over 4,300 test hours by 2003. This will complete the Engineering and manufacturing Development phase. Planned production stands at 339 aircraft to be delivered by 2013 and the F-22 has an initial operational capability date, with Air Combat Command, of 2005.

Above: As the USAF grapples with its new aerospace warfighting concepts it will look to the F-22 to gain the new high ground. If the F-22 performs as advertised, its stealth, speed, agility and lethality will go a long way towards ensuring dominance in the 21st century.

buddy here traps someone on his six, I can see it happen and save his bacon once again," the pilot adds. Alternatively, only one F-22 in a flight needs to use its radar; the three other F-22s have access to exactly the same information and can use it to launch and guide their missiles.

If any of the targets uses its own radar, it is likely to give the game away. The F-22's Lockheed-Sanders ALR-94 EW sensor suite "does not compare with anything out there today – it's vastly superior," remarks a Lockheed engineer. The fighter would look like a signals intelligence platform if the dozens of ALR-94 antennas, some of quite healthy proportions, were not smoothly blended into the skin. The ALR-94 can positively identify the target, determine its bearing and, to some extent, its range. A target which overuses its radar can set itself up for a completely silent missile attack, in which ALR-94 is the primary sensor.

The CIP computes the range of the hostile's radar against the F-22 at its current bearing. It appears on the defence screen as a blue cone emanating from the target. The CIP will do the same for any SAM radars, placing a circle around them on the defensive display. If the F-22 turns to present its more reflective side or rear to the radar, the envelope will expand visibly. The pilot can choose whether to risk detection or change course.

If the pilot decides to engage, a single tap on a throttle-mounted control instructs the inboard computers to prioritise the targets depending on their speed, position and type. Each target is marked by a white circle with a number, on both the main tactical display and the attack display.

The purpose of the automated 'shoot list' is to help the F-22 pilot make a good decision quickly, rather than making the pilot spend valuable seconds working out the best one. The pilot can override the shoot list, which was one of a number of techniques pioneered by the US Air Force's Pilot's Associate programme. One of the goals of Pilot's Associate was 'adaptive aiding' in which automation would be there to help the pilot in high-workload situations, but would not take over against the pilot's wishes.

As the attack proceeds, the computers will show the pilot the estimated range of the F-22's missiles and the range of the adversary's weapons. The pilot can make the tactical choice between a long-range shot (which keeps the F-22 safe) and a more lethal attack at closer range. The combination of the F-22 and AMRAAM is important: until the missile is in the final stages of flight, and locks up the target with its active radar, it does not emit, using its onboard inertial guidance system with periodic updates from the launch aircraft, and there is no strong signal that indicates an attack is under way. When the AMRAAM's radar does light up, it is usually too late.

Similarly, the defensive screen will show countermeasure and manoeuvre options against an imminent threat; the pilot can ignore them, evade manually or consent to the automatic use of countermeasures. The Lockheed Martin AAR-56 Missile Launch Detector (MLD), comprising six IR focal plane arrays with 128 x 128 elements located around the F-22's nose, warns of immediate threats.

Advanced radar technology

As the engagement continues, and the system needs accurate target tracks, so the computers will allow more use of the radar. The Northrop Grumman/Raytheon APG-77 is the first fighter radar with an active-array antenna, comprising nearly 2,000 finger-sized transmit and receive modules embedded in a fixed array. The USAF has pursued this technology since the early 1980s for three main reasons: power, agility and reliability.

The F-22 radar has a peak power in the megawatt range. This allows it to put a great deal of power on the target in a very short space of time, gathering data before the target's electronic jamming or surveillance systems can respond. It makes it easier to use advanced modes to identify 'non-co-operating' targets at long range.

The agility of the beam – its ability to change in direction or waveform – is better than any other type of radar. The F-22 radar can switch among its 18-plus modes so quickly

– so-called 'interleaved' modes – that they appear concurrent to the avionics system. Some of these modes are very unusual: for instance, a narrow-band interleaved search and track (NBILST) mode apparently uses sensors in the wings.

Agility opens the way to the low probability of intercept (LPI) techniques which the radar uses to perform its functions without betraying the fighter's own presence. Because the beam can scan instantly, it does not spray radiation across the sky as it sweeps from one target to another. The advanced solid-state power supply also responds quickly; an LPI radar never uses more power and never transmits longer than it must. Reliability is very important. The APG-77 has no antenna drives and no failure-prone electro-mechanical components such as rotary waveguide joints. The high-power transmitter/receiver and the single-channel amplifier and power supply are also gone. As for the transmit/receive modules, dozens of them can fail before the radar's performance is noticeably affected.

The F-22 display system has been extensively simulated since the late 1980s, including many real-time sorties using multiple interlinked dome displays. The results, says Lockheed Martin, show that the system is intuitive and easily learned, and raises the performance of an inexperienced pilot.

The EMD effort has been long and painstaking, and the schedule has slipped by four years since the contract was awarded in August 1991. Technical problems have little to do with this very deliberate pace. Development has been a success story. The engine passed its Critical Design Review (CDR) in 1992, and the aircraft did the same in February 1995. Problems, such as weight gains, RCS snags and a shortfall in engine efficiency, did occur, but they were discovered well before the first flight and were resolved without delaying the programme.

Paying for it all

Money has been a different matter. Since the EMD programme started, budget cuts moved the first flight from August 1995 to May 1997 – a date which slipped to September due to a number of individually minor problems – and have delayed initial operating capability from 2001 to 2005. The Pentagon has reduced the planned F-22 fleet twice – from 648 to 442 aircraft, in the 1993 'bottom-up review' of US defence plans, and then down to 339 in the mid-1997 Quadrennial Defense Review. This review also cut the peak production rate from 48 to 36 aircraft a year.

In July 1996, the USAF deferred development of the F-22B two-seater to save money and eliminated two F-22Bs from the test programme. This was not a painless decision, but the fighter's carefree handling and straightforward flying qualities should make it easy and safe to fly, while recording devices and the debriefing functions built into the Boeing-developed training system allow a pilot's performance to be reviewed on the ground.

The budget changes have been a tremendous problem for this tightly integrated programme. Whenever the programme is slowed down, each team has to restructure its work so that it is finished at the right time, neither too late (which delays other teams) nor too early (which is wasteful because the team will be idle). The new schedules have to be compatible, so that one team is not left waiting for another team's work, and ensure that teams are not conflicting in their use of test facilities.

The cuts have wasted hundreds of millions of dollars. The money that is cut in one year must all be spent in a later year to do the same work. Moreover, many costs are fixed – such as administration, security and the maintenance of facilities – and the total spent increases as the programme is extended. Lockheed Martin managers estimate that every dollar taken out of the programme now means three dollars of extra cost to complete the effort.

Flight test programme

The Raptor's first flight on 7 September 1997 marked only the mid-point between the start of EMD and the fighter's entry into service. Nine EMD aircraft are being built. Two of the 11 aircraft in the original contract were eliminated at the beginning of 1993; in 1998, however, when Congress insisted on the aircraft achieving certain test milestones before production could start, the first two production aircraft were redesigned as 'production representative test vehicles' to be used for operational testing.

The first three F-22s (4001-4003) are dedicated to airframe and engine testing and weapon release clearances. The first aircraft made two flights at Marietta before being flown to Edwards aboard a C-5 in February 1998, resuming flight tests on 17 May. The second aircraft flew at Marietta on 29 June and was ferried to Edwards on 26 August.

Early tests showed that the F-22 was easy to fly – on its own, in formation or in refuelling – with excellent handling qualities. Pilots describe it as combining an F-16's

The F-22's origins are firmly in the air superiority world and for most of its life the USAF has worked hard to keep it that way – not diluting its raison d'être by publicising other missions for it. For as long as possible the F-22's primary mission was shielded until the possibility that the F-22 might be cancelled altogether became a distinct possibility. Then, ironically, the budget cuts that deeply affected F-22 acquisition prompted a wide reassessment of the aircraft's real-world capabilities – and may now lead to a much-expanded range of missions for the aircraft. Lockheed Martin has already explored SEAD, deep interdiction and even Elint and tactical/strategic reconnaissance versions of the aircraft. Though the F-22 already has an air-to-ground PGM capability, to fulfil any of these missions effectively it would need several systems upgrades. The impetus for this may quite clearly come from Operation Allied Force experience over Kosovo, where US SEAD assets in particular have been sorely overstretched . The prospect of a multi-role F-22, or a family of expanded variants, may not be far away. Now that the USAF has the F-22 in its inventory, it would make sense to exploit it to the full.

The tests also cleared Congressionally mandated criteria for the start of production, allowing the USAF to award a contract covering long-lead items for the first low-rate initial production batch of six aircraft.

A clear road ahead?

The 1998 tests took the F-22 beyond the point – in flight hours and envelope – where major problems would usually begin to manifest themselves. The F/A-18E's wing-drop, for example, emerged very early in envelope expansion. USAF pilots continue to describe the aircraft as combining the agility of the F-16 with the ease of handling and stability of the F-15, and the fighter's power and acceleration are impressing its pilots and giving chase aircraft problems: F-15 and F-16 chases routinely use afterburner to stay with the F-22, particularly in climbs where the F-22 is close to full military power. Lockheed Martin chief test pilot Paul Metz summarises the F-22 as "a kick-ass rocket ship."

The next phase of flight testing, in the summer of 1999, was to involve speeds above Mach 1.5 and higher angles of attack, said General Mushala in early 1999. In terms of supercruise, he says, "we have done everything that we can do within the Edwards ranges" and the programme office is looking for expanded flight-test airspace, possibly over water, for use as the F-22 starts to prove its performance.

Even at Mach 1.5, the F-22's engines are operating below military power. General Mushala says that the programme office has selected Mach 1.5 as the threshold for supercruise "because nobody else can do it. It's going to be a lot of fun to figure out what supercruise and extended range mean to our operational capability."

The third F-22 (4003) is due to fly in late 1999. The importance of 4003 is that it is the first full-envelope F-22. The first two aircraft have about 80 per cent of full capability in terms of loads and other parameters, because of an over-enthusiastic weight-reduction effort in the initial design. Analysis after critical design review (CDR) showed that parts of the lighter structure did not provide an adequate margin of strength, and they were redesigned in time for the changes to be incorporated on the third and subsequent aircraft. After 4003 arrives at Edwards, it will continue to expand the F-22's flight envelope and will become the programme's main test vehicle for weapons separation.

Export customers for the F-22 would bolster the domestic programme, extend the production cycle and cut costs. While, officially, the F-22 is not available on the international market, many unofficial contacts have been made. Two things will count against the F-22. Firstly, its cost will make many potential customers think twice. Some will settle for reduced capabilities at a better price and shop elsewhere. Others will simply not be allowed to have the F-22, no matter how much they want it, as the technology it contains is too sensitive for all but the United State's closest allies – not all of whom can afford it.

agility with the F-15's good manners. One of the challenges for the test crew was learning the quirks of the IVSC, which exercises computer control over features such as the landing gear, brakes and canopy – items which are normally operated directly by the pilot. Brake inputs, for example, originally commanded a deceleration rate. If the aircraft was already slowing down on the runway, the system might not provide any additional deceleration when the pilot applied the brakes – leading the pilot to suspect that the brakes had failed. (The software is being changed so that brake application commands a change in deceleration rate.) In another case, a pilot found himself trapped in the cockpit: the IVSC was ignoring the command until all power was off the aircraft.

Between September and the end of 1998, the first two F-22s were used for a rapid envelope expansion programme. The first supersonic flight was made on 10 October. By the end of the year, the test team cleared the envelope to an airspeed of Mach 1.4 (without afterburning), a peak altitude of 50,000 ft, g-loadings from +6 to -1, and an angle of attack of 26°. The two aircraft had accumulated 199 hours in the air, including 4.76 hours at supersonic speed. The engines have been cycled from idle to full afterburner at 50,000 ft without problems.

The F-22 EMD aircraft will fly about as many hours as the full-scale development F-15 fleet, says General Mushala, but the programme will be very different. "We do a lot less flying in the basic aerodynamic performance areas – with the work we do on modelling and simulation, it's really validation. We do a lot more flying on integrated avionics, LO characteristics and supercruise." The entire programme will encompass more than 2,400 flights and 4,350 hours, and will continue until 2003. The busiest flight-test years will start in 2000, when aircraft 4004 enters the test programme, followed by five more avionics aircraft.

Six of the nine EMD aircraft, a modified Boeing 757 transport, and an extensive ground facility in Seattle are dedicated to avionics testing. The 757 flying testbed (FTB) carries the F-22's Northrop Grumman APG-77 radar, a forward-mounted 'wing' accommodating other F-22 antennas, a representative crew station and 30 engineering workstations. The software is developed in blocks. After being tested on the ground, each block is evaluated on the 757 before being released to the F-22 prototypes.

In early 1999, the 757 started flying with Block 1 software, which operates the radar and communications, navigation and identification (CNI) systems. This was to be checked out and delivered to Marietta in May, ready for installation on Raptor 4004, which is the first F-22 to have a radar.

Block 2 software was due to be installed in the FTB in two loads, in August and October. It adds radar modes and some EW. Block 3, originally planned as the final pre-IOC release of the software, should be released in 2000 and includes all EW functions. It will be followed by Block 3.1, which includes provision for JDAM.

Outpaced by technology

One potential snag has arisen from the huge mismatch between the pace of the F-22 programme and the progress of computing technology: components that were state-of-the-art when the fighter was designed may be obsolete, and difficult, expensive or impossible to acquire, by the time production starts. A special IPT team within the avionics programme is responsible for identifying such components and developing substitutes, using commercial technology to the greatest possible extent. "It is a tremendous challenge," General Mushala remarked in 1998, "and I don't expect that any two of the 339 aircraft that I build will be the same." The Intel I-9000 chip, extensively used in the F-22, is now out of production – "Intel got out of the military business and did something more profitable with the plant," comments Mushala. In total, 500 parts are already unavailable.

The technical orders (maintenance documentation) that accompany each F-22 are all-digital, too, so it is relatively easy to substitute new avionics modules for components that are no longer in production, as long as they are 'form,

fit and function' (F³) compatible. The aircraft will 'know' what modules are installed, and adapt its diagnostic software accordingly.

Low-rate production is due to start at the beginning of 1999; high-rate production will not be approved until virtually all the testing is finished, in late 2002, and the fighter will not become operational until late 2005.

The total EMD cost, including Lockheed Martin and Pratt & Whitney contracts, and work done by the Air Force, is now estimated at $19.2 billion in FY 1998 dollars (most of which has already been spent). Production of 339 aircraft at a peak rate of 36 per year will cost $34.2 billion, with an average unit flyaway cost (the cost of one fully equipped aircraft) of $81 million. The entire project – including Dem/Val, EMD, production and military construction – will cost $58.3 billion.

It is possible to calculate that the 'programme acquisition unit cost' of the F-22 – the total programme cost, divided

The F-22 still faces important cost hurdles as it competes for a shrinking defence budget against several other heavyweight contenders. Worries about what some observers have called a 'tactical aircraft train-wreck' have not yet gone away as the Navy's F/A-18E/F and the Joint Strike Fighter face off against the F-22 for funding. Waiting in the wings are improved versions of the Boeing F-15 and even Lockheed Martin's own advanced F-16 developments, if the F-22 should falter.

by the number of aircraft delivered – is $170.8 million, or $187.3 million in then-year dollars. This number is used by the F-22's critics, but is meaningless: cancelling a single F-22 does not save $170 million and buying an extra F-22 does not cost $170 million.

The long development process has given the F-22's critics time to marshal their arguments against the fighter. The gist of the case against the F-22 is that it is a Cold War weapon, designed to fight an enemy that no longer exists.

The Air Force's defence of the F-22 is far-reaching. In the latest revision of the Air Force's post-Soviet doctrine, air and space superiority is listed as the 'first of the USAF's core competencies'. Air and space superiority is intended to provide US forces with freedom of action, while preventing hostile aircraft and missiles from interfering with US operations and denying them sanctuary.

"Too many people fail to understand how the country depends on air dominance," Air Combat Command chief General Richard Hawley remarked in January 1997. Hawley pointed to Rivet Joint and Joint STARS, two systems which provide vital information on hostile air and ground forces, and which are carried on modified C-135 and 707 transports. "How long will that information be available if those aircraft are threatened by long-range AAMs launched from sanctuaries protected by surface-to-air missiles? Will we be able to sustain precision attack operations against adversary fighters? Will ground forces be able to manoeuvre as they did in Desert Storm if the enemy's reconnaissance aircraft can see them?"

F-15s have shot down 96 adversaries with zero losses in air combat, including 33 of 35 aircraft shot down in the Gulf. However, the Air Force argues, a more lethal and survivable replacement is needed to counter the proliferation of advanced fighters and SAM systems. Two factors support the need for a fighter which outclasses the threat, rather than matching it (as an improved F-15 could). First, US and allied forces in-theatre are likely to be outnumbered in the early stages of a conflict, as they arrive and establish their bases. Second, the US public and political leaders expect quick success and minimal losses.

The future for F-22

The Soviet threat, as we knew it, has vanished, but future adversaries will use much the same technology that the intelligence community projected for the Soviet Union when the F-22 was conceived, because the best SAMs and fighters developed for the former Soviet Union are now sold on the export market.

Where the F-22 should prove most useful is in its ability to give its pilot control of the engagement, however many adversaries may be involved. The F-22 pilot will have the speed and lethality to engage when conditions are favourable, the stealth and agility to decline combat when necessary, and the situational awareness to tell the difference.

A fundamental and often overlooked point is that the need for the F-22 is not exclusively driven by the fighter threat, and never has been. Many of its unique features – all-round stealth, supercruise and high altitude – are equally important in countering SAMs. Programme director Brigadier General Mike Mushala observes that this capability is not just important when the SAM threat is sophisticated, but also when the threat is uncertain – as is often the case in today's peacekeeping operations.

So far, the F-22 has survived. The Pentagon's 1997 Quadrennial Defense Review neither cancelled the programme nor cut it back to a token 'silver bullet' force – two options which had been mooted before the review was published. Combined with a supportive Congress, this goes a long way to stabilising the programme for the life of the present administration, and EMD will be almost complete by the time the next President is inaugurated.

Tomorrow's F/A-22

Even the cut in production was not as bad as it seemed, because the QDR encouraged the USAF to designate the F-22 as the ultimate replacement for the F-117 and F-15E; already, the USAF is talking about a requirement for 200-plus strike-modified Raptors to be delivered from 2012. It is early to talk about specific features, but the new version will probably carry new weapons, and might have some weapon bay modifications.

Exports are a possibility. Pentagon policy precludes final contracts until initial operational test and evaluation is complete, in 2001-02, but that does not prevent Lockheed Martin from briefing export customers. Potential customers include F-15 operators such as Israel, Saudi Arabia and

Japan. South Korea is considering a high-end fighter to complement the F-16, and Lockheed Martin is looking at the possibility of selling small 'silver bullet' F-22 fleets to operators of modern but non-stealthy fighters.

In 1999, with the first production contracts signed and flight testing on track, the long-running F-22 programme looks more stable than at any time in the past. As the fighter proves itself, too, the world may hear more about its performance – and the world may be surprised.

Bill Sweetman

The future of the F-22 is not assured, but is looking better. After the air power debacle over Kosovo, increases in the US defence budget are now likely. It may be that the uncertain world of the 1990s, which threw the F-22 into such confusion in the first place, may yet secure its prospects.

Ejército del Aire

Photographed by José Terol and Luigino Caliaro

Fully integrated into NATO's military alliance, the Ejército del Aire has a strength in excess of 500 aircraft, with over 29 types in service ranging from fast jets to gliders, transports to trainers. Capabilities are being improved with new procurement and upgrade programmes.

Combat assets of the Ejército del Aire consist of the C.15A/B Hornets of Grupos 12 (above), 15 (below) and 21, and the C.14 Mirage F1s of Ala 14 (below). The number of Hornets has swelled since December 1996 by the addition of 24 ex-US Navy examples, and their capabilities have been enhanced under the EF-18A+ programme, giving them the ability to fire AIM-120 AMRAAMs. A mid-life upgrade is planned which includes adding some elements of the later APG-73 radar system and new weapon capabilities. Spain's fast jets use hose-and-drogue refuelling, tanking from 312 Escuadrón's TK.10s (KC-130Hs – left) or 451 Escuadrón's T.17s (707s).

Spanish Hornets did not get the chance to fly combat missions during Operation Desert Storm, having to wait until Operación Icaro (NATO's Operation Deny Flight over Bosnia) for their combat debut. This pair is seen dumping fuel from the fin-top fuel jettison vents over the more tranquil Spanish landscape.

Above: *The Hornet's ability to carry an asymmetrical load enhanced versatility during operations over Bosnia. This example has an AIM-7M on the port conformal station, an AN/ASQ-213 HARM targeting system on the starboard next to the AGM-88A itself, wingtip AIM-9Ms, Paveway II-series GBU-10 LGBs and a pair of drop tanks.*

Right: *Fifty-five of Ala 14's C.14/CE.14 fleet are to undergo an avionics and service-life extension update to keep the type in service until 2015. C.14-91 (an F1C – below) is one of four single-seaters received from France in 1994. All will gain the overall grey scheme.*

The wing badge of Ala 14, portraying Don Quixote saluting three Mirage F1s, is displayed on the side of the intake. Although individual escuadrón badges are not normally displayed on Ala 14's aircraft, Escuadrón 142's membership of the NATO Tiger club has resulted in exceptions to this rule.

Above: The Eurofighter Typhoon (C.16 Tifón) is due to enter service with the Spanish air force early in the next century, with Spain currently committed to purchasing 87 production aircraft. The CASA-assembled, EJ200-powered XCE.16 prototype, DA6, was the first two-seater to fly and is tasked with testing the avionics and systems of that version. It was delivered to the Centro Logístico de Armamento y Experimentación (CLAEX – Weapons and Test Centre) at Torrejón for development trials.

Above, right and below: CR.12 Phantoms (RF-4Cs) are operated by 123 Escuadrón from Torrejón. The 'Rhino' has served with the air force since 1978, when four ex-363rd TRW examples were delivered, followed in 1989 by eight ex-123rd TRW aircraft from the Kentucky Air National Guard. Upgrades to the aircraft in service have included AN/APQ-172 terrain-following radar, new ECM systems, laser INS, real-time datalinks, provision for the AN/AVD-5 EO-LOROPS system and fixed inflight-refuelling probes.

Top: Talavera-based Ala 23 uses the surviving SF-5Bs primarily for weapons and advanced training of future fast-jet pilots, with a secondary close-air-support role.

Above: Since 1976 the TK.10 Hercules fleet has provided tanker support to the fast jets. Five KC-130Hs were acquired and have recently undergone a programme to extend their service life until 2005. TK.10-12, delivered in January 1980, is depicted topping up a pair of C.14s from the Los Llanos-based Ala 14.

Four Boeing 707s are in service – two as tanker/transports, one as a VIP transport (below) and one for electronic warfare. T.17-2 (right) is equipped with a pair of Sargent-Fletcher wingtip-mounted refuelling pods.

Since becoming the standard Spanish basic jet trainer, the majority of E.25s (CASA C.101EBs) have served with the Grupo de Escuela de Matacan or the San Javier academy. The academy provides the national display team – the 'Patrulla Aguila' (above). Other Aviojets are flown by CLAEX in the standard trainer silver/Dayglo scheme and Grupo 44 codes.

Above: The Escuela de Vuelo provides pupils with 48 flight hours in the CASA-assembled E.26 Tamíz (T-35C Pillán) before progressing to the Aviojet. Thirty-six of the 40 delivered from 1985 are used by the school.

Left: Ala 78 at Armilla is responsible for helicopter training of both air force and army pilots. Students undertake 50 hours on the HE.20 (Hughes H-269C) with 782 Escuadrón before progressing to the HE.24 (S-76C).

Electronic warfare assets of Escuadrón 408 include TM.11s (Falcon 20s – above) and a single TM.17 (Boeing 707-351 – left). The Falcons of this unit differ externally from those of Grupo 45 by the addition of two large aerials on the fuselage top and blacked-out windows, while the TM.17 displays an extensive aerial farm as well as the sensors mounted under the nose.

VIP and staff transportation is provided by T.11/TM.11s (above), a T.16 (Falcon 50), T.17s (707s) and the pair of T.18s (below) – all based at Torrejón with Grupo 45.

Right: Short-range SAR is undertaken by nine SA 332B Super Pumas (HD.21) in two squadrons. Twelve were originally delivered for this task from 1983.

Above: Crewed by Ejército del Aire personnel, the CL-215Ts were acquired with funds from the Ministry of Agriculture and Fishing. Of the 30 waterbombers acquired from 1971, 15 have been re-engined with PW123F turboprops.

Left: Three Fokker F27-200MPAs (D.2s) are based at Gando on Gran Canaria and provide SAR coverage out to 1,000 nm into the Atlantic. They replaced the HU-16 Albatross in service from 1979.

Below: The HD.21 has added the combat SAR mission to its tasks, but at present the fleet has few additional aids for this demanding role. The Super Pumas were repainted overall grey (instead of white) but retain the yellow SAR bands.

Above: Navigation students at the San Javier academy undertake airborne tuition in the TE.12B Aviocars of the Escuela de Navegación.

Left: Escuadrones 351 and 352 of Ala 35 (whose badge is displayed on the nose of the aircraft) – based at Getafe air base, Madrid – are the operators of the Ejército del Aire's 18 Airtech T.19B (CASA CN.235-100) tactical transports.

Below: The CASA C.295M is designed to carry 69 troops or 48 paratroopers, and a crew of two. Ala 35 will be the first unit to operate the type, passing on its CN.235s to other units. EC-295 is the first prototype.

Below: Six of the eight pre-production Aviocars were completed as CASA C.212B photographic survey aircraft (TR.12A), equipped with two Wild RC-10 aerial survey cameras. The Aviocars operate alongside a pair of TR.20s (Cessna 560 Citation V) with 403 Escuadrón from Cuatro Vientos, as part of Ala 78.

Below right: The Cabra (Goat) – as the Dornier Do 27 is known in Ejército del Aire service – was selected in 1958 to replace the Fieseler Storch, and remains in use for liaison and glider-tug duties. This Spanish-built CASA 127 has the tug attachment under the tail, and is assigned to the San Javier-based Academia del Aire.

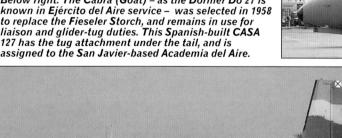

Above: Four Eurocopter HT.21As (AS 332M Super Pumas) are used for VIP transport by Escuadrón 402 from Cuatro Vientos.

Below: CLAEX, the flight test centre, uses a variety of types, including this overall-white CASA 211-200.

Below: 781 Escuadrón uses the HE.24 (Sikorsky S-76C) for advanced helicopter training. The unit has a secondary SAR/combat SAR tasking, which accounts for a quarter of flight hours.

Above: Seven D.3B Aviocars (and a pair of D.3As) are shared between the SAR units at Cuatr0 Vientos and Son San Juan.

Below: This HD.21 of Escuadrón 803 from Cuatro Vientos air base still displays the old-style white scheme, largely replaced by overall light grey.

Boeing CH-47 Chinook
Variant Briefing

In production for nearly 40 years, the Chinook has become the West's primary medium-lift helicopter. Its capacious cabin and weight-lifting capability have made it a highly versatile battlefield vehicle. Increasingly powerful engines and ever more capable systems have permitted useful loads to grow, ranges to increase and operations to be undertaken at night and at low level with greater safety. With no real competitor in its size/weight category, the Chinook is set for many more years of success.

Above: The third production CH-47A demonstrates the ability of the Chinook to deliver paratroops. A standard load was 33 fully-armed troops, although this figure was later to rise to 44. During the Falklands War, the sole in-theatre RAF Chinook once carried 81 troops.

Right: The YCH-1B development programme was to have involved five flying prototypes, but the first was badly damaged in a ground running accident. The nearest of this pair is extensively tufted on the undersides, around the nose and on the front rotor pylon to enable accurate monitoring of airflow patterns.

Left: An RAF Chinook displays the type's legendary lifting power. The British forces have routinely made heavier use of the Chinook than other operators, and their duties encompass a wide variety of roles.

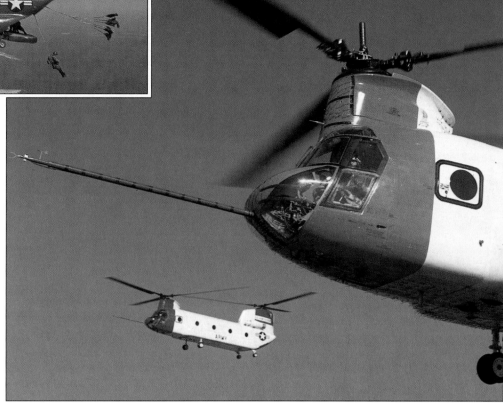

The CH-47 Chinook medium-lift helicopter is old, familiar, friendly, and on the verge of becoming one of the longest-lasting success stories in aviation. At the Boeing helicopter plant in Ridley Township, Pennsylvania – often called, simply, Philadelphia, for the city nearby – they are introducing 21st-century assembly techniques to create a new fleet of Chinook helicopters built on the airframes of the old ones. Even before overseas customers begin to take delivery of the CH-47D 'Super D' in late 1999 and the US Army begins to fly the CH-47F ICH (Improved Cargo Helicopter) in 2005, the Chinook already enjoys a record for longevity and success matched by few flying machines. When the first CH-47SD 'Super D' reaches its first international customer, Singapore, in October 1999, the crew of that helicopter will be piloting an upscale, hi-tech version of an aircraft that has changed little in appearance in 40 years. Only a handful of aircraft serve long, change little, and become so familiar they are etched into our minds – the Douglas DC-3, the B-52 Stratofortress bomber, the ubiquitous UH-1 Huey, and now the Chinook.

The aircraft has been seen in US Army colours from Germany to Korea, with a dramatic appearance in Tirana, Albania to support recent combat operations there – and, if anything, is even more visible in the livery of two dozen international military users. The fundamental capabilities of the Chinook, improved in stages over the decades, have been tested to the limit under fire in Vietnam and the Persian Gulf.

The Chinook has always had to fight for every defence dollar spent in its name because, as CH-47D flight engineer Sergeant Ralph Wood says, "A Chinook is not glorious, it doesn't have guns, missiles or bombs and there-

The Chinook's baptism of fire came in Vietnam, where the type proved outstanding in the construction and resupply of outlying bases (right), movement of artillery and vehicles, and the recovery of downed aircraft. Birth Control (above right) was one of three ACH-47A gunships deployed for operational trials with the 53rd AvDet, 1st Cavalry in June 1966.

CH-47 Chinook Variants

Chinooks regularly operate with ski undercarriage fixed to the mainwheels, as displayed by this CH-147. The skis spread the footprint of the helicopter, and can be of use on both snowy or boggy ground.

Sizeable numbers of US Army CH-47Cs were forward-deployed in West Germany and Korea. The version was improved throughout its career, especially in the field of defences.

fore will never be recognised for its importance on the battlefield. The only time a Chinook is recognised is when there is some natural disaster such as the recent hurricane in Central America [Hurricane Mitch in December 1998]."

Based on a *per capita* measurement of the Chinook fleet, it is possible that no other aircraft has performed its mission so consistently, logging so many flying hours. The Chinook is far from beautiful – its business end is perhaps its least glamorous feature, what one Boeing engineer calls "a long cabin in a short fuselage" – but there are soldiers who rate this big, twin-tandem conglomeration of machinery right up there with spouse, children, home, and bank account. "It is, next to my wife and children, the love of my life," says CW5 Ruffin C. Moore of Company D, 2/160th SOAR (Special Operations Aviation Regiment), who flies the MH-47E at Fort Campbell, Kentucky

The Chinook is a relatively forgiving aircraft to fly, and for newly-converted pilots the main problem is coping with the sheer size of the craft. Prospective US Army Chinook pilots first encounter the type at the Army Aviation Center at Fort Rucker, after having flown the TH-67A.

and has been associated with Chinooks for two decades. "It is the best aircraft in the Army inventory and will be for the next few years."

It is not widely known that the Chinook has enjoyed the lowest accident rate of any aircraft type in US Army service throughout its career, and currently has fewer than 1.0 serious mishaps per 100,000 flying hours. Other aspects of the Chinook story never made the limelight, among them the 'offshoot' XCH-62 cargo helicopter design that would have challenged every superlative in anyone's rotary-wing vocabulary but never flew, plus several other experimental variants and offspring.

The Chinook has the most available and usable cargo space of any US Army helicopter. Its fuel supply (1,028 US gal/3891 litres on US Army cargo versions, twice as much on most export Chinooks) is carried externally in pods running the length of the fuselage, which results in a constant cross-section cabin similar to that of many fixed-wing transports. The cabin measures 30 ft x 8 ft 3 in x 6 ft 6 in (9.14 x 2.51 x 1.98 m) and provides an area of 1,440 cu ft (41 m³), and is long enough to accept two of the standard tactical vehicles in use at the time the helicopter was designed, the M551 Jeep; only a single example will fit – just – of today's US Army's standard tactical vehicle, the M998 'Humvee'. A 'Hummer' inside a Chinook has

less than 1 in (2.5 cm) to spare on either side, meaning that the driver who brings it aboard – always by backing into the helicopter – is trapped inside unless he has a 'ragtop' version and can exit overhead. The larger M1097 'Humvee' vehicle will not fit in a Chinook at all.

For most routine cargoes, the Chinook's cargo space is more than ample and it is usually called the US Army's heavy-lift helicopter, although it technically falls into the medium-lift category. Around the Chinook's cargo space, the helicopter's surrounding fuselage is remarkable compact. At 51 ft (15.54 m) in length, just ¼ in (6 mm) longer than a UH-60 Black Hawk, it fits easily into restricted landing areas.

Twin-rotor design

The Chinook's tandem rotor design allows the entire length of the fuselage to be put to good use, since none of it is required as a boom for a tail rotor. Loading and unloading can be accomplished through a full-length rear ramp, which can be lowered to the ground or raised to match the level of truck beds. One soldier using a built-in winch can pull cargo in or out of the aircraft. Extremely long cargo can extend beyond the opened rear ramp, if necessary.

Above: An important role for the CH-47D is artillery placement, being able to lift the M198 155-mm howitzer, its 11-member crew and 32 rounds of ammunition for a total of about 22,000 lb (9980 kg). This capability was outside that of the earlier variants.

The Chinook's high rotor blades allow soldiers to enter or exit the helicopter quickly and safely, even with the rotors turning. The standard troop load is 33 fully-equipped troops on standard sidewall seating, but the Chinook can carry 44, 50 or 59 infantrymen by placing additional seats in the centre aisle. For medical evacuation missions, the cabin can take 24 standard NATO litters and two medical attendants. Realising the usefulness of this capability, the US Army designed a MUST (Medical Unit, Self-contained, Transportable) for rapid deployment in the field. The Chinook was able to carry these units, weighing up to 6,000 lb (2721 kg), up to 100 nm (185 km) from base and bring casualties back rapidly when required. This capability eventually fell into disuse in the Army, which relied on the smaller, more nimble UH-1 Huey (in Vietnam) and the tadpole-like UH-60L Black Hawk (today) for the battlefield medical evacuation job.

Although its four-point undercarriage is nothing more than a logical solution for an aircraft of this size and shape, it has proven aptly suited for harsh environments. The quadricycle landing gear provides good stability during loading and unloading operations, preventing roll-overs when landing at unprepared sites, including slopes up to 20°. The aircraft was initially built with six wheels (two each on the rear landing gear points), reduced to four using low-pressure tyres to which skis can be added to prevent the helicopter from sinking in snow, mud or marshy terrain.

Every Chinook's hull is sealed at the factory so the helicopter can land and take off from water in conditions up to Sea State 3; this amphibious capability enables it to operate from a larger number of locations, but is rarely used in everyday operations. The helicopter is cleared for IFR (instrument flight rules) flying, even in conditions of light icing and moderate turbulence. All current models are equipped with fibreglass rotor blades which can be repaired in rough-field conditions. The Chinook is self-sufficient in that it has an onboard auxiliary power unit to furnish electrical and hydraulic power, eliminating a need for external carts. The fuselage design includes built-in handholds, flush steps and walkways to make most maintenance possible without work stands or ladders.

History

The CH-47 Chinook had its origins as the Vertol Model 114 of 1958 (the company was originally named for Frank Piasecki, pioneer of the tandem-rotor configuration, and has been Boeing since 1960). The straightforward idea behind the Chinook was to devise a more capable follow-on development of the maker's earlier Model 107 twin-engined assault transport helicopter, better known today as the US Marine Corps' CH-46E Sea Knight, or 'Bullfrog'. The US Army did consider the

Above: With its far greater lifting power and two extra hooks, the CH-47D has vastly increased the mobility of the US Army. Here aircraft are seen carrying the Army's standard 2½-ton truck.

Above and below: The Chinook played a major part in the Gulf War, US Army CH-47Ds being heavily involved in General Schwarzkopf's famous 'left hook' encircling manoeuvre around Kuwait. The aircraft stood up well to the rigours of operations in extremely dusty conditions.

With its good lifting capability, the Chinook makes a useful fire-fighting tool. Many military users have purchased underslung fire-fighting equipment such as the Sims Rainmaker bucket. In the early 1980s US Army CH-47As were used by the Los Angeles City Fire Department to help tackle forest fires in the surrounding hills.

Model 107 in 1959 under the military designation YCH-1, but found it too small. Curiously, when the Chinook came along it was given a follow-up designation of YHC-1B, subsequently changed to CH-47A.

From 1965, the US Army relied heavily on the CH-47A, CH-47B and CH-47C for lifting duties. It is claimed that no fewer than 10,000 downed aircraft were retrieved from Vietnamese rice paddies and mountain sides, and brought home for salvage or repair slung beneath the belly of a Chinook; considering that A, B and C models were all hampered by having only one sling point to attach a load – replaced by three sling points in the post-Vietnam CH-47D – this is quite an achievement. The Chinooks became a familiar sight throughout the country, virtually all painted flat olive drab and devoid of any colour or noteworthy markings. By 1971, the Vietnamese Air Force was also equipped with the CH-47.

Gunship Chinook

An armed battlefield version, the ACH-47A, appeared briefly in Vietnam. It bristled with guns and worked perfectly but, despite its apparent potential on the battlefield, to say nothing of the success of more modern attack helicopter types, the US Army did not proceed with it.

The 1st Air Cavalry Division brought a new form of warfare to the world in 1965, creating the largest helicopter base ever hacked out of the jungle (at Anh-Khe) and launching infantry attacks in which air cavalrymen leapfrogged the enemy, enjoying a degree of mobility not even imagined by North Vietnamese regulars who moved on the ground. The UH-1 Huey was the principal player in this new kind of fighting, but the supporting role played by the Chinook was what made everything work. Anh-Khe was the main base at the time, but helicopters were

free to fan out in all directions and needed no base at all for much that they did. As early as January 1966, the 1st's Chinooks had amassed 4,400 flight hours and had successfully recovered 100 downed aircraft.

The Pentagon stepped up CH-47 production and the Army experimented with methods, tactics and crew composition. In Vietnam, a Chinook's crew complement consisted of pilot, co-pilot, flight engineer/crew chief (who also doubled as a gunner) and gunner. In the combat zone, soldiers removed the rear cabin windows, and sometimes other windows, to create rifle ports for onboard infantrymen. Chinooks in Vietnam carried a pintle-mounted 0.30-in (7.62-mm) M60D machine-gun in the port escape hatch opening and a second M60D on a swing-out mounting in the forward starboard crew door. Numerous other weapons were tried at various periods as 'search and destroy' missions became increasingly important.

Considerable innovation went into the way Chinooks were deployed and used. The helicopter could supply a hill-top observation post by landing on just one wheel or by backing up to the hill top and lowering the rear ramp to allow supplies to be offloaded and casualties taken aboard; this was done with rotors still turning and the helicopter, for every practical purpose, still airborne. Chinook pilots did not easily acquire such skills, but the helicopter could be relatively forgiving, even with a novice at the controls.

At the height of the US role in the war (when 660,000 troops were in the field in mid-1969), some 22 CH-47 units were scattered around South Vietnam. Some were used in civil action operations, which included rapid relocation of large segments of the civilian population. On one sortie, a CH-47 is reported to have carried 147 Vietnamese civilians and their belongings from a village to a new home a few miles away.

The widespread use in Vietnam and elsewhere of the CH-47C ended complaints that the type was underpowered. The CH-47C was both more powerful and more capable. It was

Aussie 'Chooks'

Having seen just what the Chinook could do while serving alongside the type in Vietnam, the Royal Australian Air Force became the first overseas customer for the CH-47 in 1970. In 1989 the type was prematurely retired from RAAF service when the support helicopter role transferred to the Army, but four years later the 'Chook' was back, and in more capable CH-47D form.

Australian military interest in a medium-lift helicopter began in the early years of the 1960s. The Chinook came under scrutiny during the Vietnam War, when RAAF and Army officers were first impressed by the lifting and load-carrying capability of in-theatre US Army machines. The RAAF, in particular, had cause to be grateful for the assistance provided by US Army CH-47As, as they recovered several of No. 9 Sqn's downed Iroquois which were then sent to Vung Tau, for rebuild and return to service, thus saving the service (and therefore the Australian taxpayer) millions of dollars that would have been required to purchase attrition replacement helicopters.

In 1969 the Australian government approved the purchase of 12 helicopters, of an unspecified type, to fulfil its Medium Lift Helicopter (MLH) requirements. The two types considered were the Boeing Vertol CH-47C Chinook and the Sikorsky CH-53C Sea Stallion; the former was eventually selected, with an announcement by the Minister for Defence on 19 August 1970 that an order for 12 of the then-current production CH-47C helicopters would be placed with Boeing Vertol. This order was duly lodged in March 1972, under the Foreign Military Sales (FMS) agreement, and the RAAF became the first export customer for the type.

At that time, however, the US Army was experiencing a series of turbine failures of the T55 engine, resulting in the RAAF order being placed on hold until the problems were sorted out. After this had happened, the order was reinstated in March 1972.

The first flight of an Australian Chinook came in the middle of 1973, when A15-001 took to the air at the Boeing Vertol plant in Philadelphia. All 12 aircraft were delivered as deck cargo aboard the aircraft-carrier HMAS *Melbourne*, departing San Francisco on 9 April 1974 and finally arriving in Brisbane on 28 April. The aircraft were then transferred to No. 3 Aircraft Depot at Amberley (their new home base) for reassembly and flight testing prior to delivery to No. 12 Sqn.

Below and below right: A CH-47D is seen working with ground units in the bush. The Chinook's long range makes it ideal for operations in Australia's vast and inhospitable terrain.

CH-47 Chinook Variants

Australia's **CH-47C**s were delivered in standard **US** Army olive drab (above), but later acquired a white topped fuselage. Later still they were painted in a tactical three-tone scheme (left).

Preparation for the introduction of the 'Chook' (the RAAF's nickname for the CH-47C is a common Australian term for chicken) saw No. 12 Squadron reform at Amberley on 1 September 1973. With the primary role of providing tactical support to the Army, the aircraft soon proved itself invaluable in the transportation of fuel, artillery pieces, troops and the like, but also played a major role in civil aid and flood relief operations. Not all aircraft were in service at any one time, an available establishment of between four and six aircraft being the norm, with airframes rotated through storage at 3 AD to even out flying hours.

The RAAF aircraft were initially delivered in the standard US Army olive drab colour scheme, but the top of the fuselage was painted white shortly thereafter, in deference to the hot Australian climate. A later disruptive scheme of green and tan (as worn by the Iroquois fleet) was applied, and the aircraft remained in these colours until its premature retirement.

It was announced in May 1989 that the battlefield support helicopter role would pass to the Army, and that the Chinooks would be withdrawn from service at the same time due to their high operating costs. This immediately caused an outcry within certain sections of the RAAF (and Army), who feared that the newly acquired Blackhawk would not be able to provide the same service, particularly in tasks such as the transportation of fuel bladders to forward logistics areas. Nevertheless, the decision stood, and the 11 surviving aircraft were retired and placed into long-term storage at 3 AD in July 1989. No. 12 Squadron passed into history from 1 July.

As predicted by those in the ADF with an intimate knowledge of the Chinook's virtues, it soon became clear that there was now a shortfall in capability, particularly in terms of mobility when undertaking large-scale deployments, and a platform with a heavier lifting ability than the Blackhawk could offer was required. The lack of a medium-lift helicopter capability in the Kangaroo 89 (K89) combined military exercise, held shortly after the withdrawal of the Chinook, was keenly felt, and pressure then began to be applied on the Minister for Defence, in an attempt to force a reconsideration. Consequently, the sale of the stored CH-47Cs was abandoned and, after at least one false start, a deal was hammered out with the US Army, whereby seven aircraft would be transferred to that service in order to partially fund the conversion of the remaining four to CH-47D standard. This deal was finally announced on 30 May 1991, for between four and six CH-47Ds, but in the event it was the lower number that eventuated after an analysis of costs. Accordingly, the aircraft were returned to the USA by merchant ship, departing Brisbane in July 1993. After conversion to CH-47D standard, the four Australian aircraft were returned to Brisbane, again by merchant ship, in May and July 1995 (two aircraft each). Following reassembly on the wharf, the aircraft were flown first to Amberley, and then to their new home at Townsville. As mentioned previously, the Army had gained control of the battlefield helicopter role in 1989, and therefore the Chinooks were delivered to C Squadron of 5 Aviation Regiment.

5 Aviation Regiment was raised at Townsville on 5 November 1987, and was to eventually operate the Sikorsky S-70A-9, after taking over the battlefield mobility role of Nos 9 and 35 Sqns, RAAF. The Sikorsky product is operated by A and B Sqns, with C Sqn flying the gunship-equipped UH-1H and latterly the CH-47D, in the aerial fire support (AFS) and medium-lift/airmobile support roles. From the end of 1998, however, the Iroquois were transferred to 171 Sqn/1 Avn Regt, leaving C Sqn solely equipped with the Chinook.

The new aircraft soon settled down into service and at once began proving their worth, though the fleet of just four airframes was felt to have limitations, particularly if one or more were away from Townsville. As a result, two more, new-build, examples were ordered in June 1998 for delivery in March 2000, in order to provide the ADF with increased capability, but also in the hope of extending the life of the existing fleet.

Apart from some minor modifications required to comply with Australian military certification, Australia's CH-47Ds are identical to their US Army counterparts, as the Army logistical management plan is for the aircraft to remain fully compatible with the US Army fleet. This is readily evidenced by the application of a US serial number on the rear rotor pylons of (at least) the rebuilt aircraft, and the standard US Army olive drab colour scheme. Australian Army helicopters are normally finished in a green/tan/black disruptive camouflage pattern that was developed especially for Australian conditions, but while it is admitted that the American scheme is less effective for local operations, the advantages of operating as part of a larger fleet appears to outweigh the disadvantages. **Nigel Pittaway**

A **C Squadron CH-47D** demonstrates the type's power by lifting the considerable bulk of a Caribou. Throughout its career the Chinook has retrieved thousands of aircraft.

CH-47 Chinook Variants

Central to the use of the Chinook in the Special Forces role is the provision of inflight refuelling. The huge, fixed refuelling probe, seen here under test using a CH-47D, leads into the starboard fuselage fuel tank.

able to carry four bladder-type internal fuel tanks in the cargo compartment, making possible a ferry range of over 1,000 miles (1610 km) when flying at 10,000 ft (3048 m). This meant the Chinook now could routinely self-deploy across the Atlantic. In 1979, as part of Operation Northern Leap, four CH-47Cs flew from Fort Carson, Colorado to Heidelberg Army Air Field, Germany, establishing a new distance record for this type of flight.

The ultimate expression of the Special Forces Chinook is the MH-47E, a purpose-built version for the US Army. Dripping with defensive avionics and low-level night penetration aids, the MH-47E also introduced a 'glass' cockpit, and bulged 'saddle' tanks based on those developed for the Model 234LR Commercial Chinook.

Curiously, the Chinook appears not to have participated in Operation Urgent Fury, the US combined-arms invasion of Grenada in October 1983, and only a handful were on the scene during Operation Just Cause, the fight in Panama in December 1989 and January 1990. In a real-world environment, it is rarely possible to self-deploy a Chinook force, and US Army personnel were frustrated during 1990's Operation Desert Shield when it took nearly 30 days to deliver Chinooks to the war zone, taking into account 'cocooning', sea lift, unloading and rebuilding needs. Still, the CH-47D proved invaluable. In Operation Desert Storm in 1991 – in company with British Chinook HC.Mk 1s, among many other types – CH-47Ds participated in the famous

'left hook' ground manoeuvre that isolated much of Saddam Hussein's army and rolled over the rest. The 101st Airborne Division from Fort Campbell, the 159th Aviation Regiment from Schwabisch Hall, Germany and other units carried equipment and personnel, brought back captured Iraqi prisoners of war, and spearheaded the ground offensive. For a time, the most famous CH-47D pilot in the world was the US Army's Major Marie Rossi, who was featured in a worldwide cable news segment in the final week of the war but who, sadly, was killed in an aircraft mishap only hours after the war ended.

Inflight refuelling to extend the range of the Chinook has always been a possibility but has been pursued only with a few specialised aircraft. Refuelling trials were conducted with one of the first CH-47D models: a six-minute transfer of fuel from an HC-130 Hercules tanker was accomplished on 35 successful hook-ups, but the refuelling feature was not adopted for standard cargo helicopters. The MH-47D and MH-47E special operations variants later appeared with refuelling booms and include air-refuelling as part of their routine tactics.

Foreign Chinooks

Although the Chinook was never quite the biggest or the best – from its inception, it was dwarfed by the giant helicopters manufactured in the Soviet Union and today it faces formidable competition from the three-engined Sikorsky MH-53E Super Sea Stallion – it was such a sensible and pragmatic design that it held

obvious appeal for other armies. The first overseas customer was Australia, which took delivery of 12 CH-47C models. The Italian firm Elicotteri Meridionali (EM), part of the Agusta group which now uses solely the latter name, acquired rights to manufacture the CH-47C in 1968, built them in Frosinone, and sold its first batch of 20 to a then-friendly Iran. Agusta-built CH-47Cs also equip the Italian army.

Under the terms of the licensing arrangement, Agusta was expected to pursue sales of

A CH-47D repositions a 'Hummer' during manoeuvres. This ubiquitous US Army vehicle only just fits inside the Chinook, meaning that it is more regularly carried as an underslung load. It is carried on fore and aft hooks to keep it stable under the helicopter.

the CH-47C model in the Mediterranean and the Middle East, and did supply CH-47Cs to Egypt, Greece, Libya and Morocco. Agusta's total production run of approximately 200 Chinooks is a little-recognised success story.

Below: The CH-47D can carry the M102 105-mm howitzer and its eight-man crew internally. Carrying cargo inside is obviously preferable in order to reduce drag, allowing such loads to be transported over long distances at high speed.

CH-47 Chinook Variants

Long after the Islamic revolution, Iran maintains around 50 CH-47Cs in its army aviation fleet. These were used during the long war with Iraq in the 1980s.

Kawasaki became a builder of Chinooks for the Japanese ground and air arms and still manufactures a few today, the only overseas builder to produce an aircraft comparable to the US Army's CH-47D. Now that 14 international users operate Chinooks, including helicopters more advanced than current or future US Army Chinooks, Boeing says it has 'no interest' in licensing Agusta to build advanced CH-47D, CH-47F, or CH-47SD models. Doing so would put Boeing in the unwanted position of competing with its own product, and the company has no such plans as long as export models continue to roll off the Ridley Township production line – which is, of course, really a remanufacturing line.

Taking advantage of the substantial upgrade of the military Chinook when it was being modified into the CH-47D, Boeing announced in the summer of 1978 that it had completed the market evaluation of a commercial version. The target was the growing North Sea oil business, in which drilling operations were being pushed farther from the mainland. The availability of the Commercial Chinook was instrumental in British Airways Helicopters (BAH) obtaining a seven-year contract from Shell to service its large Brent/Cormorant oil field to the east of the Shetland Islands. In November 1978, BAH ordered three Model 234s at £6 million each, and later increased the contract to six; the type entered service on 1 July 1981.

Since 1981, the Chinook has performed civil duties as the Model 234. This very sound helicopter design was thought to be an ideal aircraft for the resupply of oil rigs and similar short journeys. The military helicopter was changed for this role with the addition of a lengthened nose to accommodate a weather radar unit (now commonplace on non-US military variants as well), the repositioning of the forward wheels, and redesign of the fuselage side fairings enabling some civilian versions to acquire the long-range fuel tanks also associated with the military CH-47SD and MH-47E. The civil Chinook began its life with the glass-fibre rotors found only on military CH-47Cs and onwards. In addition to BAH, those ordering the civil version include Helikopter Service of Norway, Arco Alaska, ERA Helicopters and Columbia Helicopters.

Chinook licence-production has been undertaken by Elicotteri Meridionali (Agusta) in Italy (left) and by Kawasaki Heavy Industries (below) in Japan. The Italians built CH-47Cs, although some aircraft have been subsequently upgraded to D status, whereas Kawasaki built D derivatives from the outset.

A catastrophic crash occurred during an oil rig operation in the mid-1980s when a civil Chinook suffered blade failure and went down with all aboard. Since that time, the Chinook has been better known for other duties, including support of construction operations and logging.

CH-47F – for and against

The CH-47F ICH for the US Army (semi-'glass' cockpit, no radar nose, no long-range fuel tanks) is recognised by both supporters and detractors as the best way to achieve economical operation and longevity in a 'no frills' fashion. No one doubts that the CH-47F will be the best medium-lift helicopter ever offered to American soldiers, but some wish that the real-world consideration of cost (roughly two-thirds the price of the upscale 'Super D') did not have to be taken into account. The ICH programme is expected to extend the service life of about 300 of the current 431 CH-47D Chinooks at a bargain-basement tab of $3.1 billion.

"The problem really lies with the Army and its failure to recognise the importance and relatively low cost of upgrading the Chinooks the right way," says a US Army expert assigned to the factory. "I see the spanking new Chinooks that those other countries are getting and am depressed by the fact that neither today's nor tomorrow's [US] soldiers will ever see anything half as good. There are dozens of improvements over the D model that are not going to be applied to the F. All of those would enhance safety, performance, reliability, and maintenance."

The CH-47F ICH will retain the aluminium honeycomb bonded structures well known throughout the Chinook community as having corrosion and fatigue problems, and which have long since been replaced by composites on international Chinooks. It will, however, represent the most comprehensive 'facelift' of the Chinook in its chequered history, incorporating freshly manufactured sub-assemblies, structural strengthening, a replacement avionics suite, uprated engines, and new electrical wiring and hydraulic tubing. When earlier CH-47D models reach Ridley Township to be reborn as CH-47Fs, Boeing will strip away the entire nose structure forward of the main wheels, known as Section 41, and will simply build a new cockpit housing rather than refurbishing the old one. The first CH-47F, when it flies in July 2001, will be somewhat down the scale from international 'Super Ds' coming off the same line, but it will be a world-class helicopter of which its makers and users can be proud.

American forces are expected eventually to develop a JTR (Joint Transport Rotorcraft) to replace the CH-47F, CH-53D and CH-53E, with the first to be deployed in 2020. JTR is likely to look more like the tilt-rotor V-22 Osprey (albeit with five- or six-bladed rotors) than a conventional helicopter and is expected to be tasked to carry C-130 Hercules-sized cargoes. Rotary-wing (or tilt-rotor) combat and combat support aircraft rarely get top priority in the Pentagon's scheme of things, though, and no serious JTR funding has yet been allocated.

For most international customers, the future of the Chinook rests with the technical improvements associated with the CH-47SD 'Super D', alias the Model 414-100. The situa-

RAF Chinooks

The Royal Air Force has been operating the Boeing Chinook for almost 20 years, during which the helicopter has exceeded all operational expectations and has become the premier workhorse of the Support Helicopter Force. The Chinook's serviceability, lift and multi-mission capabilities continue to match or exceed planned requirements. As new global strategic and tactical missions and operational priorities change, with the emphasis turning to more mobile and flexible force structures, the RAF Chinook's versatility and mission flexibility continues to expand.

The lift capability provided by the RAF Chinook force is more in demand than ever before as the emphasis turns towards supporting out-of-area and rapid deployment forces such as the UK's newly created 16 Air Assault Brigade, along with peacekeeping, humanitarian missions, combat search and rescue and Advance/Special Forces support. Many of these missions are only capable of being undertaken by the Chinook. The RAF is the second-largest Chinook operator in the world and has a fleet of 48 aircraft in three variants, the Chinook HC.Mk 2 (31), HC.Mk 2A (nine) and HC.Mk 3 (eight). The acquisition took many years and suffered a number of setbacks as the project became the victim of adverse political and industrial lobbying and short-sighted defence spending cuts.

History

The RAF had been operating the tandem-rotored Bristol Belvedere HC.Mk 1 in the 1960s as its medium-lift tactical transport helicopter, with limited success. The Boeing Vertol Chinook was seen as an ideal replacement and the RAF lobbied hard for the new helicopter. In March 1967, the British Ministry of Defence placed an order for 15 Boeing Vertol CH-47B Chinooks but this order was cancelled in November 1967 as part of a defence spending cut. The Belvedere retired from service in 1969 (it had an airframe life of only 1,600 hours), leaving the RAF with no medium-lift helicopter; in 1971 the original order was re-placed with Boeing, only to be cancelled, yet again, by politically-motivated defence spending cuts. The RAF continued to look toward the Chinook as its ideal medium-lift tactical transport helicopter, and in 1978 the Ministry of Defence finally placed an order with Boeing for 33 new-build Chinook HC.Mk 1s (ZA670- ZA684/ZA704-ZA721).

These Chinooks were designated by the RAF as HC.Mk 1s and by Boeing as Model BV 414-352. They were similar to the US Army's new CH-47C variant but were additionally equipped with many of the new features due to be included in the latest modernised and updated CH-47D variant being offered to the US Army. The first RAF Chinook HC.Mk 1 flew on 23 March 1980, fitted with Lycoming T55-L-11E turbines and metal rotor blades. They were later updated (1986/87) with more powerful Lycoming T55-L-712 turboshaft engines and wider-chord composite rotor blades.

The first RAF Chinook arrived in the UK on 31 October 1980 and began trials at A&AEE Boscombe Down that November. The first Chinook arrived at RAF Odiham, Hampshire, the new home of the RAF Chinook, on 2 December 1980 to begin pilot conversion training with No. 240 Operational Conversion Unit (OCU). No. 18 Squadron (red Pegasus badge), the first RAF Chinook squadron, reformed at RAF Odiham on 4 August 1981 and began operational tasking in support of the British Army. No. 18 Squadron had operated the Wessex HC.Mk 2 until December 1980 and the squadron was used extensively in trials during 1978-1980 to evaluate battlefield tactics and procedures for proposed UK airmobile operations. The squadron worked closely with 5 Field Force in Germany to develop airmobile tactical doctrines which would later benefit the squadron when it converted to the Chinook and returned to Germany to undertake further airmobile trials with 6 Brigade's experimental airmobile force evaluations.

RAF Chinooks operated in two roles during Desert Storm: regular army support and Special Forces duties. For the latter, several aircraft received hastily applied 'experimental night camouflage', SATCOMs and door guns. This aircraft, ZA720, is believed to be the one that was damaged by an unexploded JP233 minelet.

RAF Chinooks have been used during several humanitarian aid programmes. Here an HC.Mk 1 sets down a Land Rover during Operation Provide Comfort in northern Iraq.

Falklands conflict

The lift capability of the new RAF helicopter was immediately put to use at the outbreak of the Falklands War, on 2 April 1982, for which they were equipped with a modified gun-mounting system to allow the fitting of the standard British Army 7.62-mm GPMG along with ex-Vulcan bomber Marconi ARI 18228 radar warning receivers (RWR). Five No. 18 Squadron Chinooks (ZA670/ZA679/ZA706/ZA715/ZA716) deployed to RNAS Culdrose in Cornwall and began providing logistical support, moving men and material around the UK's south coast as the British Task Force fleet of ships prepared to sail south. On 25 April 1982 five Chinooks (ZA706/ZA707/ZA716/ZA718/ZA719) embarked on the ill-fated MV *Atlantic Conveyor* bound for the Falkland Islands. ZA707/BP was disembarked at Wide Awake Island to assist in the vertical replenishment of the Task Force and ZA718/*Bravo November* had been flown off the *Atlantic Conveyor* to undertake a task when the ship was hit by an Exocet missile (with the eventual loss of three Chinooks).

ZA718/*Bravo November*'s exploits during the conflict and the aircraft's serviceability with only limited engineering support (comprising few saved spares and 17 maintenance engineers) and eight aircrew is now legendary. *Bravo November* operated from the San Carlos area on East Falkland and flew many missions moving troops, guns and supplies. On 30 May, returning from a night mission to move three 105-mm guns forward to Mount Kent, the Chinook hit the water and was almost lost. On another mission the aircraft flew 81 fully-equipped troops from 2 Para towards Port Stanley, then carried 75 paras, as well as moving tons of ammunition and supplies plus recovering several downed Wessex helicopters. Between 27 May and 14 June 1982, *Bravo November* flew over 110 hours, carried 2,150 troops and over 550 tons of stores and equipment.

After the Falklands

During September 1982, No. 7 Squadron reformed at RAF Odiham to become the UK Chinook Squadron, allowing No. 18 Squadron to return to RAF Gütersloh in Germany in August 1983 to continue providing support to the British Army of the Rhine (BAOR). In 1983 an order for eight Chinook HC.Mk 1s was placed with Boeing Vertol as attrition replacements for the three lost in the Falklands Conflict. These aircraft (ZD574-ZD576/ZD980-ZD984) were equipped with the new uprated Lycoming T55-L-712 turboshafts and full night

In Germany No. 18 Squadron regularly practised dispersed operations. Here three HC.Mk 1s are seen during operations from a farm, with the ops centre established in one of the buildings behind.

vision goggle (NVG) compatible cockpit lighting; they had been delivered by March 1986.

In 1985, both Nos 7 and 18 Squadrons deployed four Chinooks to Akrotiri in Cyprus for four months to assist in the evacuation of British nationals and United Nations peacekeeping troops operating in Beirut, Lebanon. RAF Chinooks also helped in the recovery of bodies in the aftermath of the Indian Boeing 747 which crashed off the west coast of Ireland. The aircraft continued to spend many hours undertaking trials and exercises evaluating the UK's proposed Airmobile Brigade as well as supporting the UK's newly formed 5 Airborne Brigade (an out-of-area intervention force), fulfilling other NATO commitments and undertaking permanent detachments in Northern Ireland and with No. 1310 Flight in the Falkland Islands. On 22 May 1986 the Chinooks of No. 1310 Flight became part of No. 78 Squadron based at RAF Mount Pleasant in the Falklands, comprising a Chinook and Sea King flight. Crews were taken from 7 and 18 Squadrons.

Airmobile

The main role for the Chinook force in the mid-1980s was to reinforce and support the BAOR, 1 British Corps in northern Germany as it attempted to block a potential Soviet advance. No. 7 Squadron Chinooks would reinforce those of 18 Squadron in Germany and the Chinook force would deploy to field flying sites or forward operating bases in farm buildings, woods or (more favoured) town centre supermarket sites which afforded large car parks and buildings. Missions would

The advent of the CH-47D created an export renaissance, and many foreign operators now fly aircraft that are significantly more capable than the standard US Army model. Depicted here are CH-47D/Model 414s of the Netherlands (left) and Thailand (below). Singapore is the first customer for the latest CH-47SD 'Super D' model, while Taiwan flies three of the Model 234MLR version, essentially a civilian cover designation for the military variant.

Above: Seen in Albania while operating in support of Kosovan refugees in May 1999, this Greek air force Chinook has the bulged 'saddle' tanks initially found on the MH-47E. The Greeks took delivery of Agusta-built CH-47Cs, but subsequently brought them to CH-47D standard, the upgrade accompanied by a change from bright three-tone camouflage to US Army-standard drab.

Below: This Spanish army CH-47D is about to demonstrate its triple-hook capability by picking up three light guns. Spain has operated three main Chinook versions: standard CH-47C, Model 414 (a C with some D upgrades) and CH-47D. To further complicate matters, the 414s have been upgraded with nose radar.

tion has become something of a nightmare for the observer who seeks to distinguish one mark from another by the appearance of bumps, bulges, nose shape or antennas. Both in the US Army and abroad, some aircraft now have the longer nose associated with a weather radar unit that is not always installed (MH-47D, MH-47E), while some do not. In the service of the US and several other countries, some Chinooks have the larger, longer-range fuel tanks (MH-47E), while some do not; some aircraft of a particular variant have a 'glass' cockpit (Dutch CH-47Ds), while some do not. These differences – from a larger perspective, all rather minor in an aircraft that has changed little externally over the years – are frequently not unique to a particular variant or model. The variants entries which follow represent an attempt to pin down these external differences – as well as differences in performance not visible to the eye – in a rational format that can serve as a quick reference.

Robert F. Dorr, with contributions from Patrick Allen, Yoshitomo Aoki, and Nigel Pittaway

include providing logistic support in bringing up ammunition and supplies, as well as flying forward anti-tank-equipped infantry, air defence and blocking forces. Other missions included bar mine-laying and casualty evacuation.

The result of the four-year airmobile validation process undertaken by No. 18 Squadron and 6 Brigade in Germany confirmed the concept of a highly mobile force, strong in anti-tank weaponry, which could be moved by helicopter at short notice to respond to massed enemy movement. This resulted in the formation of the UK's 24 Airmobile Brigade on 1 April 1988, with RAF Chinooks and Pumas providing the brigade's tactical and logistical lift capability, first moving forward anti-tank-equipped airmobile troops and then providing the logistics support. The Airmobile Brigade and its helicopters was to support the Allied Rapid Reaction Corps (ARRC) as well as I British Corp. As missions turned away from blocking a Soviet advance in Germany, airmobile tactics adapted to new Rapid Reaction Force missions, with operational theatres ranging from the arctic to the desert. The Chinook happily adapted to the ever-changing scenarios which included peacekeeping, humanitarian and support of more specialised troops.

Gulf War

The first three RAF Chinooks to deploy on Operation Granby belonged to No. 7 Squadron and were flown out of the UK by USAF C-5 Galaxy transport aircraft from RAF Mildenhall on 24/25 November 1990. They arrived in RAS Al Ghar, Saudi Arabia before moving to Al Jubayl to begin training for desert operations, and were later joined by four more Chinooks airlifted in January 1991. The first three helicopters were the advance element of six (ZA671/EO, ZA677/EU, ZA707/EV, ZA708/EK, ZA712/ER, ZA713/EN) belonging to the RAF Chinook Special Forces Flight. At least one other SF aircraft, ZA720/EP, also served on Granby. They were joined by eight Chinooks from Nos 7 and 18 Squadrons and from No. 240 Operational Conversion Unit which departed Southampton Docks on 23 December 1990, arriving in Saudi Arabia on 8 January 1991. Eight RAF Chinooks formed part of the Support Helicopter Force (Middle East) working with Royal Navy Commando Sea Kings and RAF Pumas.

The first priority for the Chinook Special Forces crews was to perfect their low-level desert night-flying capabilities, using NVGs, as they had to be able to operate below 50 ft (15 m) on even the darkest nights. They also needed to get acquainted with their newly-acquired GPS navigation systems (RNS-252 Super TANS), Sky Guardian RWR, missile approach warners (MAW), new chaff and flare dispensers, ALQ-157 IR Jammers, satellite communications, improved IFF and secure speech radios. Other additions to the Special Forces Chinooks were 7.62-mm M134 Miniguns and MD60s, plus recently acquired 800-Imp gal (3637-litre) Robertson extended range tanks. All RAF Chinooks deployed to the Gulf were equipped with GPS system (Trimble) and Centrisep Engine Air Particle Separators (EAPS).

They were painted in an all-over desert pink camouflage, first used on Special Air Service desert Landrovers known as 'Pinkies'. When mixed with a detergent this paint is easily removed, hence it is known as an Alkali Removable Temporary Finish (ARTF). After several NVG training missions by the SF Flight, it was found that the pink paint glowed under IR lighting conditions; the flight commander decided to copy a paint scheme adopted by German night-fighters during World War II and had the new pink colour overpainted with black in a speckled pattern. This not only improved the Chinooks' camouflage at night, but proved highly effective in daylight.

By mid-January the Special Forces Flight had moved to the United Arab Emirates to support Special Forces training missions near Al Minhad. The Chinooks of the SHF (Middle East) moved to a main operating base at King Khalid Military City, located in the desert north of Riyadh, and prepared for their support of the 1st (British) Armoured Division. Main missions would be casualty evacuation and logistics support involving bringing forward fuel and ammunition for the Armoured Brigade. By mid-February the RAF Chinooks were assisting in the secret move by coalition forces out to

the west for their outflanking manoeuvre, which was launched on 24 February. During the land phase of the war RAF Chinook missions provided the logistical resupply of the rapidly advancing armoured units as well as flying POWs to the rear. During the brief land war the Chinooks moved over 3,000 prisoners, often 80 at a time. In the first seven weeks of operations, RAF Chinooks from the SHF (Middle East) flew over 1,000 hours and moved over 2.5 million lb (1 million kg) of material, over 84 per cent of the total carried by all the UK helicopters in-theatre.

The RAF Chinook Special Forces Flight undertook its first mission into Iraq on the night of 17 January 1991 when a Chinook flew into Baghdad, deploying troops to destroy Iraqi communications systems around the capital. The first SAS Bravo Patrol was deployed on the night of 20 January, followed by several more Bravo Patrol deployments as SAS troops were sent out to keep watch on the Iraqi main supply route between Baghdad and Jordan. They also undertook several diversionary raids and destroyed communications systems between Baghdad and Basra and throughout the western desert region, as they attempted to draw the Iraqis into thinking the main push by the coalition force would be in the east. Numerous other missions were flown by the SF Chinooks in support of Special Forces as they inserted, resupplied and extracted patrols. Once attention turned to destroying the Iraqi 'Scud' missile threat, Chinooks began to support the larger fighting patrols being deployed to find and destroy these weapons and by mid-February large numbers of British and American Special Forces were

operating in the desert. The last mission to involve the Special Forces Flight was Operation Trebor on 27 February, when SBS troopers were fast-roped onto the roof of the British embassy in Kuwait; the British Ambassador was later flown by SF Chinook back to his embassy.

During the conflict, no RAF Chinooks were lost and only one received (repairable) damage when it disturbed an unexploded JP233 bomblet with its downwash while landing at an Iraqi military airfield.

Kurdish humanitarian missions

In early April 1991, almost immediately after the Gulf War, a huge coalition effort was launched to provide humanitarian assistance to the thousands of Kurdish refugees who had fled to the mountainous region between Iraq and Turkey to escape Saddam Hussein. The region was inhospitable and the poor weather conditions that spring meant the Kurdish refugees began to suffer, and the only way to deliver urgently needed humanitarian and medical aid was by dropping it from C-130 Hercules. Preparations were made for the deployment of a huge Allied helicopter force, together with troops, their mission being first to assist the refugees and help prevent further deaths, and then to establish a 'safe haven' within northern Iraq for the returning Kurds. These missions went by the names Operation Provide Comfort and Operation Haven.

The first four RAF Chinooks arrived at Diyarbakir in eastern Turkey on 9 April 1991, having self-deployed from their home base at RAF Odiham. Another five Chinooks arrived in Turkey a few days later, having

Above: Since December 1995 RAF Chinooks have flown from Divulje Barracks in Croatia on IFOR/SFOR duties. Operations over Bosnia required an upgrading of the aircraft's defences.

Two Chinook HC.Mk 2s are flown by 'A' Flight of No. 78 Squadron from Mount Pleasant in the Falklands. Among the assigned tasks is firefighting, using the Sims Rainmaker bucket.

been diverted from their return to the UK from Saudi Arabia aboard the ship MV *Baltic Eagle*. The nine RAF Chinooks and their crews and engineers came from No. 240 OCU and Nos 7 and 18 Squadrons, with additional support from the Joint Helicopter Support Unit (JHSU) and the Tactical Support Wing (TSW). The Chinooks arriving from the UK and Germany retained their normal camouflage scheme, with the addition of a Union Jack on the aft pylons, while the Chinooks which had been diverted from their return from the Gulf still wore their desert paint schemes.

As one of the first helicopter units to arrive in-theatre, the RAF began flying missions on 14 April 1991, operating from Diyarbakir but forward deploying to Silopi on the Turkey/Iraq border where, within a few weeks, the entire coalition helicopter force was based. Using their internal 800-Imp gal (3637-litre) extended range tanks, the RAF Chinooks were able to operate in the more remote regions in the east of Iraq, as far as Hakkari and Yukesova close to the Iranian border, delivering urgently needed supplies.

During the early days before the UNHC became established, RAF Chinooks delivered bread, food, clothes and medical supplies provided by the local Turkish population. With no ground troops to receive

the Chinooks as they arrived at the mountain refugee camps, there were several occasions when refugees were in severe danger of being struck by the forward rotor blades as they rushed the helicopters. Eventually, pilots resorted to hovering over the crowds and having the supplies thrown off the rear ramp to reduce the risk of killing people. As more Allied troops arrived and the UNHCR logistic chain became established, US Army Special Forces and Royal Marine M&AW cadre troops were deployed to the mountain camp sites to help organise the helicopter landing sites and to distribute food.

Once the Silopi UNHCR food distribution centre became established, the Chinooks began to maximise their enormous lift capability by flying triple and double netted loads of UNHCR supplies from Silopi, high into the mountain camps at heights that often reached 8,000 ft (2438 m). In a single day, they could move over 130 tons of cargo and undertook 93-mile (150-km) transits from Silopi into the high mountains, even in the late spring when 'hot and high' conditions affected the performance of other helicopters. Between 14 April and 4 May, RAF Chinooks flew over 380 sorties and completed 737 flight hours, moving over 1,300 tons of UNHCR supplies and over 1,400 troops.

By June 1991 the Kurds had been moved off the mountains and the 'safe haven' had been established, and the RAF Chinooks left the region as responsibility was transferred to the United Nations.

Return to normal operations

After the Gulf War and Operation Provide Comfort, the RAF Chinook force returned to its normal operations supporting the British Army, mainly undertaking 24 Airmobile Brigade exercises as the fleet began preparations for the $250 million RAF Chinook Mid-Life-Update programme, signed in November 1990. This update would bring the entire fleet of 32 RAF Chinook HC.Mk 1s to HC.Mk 2 standard, similar to the CH-47D.

The programme had a through-put rate which would allow the RAF to maintain an adequate operational capability, and first HC.Mk 1(ZA718/BN) returned to the US in late 1991. It arrived back in the UK on 20 May 1993 and was sent to the Defence Evaluation and Research Agency (DERA) at Boscombe Down to undertake Initial Military Aircraft Release (IMAR) trials. The second Chinook HC.Mk 2 (ZA681) returned to RAF Odiham on 10 September 1993 to operate with No. 27 Squadron, the newly commissioned RAF Chinook training squadron which was reformed at Odiham on 1 October 1993, replacing No. 240 OCU. RAF Chinooks returned from Boeing Helicopters at the rate of one a month until the programme was completed in mid-1995. On 1 September 1995 the UK Ministry of

Defence completed contract negotiations with Boeing for the procurement of another 17 Chinooks. This would include three attrition replacement Chinook HC.Mk 2s (ZH775-ZH777), six new-build HC.Mk 2As (ZH819-ZH896) and eight Special Operations Force Chinook HC.Mk 3s (ZH879-ZH904).

Bosnia

On 8 August 1995 six RAF Chinook HC.Mk 2s, painted with United Nations markings, deployed from their Odiham base to Ploce in Croatia in support of the UK's 24 Airmobile Brigade. They were part of a UN protection and rapid reaction force to protect UNHCR missions in the former Yugoslavia, tasked with assisting in any withdrawal of UNHCR/UNPROFOR personnel should the situation become untenable. The Chinooks self-deployed to Ploce and held regular training exercises, by day and night, as the airmobile troops undertook their theatre work-up training. In the event, this force was never used and the airmobile troops returned to the UK in October, although the Chinooks were ordered to remain in-theatre, ready to support a new NATO Peace Implementation Force.

For these missions the helicopters were equipped with 550 lb (250 kg) of armour plating on the floor to protect the cockpit and forward crew/gunners positions, and featured improved aircraft survivability equipment that included upgraded GEC-Marconi Sky Guardian 2 RWR, relocated AN/ALE-40 chaff and flare dispensers, AN/ALQ-157 IR jammers, Mode-4 IFF, SATCOM and secure speech radios, and later the ADS Inmarsat satellite-based CAPSAT flight following system. Some were also equipped with the covert personnel locator system homer, AN/ARS-6 to provide covert homing, and the two-way voice communications with a hand-held PRC-90 or PRC-112 radio first fitted to the Special Forces Chinooks during the Gulf War. They were also armed with the M134 Minigun.

During the Ploce detachment, two No. 7 Squadron RAF Chinooks were painted in all-white UN colours in preparation for undertaking UN humanitarian missions in the Krajina region. In mid-August both Chinooks deployed from Ploce to Zagreb to fly humanitarian missions to Banja-Luka airport to deliver tents and clothing and UNHCR supplies to the large numbers of Serbian refugees trapped in the region as Croatian forces advanced through Krajina. The detachment lasted some three weeks, with the first mission flown from Zagreb to Banja-Luka on 16 August before the Chinooks were ordered to deliver their supplies to the border town of Bosanski Gradiski. This mission lasted three weeks, the Chinooks flying around three missions per day.

IFOR/SFOR

On 20 December 1995 the NATO-led Multi-National Implementation Force (IFOR) took over from the United Nations under Operation Resolute, its mission being to implement the Dayton peace agreement, by force if

need be, throughout the former Yugoslavia. Six RAF Chinooks from No. 7 and No. 18 Squadrons deployed to Divulje Barracks, near Split, Croatia to support missions within the UK's Multi-National Division (MND) South West sector. The Chinooks yet again proved their outstanding capabilities by being the only helicopters during that winter with the range, versatility and lift capability to operate in the difficult mountainous region, which required long-distance transits. Missions included resupplying patrol bases, moving troops and providing routine logistics support. RAF Chinooks were also used to provide forward refuelling for Army Lynx helicopters, and regularly operated from Royal Navy ships in the Adriatic, moving international troops ashore and undertaking maritime logistic resupply missions. They still operate in the region as part of the new SFOR under the designation No. 1310 Flight Chinook Detachment (Operation Palatine).

In March 1997 two HC.Mk 2s deployed from their Split base to Gioia del Colle air base in southern Italy, from where they flew British troops into Tirana, Albania to reinforce and then evacuate the British embassy, undertaking a classic 'intervention and protection of British nationals' role. An RAF C-130 Hercules acted as an airborne command and control platform while Commando Sea Kings provided CSAR cover. RAF Chinooks were placed on standby in 1998 during the Kosovo crisis.

Current operations

Over the past few years RAF Chinooks have continued to expand their operational missions and areas of operations, making regular deployments to Norway in winter for arctic flying training, to the deserts of Jordan and Oman to practise desert and hot weather operations, and to Malaysia to perfect jungle operations. They also regularly practise their maritime capabilities, operating from the Royal Navy's aircraft-carriers. The RAF Chinook force continues to expand its operational capabilities and is preparing to support the UK's newly formed Joint Rapid Reaction Force (JRRF) and the recently created 16 Air Assault Brigade; the latter will be equipped with the new Boeing WAH-64D Longbow Apache and takes over from the UK's former 5 Airborne and 24 Airmobile Brigades.

In the past two years the RAF Chinook force has seen further changes as the Support Helicopter Force (SHF) reorganises for the next century. In 1997 Pumas moved from RAF Odiham to RAF Benson as No. 18

Squadron returned to Odiham from RAF Laarbruch as an all-Chinook squadron. Odiham is now the home of the RAF Chinook force following the creation of a Chinook wing.

Both No. 18 and No. 27 Squadrons had previously operated a Puma Flight, which have now been replaced with Chinooks. Odiham is now home to three Chinook squadrons – Nos 7, 18 and 27 Squadrons – providing four operational Chinook flights. No. 27 Squadron continues to operate its 'B Flight' as a Chinook Operational Conversion Unit, responsible for training RAF Chinook pilots, navigators and crewmen.

With four operational Chinook flights now available, the Chinook force has been able to restructure its training, tasking and operational commitments to provide a more effective service and a more stable working environment for the squadrons. The new system is known as 'Fighting by Flights' and provides a much better distribution and sharing of an increasingly busy workload. Permanent detachments are still provided in Bosnia (No. 1310 Flight – Operation Palatine), Falkland Islands (No. 78 Sqn) and Northern Ireland, in addition to the day-to-day commitments within the UK, NATO and out-of-area operations in support of the British Army. The new Fighting by Flights system gives each flight six-week roulement periods split into three main phases: work-up training/UK

standby (national disasters/long-range SAR, etc.); a UK tasking phase; a final six-week detachment to Bosnia, the Falkland Islands or Northern Ireland.

The eight new Chinook HC.Mk 3s are due for delivery in 2000 and are based around the Boeing Helicopter International CH-47E variant, an outgrowth of the US Army's Special Operations MH-47E featuring additional long-range fuel tanks, full 'glass' cockpit and digital databus with avionics cockpit and mission management and control systems, nose-mounted FLIR, terrain-avoidance radar, aerial refuelling, provision for fast-roping and internal cargo handling systems.

Future improvements to the RAF Chinook HC.Mk 2 fleet include the fitting of a new Smiths Industries health and usage monitoring system and a fully integrated defensive aids suite. Other modifications (subject to funding) may include a new 'glass' cockpit and a digital databus, to ready the entire RAF Chinook fleet for the new digital battlefields on the 21st century. The RAF Chinook force is now considered an essential element to almost any future UK military, peacekeeping or humanitarian operations as well as being responsible for a host of other missions such as special forces and combat search and rescue. The Chinook has exceeded all operational expectations and continues to provide the RAF with one of the most effective tactical support helicopters in operation today.　**Patrick Allen**

In the assault role, the quickest method of delivering troops is by fast-roping, demonstrated here by a No. 18 Squadron aircraft. In this procedure, the Chinook comes to a low hover, the troops disembarking by abseiling down ropes. As soon as the troops are on the ground the Chinook can retreat, the operation having taken only seconds. Up to five ropes can be used, three from the open rear ramp, one through the centre cargo hatch and one from the forward door. An alternative approach used in open spaces is a rolling assault landing. The HC.Mk 2s do not have the parachute static lines previously fitted to HC.Mk 1s.

CH-47 Chinook Variants

YHC-1B (YCH-47A)

YHC-1B was the initial military designation for the Vertol Model 114 helicopter, eventually named the Chinook. The designation is part of a unique system employed by the United States Army prior to 1 October 1962. The Army ordered an initial batch of five YCH-1B helicopters (59-4982/4986) in June 1959 and work on the YCH-1B was well under way in March 1960 when Vertol Aircraft Corp. of Morton, Pa., became a division of Boeing.

That year, the company began a protracted move from Morton to its current location in Ridley Township, Delaware County, Pennsylvania. Boeing subsequently operated a flight test facility at Wilmington, Delaware, so the names of Morton, Ridley and Wilmington recur throughout the Chinook story.

Powerplant of the YCH-1B was two 1,940-shp (1447-kW) Avco Lycoming T55-L-5 turboshaft engines driving three-bladed rotors. As with all Chinooks to follow, the twin engines drove twin rotors in tandem configuration. Apart from establishing a highly successful configuration, this was also the beginning of a remarkable story of success and growth by the durable T55 engine paired with the aircraft since its inception, though its manufacturer has changed names over the years from Avco Lycoming to Textron Lycoming to Garrett (a division of AlliedSignal).

The manufacturer of the Chinook (known at different times as Piasecki, Vertol, Boeing Vertol and Boeing) had more experience than any other builder with the tandem-rotor configuration favoured by aviation pioneer Frank Piasecki and employed on earlier helicopters like the XH-16, HUP (H-25) and H-21. The Chinook's counter-rotating blades cancel out the torque created by each set of blades, whereas torque created by single-rotor helicopters must be counteracted by a tail (anti-torque) rotor which does not contribute to the helicopter's overall performance. Tandem rotors also improve

hovering precision and permit take-offs and landings regardless of wind direction. The Chinook's tandem-rotor arrangement also gives the broadest centre of gravity of any helicopter, allowing greater flexibility for managing internal and external loads.

Like so many important aircraft, the future Chinook helicopter first took shape in the form of a mock-up of the YHC-1B illustrating the planned maximum gross weight of 33,000 lb (14968 kg), a figure which was to increase with each new model until it was nearly doubled in the eventual CH-47D variant. Built at Boeing's former location in Morton, the mock-up was painted in Army olive drab and looked little different from production Chinooks of four decades later.

Early publicity linked to the mock-up stressed the new helicopter's rear loading ramp, its tri-service applicability (Air Force, Army, Marine Corps), and its ease of maintenance.

The first YHC-1B (59-4982) was rolled out on 28 April 1961 and was bailed to Vertol. During a pre-flight engine run-up, it suffered extensive damage to its drive train, rotor blades, fuselage, and lubrication system. Scheduled to become the first YHC-1B to fly, ship no. 1 had to be relegated instead to structural evaluation duties as a GTA (ground test article). After being delayed for several months, the maiden flight of a YCH-1B, launching the incredibly successful Chinook series, was made by ship no. 2 (59-4983) on 21 September 1961 at the Pennsylvania plant with Vertol test pilot Leonard La Vassar at the controls.

The five YCH-1B service-test helicopters were redesignated YCH-47A on 1 October 1962. One aircraft in this quintet (59-4984) later served as a flying testbed for the CH-47B model.

YCH-1B serial numbers: 59-4982/4986 (c/n B-001/005)
Total built: 5

An early flight of the first prototype shows the diminutive twin-rear wheel arrangement initially used. The second prototype is seen below after conversion to CH-47B standard.

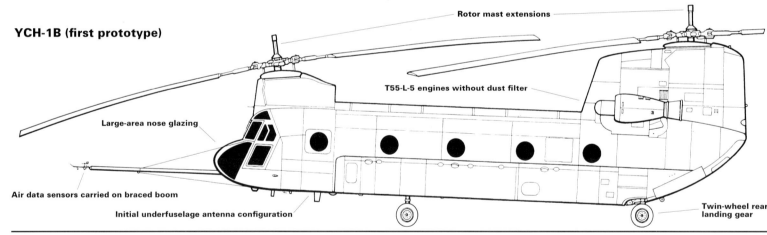

YCH-1B (first prototype)

Rotor mast extensions

T55-L-5 engines without dust filter

Large-area nose glazing

Air data sensors carried on braced boom

Initial underfuselage antenna configuration

Twin-wheel rear landing gear

CH-47A

The CH-47A was the first production Chinook, and the first designation for the helicopter following an overhaul of the US military designation system on 1 October 1962. In addition to the first five helicopters (which had been initially dubbed YHC-1B and from which a 'Y' prefix, meaning 'service test', was eventually dropped) the series included 350 aircraft manufactured in Philadelphia in the early 1960s.

Powerplant of the CH-47A was a pair of Textron Lycoming T55-L-5 turboshaft engines based on those in the earlier helicopters. From FY 1963, slightly more powerful T55-L-7 models enhanced the helicopter's capability. CH-47A helicopters were initially built with just one cargo hook for the carriage of underslung loads, but many were retrofitted with the current standard of three hooks. The Chinook has always had a sealed fuselage, and the CH-47A demonstrated this capability to land on water early in its flight test phase.

The CH-47A was meant for a crew of

three, consisting of pilot, co-pilot, and crew chief. Internal cabin space was sufficient to carry up to 33 combat equipped troops, although early company literature spoke optimistically of carrying 44, 50 or 59 in various high-density internal configurations. Alternatively, the CH-47A was designed to carry 24 litter patients plus two medical attendants. The cabin was 30 ft 2 in (9.19 m) in length with an unobstructed cross-section of 6 ft 6 in (1.98 m) and height of 7 ft 6 in (2.29 m).

Before entering service, the A model Chinook went through a series of tests

beginning in 1961. Extreme temperature evaluation from -65°F to 125°F (-54°C to 52°C) took place in the Eglin AFB, Fla. climatic test facility. In addition, high-altitude tests were performed at Fort Carson, Colo., arctic tests at Fort Greely, Alaska, and operational evaluation at Fort Benning, Georgia.

The first production CH-47A entered Army service on 16 August 1962. The 11th Air Assault Division at Fort Benning, Ga., incorporating revolutionary airmobile concepts pioneered by General Hamilton Howze, was the forerunner of the First

Cavalry Division (Airmobile) which took the CH-47A into combat in Vietnam in 1965. Initially delivered in gloss olive drab with international orange panels and stencilling and other high-visibility markings, and with open air intakes for its turbine powerplants, the CH-47A in Vietnam acquired low-visibility drab paint and protective dust/debris air filter screens to cope with the persistent and corrosive dust of Southeast Asia. After being introduced into service, the A model also acquired an air-to-ground towing kit which allowed the helicopter to tow large ground equipment, and a rear landing gear 'kneeling' kit which reduced the Chinook's overall height by 1 ft 6 in (46 cm) to permit storage on the hangar deck of 'Thetis Bay'-class aircraft-carriers.

While Chinooks went to war in Vietnam, on the home front one task allotted to a CH-47A was the transport of the bulky LEM

Boldly emblazoned with the Air Force Flight Test Center badge, the first production CH-47A is seen during a test flight from Edwards AFB. The aircraft initially flew with twin wheels.

A CH-47A is seen (above) in early 1960s' US Army colours. These soon gave way to the muted scheme displayed by this Army Reserve aircraft (right), which has the original small engine filters fitted.

(Lunar Excursion Module) for the Apollo programme from Tulsa, Okla., where it was built, to Cape Kennedy, Fla.; it took 15 hours of flight time to cover the 940 miles (1513 km). This was not easy for the A model as it had only a single lift hook and therefore no way to effectively stabilise a troublesome load. Subsequently, the transport of other LEM adapters, as well as the carriage of a multitude of outsized cargoes, became a standard duty for the Chinook.

In January 1964 the CH-47A (and 18 other helicopters) responded to a flood emergency in California – the single Chinook transported a total of 276,335 lb (125346 kg), 43.4 per cent of all helicopter-carried loads. In February 1965, the CH-47A demonstrated its ferry capability with a non-stop flight of 1,002 nm (1856 km) from Fort Rucker, Alabama to Shreveport, Louisiana and back in eight hours 59 minutes, at a take-off weight of 35,217 lb (15974 kg). At the end of the flight, 1,267 lb (575 kg) of fuel remained in the tanks, indicating that the helicopter could have made a flight across the Atlantic with stops in Greenland and Iceland had it been necessary to support US troops in Europe.

As the US build-up in Vietnam progressed in 1966, CH-47As became more numerous and gained a reputation for being dependable, adaptable to adverse weather conditions, and able to haul respectable loads to the battlefield, often under fire, and survive. For combat operations, crews often removed the rear cabin windows to create gun ports for onboard troops. CH-47As in Vietnam routinely carried a pintle-mounted

7.62-mm M60D machine-gun in the port side escape hatch opening and a second such gun on a swing-out mounting in the forward starboard crew door. This armament sub-system was embraced by the term XM24 and contained mechanical stops to prevent the gunners from inadvertently firing into the rotors or fuselage. The M60Ds were equipped with bipods and were capable of being detached and hand-held in case the Chinook went down and the crew needed firepower.

Four helicopters in the CH-47A series were modified to become ACH-47A

gunships (separate entry). One CH-47A (65-7992) was extensively rebuilt to become the sole Model 347 technology demonstrator (separate entry). Another CH-47A (60-3449), the second ship in the series, was redesignated JCH-47A when employed for temporary flight tests.

CH-47A serial numbers: 60-3448/3452 (c/n B-007/011); 61-2408/2425 (c/n B-012/029); 62-2114/2137 (c/n B-030/053); 63-7900/7923 (c/n B-054/077); 64-13106/13165 (c/n B-078/137); 65-7966/8025 (c/n B-138/197); 66-0066/0125 (c/n B-198/257); 66-19000/19097 (c/n B-258/355)
Total built: 350 (not including five prototypes)

CH-47A

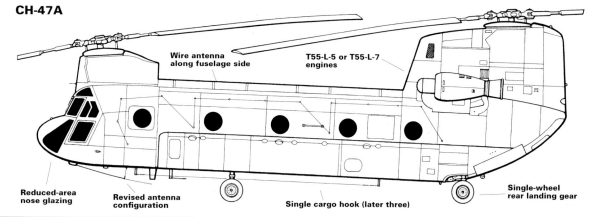

Wire antenna along fuselage side

T55-L-5 or T55-L-7 engines

Reduced-area nose glazing

Revised antenna configuration

Single cargo hook (later three)

Single-wheel rear landing gear

South Vietnam received 20 CH-47As in late 1972 under the Enhance Plus programme. They served with the 237th Helicopter Squadron.

Thailand acquired four CH-47As in 1972. Two of the survivors (and an ex-US Army CH-47B) were later upgraded to CH-47C standard and still serve.

ACH-47A

The ACH-47A, initially known simply as the 'Armed CH-47A', was the battlefield gunship version of the Chinook, powered by the same duo of Textron Lycoming T55-L-5 turboshaft engines. Boeing modified four helicopters in 1965 for operational evaluation in Vietnam. In the ACH-47A, engineers deleted all cargo-handling equipment, soundproofing, and all but five troop seats, then added 2,000 lb (907 kg) of

The first of the four ACH-47A 'Go-Go Birds' is seen during tests at Eglin. It carries a Minigun pod on its starboard pylon. In addition to its fixed, forward-firing armament the ACH-47A mounted 0.50-in (12.7-mm) machine-guns in four window positions, plus the option of a fifth on the rear ramp. The result was a very powerfully armed 'flying battleship', able to suppress fire from all directions.

CH-47 Chinook Variants

armour plating and weapons pylons on each side of the aircraft outboard of the front wheels, plus a nose gun installation.

Nicknamed 'Guns A Go-Go', the ACH-47A carried two 20-mm fixed forward-firing, pylon-mounted cannons, up to five 0.50-in (12.7-mm) machine-guns with 4,000 rounds (two on each side of the aircraft plus one firing down from the ramp), and two pylon-mounted XM128 19-round pods of 2.75-in rockets, plus a single chin-mounted M5 40-mm automatic grenade launcher weighing 630 lb (285 kg) which provided 500 rounds for two minutes of fire. The grenade launcher was controlled by the pilot, who was able to cover an extensive area on either side of the flight path. The total armament package for the ACH-47A typically weighed 3,595 lb (1630 kg).

In February 1964, the Army established a requirement for the use of a heavily armed helicopter in combat operations. The Army ordered four modified CH-47As in June 1965, and in October put out a field manual setting forth its expectations for all armed helicopters. An officer wrote about the tactics foreseen for the armed Chinook: "The ACH-47A will operate in fire teams consisting of two aircraft. One will furnish a vase of fire while the other manoeuvres into an advantageous attack position." The prototype ACH-47A made its initial flight on 6 November 1965 and an official roll-out ceremony was held four days later. The First Air Cavalry Division took three of the four ACH-47A gunships to Vietnam in June 1966.

The Vietnam detachment of 'Guns A Go-Go' was the 228th Aviation Battalion of the First Cavalry Division, which flew numerous sorties providing direct support to American and Australian ground combat troops.

Eventually, the development of the smaller, more nimble AH-1 Cobra made a Chinook gunship unnecessary, and the concept was not developed further. The theatre commander wanted up to 24 additional 'Go-Gos' but the political situation underlying Cobra development precluded this.

ACH-47A serials: 64-13145, 64-13149, 64-13151, 64-13154

Total modified (from CH-47A): 4

ACH-47A

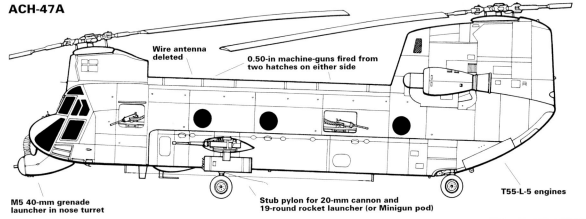

Wire antenna deleted

0.50-in machine-guns fired from two hatches on either side

M5 40-mm grenade launcher in nose turret

Stub pylon for 20-mm cannon and 19-round rocket launcher (or Minigun pod)

T55-L-5 engines

Top: Two of the 'Go-Go Birds' are seen during testing in the US. The airborne aircraft is fully armed with nose grenade launcher, 20-mm cannon and rocket pods on the stub pylons and has 0.50-in (12.7-mm) machine-guns mounted in the open hatches.

Above: Over the Eglin sea range an ACH-47A lets fly with 2.75-in rockets from the XM129 19-round launchers. An alternative store for the fuselage-side pylons was a Minigun pod firing 7.62-mm ammunition. The ACH-47A was a powerful gunship, but its extra firepower was more than offset by the agility of lighter gunships such as the Bell AH-1.

CH-47B

The CH-47B, the second principal version of the Chinook to enter production, was Boeing's response to a need for greater performance and payload, identified after combat experience in Vietnam. It apparently had a sea-level payload of 14,500 lb (6577 kg), which Boeing said was 42 per cent greater than the CH-47A. The B model was essentially an update in two phases. First came improvements to the airframe, next an updating of the powerplant. Engineers altered the exterior shape of the Chinook by adding rear-fuselage strakes and a squared-off rear rotor pylon. These minor changes improved directional stability in cruising flight.

The CH-47B's pair of Textron Lycoming T55-L-7C turboshaft engines rated at 2,850 shp (2126 kW) significantly enhanced the Chinook's performance under combat conditions. To complement the increased power, the engineers added new rotor blades with slightly increased span and cambered leading edges, producing a new airfoil shape for improved stability. The CH-47B also introduced strakes on the dorsal area of the rear fuselage (located on the rear ramp) to improve longitudinal stability, a feature found on all subsequent Chinooks.

The principal features of the B model were incorporated in the third prototype YCH-1B/YCH-47A (59-5984), which flew in the original white paint scheme with Dayglo trim on the fore and aft portions of the helicopter; the bright colours were necessitated by the proximity of the Philadelphia airport, with its heavy civil

The CH-47B offered a small but significant all-round improvement performance over the A. It could be identified by the rear ramp strakes and straightened trailing edge.

activity, during flight testing. Replete with an instrument probe extending from the left side of the nose, this aircraft made its first flight on 9 September 1966 at Boeing's Morton facility.

The first CH-47B was delivered to the US Army on 10 May 1967, and the first reached Southeast Asia in February 1968, many going to the 101st Air Assault Division. The B model joined earlier Chinooks in Vietnam. The minor improvements to the CH-47B were the direct result of Vietnam combat experience, giving soldiers a helicopter with somewhat better lift capacity, greater reliability, and slightly improved performance. Very simply, the CH-47B

CH-47B

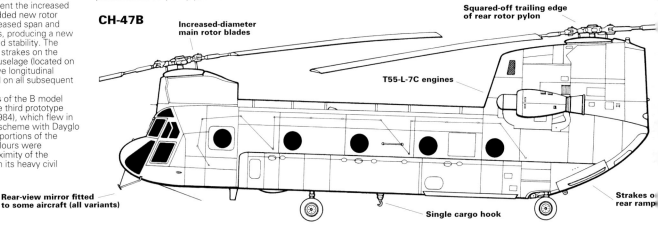

Increased-diameter main rotor blades

Squared-off trailing edge of rear rotor pylon

T55-L-7C engines

Rear-view mirror fitted to some aircraft (all variants)

Single cargo hook

Strakes o rear ramp

CH-47B 66-19138 flew with NASA Langley from 1974 to August 1979 for a variety of rotary-wing test programmes. At that time it was transferred to NASA Ames at Moffett Field, California. It flew from Moffett for another 10 years before returning to the Army in 1989.

could go a little faster and a little farther and offered a snappier response in hot weather.

The CH-47B was always regarded as something of an interim Chinook while Boeing developed the improvements that went into the subsequent CH-47C (below).

CH-47B serial numbers:
66-19098/19143 (c/n B-356/401); 67-18432/18493 (c/n B-402/463)

Total built: 108

CH-47C

The CH-47C was the third basic US Army model of the Chinook and provided the foundation for a number of export versions of the Boeing helicopter. Its power was provided by two Lycoming T55-L-11 engines developing 3,750 shp (2797 kW). One reason for developing the CH-47C was that earlier Chinook variants could not haul the US Army's standard 155-mm towed howitzer of the era – the M198 – which weighed more than 15,000 lb (6800 kg) on any sort of realistic mission. The earlier models could lift such a weight (with some difficulty) but could not meet an additional Army requirement to carry it a distance of 34 miles (55 km).

Thus, although external differences are few, the C model reflects relentless progress in the size of cargo a Chinook could realistically handle. According to Boeing figures, cargo capacity on a real-world Army sortie rose from 12,000 lb (5443 kg) on the CH-47A to 15,900 lb (7212 kg) on the CH-47B to 24,000 lb (10886 kg) on the CH-47C. The last of these figures is somewhat high because, like earlier Chinooks, the CH-47C had only one cargo hook, normally rated for a capacity of 20,000 lb (9071 kg). Not until a later model, the future CH-47D, did the number of hooks increase to three. As for the CH-47C in the real world, it was capable of hauling 23,100 lb (10478 kg) on a 10-nm (18-km) radius and 19,100 lb (8663 kg) on a 100-nm (185-km) radius. Boeing literature in 1968 credited the CH-47C with a maximum speed of 164 kt (304 km/h) as compared with just 100 kt (185 km/h) in the earlier CH-47A.

Some aircraft in the CH-47C series (among them, Canadian CH-147s) are identified in documents as 'Super C' Chinooks and are distinguished by an external hoist mounted above the crew door. Retroactively, CH-47Cs and subsequent models acquired crashworthy fuel systems and ISIS (integral spar inspection systems) which became standard for later variants. A CH-47C first flew with glass-fibre rotor blades (later standard on the CH-47D) on 22 May 1978, such blades being retrofitted to many C models from 1980.

The first flight of a US Army CH-47C was accomplished on 14 October 1967, and the first of 270 was delivered on 30 March 1968. It was the final model to be used during the Vietnam War.

The first overseas user of the CH-47C Chinook was Australia, which took delivery of 12 (A15-001/A15-012 alias 73-12970/73-12981, c/n B-698 and B-700/710), where it is known as the 'Chook', a term for chicken. Only one aircraft was lost in RAAF service: on 4 February 1985, A15-001 crashed into the spillway of the Perseverance Dam near Toowoomba in Queensland, killing the British exchange pilot. In May 1989, the battlefield support helicopter role passed from the RAAF to the Australian Army. The 11 survivors were retired and placed in long-term storage; eventually, seven Chinooks were transferred back to the US Army in a deal that partly funded conversion of the remaining four to CH-47D standard.

Eight CH-47Cs were delivered to Canada and operated under the designation CH-147. Forty-one CH-47C models were delivered to the Royal Air Force as Chinook HC.Mk 1 and HC.Mk 1B aircraft. The three Chinooks delivered to the Fuerza Aérea Argentina and employed primarily in the rescue and recovery role, rather than for battlefield hauling) are listed on Boeing ledgers as Model 308s but are, in fact, standard CH-47C models.

The CH-47C also formed the basis for licence production in Italy by Elicotteri Meridionali (Agusta).

The first CH-47C lifts off on its maiden voyage. The aircraft was actually a converted CH-47B (66-19103), re-engined with the uprated T55-L-11s that constituted the main change from the earlier model.

CH-47C serial numbers:
67-18494/18551 (c/n B-464/521),
68-15810/16022 (c/n B-522/614),
69-17100/17126 (c/n B-615/641), 4-201/202 (c/n B-642, B-665), 70-15000/15035 (c/n B-643/663, B-666/668, B-670/678, B-680/682), EL180822 (c/n B-664), 4-801/804 (c/n B-669, B-684, B-688, B-691), 71-20944/20955 (c/n B-683, B-685/687, B-689/690, B-692/695, B-712, B-719)
Spain: ET401/417 (c/n B-696/697, B-699, B-713, B-717, B-724, B-792/794, B-855/857, B-870/871, B-878/879, B-877)
Australia: A15-001/012 (c/n B-698, B-700/710, 73-12970/12981)
Iran: 5-4056/4057 (c/n B-711, B-714), 5-4059 (c/n B-716), 5-4061/4063 (c/n B-720/722), 5-4065/4084 (c/n B-727, B-730, B-735/736, B-751, B-756/758, B-761/762, B-765, B-769, B-774, B-776, B-772, B-778), 5-4092/4097 (c/n B-780, B-782, B-784,

Right: Equipped with ski undercarriage for snow operations, this CH-47C was operating from Fort Richardson, Alaska, in 1976.

Below: A CH-47C demonstrates the Chinook's ability to land on water. In practice this is rarely done, as the aircraft is not corrosion-proofed, and requires a major internal washdown after a sea landing.

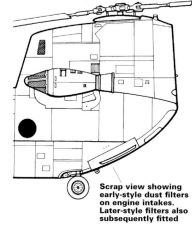

Scrap view showing early-style dust filters on engine intakes. Later-style filters also subsequently fitted

CH-47C

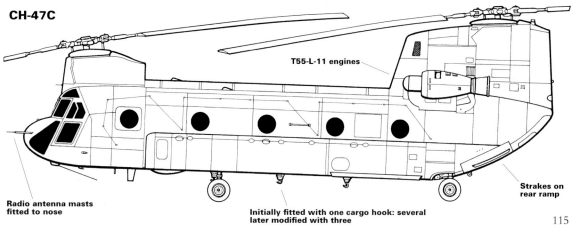

T55-L-11 engines

Radio antenna masts fitted to nose

Initially fitted with one cargo hook: several later modified with three

Strakes on rear ramp

Cs for Export

The CH-47C was the first major export model, and was supplied directly to Australia (12 – top left), Spain (initial batch of 13, locally known as HT.17 – top right) and Argentina. The latter country acquired two for the army, of which one was lost in the Falklands War, and three for the air force. Two now serve with the FAA (right) having been upgraded with nose radar, and flying with Grupo 7 on Antarctic duties.

B-786, B-788, B-790), 74-22271/22294 (c/n B-733/734 (plus?), B-747/750, B-752/755, B-759/760, B-763/764, B-766/768, B-770), 76-22673/22684 (c/n B-771, B-773, B-775, B-777, B-779, B-781, B-783, B-785, B-787, B-789, B-791, B-795)

Argentina: AE500/501 (c/n B-797/798), H91/93 (c/n B-800/802), 79-23394/23401 (c/n B-803/805, B-808, B-810/811, B-813/814), 091/093 (c/n B-806/807, B-809)
United Kingdom: ZA670/684 (c/n B-812,

B-815, B-819/825, B-827/828, B-830/833), ZA704/721 (c/n B-834/838, B-840/852), ZD574/576 (c/n B-866/868), ZD980/984 (c/n B-872/876),
Others: unknown (c/n B-877), NAF540/543 (c/n B-858/859, B-863/864), 7201/7203 (c/n

B-862, B-865, B-869), 52901/52902 (c/n B-878/879)
(not including eight Canadian CH-47Cs delivered as CH-147 and not including a non-flyable mock-up completed as c/n B-799)

CH-147

CH-147 is the military designation for the Canadian Armed Forces' Chinook which is included in production totals for the CH-47C model. Canada first purchased nine CH-147s, delivered in September 1974. Of the nine aircraft, two crashed: one on delivery (147001) and the other (147002) in Resolute, when it struck a light standard. The remaining seven were split between two locations: three went to 447 Sqn, CFB Edmonton, Alberta (formerly a BOMARC missile squadron), the other four to 450 Sqn, CFB Ottawa. Both squadrons were part of the Tactical Helicopter Division of

Ten Tactical Air Group (10TAG).
The Canadian CH-147 had an external hoist mounted above the crew door, making it a 'Super C'. The engines were Textron Lycoming T55-L-11Cs. Significant features included integrated spar inspection system, a redesigned crashworthy fuel system, a rescue hoist, advanced flight control system and a rear water dam for water operations. The Canadian Armed Forces utilised

Right: As first delivered, CH-147s wore high-visibility national insignia. The surviving fleet of seven aircraft was retired from service in mid-1991 on cost grounds.

CH-147s frequently for Arctic operations and equipped them with skis for landing on both snow and swampy ground.

CH-147 serial numbers: 147001/147009 (c/n B-718, B-723, B-725/726, B-728/729, B-731/732, B-796)

Left: Canada's CH-147s were essentially to 'Super C' standard, equipped with a starboard-side rescue hoist and fitted with the later-style engine filters. This example served with 450 Squadron, based at CFB Ottawa.

JCH-47C/D

The 'J' prefix, referring to temporary test duties, has been applied to at least two Chinooks used for icing tests by the US

Army Aviation Engineering Flight Activity at Edwards AFB, California. The JCH-47C (68-15814) was replaced by the JCH-47D (84-24159) in the early 1990s. The icing rig is carried on a large gantry mounted (second from front) cabin window apertures

and the rear ramp. Water for the icing rig is carried internally. Test equipment for recording the effects can be carried on panels which can fit into the forward doors, and on the rear ramp.

The JCH-47D serving with the USAAEFA at Edwards AFB is seen with its icing rig attached (below), and carrying the name Trash Ice Ice Baby *(left).*

Above: Preceding the JCH-47D, this JCH-47C (68-15814) served as the Edwards ice test aircraft.

CH-47D

The CH-47D is the US Army's current Chinook version, a product of an extensive 'rebuild' programme launched in the 1980s by remanufacturing earlier airframes. It is powered by two Textron Lycoming (now Garrett) T55-L-712 engines rated at 3,750 shp (2797 kW); the ratings depend on a multitude of factors and the manufacturer rates the -712 at 4,075 take-off shp (3039 kW).

The CH-47D has three cargo hooks – the centre hook rated for a 28,000-lb (12700-kg) load and the forward and aft hooks rated for 20,000 lb (9071 kg). Because the helicopter has an intended maximum gross weight of 50,000 lb (22680 kg), which is itself 16,000 lb (7257 kg) or about 35 per cent greater than the outer maximum for the original Chinook design, all three hooks cannot carry their full rated loads at the same time. Nevertheless, the three-hook arrangement is a significant change and a tremendous enhancement over the single hook on the CH-47C and other earlier models. The triple-hook arrangement, adopted in virtually every subsequent US and international Chinook variant, enables outsized cargoes to be flown with greater stability at speeds up to three times faster than earlier Chinooks – more than 115 kt (212 km/h) compared to the previous limit of 40-60 kt (74-110 km/h). Three hooks also permit multiple-destination resupply missions, allowing fuel blivets, cargo containers, or ammunition pallets to be positioned at up to three separate destinations per sortie.

Introduction of the forward and aft hooks came from the need to rig bulky, aerodynamically unstable loads from the aircraft with a two-point suspension. Earlier Chinooks became aerodynamically unstable and performed poorly, if at all, when tasked to carry odd-sized loads from their single-point hooks. As for the improved lift capacity, Boeing took the position that one CH-47D Chinook was as effective in hauling cargo as three Sikorsky UH-60 Black Hawks. Citing the way the Chinook's hauling capacity saves time for Army personnel prior to and following a lift mission, Boeing pointed out that a D5 Caterpillar tractor, which weighs 24,750 lb (11226 kg), can be carried intact on the aircraft's centre cargo hook, so that no valuable time is lost disassembling and reassembling urgently needed heavy equipment.

The CH-47D incorporated two Lucas 40-kva generators to produce inflight electrical power, in contrast to earlier Chinooks with two 20-kva generators. All US Army CH-47Ds were built with new-design fibreglass rotor blades and single-point pressure refuelling. The chord of rotor blades was increased slightly.

The CH-47D programme began in 1976 and, like previous efforts to spruce up the Chinook, was a rebuilding effort that meant

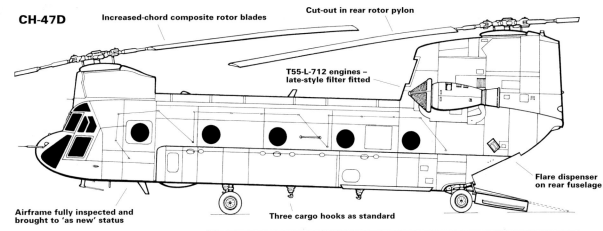

CH-47D

Increased-chord composite rotor blades

Cut-out in rear rotor pylon

T55-L-712 engines – late-style filter fitted

Flare dispenser on rear fuselage

Airframe fully inspected and brought to 'as new' status

Three cargo hooks as standard

Three early test CH-47Ds are seen at the Wilmington facility. The D is easily recognisable thanks to the large cut-out in the rotor pylon which provides cooling air for the transmission.

bringing older aircraft back to the factory -- high-hour examples were plucked from Army inventory first for this purpose -- putting them on a new production line and completely rebuilding them. Chinook airframes were selected for induction into the production line several months before they became due for their next scheduled major overhaul. Rebuilding involved removing the rotors, engines, transmissions and other assemblies, stripping the airframe down to bare skin and ribs, and inspecting virtually every square inch. Any defects discovered were replaced with new materials or components. The helicopters were then reassembled to include 11 major new systems that gave the resulting CH-47Ds greater reliability, availability and maintainability, extending realistic service life by about 20 years. CH-47Ds received new constructor's numbers and new military serials.

The first CH-47D was rolled out on 6 March 1979 and made its 55-minute initial flight four months ahead of schedule, on 11 May, with pilots Ron Mecklin and Phil Camerano. On 14 May, the first D model demonstrated its ability to fly at a gross weight of 50,127 lb (22737 kg) for 63 minutes. The initial flight of a fully-fledged production model was on 26 February 1982. The first operational unit for the D model was the 159th Aviation Assault Battalion, 101st Airborne Division (Air Assault) at Fort Campbell, Kentucky. The CH-47D had become the US Army's standard heavy-lift and transportation helicopter by the end of the 1980s.

The US army sought to modernise 472 Chinooks to the D model standard, a figure which from the beginning may have been

meant to include some aircraft purchased for overseas users in programmes managed by the Army. The exact number of CH-47Ds for American use is 403, but the total number of D models is more elusive, depending on what gets counted. For example, helicopters operated by the Netherlands are CH-47Ds but have

significant differences in powerplant, cockpit and flight management system.

In the 1980s, work was undertaken on two sub-variants of the CH-47D with mission packages optimised for the SOA (Special Operations Aircraft) role. Development of these platforms was initiated by a discreetly titled Operational

This is the cockpit of a regular US Army CH-47D, which retains dial-type instruments. The proposed CH-47F upgrade would see a 'glass' cockpit fitted. The pilots have an excellent view thanks to the extensive glazing.

By contrast, the cockpit of the 'CH-47D+' flown by the Netherlands has only three dials in the central console, displaying vital data as a back-up to the full-EFIS cockpit. The central comms panel has also been modified.

Enhancement Program (OEP). The CH-47Ds that initially emerged from this effort featured upgraded communications, navigation and cockpit management systems, radar warning systems, electronic and infra-red countermeasures systems and satellite communications links. With the exception of the SATCOM antenna

mounted above the dorsal fuselage, the aircraft resembled standard transport variants. Known as CH-47D SOA (Special Operations Aircraft) aircraft, the first of 16 to 24 aircraft modified to this configuration entered service in 1985. Subsequently, the OEP effort produced a second sub-variant, the MH-47D (separate entry).

The Australian Army's four CH-47Ds were former RAAF CH-47C Chinooks that were returned to the US, rebuilt and shipped back to Australia in 1995. They were numbered A15-102/104 and A15-106 (c/n M3451/3454, also numbered 93-0924/0927, and were formerly A15-002/004 and A15-006). Apart from some minor modifications in order to comply with Australian military certification, Australia's CH-47Ds are identical to their US Army counterparts as the logistical management plan is for the aircraft to remain fully compatible with the US Army fleet. Australia now considers its fleet of just four D models insufficient, especially when one or more is away from home base at Townsville, for example providing drought relief in Papua New Guinea. As a result, two more new-build examples were ordered in June 1998 for delivery in March 2000, to provide the ADF with increased capability, but also in the hope of extending the life of the existing fleet. These latest two examples are to be serialled A15-201 (c/n M4036), and A15-202 (c/n M4037). The US Army has acquired seven CH-47Ds that formerly served in Australia as CH-47Cs, these being 93-0928/0934 (c/n M3455/3461).

The Netherlands had acquired 13 CH-47D Chinooks with more powerful engines and other improvements, compared to US Army D models. These differences mean the Dutch CH-47Ds are sometimes referred to by the manufacturer as Model 414-100s. Six of the Netherlands' 13 aircraft are hybrids, with some of the features of the yet-unbuilt CH-47SD (separate entry), while seven are upgraded ex-Canadian aircraft incorporating monochrome 'glass' cockpits, T55-GA-714A engines and modified structures.

Following acquisition of seven helicopters in the 1980s (former Canadian CH-47Cs rebuilt to CH-47D standard), in December 1993 the Netherlands Ministry of Defence approved the purchase of six more CH-47Ds for its airmobile brigade,

temporarily giving them priority ahead of Holland's eventual purchase of McDonnell Douglas AH-64C Apache attack helicopters for the same brigade.

All 13 Dutch aircraft are powered by 3,100-shp (2313-kW) Textron Lycoming T55-L-714 engines instead of the less expensive -712. The heavier 714 engine provides greater range and lift, lower fuel consumption and reduced maintenance. Like US Army CH-47Ds, the Netherlands' helicopters have wide-chord composite rotor blades and single-point pressure refuelling. They also have crashworthy fuel tanks. The Netherlands aircraft were the first Chinooks (with the sole exception of US Army special operations MH-47Es) to have 'glass' cockpits; they incorporate the Boeing Honeywell ACMS (Advanced Cockpit Management System). Boeing rolled out the first Netherlands CH-47D in the second batch on 26 September 1994, began deliveries in January 1995, and completed deliveries before the end of that year.

CH-47D serials

US Army: 84-24152/24187 (c/n M30563091) (36), 85-24322/24369 (c/n M3092/3139) (48), 86-1635/1682 (c/n M3140/3187) (48), 87-0069/0116 (c/n M3188/3235) (48), 88-0062/0083 (c/n M3236/3257) (22), 88-0085/0109 (c/n M3259/3283) (25), 89-0130/0177 (c/n M3284/3331) (48), 90-0180/0226 (c/n M3332/3378) (47), 91-0230/0271 (c/n M3379/3420) (42), 92-0280/0309 (c/n M3421/3450) (30), 93-0928/0934 (c/n M3455/3461) (7), 92-0367/0368 (c/n M4301/4302) (2)

Australia: 93-0924/0927 (c/n M3451/3454) (4)

Spain: HT.17-02/10* (ET-401/409) (c/n M3501/3509) (9)

Greece: 001/009* (c/n M3561/3569) (9)

Netherlands: NL001/007 (c/n M3661/3667) (7)

Korea: 001/006 (c/n M4008/4013) (6), 90-0838/0849 (c/n M4014/4025) (12), (None assigned) (c/n M4061/4069) (9), (RoKAF)

Troops exit at the double from a CH-47D, just after the helicopter has deposited the artillery piece. Extremely versatile, the Chinook can also be easily airlifted by C-5 Galaxy.

CH-47 Chinook Variants

Foreign Ds

Above: Equipped with EFIS cockpit, nose radar and T55-L-714 engines, the Dutch Chinooks are among the most advanced in service. The first seven were rebuilt from ex-Canadian CH-147s.

Above right: Thailand ordered five CH-47Ds in 1988, which were delivered in 1989 to serve with the Army Aviation Battalion at Lop Buri. They are equipped with nose radar.

Right: Nine of Spain's CH-47Cs were upgraded to D standard for continued service with BHELTRA V, serving alongside six Model 414s and a pair of CH-47Cs.

Below right: South Korea acquired 18 standard CH-47Ds for the army, and a further number (believed six) for the air force's 235th Squadron (illustrated). Dubbed HH-47D, the air force aircraft are used for SAR work and have large tanks and radar.

Below: Australia traded in its old CH-47Cs for six CH-47Ds, operated by the Army with C Squadron/5 Aviation Regiment.

(None assigned) (c/n M4501/4506) (6), (None assigned) (c/n M4517/4522) (6)

Korea/Australia**: (None assigned) (c/n M4032/4037) (6)

Thailand: 90-111 (c/n M4026) (1), 90-222 (c/n M4027) (1), 90-333 (c/n M4028) (1), 90-444 (c/n M4029) (1), 90-777 (c/n M4030) (1), 90-888 (c/n M4031) (1)

Netherlands: (None assigned) (c/n M4101/4106) (6)

UK RAF: ZH775/(?783?) (c/n M4451/4459) (9), (None assigned) (c/n M4476/4483) (8), (Various) (c/n M7001/7032) (32)

(Undisclosed): 95-88180/88183 (c/n M4511/4514) (4), 95-88186 (c/n M4515) (1), 95-88188 (c/n M4516) (1)

*serials and c/n not in corresponding sequence
**M4036/4037 listed as Korea in some documents, Australia in others

Model 414 late configuration (CH-47D)

Cut-out in leading edge of rear rotor pylon
Broad-chord rotor blades
T55-L-712 or T55-L-714 engines
Weather radar in extended, bulged nose radome
EFIS cockpit optional
Revised ventral antenna fit
Three cargo hooks as standard
Slightly enlarged fuselage-side tanks

119

MH-47D

MH-47D is the designation set aside for a dozen D model Chinooks modified for special operations duty, of which 11 survive today. These aircraft can be recognised externally by laser, missile and radar warning antennas, and by a raised, circular SATCOM antenna on the dorsal fuselage above the cabin, as well as the longer pointed nose for optional radar found on many overseas Chinooks.

Developed from the CH-47D SOA (covered in the CH-47D entry), the more capable MH-47D also incorporated the OEP package, a colour weather radar and a FLIR turret. A rescue hoist was installed above the starboard forward cabin door. A detachable inflight-refuelling probe, the first ever installed on an Army aircraft, is a distinguishing feature of this variant. Unique to the D model is an M60 0.50-in (12.7-mm) machine-gun located on the ramp. The first of 12 aircraft in this series acknowledged to be in inventory was delivered in 1985.

The MH-47D has a Rockwell Collins cockpit simpler than the Honeywell cockpit found in overseas Chinooks and similar to that planned for the CH-47F (below). US Army soldiers often refer to this variant as the MH-47D AWC (for all-weather cockpit). The fuel system is the same as the CH-47D, with half the capacity of the subsequent MH-47E (below).

MH-47Ds are operated by the 3/160th

SOAR detached from Fort Campbell (where three airframes reside for training purposes) to Hunter Army Air Field in Savannah, Georgia, with a detachment reportedly deployed on a semi-permanent basis to Howard AFB, Panama. The 160th had previously been equipped in part with CH-47C models modified with a non-standard rack for electronic warfare systems, a feature which was refined on the MH-47D; these have been retired.

Some sources say that the US Army has at least 12 and possibly 20 more CH-47Ds than the 11 it has acknowledged. The Army denies this but acknowledges that one

MH-47D (83-24110) crashed in 'approximately' December 1989.

These special-duty Chinooks routinely operate without refuelling probes, making it somewhat difficult to distinguish them from ordinary CH-47Ds, although the pointed nose is one give-away. The Army also has a number of CH-47D SOA (Special Operations Aircraft) with digital electronic warfare systems, new radar warning receivers, and the EW rack.

MH-47D serials
82-23763 (c/n M3014) ex-CH-47A 66-19049
83-24110 (c/n M3040) ex-CH-47A 64-13111

Boeing used a demonstrator CH-47D to test the refuelling probe of the MH-47D, tanking from an HC-130.

83-24118 (c/n M3048) ex-CH-47C 70-15010
85-24342 (c/n M3112) ex-CH-47A 66-19071
85-24360 (c/n M3130) ex-CH-47A 66-19018
85-24361 (c/n M3131) ex-CH-47C 68-16021
85-24367 (c/n M3137) ex-CH-47A 65-08010
86-1635 (c/n M3140) ex-CH-47A 64-13137
89-0131 (c/n M 3285) ex-CH-47C 69-17106
89-0146 (c/n M3300) ex-CH-47C 70-15031
89-0160 (c/n M3314) ex-CH-47C 67-18500
89-0161 (c/n M3315) ex-CH-47C 67-18532

MH-47E

The MH-47E is the specialised Chinook variant for US Army special operations forces, all 26 being remanufactured from CH-47Cs or earlier models. Criticism of the reliability of American and British Chinooks prompted the US Army to put the purpose behind the E model into a few simple words: "The primary objective of the MH-47E programme is to meet the Army's requirement of a 90 per cent probability of successfully completing a five-hour, deep-penetration, clandestine mission over a 300-nm [553 km] radius." The MH-47E was tailored for the 160th Special Operations Aviation Regiment (Special Operations), the 'Night Stalkers', at Fort Campbell, with which it still serves.

A distinctive recognition feature is a huge air-refuelling probe on the front right of the aircraft. Other distinguishing features include twin Textron Lycoming T55L-714 engines rated at 4,085 maximum continuous shp (3047 kW), long-range all-composite fuel pods, the already-mentioned air-refuelling probe, internal auxiliary fuel tanks, an internal cargo-handling system, Texas Instruments multi-mode radar, FLIR, and standard internal armament of two M134 Miniguns for defence. Unique to the E model, the 0.30-in (7.62-mm) M134 is air cooled, link fed, and has a maximum effective range of 1500 m (4,920 ft) with tracer burnout at 900 m (2,953 ft). Reports that the aircraft is equipped with an onboard oxygen-generating system are incorrect.

A roll-out ceremony for the first MH-47E took place on 6 December 1989. The first ship in the MH-47E series (88-0267, c/n M3258, a former CH-47C 68-15838 c/n B-540) made its maiden flight on 1 June 1990. One source indicates that the aircraft may have briefly become airborne for the first time the previous day, 31 May 1990. On the 1 June sortie (generally regarded as

The MH-47E is optimised for covert low-level penetration, usually undertaken at night. As well as Special Forces insertion, it has an important 'fat cow' forward refuelling point role.

the E model's first trip aloft), Boeing test pilots Ron Mecklin and John Tulloch flew the aircraft from the Ridley Township factory to the company's test centre at Wilmington, Delaware.

The first production MH-47E to enter service (the fourth MH-47E to come off the line) was delivered to the 160th at Fort Campbell in January 1994. The first was a flight-test prototype and two others underwent electromagnetic effects and aircraft survivability equipment testing at the Naval Air Warfare Center, Patuxent River, Maryland before belatedly reaching the 160th.

Crew of the MH-47E consists of pilot, co-pilot, two side gunners, and crew chief in the back. The rear of the E model is a large compartment, ideal for a Special Forces unit of 10-12 men. Farther forward is a 'black box' about 7 ft (2.13 m) tall and 5 ft (1.52 m) long. The crew is positioned forward of the 'box'. The E model has a package of internal fuel tanks made by Robertson, known as CCERFS (Cargo Compartment Expanded Range Fuel System), consisting of one to three ballistic-tolerant, self-sealing tanks. Each tank holds 780 US gal (2953 litres) of fuel, refuellable during aerial refuel operations.

Contrary to published references which make the E model more hi-tech than it is, door gunners have computer terminals that feed into the mission equipment package. Up front, a 'glass' cockpit set up for night, low-light flight operations.

The US Army intended to purchase 50 MH-47Es as of 1990, but the number was later cut virtually in half. One MH-47E

(92-0465, c/n MN3713) was lost in a mishap at Fort Campbell on 7 March 1996 and 25 remain in service.

MH-47E serial numbers: 88-0267 (c/n

All 25 surviving MH-47Es serve with the 160th SOAR at Fort Campbell, Kentucky. The aircraft are electronically hardened for compatibility with ships, and have new, rapid-fold blades for shipborne operations.

M3258) formerly 68-15838 (c/n B-540) (1), 90-0414 (c/n M3701) (1), 91-0496/0501 (c/n M3702/3707) (6), 92-0400/0403 (c/n M3708/3711) (4), 92-0464/0477 (c/n M3712/3725) (14)

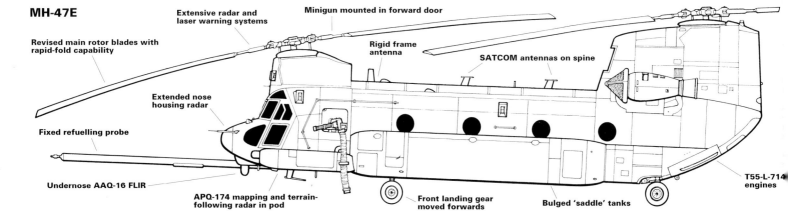

MH-47E

- Extensive radar and laser warning systems
- Minigun mounted in forward door
- Revised main rotor blades with rapid-fold capability
- Rigid frame antenna
- SATCOM antennas on spine
- Extended nose housing radar
- Fixed refuelling probe
- Undernose AAQ-16 FLIR
- APQ-174 mapping and terrain-following radar in pod
- Front landing gear moved forwards
- Bulged 'saddle' tanks
- T55-L-714 engines

CH-47F

CH-47F is the designation assigned in 1998 to the ICH (Improved Cargo Helicopter), a no-frills effort to provide an upgraded Chinook to the US Army capable of remaining in service for the next 30 years. The CH-47F will have some of the features of the upscale CH-47SD – such as more powerful engines – but will lack others, such as long-range fuel tanks. The F model is considered a compromise on grounds of cost, and will provide American soldiers with a modernised helicopter that is somewhat less capable than the export Chinook.

The CH-47F will finally address a problem associated with the Chinook series from the beginning – the helicopter's high level of vibration. CH-47F improvements include fuselage 'tuning' to reduce the effects of vibration on aircraft systems, installation of a Military Standard 1553 databus to permit eventual digital integration of the Chinook's flight controls and cockpit management systems, and repair and replacement of structures as needed. The 'rebuild' of the aircraft will be accomplished by stripping off the '41 section' – the forward section of the aircraft including the flight deck – and building a new one, strengthening fuselage panels to 'deaden' the fuselage so it will not vibrate harmonically when the aircraft is

operating, and other structural improvements aimed at decreasing structural degradation from the upgraded engine.

Powerplant will be the AlliedSignal/ Garrett (formerly Textron Lycoming) T55-GA-714A engine, the A suffix indicating that the engine is 'marinised', or more capable of enduring a corrosive maritime environment. The engine is rated at 4,085 maximum continuous shp (3047 kW) and will have FADEC (full authority digital engine control). This is the engine found on the MH-47E and on most export Chinooks but, even with the increased power, the US Army intends to keep useful load at the same 25,000 lb (11340 kg) figure as its current CH-47D.

As for the addition of FADEC, the Royal Air Force learned with its Chinook HC.Mk 2 variant (separate feature) that it improved engine response times and enhanced power management throughout the entire engine operating range, increasing the helicopter's response and handling characteristics. It also replaced the need for the pilot to operate 'beep' switches on the collective to help control engine torque and rotor speeds. FADEC automatically matches engine torques and temperatures, and provides complete engine power management together with precision rotor speed control throughout the entire operational flight envelope. The system

would improve engine power control which, in turn, would save fuel and reduce lifecycle costs. FADEC also ensures automatic emergency single-engine performance should one engine fail. Estimates suggest that FADEC will give the new Chinook a 600 per cent increase in engine reliability over earlier US Army models or British HC.Mk 1s (separate entry), while engine-related lifecycle costs may be reduced by 40-50 per cent.

Rockwell Collins is developing the CH-47F cockpit management system, drawing in part on components in the cockpit of the Beech RC-12 Huron reconnaissance aircraft. It includes a moving map but not digitised engine controls, and will rely in part on analog instruments, unlike the full 'glass' cockpit developed for the export Chinook by Honeywell.

The first of two aircraft slated for conversion to CH-47F EMD (engineering manufacturing development) standard were brought to the Philadelphia plant the first week of January 1999. The first aircraft, 83-24107 known in plant jargon as ICH #1, wore 'ICH INDUCTION # 1' in white lettering on the side of the fuselage and was brought to the factory by Lieutenant Colonel Tom Crosby. The second, alias ICH # 2, is 83-24115. Both are among the earliest CH-47Ds produced by Boeing, having been delivered in 1983, shortly after the inception of the D model programme.

During the EMD phase of the ICH programme, Boeing will modernise the first two CH-47F pre-production aircraft, manage initial flight tests, evaluate system improvements, and prepare for full-scale production.

The CH-47F programme will modernise and improve the CH-47D fleet to ensure the US Army retains its heavy-lift helicopter capability whether or not the long-contemplated JTR (Joint Transport Rotorcraft), the notional replacement for the Army CH-47 and Marine Corps CH-53E, materialises to begin service in 2015 or later. CH-47Fs will remain in service until 2040.

The ICH programme calls for upgrading 300 Chinooks and includes installation of a digitally compatible databus to make cockpit instrumentation compatible with the Army's digital battlefield requirements and to improve navigation. The manufacturer claims that these improvements will reduce ICH Chinook operating costs by 22 per cent compared to the costs of operating a D model today.

The first CH-47F was once scheduled to be delivered in 2003, although it is unclear whether this schedule remains firm. This will be followed by a ramp-up to at least 24 deliveries per year until Army fleet requirements are met.

'HH-47'

The HH-47 designation – the H prefix signifying a dedicated rescue aircraft – was applied to Boeing studies for an aircraft for the US Air Force and Canada that was never purchased or built. It was inevitable that such an aircraft would at least be considered. Vietnam experience showed the HH-3C/E 'Jolly Green Giant' to be a guardian angel, but one with less range,

capacity and flexibility than the USAF wanted. It appears that the HH-47 concept was being studied at the same time that the USAF developed the HH-53B/C 'Super Jolly Green', which became its primary combat rescue craft. A surviving drawing of an 'HH-47 Air Force Recovery Helicopter' shows a Chinook with an air-refuelling probe and pointed, streamlined long-range fuel tanks, both in a shape and size never adopted on any real Chinook. As a postscript, the CH-47Ds operated by the

Boeing proposed this version of the Chinook for Canada's SAR helicopter competition, which was eventually won by the EH101. With refuelling probe, nose-side pod for radar and undernose FLIR, it closely resembled the Special Forces MH-47E.

Korean air force in the SAR role are designated HH-47Ds.

HH-47 proposal for US Air Force

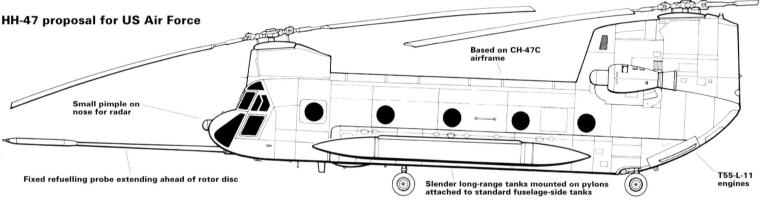

Based on CH-47C airframe

Small pimple on nose for radar

Fixed refuelling probe extending ahead of rotor disc

Slender long-range tanks mounted on pylons attached to standard fuselage-side tanks

T55-L-11 engines

CH-47SD

The CH-47SD is the top-of-the-line Chinook upgrade being offered to overseas purchasers with a bigger budget than the ICH-limited US Army. Powerplant for this series is the FADEC-equipped Garrett T55-G-714A turboshaft engine rated at 4,900 shp (3655 kW). The CH-47SD will have a Honeywell 'glass' cockpit (more advanced than the Rockwell Collins unit being prepared for the US Army's CH-47F), simplified airframe structure, the long-range fuel system, numerous provisions for optional equipment, and a cabin and cockpit fully compatible with night vision goggles. The cockpit is referred to as a fully integrated ACMS (Avionics Control and Management System) with colour multi-function displays, dual air data computers with standby flight displays, EFIS (electronic flight instruments system), and dual imbedded GPS/INS navigation capability. The standard interior is 1,474 cu ft (42 m³) with 37 troop seats; this is apparently the same dimensions as previous Chinooks and could no doubt be expanded for high-density seating of 44, 50 or 59 troops.

The CH-47SD (not a US military designation) will have the long-range fuel system already found on some international Boeing 414-100 aircraft and the US Army

MH-47E (separate entries), nearly double the size of the tanks on all other US Army variants. This two-tank configuration raises fuel capacity to 2,068 US gal (7828 litres) in contrast to the 1,034 US gal (3914 litres) of the standard CH-47D. The CH-47SD also has the longer, thinner nose associated with a number of international and civil variants, capable of holding any of several radar units. Options include the M130 chaff/flare dispenser.

The first CH-47SD model was scheduled to roll out at the Ridley Township plant in October 1999 and is one of six helicopters ordered by Singapore. That country already operates six CH-47Ds which it is considering upgrading. Singapore has a facility to train its CH-47D/SD Chinook pilots at Grand Prairie, Texas. Taiwan is slated to receive three 'Super Ds', which are listed on company records as Model 234MLRs to give them a 'civilian' title.

Boeing's demonstrator CH-47D/ International Chinook incorporates many of the features to be found in the CH-47SD. The 'Super D' will feature a full 'glass' cockpit and the enlarged fuel tanks of the MH-47E, Korea's HH-47Ds and Greece's CH-47Ds. Singapore will be the first operator.

British Airways Helicopters was the launch customer for the 234LR, employing the type until a fatal crash brought an end to oil support operations in the North Sea.

Model 234

The Model 234 designation applies to Chinook helicopters produced for commercial use. The first Commercial Chinook flew on 19 August 1980 and received Federal Aviation Administration and British Civil Aviation Authority certification on 19 and 26 June 1981, respectively. Although based on the CH-47D, the Model 234 introduced many new features. The most notable were the replacement of metal rotor blades by wide-chord glass-fibre blades, a redesign of the fuselage side fairings to incorporate larger fuel tanks, a lengthened nose to house the weather radar antenna and a repositioning farther forward of the front landing gear. Duplicated blind-flying instrumentation, weather radar and a dual, four-axis automatic flight control system ensure all-weather capability. The fuselage is of all-metal semi-monocoque construction with a basically square section and a loading ramp built into the upswept rear. Landing gear is a non-retractable quadricycle type, with twin wheels on each forward gear, and single wheels on the rear units.

Power for the Model 234 is provided by two Avco-Lycoming AL 5512 turboshafts, pod-mounted on the sides of the rear rotor pylon. Each is rated at 4,075 shp (3040 kW) on take-off, and has a maximum 30-minute contingency rating of 4,355 shp (3249 kW).

The rotor system comprises three-bladed rotors in tandem, turning in opposite directions, driven through interconnecting shafts which enable both rotors to be driven by either engine. The front half of each blade is made of glass-fibre, and the rear half filled with Nomex honeycomb. An aluminium screen inserted in the skin provides lightning protection by discharging strikes through the titanium leading edge. Blades also embody electric de-icing blankets. Two blades of each rotor can be folded manually. Power transmission from each engine is accomplished through individual clutches into the combiner transmission, providing a single power output to the interconnecting shaft. An auxiliary transmission lubrication system ensures that flights can be completed even after a total loss of oil in the primary system.

Accommodation is provided for two pilots side-by-side on the flight deck, with dual controls, and for up to 44 passengers (depending on the variant) in the cabin, three-abreast with a central aisle. Each seat has an overhead bin and under-seat stowage for carry-on luggage, with larger items carried in the main baggage compartment. A galley with cabin attendant's seat and toilet between the flight deck and the cabin are standard. Heating and ventilation provide a comfortable environment for pilots and passengers, and a specially-tuned floor construction reduces vibration. Passenger access to the cabin is via a single door on the right-hand side, while the crew has a door on each side of the flight deck. All passenger facilities can be removed and replaced by a heavy-duty floor for cargo-only service. Various arrangements of external cargo hooks are possible, including a single central hook for loads of up to 28,000 lb (12700 kg); tandem hooks for better load stability in high-speed flight; and three tandem hooks for multiple loads.

The first Model 234, registered N234BV and finished in natural metal, made its first hover flight at the Ridley Township factory on 19 August 1980. The Commercial Chinook entered service with British Airways Helicopters on 1 July 1981, and deliveries of all six Model 234LRs had been completed by 29 June 1982. The long-range LR version can be distinguished by large continuous fuselage side-fairings of advanced composites, which contain one fuel tank in each with a total capacity of 2,100 US gal (7950 litres), about twice that of the military Chinook. Internally, the 234LR was fitted out with 44 airliner seats – the same as those used on the Boeing 727 – and walk-on baggage bins on the rear ramp. It could be used in the all-cargo configuration or as a passenger/freight combination (the 234LR Combi was certificated by the FAA in summer 1982). BAH used the Chinook primarily from Aberdeen in Scotland, flying directly to rigs some 250-300 miles (400-480 km) into the North Sea, obviating the need to fly rig personnel via Sumburgh.

Chinook operations to oil rigs ceased when one machine was involved in a fatal crash in the North Sea on 2 May 1984. On 23 March 1982, Boeing announced an order for two 234LRs from Helikopter Service of Norway, with an option for one more, which was later taken up. Helikopter Service used its Chinooks in the North Sea region, flying out of Stavanger. Two 234ER extended-range models were delivered in 1983 to Arco Alaska, also for use in offshore oil rig support operations. This version featured two internal drum tanks in addition to those in the fuselage sides, increasing the range to 1,000 miles (1600 km). Seating was typically provided for 17 passengers, or for 32 with a single internal fuel tank. It received its FAA certification in May 1983. A 234MLR multi-purpose long-range aircraft was also offered but had no takers; it was designed with a utility interior and the capability of being reconfigured in eight hours. Four men could handle the cabin fuel tanks and ramp baggage bins.

Customers could also not be found for the 234UT utility. The eight 234LRs initially acquired second-hand by Columbia Helicopters in the USA, and the only ones now in civil service have all been converted to this configuration, designed specifically for enhanced lifting capability. The fuselage side tanks have been replaced by two drum tanks in the forward fuselage and the side-fairings removed, leaving only a blister around each landing gear mounting. The 234UT received supplemental FAA type certification in October 1981. Perhaps the most striking of these aircraft was the glossy-black N224TA, operated by Trump Airlines in 1990.

Model 234 production
G-BAJC c/n B-816, G-BISO c/n B-817, G-BISR c/n B-818, G-BWFC c/n B-826, G-BISN c/n B-829, G-BISP c/n B-839, LM-OMA c/n B-853, LM-OMB c/n B-854, N234BV c/n B-860, N242BV c/n B-861

'Chinook crane' family

In 1967, Boeing began studies for a huge, crane-equipped, cargo-hauling helicopter as an intended follow-on to the CH-47 helicopter. The 'Chinook crane' family, actually a totally new design with little in common with the Chinook but for tandem-rotor design, was based on an expectation that the Pentagon would issue a tri-service (Air Force, Army, Marine) requirement for a new heavy-lifter in 1969. The 'Chinook crane' family never emerged as a fully-fledged aircraft, but the design work led to the eventual XCH-62 and Model 301 design efforts (separate entries).

Included in the 'Chinook crane' family were the Boeing Model 297 Chinook Crane (the only model actually identified by this name, according to company documents) powered by three 3,750-shp (2797-kW) Lycoming T55-L-11 gas turbine engines with a rotor radius of 30 ft (9.14 m), and the Model 298, with the same engines but larger rotor having a radius of 35 ft (10.66 m) or more.

With a standard Chinook model for size comparison, these models show the Model 237 (centre), intended primarily for crane operations, and Model 227 (left) which could carry loads internally.

The Model 297 Chinook Crane would have employed many of the features then being developed for the CH-47C, but featuring a tall landing gear unit with a 'kneeling' capability, an external hoist system, a rearward-facing loadmaster's station beneath the cockpit (much in the manner of the Sikorsky CH-54A Tarhe), and a lengthened fuselage compared to the standard Chinook. It was to have a twin-winch system with two lift points. The 'kneeling' feature was meant to enable the Model 297 to be lowered onto podded loads from a straddle position. By 'kneeling', the height of the Chinook Crane would be reduced to 19 ft 6 in (5.94 m), sufficient to clear the 20-ft (6.09-m) hangar deck of US Navy LPH-2 class helicopter-carriers. The Model 297 would have had rotor blades able to be folded manually for deck storage. Although the smallest of the three designs that reached a fairly advanced stage within this family, it was so big that the bottom of its fuselage stood 9 ft 4 in (2.84 m) off the ground, and its tail rotor was some 27 ft (8.22 m) in height.

The Model 298 was a larger design and was the first in this new series of heavy-lift concepts to be studied for both military and civilian use, the latter in a 100-passenger version which would have had approximately the same capacity as a Lockheed L-188 Electra turboprop airliner. Diameter of rotor blades on the Model 298 would have been about 15 per cent greater than the Model 297.

This family of designs which came ahead of the US Army's HLH (Heavy Lift Helicopter) requirement – and which anticipated far more Air Force, Navy and civil interest than may have existed – also included the Boeing Model 299, a version that would have been larger yet. Apparently never finalised even on the drawing board, the Model 299 would have been meant to haul cargoes of up to 78,000 lb (35380 kg) over distances of perhaps 200 miles (320 km) or more.

Other company designations for aircraft in this family of never-built heavy-lifters included the Model 227, which was essentially an outsized Chinook, and the Model 237, which was similar in appearance to the Model 297 discussed above.

XCH-62

The XCH-62, or US Army HLH (Heavy Lift Helicopter), was an outgrowth of Boeing's years of experience with the Chinook design and was a bigger and wholly new aircraft in every respect. As expected, this aircraft resulted from a tri-service arrangement aimed at avoiding the duplication which had occurred just a few years earlier when the Army invested in the Chinook and the Marines in the Sikorsky CH-53A Sea Stallion.

This impression shows a CH-62A deploying a mobile SAM battery, just one of the many battlefield tasks envisaged for the type.

The XCH-62 was a tandem-rotor helicopter powered by three Allison XT701-AD-700 gas turbine engines rated at 8,079 hp (6027 kW) each. Due to its size and imposing bulk, the XCH-62 was often compared in literature of the 1970s to the outsized Boeing 747 and Lockheed C-5 Galaxy. Its design gross weight was 118,000 lb (53525 kg) and its primary mission payload was 45,000 lb (20412 kg), which apparently could be nearly doubled to 70,000 lb (31751 kg) for short-distance operations. A heavier version at 148,000 lb (67133 kg) was also contemplated. It was to employ a redundant fly-by-wire control system, an early version of which was evaluated on the Boeing Model 347 technology demonstrator ;the system was expected to reduce weight and maintenance costs.

Crew of the XCH-62 was to number four, consisting of pilot, co-pilot, load controlling crewman and crew chief. The helicopter would also have offered an internal cargo compartment with sufficient space for 12 troops. Its dimensions were: length (blades turning) 162 ft 3 in (49.50 m), length with rotors folded 89 ft 3 in (27.20 m), rotor diameter 92 ft (28.04 m) and a landing gear width of 29 ft 10 in (9.10 m).

The XCH-62 would have been able to carry numerous standard Army items too heavy or too bulky for the standard Chinook. These included the Chaparral self-propelled anti-aircraft missile system, weighing about 26,600 lb (12065 kg), and the M107 self-propelled 175-mm howitzer, which tipped the scales at an impressive 62,200 lb (28213 kg).

In 1971, just as the US was withdrawing from Vietnam, the Pentagon chose Boeing, in preference to Sikorsky and Hughes, to proceed with a technology programme for design and fabrication of an HLH. The initial effort did not involve construction of an actual aircraft, but a single austere prototype was placed under contract in 1973 with the objective of evaluating and validating HLH technology. By then, one observer had opined that "the choice of a single company at such an early stage almost guarantees that Boeing will go forward to production since no other firm has shown a willingness to invest [in such a helicopter]". However, the Department of Defense was underwriting something less than an actual flight test programme, at least a fully-fledged one, although a first flight date of August 1975 was announced and anticipated. It should be remembered that the XCH-62 was considered a venture into advanced technology, as the first aircraft ever to utilise bonded honeycomb for all primary airframe structure in place of

CH-47 Chinook Variants

Congress abruptly cut funds for the huge cargo helicopter in the FY 1976 budget after the US Army had spent $179 million on the prototype, which was about 90 per cent complete. This was not a surprise, since Capitol Hill legislators had long expressed dismay over the cost of the programme relative to its benefit and had attempted much earlier (in 1970) to end development. In August 1975, they succeeded – for the time, at least – when Boeing cordoned off the unfinished prototype and released about 500 employees. The uncompleted and unflown XCH-62 was placed in storage and many who believed in this outsized helicopter design hoped that it could be resurrected. This seemed to happen in the mid-1980s when NASA, the Defense

Advanced Research Projects Agency and the US Army teamed up to spend $71 million to permit completion of the XCH-62, with the goal of achieving a first flight in 1987 and conducting a 115-hour flight test programme. Once again, however, politics intervened and the aircraft was neither completed nor flown. At the time, the Cold War was under way and the Soviet Union was operating several heavy-lift helicopters that were larger than any lifter in US service. The Soviet Mi-12 of the 1950s had been a comparable twin-rotor design, although much larger, while the Mi-6 was a conventional, single-rotor type.

XCH-62 serial: 72-2012 (not completed)

The XCH-62, seen here at the Ridley Township works, had reached this hardware stage at the time of its cancellation in 1976.

conventional skin and stringer construction. The 92-ft (28.04-m) fibreglass rotor design was, itself, considered more advanced than anything previously attempted.

The Pentagon's effort to achieve a high-technology heavy-lifter for tri-service use was under threat from the beginning by the service branches' differing expectations of payload capacity. The Army was calling for a 54,000-lb (24493- kg) payload at 4,000-ft (1219-m) altitude in 95°F (35°C) (equivalent to 70,000 lb/31751 kg at sea level), which corresponded essentially to what Boeing's goal had been all along. The Marine Corps,

pondering operations from LPH class helicopter-carriers, saw 34,000 lb (15422 kg) as the maximum cargo weight it was likely to attain in an aircraft that would be practical for their needs – and, indeed, this figure is slightly beyond the capability of today's later-generation CH-53E Super Sea Stallion. In due course, the Marines gained access to the larger and more capable LHA helicopter assault ships, but they were not yet in service when the XCH-62 was taking shape.

Boeing announced a major milestone on 21 April 1975 when major fuselage sections of the XCH-62 were joined at the Ridley Township factory. By then, the company was testing the HLH rotor on a whirl test tower which resembled a Dutch windmill with the blade pointed upward. At that time, the expected first flight date had slipped to early 1976.

Model 301

The Boeing Model 301 was the manufacturer's proposed civil version of the US Army XCH-62 HLH (Heavy Lift Helicopter). The company perceived the Model 301 to be the heavy-lift champion of the commercial world, able to carry cargoes many times greater than civil Chinooks, in some cases as great as 70,000 lb (31751 kg). At one time, an application was on file with the FAA for civil certification of the helicopter. Had a first flight of the military version taken place in August 1975 as once contemplated, Boeing was prepared to go ahead immediately with the civil aircraft.

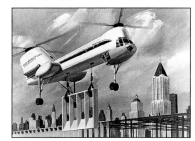

The Model 301 was envisaged for work in the heavy construction field, with a 70,000-lb lift capability.

Model 347

The Boeing Model 347 was a Chinook development with a longer fuselage, four-bladed rotors, and a higher rear pylon with extensively modified systems. The programme was established in early 1969 to provide full-scale flight evaluation of an advanced technology helicopter which would have better handling qualities under instrument flight rules conditions, improved stability, control and manoeuvrability, elimination of rotor bang, reduced vibration and an improved cockpit. The aircraft was a CH-47A (65-7992) returned to the factory in July 1969 and modified to the Model 347 configuration; it became a technology demonstrator which, in turn, contributed substantially to Boeing's work on a family of heavy-lift helicopters, the Chinook Crane, XCH-62, and Model 301 (separate entries). The Model 347 made its maiden flight on 27 May 1970 at Boeing's Center 3 flight test facility at Eddystone, Pa.

As viewed initially, this technology programme was to have two phases. Phase I was the 'Advanced Helicopter' portion, and Phase II, the 'Winged Helicopter' component. For Phase I, modifications to the one-time CH-47A airframe included four rotor blades in lieu of three per rotor head, a fuselage extended by 9 ft 2 in (2.77 m), provisions for later installation of a wing, an upgraded Textron Lycoming T55-L-11 engine, a sponson extended by 2 ft 6 in (76 cm), an uprated CH-47C transmission, an improved cockpit and retractable landing gear. In this configuration, the Model 347 carried out flight tests in the helicopter mode while engineers completed plans to fit the aircraft with a wing.

Although flown initially with a conventional control system, the Model 347 eventually demonstrated a FBW system to replace the conventional helicopter control arrangement, in Boeing's words, "alleviating the risk that helicopter handling qualities might change with mechanical wear, slop, and friction". Internally, the Model 347 had the capability for 44 troop seats as compared with 33 on a CH-47A.

In Phase II, initially scheduled for mid-1971, the Model 347 was to fly with a wing having a span of 45 ft (13.71 m), more than some fighters. The wing had an area of 340 sq ft (32 m²) enabling the aircraft to demonstrate a 60° banked turn (a 2g manoeuvre) at a gross weight of 45,000 lb (20411 kg). The wing was essentially a tilt wing having four modes for hover, cruise, manoeuvre and auto rotation.

The Model 347 made its first hover on 27

Above: Much more than just a stretched Chinook, the Model 347 was a technology demonstrator which ultimately tested fly-by-wire systems and winged flight. The large wing swivelled, being held almost vertically when the aircraft was in the hover.

Right: Equipped with a fly-by-wire control system and retractable pilot cupola for crane operations, the Model 347 demonstrates its lifting capability. The mounting for the wing is of note.

May 1970 and its first extended flight the following day. Eventually, over 160 people flew the Model 347 in its Phase I configuration (minus wing) and it appeared briefly in company-applied US Army markings with the legend 'HLH Fly By Wire' painted on the forward fuselage, a reference to the outsized XCH-62.

After the wing was installed, the Model 347 was briefly equipped with the three-bladed rotor when it appeared at an air show in May 1972.

Model 414-100

Boeing uses the term Model 414-100 to refer to most of its export Chinook helicopters, even to those with other company designations, such as the British Chinook HC.Mk 1 (separate entry) which is officially on the company''s books as the Model 414-352. The term is sometimes interchangeable with the unofficial (as far as the US military is concerned) designation CH-47SD (separate entry). It is best understood as a generic reference to all Chinooks not operated by the US Army.

Some Boeing 414-100s have the long-range fuel system (much bigger, bulging side-fuselage fuel tanks) with fuel capacity

Spain's second batch of Chinooks was the first officially designated Model 414 International Chinook, although they were essentially CH-47Cs with some CH-47D features. The aircraft have recently had nose radar added.

raised to 2,068 US gal (7828 litres) or almost double that of standard Army Chinooks, a feature also found on the MH-47E and CH-47SD (separate entries).

In this account export Chinooks are covered under their basic build variants (CH-47A, C or D) or under specific entries (CH-147, HC.Mk 1/2, CH-47J/JA and Agusta).

Chinook HC.Mk 1

The Chinook HC.Mk 1 is Britain's improved version of the CH-47C model. The Royal Air Force originally intended to purchase the CH-47B in 1967, but delays in the procurement process finally led to it buying a fleet of 33 new-build CH-47C variants, ordered in 1978 for delivery from 1980. The first RAF Chinook HC.Mk 1 (ZA670) flew on 23 March 1980.

Boeing marketed the CH-47C variant to overseas customers as the Boeing Vertol International Military Chinook Model 414/CH-47C, the basic variant purchased by the Royal Air Force but with many additions. During this period Boeing was designing and developing an even more powerful and capable CH-47D variant which would allow the entire US Army's fleet of over 472 CH-47A/B and C variants to be updated and modernised to this new standard and would provide the US Army with an enhanced medium-lift capability beyond 2000. This design study began in 1976 and many of the features proposed for the new CH-47D variant were offered to the RAF.

The RAF Chinook HC.Mk 1, although similar to the CH-47C variant, featured an uprated automatic flight control system, Lucas oil-cooled generators, rotor brake, engine and windscreen anti-icing, single-point pressure refuelling and crash-resistant fuel tanks, triple-hook external load system

This aircraft (ZA708) was used at CFB Shearwater to test a rotor blade heating system for de-icing. It carries cameras on the rotor masts to record the movements of the blades and operations of the de-icing mats.

and NVG-compatible cockpit lighting. It also featured a hydraulically-powered rear ramp and seating for 44 troops. The RAF equipped its Chinooks with a full IFR cockpit which would allow them to transit Europe's airways and fly long-range self-deployment transits of over 900 nm (1666 km) when fitted with 7,500 lb (3400 kg) of internal fuel provided by fuel tanks from redundant Andovers. The cockpit specification included four separate radio systems (for pilot/navigator/jump-seat and forward crewman positions) comprising HF, AM, FM and UHF communications and homing systems, TACAN, ADF and Doppler Tactical Air Navigation System, radar altimeter, barometric altimeter and automatic barometric height hold capability, IFF and ILS/VOR systems.

The first batch of RAF Chinook HC.Mk 1s was delivered with metal rotor blades and Textron Lycoming T55-L-11E turboshafts. They were later retrofitted with uprated

T55-L-712s developed for the CH-47D programme, providing 3,750 shp (2797 kW), along with a Cobra engine fire prevention system. The original metal rotor blades were replaced by larger, 25-in (64-cm) chord glass-fibre rotor blades with titanium leading edges which were 5 in (12.7 cm) wider than the original metal blades, and provided reduced maintenance and an increased operational life of over 3,000 hours. The HC.Mk 1 could operate at a maximum all-up

weight of 50,000 lb (22680 kg), carrying 28,000 lb (12700 kg) on the centre hook and 17,000 lb (7711 kg) on the fore and aft hooks, or 25,000 lb (11340 kg) as a forward and aft dual-point load or, alternatively, a 19,550-lb (8863-kg) internal load. RAF HC.Mk 1s have lifted loads of more than 22,045 lb (10000 kg) and all are equipped with a 3,000-lb (1360-kg) capacity hydraulically operated cargo winch which is housed on the floor behind the cockpit. All three cargo hooks and winch can be operated by either pilot or by the crewman in the rear.

RAF Chinook HC.Mk1s were painted in a two-tone camouflage scheme which suited the main operational environment of the time in Central Europe. The two-tone scheme had an infra-red quality which helped break down the helicopters silhouette in the infra-red wave-bands. RAF Chinooks were also fitted with engine intake screens to help reduce foreign object damage and an engine intake de-icing system using ducted hot air from the turbines. During the mid-1980s the RAF and A&AEE Boscombe Down deployed Chinook HC.Mk 1(ZA708) to the Canadian Forces Base at Shearwater in Canada to undertake rotor blade de-icing trials, in which electrically heated mats were fixed to the rotor blades. These cold weather trials helped to explore the RAF Chinook's icing limitations, allowing the Chinook HC.Mk 1

This HC.Mk 1 carries extra antennas and a hastily applied night camouflage for its Desert Storm Special Forces role. The IRCM turret below the engines is noteworthy.

Chinook HC.Mk 1

Original narrow-chord blades later replaced by wide-chord glass-fibre blades

T55-L-11E engines, later replaced by T55-L-712E

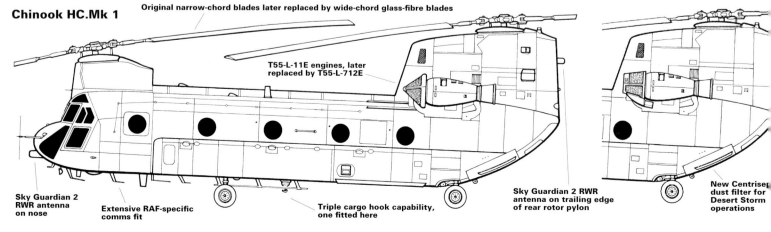

Sky Guardian 2 RWR antenna on nose

Extensive RAF-specific comms fit

Triple cargo hook capability, one fitted here

Sky Guardian 2 RWR antenna on trailing edge of rear rotor pylon

New Centriser dust filter for Desert Storm operations

An HC.Mk 1B at work displays the chaff/flare dispenser boxes fitted on the fuel tank sides and rear rotor pylon.

to operate down to minus -6°C (21°F) in potential icing conditions. The rotor blade heating system has never entered operational service. Britain's Chinooks were the first to introduce triple cargo hooks, a rotor brake, NVG-compatible cockpit, an automatic fuel fire suppression system, and pressure refuelling.

The Chinook helicopter has been vital to British forces virtually since its introduction: a single example (ZA718) belonging to No. 18 Squadron gained fame for its achievements in the 1982 Falklands War after other Chinooks *en route* to the battle zone were lost when the MV *Atlantic Conveyor* was sunk by an Argentine Exocet missile. In Operation Desert Storm in 1991, they were responsible for transporting army personnel and equipment prior to and during the land war against Iraq. Chinooks carried 3,500 prisoners of war, as many as 85 at a time in a single helicopter. Chinooks have also figured extensively in humanitarian relief operations, and improved models (below) will do so well into the next century.

Chinook HC.Mk 1B

The HC.Mk 1B designation was assigned to Royal Air Force Chinook HC.Mk 1 helicopters after retrofit of glass-fibre rotor blades in 1980.

Chinook HC.Mk 2/2A

The Chinook HC.Mk 2 is the RAF's equivalent to the US Army CH-47D helicopter, essentially brought up to the standard of the future CH-47SD but with minor differences. The Mk 2 was the result of the US Army modernising its entire Chinook fleet to updated CH-47D standard in the 1980s, meaning that Americans were no longer flying an aircraft corresponding to Britain's HC.Mk 1 (CH-47C). RAF officers concluded that the cost of supporting an ageing Chinook fleet would become unacceptably high beyond 1996. This prompted the RAF to take a close look at Boeing's International Chinook modernisation programme, which resulted in the Ministry of Defence and Boeing Space and Defence Group, Helicopters Division signing a $224 million contract in the spring of 1990 to modernise and update the RAF's fleet of 32 Chinook HC.Mk 1s to HC.Mk 2 (CH-47D) standard.

The mid-life update was similar to the US Army's CH-47D mid-life update and modernisation programme. Although externally similar to the HC.Mk 1, except for the large intake on the aft pylon leading edge which provides air cooling to the aft transmission, internally, the HC.Mk 2 is effectively a new helicopter with improved systems and components.

The RAF returned Chinook airframes to Boeing where the aircraft were completely dismantled, rebuilt and returned as zero-timed airframes without regard to their prior history or flight hours. The variant received a new powerplant: the original Lycoming T55-L-712E turboshafts were removed and sent to the RN Aircraft Yard at Fleetlands, Hampshire for rebuilding to the new enhanced T55-L-712F standard. This involved replacing the 'hot' end of the engine to allow higher temperatures and increased engine performance.

One major improvement to the HC.Mk 2 variant was the replacement of the original hydro-mechanical fuel system with a FADEC system.

Apart from the engines, improvements included an uprated 7,500-shp (5595-kW) transmission and drive system. This has helped to increase the aircraft's emergency single-engine performance and includes several additional safety features. A much simplified and improved modular hydraulic system reduces the risk of leaks and also improves reliability, while a new maintenance panel in the aft cabin provides 26 separate monitoring and inspection functions. Other improvements include a redundant and improved electrical system and additional generator. A new 95-shp (70-kW) Solar T62-T-2B APU mounted in the aft cabin above the ramp drives a generator and hydraulic pump to furnish hydraulic and electrical power for ground operations. The two improved advanced flight control systems contribute to the stabilisation of the aircraft and enhances control responses throughout all axes. The AFCS maintains desired airspeed, altitude, bank angles and heading and can be coupled to either the pilot or navigator/co-pilot's horizontal situation indicator. With two systems, each operate at half-gain, and if one fails the remaining system will increase to three-quarters gain. This, along with an improved cockpit layout, has helped to reduce pilot work-load.

A trials RAF Chinook HC.Mk 1 first flew with a FADEC at Boeing Helicopters on 16 October 1989. The RAF FADEC was produced to a Chandler Evans design using an electronic unit provided by Hawker Siddeley Dynamics, and the system was adapted by a team consisting of Chandler Evans, Lycoming and Boeing Helicopters for use with the Textron Lycoming T55-L-712 engines. The RAF was the lead customer for this particular FADEC system. A similar FADEC was fitted to the US Army's Special Operations MH-47E variant, retrofitted to some CH-47Ds, and is slated for the CH-47F – all the subjects of separate entries.

Chinook HC.Mk 2s regularly lift ISO containers in the course of their duties. Such loads are supported fore and aft to keep them stable during lifts.

Above: RAF Chinooks undertake all forms of flying, including mountain work. The fleet has a secondary SAR capability, and can be called upon when either long-range or heavy-lift capability is required, or during large-scale emergencies when the SAR-dedicated Sea King fleet is overloaded.

Left: This white-painted HC.Mk 2 is in 'Bosnia fit', with spent-case ejector chutes for the guns normally mounted in the forward hatches.

Above: The HC.Mk 2As serve with No. 27 Squadron. They have strengthened forward fuselages but are otherwise similar to the HC.Mk 2.

The first HC.Mk 2 (ZA718/BN) returned to the United Kingdom in its new guise on 20 May 1993 to undertake acceptance trials with DERA at Boscombe Down, followed by the second example (ZA681) on 10 September 1993 which would be operated by No. 27 Squadron undertaking RAF Chinook HC.Mk 2 aircrew conversions at RAF Odiham. These were followed by one Chinook a month returning to RAF Odiham. During this period there were several FADEC-related incidents both at Boscombe Down and at Odiham, resulting in digital engine control units (DECU) fault codes, engine over-temperature on start-ups, engine torque mismatch, engine run-up and spurious engine failure captions, many related to the FADEC software. The Chinook FADEC has two separate computers, a primary lane for normal control and a reversionary lane for use when the primary lane is out of action. The intelligence of both computers is the result of the software, which is different for each lane. Both computers and electrical power supplies were built into one DECU – one for each engine, which are located in the rear cabin. It was soon realised that there were problems with the software, exacerbated by the difficulty in reading and analysing it. This problem has now been resolved.

Other than the FADEC problem, the introduction of the HC.Mk 2 into service was trouble-free, and RAF Chinook reliability and operational availability increased substantially. Figures released by Boeing show that, compared to the CH-47C, the modernised CH-47D/HC.Mk 2 offers 58 per cent improvement in operational effectiveness, a 56 per cent improvement in meantime between unscheduled maintenance, a 45 per cent reduction in maintenance man-hours per flight, and a 22 per cent improvement in the elimination of aborted flights. When costs of labour, materials, spares replenishment and transportation costs are considered, the modernised CH-47D/HC.Mk 2 provides a 42 per cent reduction in unit and depot level maintenance, repairs and overhaul. These figures help to vindicate the 'spend-to-save'

modernisation programme in which increased aircraft availability and savings are set against projected life-cycle operating costs. The RAF is the highest-time user of the Chinook, its aircraft operating far above the flight hours flown by any other user and undertaking a more diverse range of missions than any other customer.

Only two RAF HC.Mk 2s have been lost to date: one crashed at Hanover, Germany and the other (ZD576) crashed into the Mull of Kintyre on 2 June 1994. The latest RAF Chinook – HC.Mk 2As (ZH775-ZH896) ordered in 1995 – arrived in the UK during 1997/98. The only difference between a normal HC.Mk 2 and HC.Mk 2A is additional strengthening of the front end of the fuselage section around the cockpit area, which could possibly allow the addition of an aerial refuelling boom at a later date.

Chinook HC.Mk 2 – 'war fit'

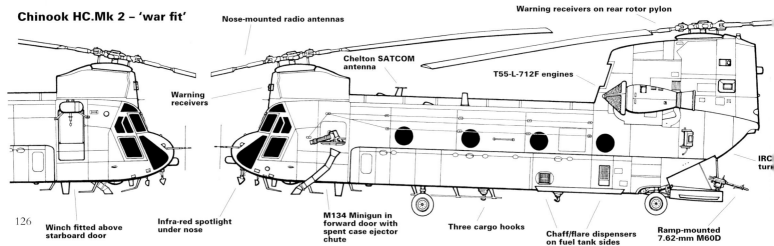

Warning receivers on rear rotor pylon

Nose-mounted radio antennas

Warning receivers

Chelton SATCOM antenna

T55-L-712F engines

IRC tur

Winch fitted above starboard door

Infra-red spotlight under nose

M134 Minigun in forward door with spent case ejector chute

Three cargo hooks

Chaff/flare dispensers on fuel tank sides

Ramp-mounted 7.62-mm M60D

HC.Mk 2 details

The capacious cabin of the Chinook can accommodate small vehicles, cargo or up to 80 standing fully-equipped troops (left). Floor belts are provided for troops not able to get a sidewall seat. On long-range missions the aircraft can be fitted with an internal Robertson 800-Imp gal (3028-litre) ERT (Extended Range Tank) in the cabin (below right). RAF HC.Mk 2s are extremely well protected with an extensive warning suite and chaff/flare dispensers (right). For suppressive fire the aircraft are routinely fitted with M134 Miniguns (below left) in the forward doors and an M60D on the rear ramp (below), fired by a crewman on a dispatcher. The Minigun is aimed by the LC-100-400 sight, and is usually provided with four cases of ammunition totalling 8,000 rounds.

Chinook HC.Mk 3

The RAF ordered eight special operations Chinook HC.Mk 3s in 1995 with delivery expected in early 2000. They are based on the Boeing export Chinook models, variously known as Model 414-100 and CH-47SD, and will be used for Special Forces/combat search and rescue support, and are the first dedicated special operations helicopters to be purchased by the Ministry of Defence. They essentially employ 'Section 41' (the nose component of the aircraft) identical to the US Army's MH-47E special operations aircraft.

The HC.Mk 3 will have many of the features found on the CH-47SD, MH-47E and 414-100, including two 1,030-Imp gal (4682-litre) long-range, side fairing fuel tanks, internal 'plumbing' for an aerial refuelling probe (though the probe itself is not installed), additional weapon mounts for 0.50-in/12.7-mm machine-guns, provision for fast-roping and an internal cargo handling system. With a maximum gross weight of 54,000 lb (24500 kg), the HC.Mk 3 will be fitted with uprated Textron Lycoming T55-L-714 (4,168 shp/3109 kW continuous, 4,867 shp/3630 kW max), FADEC and uprated 7,500-shp (5595-kW) transmission providing a useful load of 27,082 lb (12284 kg).

The two long-range fuel tanks will give the HC.Mk 3 a standard fuel capacity of over 2,060 Imp gal (9365 litres), giving a radius of operations in excess of 600 nm (1111 km) with an endurance over 5½ hours and a ferry range unrefuelled of 1,260 nm (2333 km). This gives the HC.Mk 3 over twice the range/endurance of the HC.Mk 2 and can be further increased with the fitting of up to three Robertson 800-Imp gal (3636-litre) internal extended range tanks, although these reduce the cabin space for troops and cargo. The normal operational fit for RAF Chinooks (HC.Mk 2/HC.Mk 3) is a single 800-Imp gal ERT; together with aerial refuelling, it will give the HC.Mk 3 unlimited range.

The RAF's HC.Mk 3 will feature a customised UK cockpit comprising digital EFIS 'glass' cockpit which will almost certainly feature a comprehensive avionics control management system. The cockpit will be fully NVG-compatible with MIL-STD 1553 databus and secondary ARINC 429 databus, with EFIS cockpit displays comprising air vehicle multi-function and mission management displays in which mission and air vehicle information is entered via a pair of control display units. Navigation and mission capability will be further enhanced by a combination of a laser ring gyro and inertial navigation system, which will be linked to a Doppler and GPS navigation computer. A data transfer device using a ground station computer will automatically download aircraft and mission details such as digital maps, routes/waypoints, RVs, heights, radio frequencies and threat analyses, allowing mission planning to be finalised pre-flight and not on start-up.

The mission management system will allow the full integration of other operational equipment such as SATCOM and aircraft defence aids suite. The HC.Mk 3 will also benefit from a nose-mounted FLIR system to complement the pilot's night vision goggles, and will be used for route flying and to permit operations in the worst of weathers. It is yet to be confirmed which type of terrain-following or terrain-avoidance multi-mode radar will be fitted. The HC.Mk 3 will have an aerial refuelling capability and will work with the new C-130J Hercules using a wing-mounted hose-and-drogue system.

CH-47J

The Kawasaki CH-47J is Japan's licence-built equivalent to the CH-47D Chinook, with minor changes including different navigation equipment. It is powered by two 3,750-shp (2797-kW) Textron Lycoming T55-L-712 turboshaft engines, also referred to as T55-L-11B in Japanese documents. Used by both ground and air force units, the

This JASDF CH-47J of the Misawa HAS was tested in 1993 with this light grey camouflage for winter operations, but the scheme was not adopted.

CH-47J serves alongside the CH-47JA (separate entry), which is equivalent to the CH-47SD/Model 414-100. Manufacturer Kawasaki Heavy Industries (KHI) is located in Gifu.

Japan's experience with the Chinook began with the delivery of two aircraft manufactured by Boeing which set forth for Japan on a ship in March 1986 and arrived at Nagoya the following month. The two Boeing-built helicopters for Japan are identified in published reference sources as CH-47Cs or CH-47Ds, but in Boeing documents are listed simply as CH-47Js. The two Boeing-built aircraft were assigned Japanese military serial numbers 52901 (c/n M4507, the first aircraft, delivered to the Japan Ground Self-Defence Force), which made its first flight at the factory in January 1986, and 67-4471 (c/n 4508, the second aircraft, delivered to the Japan Air Self-Defence Force), which made its first flight fully fitted-out in July 1986, after temporarily wearing registry no. N7425J.

The CH-47J filled Japan's HH-X requirement of the mid-1980s to replace Kawasaki KV-107/II-5 helicopters with the JASDF for logistic support of radar sites, utility and SAR duties. In addition, the JGSDF sought CH-47Js for transportation duties. Japan's army and air force chose the Chinook after studying other heavy-lift helicopter candidates, including the Sikorsky CH-53E Super Sea Stallion. The first five Kawasaki-built CH-47Js were made as knock-down kits in the US and assembled in Gifu. After 1986, the helicopters were manufactured in Japan. Beginning with these ships, the engines (Lycoming T55-L-712) were manufactured by KHI under licence, marking the first time that both airframe and engine had been manufactured under licence by same Japanese company.

The first two CH-47Js, one for each of the JASDF and JGSDF, were delivered simultaneously on 26 December 1986. After

The JASDF CH-47Js differed from those of the JGSDF by having INS. This example serves with the Iruma Herikoputa Kuyu-tai, one of four airlift squadrons operating four CH-47Js each.

This was the first CH-47J, one of two built and assembled by Boeing. It wears the standard camouflage of the JGSDF. Most army CH-47Js serve with Dai 1 Herikoputa-dan at Kisarazu AAB.

technical and operational tests, the first operational unit in the JGSDF, the 1st Helicopter Brigade, received its CH-47J on 10 March 1988 and started conversion from the KV-107. The first Chinook unit in the JASDF was the Provisional Iruma Helicopter Airlift Squadron, which received its aircraft on 1 October 1987.

The more numerous JGSDF Chinooks have received considerable attention flying civilian relief missions, such as in response to the 1994 Hanshin earthquake which hit Kobe Bay in western Japan, killing 5,300 people, injuring 27,000 and leaving 300,000 homeless. The army provided eight CH-47Js that performed hundreds of sorties, including deliveries of emergency shelter provisions and food supplies to the victims. The Emperor and Empress of Japan personally requested to be transported by an army CH-47J to visit the devastated areas. Japan uses its air force Chinooks primarily for their intended mission of resupply of remote radar bases, as well as in rescue work.

The Japanese Chinook is still in production. Most sources list 51 delivered so far of an intended 56, of which 50 can be identified (two by Boeing, 48 by Kawasaki). Plans for FY 2000 call for two CH-47Js for the JASDF, apparently ships numbers 52 and 53, in addition to two CH-47JA models (separate entry) for the JGSDF. The current total of 50 breaks down by service branch as 16 aircraft for the JASDF and 34 for the JGSDF. The eventual total of 56 will comprise 16 plus 40.

CH-47Js in both the JGSDF and JASDF wear a camouflage scheme but the JASDF's colour is much brighter, reflecting the differences in operational circumstances and role. In the Japanese serial system, the first digit indicates the calendar year an aircraft was received, using the Western calendar, i.e., the first digit in 67-4486 means that the aircraft was received in 1996 (not FY 1996).

CH-47J serials
Boeing-built aircraft: M4507 (52901) (1) JGSDF, M4508 (67-4471) (1) JASDF
Total built: 2

Kawasaki-built aircraft: 52902/52934 (33) JGSDF, 77-4472 (1) JASDF, 87-4473/4474 (2) JASDF, 97-4475/4476 (2) JASDF, 07-4477/4478 (2) JASDF, 17-4479/4480 (2) JASDF, 27-4481/4482 (2) JASDF, 37-4483/4484 (2) JASDF, 47-4485 (1) JASDF, 67-4486 (1) JASDF
Total built: 48

CH-47JA

The CH-47JA is the improved Japanese Chinook with the long-range fuel tanks found on other advanced models (MH-47E, Model 414-100, CH-47SD, RAF Chinook HC.Mk 3, some Model 234s) plus numerous other changes aimed at improving performance, all instigated by the JGSDF, which shifted to the CH-47JA with its FY95 budget request. The distinguishing changes are obvious: enlarged fuel tanks on each side of the fuselage, weather radar, an RWR and a AN/AAQ-16 FLIR unit. The main navigation equipment was changed to IGI (Integrated GPS and INS) and colour liquid crystal MFDs were introduced as cockpit instrumentation.

Principal external differences found in the CH-47JA (as compared to the CH-47J) are enlarged side sponsons, radar nose and FLIR turret (non-retractable) under the nose. Some Chinook pilots in the JGSDF claim that forward downward view from the A's cockpit is worse than from the CH-47J because it is obscured by the radar nose, making rough-field landings more difficult.

As in other Chinooks having the longer-range fuel system, fuel tank capacity was increased to 2,086 US gal (7896 litres) from 1,028 US gal (3891 litres). The KHI-designed sponson, not identical to that on Boeing-built long-range Chinooks, was based on Boeing Vertol's Model 234LR long-range Commercial Chinook's sponson. The change in fuel capacity doubled range to about 1,080 nm (2000 km) but payload capability was decreased on the CH-47JA because the allowed maximum take-off weight was not changed. These enhancements in range and fuel were prompted in part by JGSDF operations in Okinawa, where range is a consideration.

Both Boeing and Kawasaki reported the first flight of the CH-47JA model in October 1995, but did not specify the date. It appears the aircraft really flew as early as August 1995. In December 1995, the first CH-47JA was delivered to the School Support Squadron at Akeno Army Air Base for performance confirmation and other tests. Two CH-47JAs were used for a series of tests – including mission adaptability – lasting almost one year. The first delivery of CH-47JAs to an operational unit, the 101st Squadron at Naha Army Air Base, was made on 17 December 1996. The JASDF also deployed a CH-47J to Naha AB in Okinawa but no improvement modification had been done. JASDF CH-47Js deploying to Naha AB carry additional fuel tanks in the front of the cabin, consisting of two barrels of 500 US gal (1892 litres) each. This brings another 1 hour and 10 minutes of flight endurance time to the CH-47J.

The JASDF resumed its acquisition of Chinooks in 1999. Although their designation by the JASDF remains CH-47J, they are identical to JGSDF CH-47JAs because KHI has closed down the CH-47J production line and transitioned to the CH-47JA. Another order consisting of two CH-47JAs for the JGSDF and two CH-47Js for the JASDF is currently planned for FY 2000.

Above: The CH-47JA has radar, AAQ-16 FLIR and long-range tanks to greatly expand the operational capability of the type in JGSDF service. In addition to the Kyoiku Sien Hiko-tai at Akeno, CH-47JAs serve with the JGSDF's Dai 1 Konsei-Dan (Naha, Okinawa) and Dai 1 Herikoputa-dan (Kisarazu). The Seibu Homen Herikoputa-tai (Western Army Helicopter Squadron) will receive this advanced variant in 1999 to replace KV-107-IIs.

Right: The CH-47JA's cockpit is a mix of dials and screens, with one MFD for each pilot. Note the RWR display in the central console.

CH-47JA

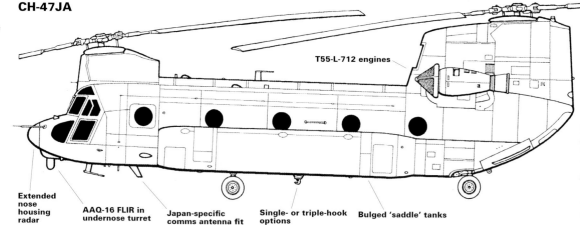

T55-L-712 engines

Extended nose housing radar

AAQ-16 FLIR in undernose turret

Japan-specific comms antenna fit

Single- or triple-hook options

Bulged 'saddle' tanks

Agusta-built Chinooks

Italy's Elicotteri Meridionali (EM), a part of the Agusta group, acquired rights to manufacture the CH-47C Chinook in 1968. In collaboration with SIAI-Marchetti, EM manufactured the CH-47C Chinook beginning in 1970s, initially with a batch of 20 helicopters for Libya, and by the late 1970s was producing about one Chinook per month. Morocco was the second customer. Agusta subsequently dropped the EM name in connection with its manufacture of an improved C model powered by two AlliedSignal (Garrett) T55-L-712E turboshaft engines. The Italian-built Chinook is virtually identical to the American CH-47C, having a maximum take-off weight of 50,000 lb (22680 kg), a useful load of 27,016 lb (12254 kg) and a maximum external cargo load of 27,015 lb (12254 kg), although the last figure seems high for any

practical mission. Like its Boeing-built equivalent, it was designed to carry 33 combat-equipped troops, or up to 44, 50 or 59 in high-density configurations.

Agusta is licensed to build the C model only, Boeing having refused to license it for the CH-47D variant since that would mean direct sales competition. The Italian company maintains the capability to manufacture CH-47Cs for export customers and for the Italian air force. Some of these have become a familiar sight during United Nations operations, painted white. Some Agusta-built aircraft have been upgraded to CH-47D status by Boeing. Agusta continues to actively promote a hospital version of the CH-47C as an Emergency Surgery Flying Centre, and also a fire-fighting version with a distinctive nozzle protruding below the fuselage.

The biggest customers for the Agusta CH-47C were the Italian army (right) which took 35 (plus two Boeing-built aircraft) and Iran (below right), which acquired 38 assembled from Boeing kits and 30 wholly built by Agusta.

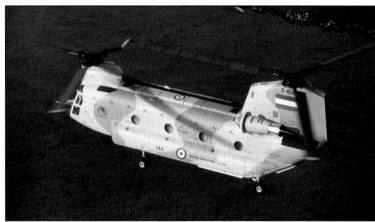

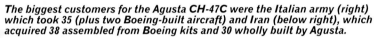

Greece's CH-47Cs have all now been upgraded by Boeing to CH-47D standard.

Agusta CH-47C   Based on standard CH-47C airframe

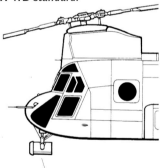

Greek aircraft optionally fitted with undernose Nitesun searchlight

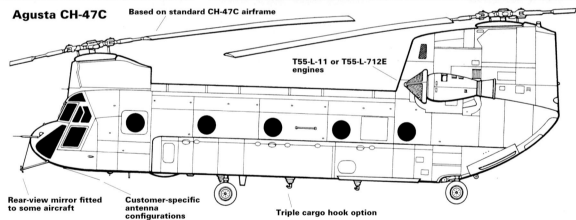

T55-L-11 or T55-L-712E engines

Rear-view mirror fitted to some aircraft

Customer-specific antenna configurations

Triple cargo hook option

Egypt acquired 15 aircraft from the Agusta line, seven of which are seen here outside the Frosinone works.

Libya was Agusta's first overseas customer, buying 20 for the air force. The survivors are now believed to have been passed to the army.

Morocco was another North African operator, buying a fleet of nine. Agusta also built 11 aircraft for the US Army National Guard.

'Bearcat III'

'Bearcat III' is a non-standard aircraft that has flown in a number of demonstration and

test programmes and is currently flight-testing CH-47F Improved Cargo Helicopter features; the US Army Aviation Center is conducting flight tests at Fort Rucker, Alabama. The aircraft has completed Boeing

evaluation of fuselage tuning and vibration reduction trials. 'Bearcat III' (86-1678) is a CH-47D (a former CH-47C) modified in 1986 to D model standard: it served in Germany, in Operation Desert Storm, in Germany

again, and then in Maryland before being leased by Boeing in March 1995. The US Army refers to this one-of-a-kind ship as the Vibration Reduction Test Aircraft (VRTA).

Golden State Guard

Above: Probably the best known of all Golden State Guard aircraft are the F-16s of the 144th FW, 194th FS. The unit flew the Block 15 F-16A/B ADF until 1994, when it began the conversion to the current Block 25 F-16C/D. All the squadron's 'Vipers' have carried this striking eagle motif on their fins.

Left: All AH-1F Cobras flying in the US today are operated solely by Army Guard units. In California, the 'Snakes' are flown by 1-18 CAV.

Known as the 'Golden State', California became the United States' 31st state in 1850. The excellent climate makes California arguably one of the best places in the world to live, but its location also leaves it vulnerable to earthquakes, floods and other natural disasters. The California Air National Guard and Army National Guard consistently provide vital aid and support in times of need. In addition to coping with their state-wide duties, California Guard members daily fulfil a host of national and international taskings.

California's network of National Guard units with an aviation component is divided into two groups, the Air National Guard (ANG) and the Army National Guard (ArNG). Guard units are federally funded and their federal mission is their primary role. Units may subsequently be called upon to support the state in times of need. Their military training goes to good use when a Guard unit performs a state mission such as SAR or evacuation. The Office of Emergency Services is the state organisation that receives direction from the California Governor and will call up and activate Guard units for state emergencies

The Deputy Adjutant General for the California Air National Guard and Commander of the California Air National Guard is MGEN

Bob Barrow, who works at State Headquarters in Sacramento. He is a Vietnam veteran, flew 137 combat missions in the F-4 with the 433rd TFS, and also served with the 163rd TFS at March AFB, flying F-4Cs. He reports to Adjutant General MGEN Tandy Bozeman. His responsibilities include making sure that the five ANG units are running smoothly and meeting their requirements.

When asked about the California ANG, Barrow said, "The California Air National Guard, along with the California Army National Guard, participate in the humanitarian role in times of disaster. We have a responsibility to support the Governor and the Office of Emergency Services at any time. The missions that we do are primarily military and when we

perform state support missions, the military training is applied. The US Air Force has lost about 30 per cent of its force structure in the last 10 years. Their operational requirements have increased 400 per cent and they now call upon the Guard forces very often."

The Guard itself is not immune from cuts, and force levels in California have been cut from 6,000 to 4,900 personnel over the same 10 years. At the same time, the demands made of it are ever increasing. For example, the California Air National Guard may possibly gain a new information operation (space mission) unit at Vandenburg AFB. As General Tandy reflected, "Over 70 per cent of our people are part-time, yet we still make demands of our units that are comparable to active-duty units. It is amazing that we can do so much with so few people."

Channel Islands ANGB, 146th AW/115th AS

Known as the 'Hollywood Guard', the 146th Airlift Wing operates 12 Lockheed C-130Es and is based at the Channel Island ANGB, California. The base is co-located with NAS Point Mugu and the ANG and the Navy share the same runway. The two squadrons under the 146th AW are the 115th Airlift Squadron and the 146th Aeromedical Evacuation Squadron. The official primary role of the 146th AW is airdrop, airland and medical evacuation.

The airdrop role (personnel, equipment, resupply) is practised most often in the C-130Es, since it is the most challenging. Most airdrops are done at 400 to 1,000 ft (122 to 305 m) by day and night; for low-level sorties, the C-130Es can get down to 300 ft (91 m) in the day. In 1994, the unit had 16 Hercules but was down-sized to 12, all of which are FY61 and FY62 aircraft. There is a chance that the E models will be upgraded to a 'glass' cockpit standard and, in the long term, the unit may transition to the C-130J, but that is still far in the future. Two of its C-130Es are equipped with a GPS and the remainder are being modified. One aircraft is trialling a new autopilot that has audible cautions.

The aeromedical evacuation squadron is made up of medical aircrews and radio operators, charged with setting up a command and control system and an MASF (Mobile Air Staging Facility). An MASF – a self-contained medical group – works in conjunction with the Army to prepare patients for transportation/airlift to hospitals or other facilities, and can operate with any kind of medevac aircraft. The unit served in Desert Storm and is fully combat-ready, trained for chemical warfare, and participates in many state exercises. A C-130E can be litter-rigged for the unit in about an hour. The squadron was instrumental in helping Chile to set up a similar unit.

One of the unit's specialities for the state is the MAFFS (Modular Airborne Fire-Fighting System) role, very much in demand during California's volatile summer fire season. The MAFFS aircraft wear temporary bright orange numbers for identification. The 146th AW is one of four MAFFS units and has two of the 2,800-US gal (10600-litre) MAFFS modules. During a fire it works for the US Forest Service and California Department of Forestry, and when all of their fire-fighting tanker assets have

been deployed, the MAFFS units are activated. The 1970s-vintage MAFFS modules are getting old and the unit would be happy to get lighter and newer modules; despite this, the unit was awarded the National Guard Association's 1996 Spatz trophy as the outstanding National Guard. The same year, the unit marked its 250,000th accident-free flying hour, in 1997 it was awarded the Air Force Association's Outstanding Airlift Unit Award, and in 1998 it was awarded its fourth Outstanding Unit Citation.

Fresno ANGB, 144th FW/194th FS

Nicknamed the 'Griffins', this wing operates 20 F-16C/Ds – although its single F-16D is currently on loan to the Arizona ANG. The unit also has a single C-26B Metro III that replaced its previous C-26A in 1992. This is the only F-16C unit in the USA to operate the F-16C in a dedicated air superiority role, which is strictly an air-to-air function. With a primary unit role of air defence, the 'Griffins' defend America's southwest against any violations of airspace. The unit's secondary state role is to help out in times of emergency and support the community.

A detachment of armed F-16Cs at March ARB stands 24-hour alert in support of NORAD's western air defence sector. A few years ago the unit operated the AIM-7-armed F-16A ADF (Air Defense Fighter) variant, and now transitioned to the F-16C and is now fully combat-capable with the AIM-120 AMRAAM. In the future, the 'Griffins' might transition to the F-15C, should enough airframes become available.

The 144th FW Vice Commander and Air Operations Officer of the 144th Fighter Wing, Colonel Al Heers, said, "We are on the leading edge of the air defence business and will stay on the forefront so we can hopefully get the F-22. That is a major goal for this unit, and under the Total Force scheme, the Air Guard will get the F-22 fairly soon after the active duty receives theirs. The Guard is under a fair amount of pressure from the Air Force to fill in the voids from the downsizing. In the air defence community, we are viable anywhere in the

world performing our air-to-air role. This could include offensive counter air, defensive counter air and air-sovereignty in places such as Southwest Asia. The people here are rising to the challenge whether it be an ORI or going to war."

March Air Reserve Base, 163rd ARW/196th ARS

The 'Grizzlys' operate the KC-135R and have some nine examples on hand, though they are slated to receive a 10th airframe soon. Their nine Boeing KC-135Rs, which now all sport nose-art with names, are all FY57 and FY59 Stratotankers. One of the more recent upgrades to the unit's aircraft was the conversion of KC-135Es to KC-135Rs, including changing the engines to the more powerful CFM56s (F108s). They also previously operated a rare KC-135D, which eventually went to Kansas.

The primary federal role of the 163rd ARW is to provide air refuelling, air cargo, passenger hauling and a SIOP (Single Integrated Operational Plan) capability according to Air Force and AMC requirements. In the event of a state disaster, a secondary role for the 'Grizzlys' is to perform similar missions in response to the Office of Emergency Services via the Governor. The 163rd KC-135Rs are due for the Pacer Crag upgrade, which adds a 'glass' cockpit to the aircraft and a dedicated GPS. The new system will also have TCAS (Terminal Collision Avoidance System), and ground collision avoidance systems, and a new HF radio system with cell call capability. All of the new systems coupled together will eventually replace the navigator position and add extra duties for the boom operator.

The 163rd ARW has been instrumental in the Pacer Crag programme and participated in early testing of the system. The wing now manages the contractors working on four Pacer Crag lines underway at March ARB. The first 163rd ARW KC-135R is slated to receive the Pacer Crag upgrade in the autumn of 1999 and all of its Stratotankers should be upgraded by spring 2000. Another modification to three of its KC-135Rs will be the addition of wingtip HDU refuelling pods, to start around 2000.

The 163rd ARW is responsible for providing administration, financing and medical support for the 162nd Combat Communications Group.

The unit can often be found working around the globe and provides security teams and disaster relief teams when required by the state

Seen before the 'Grizzlys' upgraded to the KC-135R model, a 196th ARS KC-135E refuels a trio of F-16Cs. The unit is due to receive three drogue-equipped tankers.

– most notably during the Olympics and after the Northridge earthquake. The commanding officer of the 163rd ARW is Colonel Putt Richards, who commented, "We just came back from a five-week deployment to France, provided air refuelling over Bosnia, and we did it without any problems. We have great people who work here and I don't have to worry about much because our people are always taking care of the details. Our crews averaged 65 days each per year TDY [away from the base] in 1997."

Moffett Federal Air Field, 129th RQW/129th RQS

This unit operates four HC-130P Hercules and six FLIR-equipped HH-60G Pave Hawks. The HC-130P crews use the title/callsign KING and the HH-60G crews use JOLLY (a reference to the 'Jolly Green Giant' heritage). The HC-130Ps are vital to SAR sorties as they can aerial refuel the HH-60Gs, and can drop rafts and supplies to survivors in the water. Planned upgrades to the HC-130Ps include TCAS and additional defensive systems. The HH-60Gs have the older T700 engines, and will eventually receive the newer and higher-performance T701-C engines. The NVGs in use by the unit are the newer 4950s, which have a wider field of view than the ANVIS-6.

A very important part of the organisation are its PJs (para jumpers), who routinely train with the aircraft and perform an array of specialised skills. Their job is to drop to downed aircrew, injured personnel or accident/disaster survivors and stabilise them for recovery. All 35 PJs are medically trained and capable of performing emergency surgery, and each takes about one and a half years to train. Since the unit stood up in the early 1970s, it has saved 266 lives.

The 129th RQW is spread thinly because of the limited number of HC-130Ps and HH-60Gs available to it. They are often tasked to support operations abroad, and if one or two aircraft are undergoing routine maintenance, that represents a significant percentage of the fleet. The unit could gladly use more HH-60Gs, and more HC-130s in particular. The wing and its units stand combat-ready, deployable on very short notice – which is part of their federal mission.

The official military role of the unit is CSAR (combat search and rescue) in both 'permissive' and 'non-permissive' (hostile) environments. The unit can be found operating from such places as Turkey and Bosnia, and works daily with its active-duty counterparts. The unit is currently supporting Operation Northern Watch in Turkey, where about 100 squadron personnel deploy for one to three months per rotation.

Another rotational deployment site is Keflavik, Iceland, where a C-130 is kept on station to support possible rescues. The 129th deploys personnel to Keflavik 11 times a year.

The HC-130Ps are sometimes used to help with both active-duty and Air Force Reserve HH-60G pilot training, for aerial refuelling qualification and general operational currency work. The secondary role and civilian tasking is civil SAR, and the 129th typically undertakes a civil rescue mission about once a month.

The 129th RQW Vice Commander, Colonel Tommy Williams, said, "We had not had an ORI [Operational Readiness Inspection] in 10 years and [the last one] was not too good. About a year ago we had our first ORI (12th AF full inspection team) and we deployed to Beale with all 10 aircraft. There were many scenarios and it was one of the most challenging inspections we could have had. Not one mission was cancelled and when the ORI was finished, we achieved

From Channel Islands ANGB (NAS Point Mugu), the 115th AS flies tactical airdrop missions with C-130Es. A speciality role is fire-fighting with the MAFFS equipment, as demonstrated (left) by a C-130E complete with large codes applied for this role. Retardant can be dropped in a single drop or up to five smaller discharges. Reloading takes 90 to 120 minutes.

the highest possible score of 'outstanding'. We are proud of how well we did."

From October 1999 the 129th will transition to the MC-130P Hercules with undernose FLIR, ANVIS-compatible lighting and better defences. They will not, however, be capable of receiving fuel in flight.

California ArNG flying units

Most of the California Army National Guard flying units and assets fall under the control of the 40th Infantry Division (Mechanized), with a few exceptions like OSACOM Det 32, RAID and AVCRAD. In the event that the 40th ID is mobilised, its organic units to the division would be called up, too, including the California-based 1-18th Cavalry Squadron, 1-140th Aviation Battalion, and the F/140th Aviation Brigade. Additional ArNG units in Arizona, Kansas, Montana and Washington fall under the 40th Infantry Division's command.

The Assistant Adjutant General of the California National Guard and the Commander of the California Army National Guard is MGEN Bob Brandt, who also works at State Headquarters in Sacramento. MGEN Brandt has flown an array of aircraft including the UH-1, H-13, H-19, H-21, H-23, H-34, T-42, U-8 and C-12. MGEN Brandt reports to MGEN Bozeman and is responsible for the command of the entire California Army National Guard.

When asked about the California Army National Guard, he replied, "In California we are prepared for just about anything in regards to natural disasters. We will grow in strength by over 1,000 soldiers [compared to] what we have now and we will be getting some new equipment. The versatile Chinook fleet at Stockton will be growing to 16 aircraft and the unit will expand accordingly.

"Our soldiers have responded very professionally to civil authorities during emergencies such as floods, fires and riots. The success of the California National Guard is because we have first class knowledgeable people operating good equipment in support of civil authorities.

"An example was during the LA riots when the Guard was instrumental in quickly moving 1,000 Highway Patrolmen from northern California to southern California using 146th AW C-130Es. The second military police unit in LA was from Eureka and they, too, were flown to Los Alamitos quickly via a C-130. Some 12,000 Air and Army Guard troops were

When the ANG Hercules fleet adopted ACC-style two-letter tactical unit codes, the 115th AS chose 'CI' in recognition of its base. The C-130E fleet is gradually changing from 'lizard' (illustrated) to the standard overall-grey scheme.

moved to LA within 36 hours, a very impressive undertaking."

Fresno – AVCRAD, 1106th Aviation Classification Repair Activity Depot

This facility is responsible for depot level maintenance of 13 different states' Army National Guard helicopters. The AVCRAD in Fresno is one of four AVCRADs in the nation, located in California, Connecticut, Missouri and Mississippi. Fresno AVCRAD supports Alaska, Arizona, California, Colorado, Hawaii, Idaho, Montana, Nevada, New Mexico, Oregon, Utah, Washington and Wyoming (22 flight facilities).

The AVCRAD reports to OTAG in peace-

A pair of HH-60G Rescue Hawks takes on fuel from an HC-130P at low level. The probe of the HH-60 is semi-retractable, extending beyond the rotor disc. The thimble radome on the port side of the nose houses Bendix weather radar.

time and its primary role is to administer depot level maintenance and avionics upgrades to Army rotary-winged aircraft. All the states combined send almost 600 helicopters to AVCRAD for periodic maintenance, including the AH-1F, UH-1H, CH-47D, OH-58A+/C, UH-60A/L and AH-64A.

In a secondary role, the unit can be found in places like Germany or South Korea, inspecting Army helicopters when, for example, said helicopters are being turned over to the Guard and it must be determined that they meet minimum standards. AVCRAD personnel have been sent around the world (Egypt, Somalia, Desert Storm, Haiti, Panama, etc.) to support active-duty units, undertaking helicopter shipping, test flights, rotational duties and other activities. AVCRAD also performs a limited amount of support work on some of the Army's active-duty helicopters, which may include painting aircraft and helping with major maintenance.

Flying from Moffett, the 129th RQS is the West Coast ANG rescue unit, equipped with a mix of HC-130Ps (illustrated) and HH-60G helicopters. The HC-130s provide rescue top cover, inflight refuelling, long-range search and survival equipment air-dropping capacity.

Recent projects the unit has accomplished include painting a US Navy UH-1N and a NASA C-130.

Two C-23B Sherpas of Det 1, Co. I, 185th Theater Aviation are permanently based at AVCRAD. The Sherpas used to fall under the 1106th AVCRAD, but were reassigned during a recent restructuring. In the event that these aircraft were ever mobilised, they would report to the Mississippi National Guard which would ultimately report to the European theatre.

When the two overall-grey Sherpas rolled off the assembly line, they both saw duty in Operation Desert Storm before finally finding their way to the 'Golden State' and their home

at AVCRAD. One of the Sherpas has Desert Storm nose-art while the other wears 'Lucky 13'. The C-23Bs deliver parts (engines, rotor blades, transmission) to the 11 western states, and are very busy: between them, they can fly as many as 1,200 hours per year. The type can fly at altitudes up to 18,000 ft (5486 m).

The 1106th AVCRAD owns two UH-1Hs (these Hueys are part of 1-140th), and the HQ, Aviation Brigade, 40th Infantry Division (Mechanized) also has two UH-1Hs permanently based there in addition to two 'float' OH-58Cs. Thus, between all of the units at AVCRAD, the based aircraft include four UH-1Hs, two OH-58Cs and two C-23Bs. The 'float' aircraft are loaned to units to cover the period their own spend in overhaul.

In the long term, there is a chance that the UH-1Hs at AVCRAD will be replaced by UH-60As should they become available. The UH-1Hs and OH-58Cs are used for maintenance training and help pilots maintain currency. When there are floods, fires or earthquakes, AVCRAD will often send a 10/12-person team which does maintenance at night, to help relieve the pressure on other units' maintenance mechanics and to keep the helicopters ready to go the following morning. AVCRAD has been training Mexican air force UH-1H maintenance personnel on a rotational basis.

Los Alamitos – Los Alamitos Army Airfield

Los Alamitos Army Airfield (KSLI) is centrally located in southern California. This former naval air station has two all-weather, instrumented runways and serves as a large-scale deployment location and a designated DSA (Disaster Support Area). Los Alamitos has two dynamic, full-motion UH-1 flight simulators,

Although not as extensively equipped as the Special Forces-dedicated MH-60G Pave Hawk, the HH-60G is nevertheless capable of low-level nocturnal missions, using the undernose FLIR and pilot's NVGs. Military SAR is the 129th's main mission, but the unit is regularly called upon to undertake civilian rescues.

which aviation units from 13 different states come to use (the same states supported by AVCRAD). The base can accommodate large aircraft such as C-5, C-17, C-141B and, on occasion, the 'Air Force One' VC-25A. With the closure of nearby MCAS El Toro, Los Alamitos will be the only military airfield on the Pacific Coast between MCAS Miramar in San Diego and NAS Point Mugu in Ventura County.

The Airfield Commander at Los Alamitos is

LTC Thomas E. Lasser, who commented, "With Los Alamitos's strategic location in southern California, the airfield is not only very valuable to the National Guard and the State of California, but to the rest of the Department of Defense as a national asset. The high visibility and utilisation of Los Alamitos makes it one of the busiest aviation operations in DoD."

Los Alamitos is home to the 40th Infantry Division (Mechanized), which is commanded by MG Edmund C. Zysk. All aircraft assigned at

HH-60Gs routinely work as a pair, supported by one HC-130P. For combat SAR tasks they would usually operate as the focal point of a CSAR package which would include A-10s and F-16s. The HH-60Gs can undertake their own fire suppression in the form of door-mounted guns.

Golden State Guard

The CH-47Ds of G Company, 140th Aviation Battalion from Stockton are regular sights throughout the state, especially during the fire season when they are tasked with fire-drop missions. Their normal mission is support of the 40th Infantry Division.

Los Alamitos fall under the 40th Aviation Brigade, except for the RAID detachment. A total of 18 AH-1F Cobras is based here, nine belonging to D Troop 1-18th Cavalry Squadron and the other nine to E Troop 1-18th Cavalry Squadron. The primary role of the 1-18th CAV is reconnaissance and attack helicopter support; F Troop 1-18th Cavalry Squadron is responsible for aircraft maintenance of the Cobras. Proposed AH-1F upgrades include enhanced weapon systems, Hellfire missile system and avionics upgrades.

The 1-140th AV (Aviation), the division's general support aviation battalion, has its headquarters and two units at Los Alamitos. Two other units are located at Mather Field in Sacramento. Eight UH-60As are operated by the B/1-140th AV, whose primary role is air assault. The 1-140th's tactical role is combat support, troop and supply moving, with

Two of the 1-140th AV's four aviation companies are based at the 40th Division's headquarters at Los Alamitos on general support duties. C Company flies the ubiquitous UH-1H alongside OH-58C Kiowas.

secondary functions that include supporting the state with fire-fighting UH-60As that use large 600+-US gal (2271+-litre) water buckets. The Blackhawks can also be used for medical evacuations. In the next five years, the B/1-140th UH-60As may be candidates for an exchange for the more powerful UH-60Ls.

C/1-140th AV, the general support company of the battalion, has 11 UH-1Hs and eight OH-58Cs. In five or six years there is a chance that the unit could transition to the OH-58D. Also in the distant future, the Hueys may be upgraded with T800 engines, new transmissions, and new four-bladed rotor systems.

A FLIR-equipped RAID (Reconnaissance And Interdiction Detachment) OH-58A+ helicopter is usually to be found at Los Alamitos, and most major RAID maintenance is performed by DET 3 RAID and its own mechanics there. The RAID unit does not fall under the 40th Infantry Division (Mechanized), but is under operational control of the National Guard Bureau.

Los Alamitos trains with National Guard organisations from other states and active-duty components for drug interdiction, earthquakes, floods and riots, in addition to fire-fighting. They have participated in all of the recent major state disasters in the area. F Company 140th Aviation Brigade has two assigned UH-1Hs and undertakes aircraft maintenance. Both the HQ

1-140th Aviation Battalion and DET 3 STARC (State Area Readiness Command) are located at the airfield, though they do not have aircraft attached to the unit.

NAS North Island

RAID personnel call this location AAFOB, for Army Aviation Forward Operating Base, and it is the home of Det 2 RAID which operates OH-58A+s, usually with two aircraft on hand. The RAID OH-58A+s are FLIR-equipped so have higher skids to ensure FLIR turret ground clearance. The A+s also have the more powerful C model engine (T63-A-720), though it still retains the A model instrument panel. The RAID OH-58A+s are equipped with GPS and

are NVG capable. RAID has some 'straight' OH-58A+s (i.e., non-FLIR machines) that are used for the marijuana suppression season and for training. Some additional UH-1H, OH-58C and UH-60A assets may be employed from other sister units for various seasonal duties.

Sacramento – AASF (Mather Field)

A Company, 1-140th Aviation Battalion operates eight UH-1Hs from the Army Aviation Support Facility (AASF) at Sacramento. The company's primary mission is combat assault support and it often works with the 184th Infantry Battalion, part of the 40th Infantry Division (Mechanized). The Hueys are used for troop transport and reconnaissance, performing a limited amount of transport evacuation. A long-term change for the A/1-140th will be to transition to the UH-60, should some airframes become available.

The 126th Medical Company (Air Ambulance) has 15 UH-60As, and previously also had UH-1Vs. Its Blackhawks are typically identified by their trio of large red cross markings, unlike the Los Alamitos machines. The crews use ANVIS-6 NVGs and are trained to operate by day and night. The primary mission of the 126th is medical evacuation, with a secondary state mission of evacuation (similar to their military function) and fire-fighting, using 660-US gal (2498-litre) water buckets slung under the

UH-60As. The unit trains for this role with the California Department of Forestry and the US Forest Service. The California Guard no longer uses its ageing UH-1Hs with 350-US gal (1325-litre) water buckets for fire-fighting. The 126th flies SAR missions in the state about once a month and has saved many lives. The lightweight Army Blackhawks make an excellent high-altitude SAR platform for searches conducted around Californian mountain ranges such as the Sierras and Mount Shasta area, and are capable of altitudes up to 12,000 ft (3657 m).

Det 1 RAID operates OH-58A+s from Sacramento and has a total of three FLIR aircraft and five OH-58A+ 'straights'. One FLIR example is usually based at Sacramento. OSACOM (Operational Airlift Support Command) Det 32 flies a single pristine C-12F.

D Company, 1-140th Aviation Battalion does

not have aircraft assigned, but is responsible for aircraft maintenance. The Det 1, HQ, 1-140th Aviation Battalion also resides at the facility, but no aircraft are directly assigned.

Stockton – AASF (Army Aviation Support Facility)

G Company, 140th Aviation Battalion operates eight CH-47D Chinooks and is the parent unit at Stockton. The unit originally had 16 Chinooks but lost eight to the Nevada ArNG at Reno, which is a sister unit. The company's unofficial nickname is the 'Delta Schooners', derived from their SCHOONER callsign. To regain its former strength G/140th AV is expected to receive an additional eight CH-47Ds in early 2000, which are due to become available due to the downsizing of the active-duty forces and the transfer of equipment to the National Guard.

Above: Used for staff transport, this single Beech C-12F is assigned to Det 32, OSACOM. It is based at the California Regional Flight Center, Mather Field, Sacramento (previously Mather AFB and home to the B-52s of the 320th Bomb Wing), but is a regular sight at other Californian military airfields.

Left: Mather is also home to the 126th Medical Company (AA) and its UH-60As, readily identified by the red cross markings. In 1999 the unit returned from a six-month deployment to Bosnia.

The GPS-equipped Chinooks may get an engine upgrade sometime in the next few years that will increase the lifting capability of the type. The upgrade to the engine will result in greater horsepower and involves fuel control changes.

Nine UH-1Hs are flown by B Company, 2-104th General Support Aviation Company. In the event that this unit was mobilised, it would report to the Pennsylvania ArNG. There is a chance that the B/2-104th may stand down if the eight additional CH-47Ds do indeed materialise for the 140th Aviation Battalion. D/1-1112th LUH (Light Utility Helicopter) also flies nine UH-1Hs and, in the event of a mobilisation, would report to the North Dakota ArNG. This unit may possibly get an engine upgrade and enhanced avionics for their Hueys if the money is appropriated. The Hueys' primary role in both units is personnel.

Stockton is also home to the HQ of 3/140th Aviation Battalion, though no aircraft are assigned to this unit. Stockton used to be home to the AH-1S Cobras of the 1-140th Attack

The primary role of G Company is combat support. The 140th Aviation Battalion reports to the 40th Infantry Division for administrative purposes only. If mobilised, G Company, 140th Aviation Battalion would report to 1 Corps at Fort Lewis, 66th Brigade.

Like the Channel Island ANG and its C-130Es, the 'Delta Schooners' deploy their CH-47Ds to areas all over the state when the fire season begins. The heavy-lift Chinooks carry both rigid and collapsible 2,000-US gal (7570-litre) water buckets, which is about three times what a Blackhawk carries. Buckets of 1,300-US gal (4921-litre) capacity can also be carried. Not only are the CH-47Ds great for fire-fighting, but they can be used to perform SAR sorties in high-altitude areas of the Californian ranges. The CH-47Ds are usually called upon for rescues over 12,500 ft (3810 m), beyond the UH-60A's safe operating parameters. During floods around the state, G/140th Aviation Battalion can usually be found helping out.

Designated OH-58A+, the Kiowas of the RAID (Reconnaissance And Interdiction Detachment) are equipped with AAQ-21 FLIRs for use in the anti-drug war. They have the communications equipment necessary to work closely with law enforcement agencies, and have heightened 'bush skids' to provide sufficient ground clearance for the FLIR turret. RAID aircraft are based at Sacramento (Det 1), North Island (Det 2) and Los Alamitos (Det 3).

A recent mishap (class C) occurred when a civil Beech Bonanza hit a Chinook in mid-air, striking the aft section of the CH-47D and tragically killing the Bonanza's 80-year-old pilot. The rugged Chinook made an emergency landing, was repaired on site, and ferried back to base for further repairs.

Battalion, but all of the AH-1Ss have been retired and the unit was deactivated in September 1996.

OTAG

Situated just a few miles from Mather Field in Sacramento, OTAG (Office of the Adjutant General) is the California ANG and ArNG headquarters. It is also located near the state capitol building. In addition to administration and various California Guard command centres, this is where the top three California ArNG and ANG commanding generals work.

When asked about the OTAG function, Public Affairs Chief Lieutenant Colonel Doug Hart stated, "The California National Guard came into existence in July of 1849, nearly 150 years ago. California Guard members have participated in nearly every American conflict since that time. We are a combined operation – we have an ANG Air Wing and an Army NG Wing. Our role is to interface directly with the National Guard Bureau and secure funding, programmes and equipment for our units. The CA ANG has 4,900 people in the state within the four flying units and the 162nd Combat Communications Group. The Army National Guard, with the 40th Infantry Division, the 100th Troop Command, and 115th Troop Command, have about 16,500 soldiers. During the floods we had over 1,300 Guardsman working, both ANG and ArNG.

"We have a counter-drug programme and are instrumental in helping and supporting other agencies such as the Border Patrol and Customs Service, (including) a state-wide marijuana eradication programme.

"Fifty per cent of all national (natural) emergencies happen in California. That keeps us very busy. Things to contend with here include floods, earthquakes, forest fires and even riots. We have one of three MAFFS units (146th

AW/115th AS) in the entire ANG. We have a state partnership for peace programme, which is like NATO's own PfP. Different state Guard units are partnered with a former Soviet Block nation, California's partner being Ukraine. We train with them and they train with us and we learn from each other. Last November we held a computer-driven peacekeeping exercise with them called Peace Shield."

The Golden State Guard is busier than ever. The Guard is often called upon to fill the void left by the reduced number of active-duty organisations today. The Guard and active-duty units working together has become a crucial requirement for the federal mission. A low-profile and rarely-publicised role in which many Guardsmen are involved is the war against drugs (counter-drug/drug interdiction). This involves both personnel and various aircraft from just about every Guard unit working hand-in-hand with other agencies. Anti-terrorism and response to weapons of mass destruction are other areas for which the state is prepared to counter and now train.

The OTAG Commander is MGEN Tandy Bozeman, who was appointed by and reports directly to the Governor of California. He is responsible for all CA ANG and CA ArNG organisations for both federal and state require-

For the rapid transport of spare parts and other light cargo around the western states, Det 1, I Co., 185th Theater Aviation flies two C-23B Sherpas from Fresno. This base is also home to the 1106th AVCRAD, previous 'owners' of the two Sherpas until a recent reshuffle.

ments, which includes ensuring that all of the individual units are capable and properly trained. Over the years, MGEN Bozeman has flown the T-33A, T-37B, T-38A, T-41A, C-97 and C-130A, and spent years with the 146th's Channel Island Air National Guard unit.

When asked about his job, MGEN Tandy Bozeman said, "On the state side and as the Director of the California Guard and Adjutant General, we have to be prepared for disasters and respond quickly and competently to the Office of Emergency Services. When people have asked me how long I have been the Adjutant General, I sometimes reply, just after the Los Angeles riots, during the Rodney King trial, the Northridge earthquake, the Malibu fire, the Russian River floods, the Great Central Valley floods, and most recently El Niño. We are in a period of fundamental change and, with down-sizing, the Guard and Reserve forces are becoming more integral to the active-duty forces. I am proud of our people."

Ted Carlson

The California National Guard forms a powerful air arm in its own right, with the following types on strength: F-16C/D, KC-135R, C-130E, HC-130P (illustrated), HH-60G, CH-47D, UH-1H, UH-60A, AH-1F, OH-58A+, OH-58C, C-12F, C-23B and C-26B.

Australia

Despite its seemingly remote geographical position and limited influence on world affairs, Australia is at the heart of several of the most influential defence procurement programmes in the world today. The outcomes of the RAAF's search for a new AEW&C aircraft and the AAAC's combat helicopter competition (to name but two) will have a profound effect on the decisions other nations make on their new aircraft in the future. Against this background of major changes, most other aviation assets of the Australian Defence Forces are undergoing upgrade and overhaul, to maintain and improve their operational capability.

As the new millennium approaches, the three aircraft-operating services of the Australian Defence Force (ADF) are entering a period of great change. In addition to a cut in manpower (an Australian version of the programmes that have become almost *de rigueur* for post-Cold War Western nations), many units are in the process of reorganisation and almost every type is being upgraded or replaced.

In comparison to the last review of the Australian military (*World Air Power Journal*, Volume 16), the total number of uniformed personnel fell from 58,188 to 55,174 (in 1998), and will plateau at 50,000 upon the completion of the Defence Reform Plan in the early years of the next decade. Of that total, the Army will have 23,000 people, the Navy 14,000, and the Air Force 13,000. The total defence budget in 1994 was A$9.77 billion, and will have increased to A$10.94 billion in 1998/99 (1.9 per cent of GDP). These changes, coupled with the introduction of new capabilities (Project Wedgetail, the AEW&C programme, being just one example), makes an analysis of the ADF a difficult task. The next decade will see a complete overhaul of RAAF, RAN and Army capabilities, that will hopefully retain a degree of technical superiority in the Asia-Pacific region.

The spectre of 'block obsolescence' looms large, however, as many of the platforms currently in the process of being upgraded will be nearing the end of their useful lives around 2015. It would appear to the casual observer that defence spending will have to be increased in the years leading to this date, in order to avoid a situation that has the potential to become a vexing problem.

Although Australian defence planners do not perceive a direct threat to the island continent, there has been much upheaval (both financial and political) among neighbours and allies in recent times. Several of these countries have also embarked on re-equipment programmes that could see Australia's military standing in the region diminished. In light of this, it is timely perhaps that Australia has recently completed construction of a chain of Bare Bases in the north of the country that could conceivably be used for both military and humanitarian relief purposes. The last base in this chain, RAAF Scherger near Weipa on Cape York Peninsula, was declared operational in August 1998 (*World Air Power Journal*, Volume 36), and work is currently underway to bring Learmonth, the oldest of these bases, up to the standards of Curtin and Scherger.

In addition to the Bare Base programmes, major upgrades are either underway or planned for Amberley, Darwin, and Townsville (RAAF); Nowra (RAN); Darwin and Oakey (Army). On the debit side, Richmond and possibly either East Sale or Edinburgh are due for closure in the next few years and, since the last review in Volume 16, Laverton has closed and Point Cook is no longer an active RAAF airfield.

Australia sees itself as a steadying influence in the Southeast Asia/Pacific region, and actively supports defence ties with its neighbours. As well as the ANZUS alliance with the United States and New Zealand, Australia remains part of the Five Power Defence Arrangement with the United Kingdom, Singapore, Malaysia and New Zealand. This latter alliance sees a regular RAAF presence at Butterworth, in Malaysia, with a rotational detachment of P-3C Orion aircraft from No. 92 Wing at Edinburgh, and regular deployments of F/A-18s and F-111s. In the most recent joint exercise, No. 77 Sqn F/A-18s and No. 82 Wing F-111s deployed to Kuantan in October 1998 for Exercise Churinga 98-2, operating with TUDM aircraft including the MiG-29s of No. 17 Sqn.

As well as military exercises, all three ADF services have participated heavily in aid and relief efforts throughout the region in recent times, with large efforts in particular being made in Papua New Guinea on drought relief and post-tsunami assistance operations. The life-saving efforts of the RAAF's Orion fleet have also received a great deal of publicity over the last three years, and several mariners (including yachtsmen Bullimore, Dubois and Autissier) owe their lives to the crews of Nos 10 and 11 Squadrons.

Budget constraints are a fact of life in these times, and the personnel of the ADF have experienced their share of the cutbacks. The Australian military has always enjoyed a reputation of quality (if not quantity), and the modernisation programmes in hand should ensure that this reputation is not diminished. **Nigel Pittaway**

Royal Australian Air Force (RAAF)

The Royal Australian Air Force is arguably about to receive its biggest-ever leap in capability with the introduction of an AEW&C platform in the early years of the next decade, and it is this, coupled with a far-reaching reorganisation of support assets, that provides the service with its greatest challenge. Currently under the scrutiny of the Project Air 5077 (or more commonly, Project Wedgetail) team, the AEW&C aircraft and radar combination is yet to be selected, but is due to be operational by the end of 2003. Initial Design Contracts were awarded to Boeing (737-700/Northrop Grumman ESSD MESA), Lockheed Martin (C-130J/ADS-18 AURA), and Raytheon/E-Systems (Airbus A310-300/IAI Elta) in January 1998, the selection of the successful contractor being due in the third quarter of 1999.

A new Group has been formed, in a major reorganisation of the surveillance and control assets of the RAAF. This Group will be known as the Surveillance and Control Group (SCG) and will combine the 'tactical' Control and Reporting Units (41 Wing and the 'strategic' capabilities of the Jindalee radar, of No. 12 RSU. In addition, the new AEW&C aircraft will be operated by the reformed No. 2 Squadron.

By the time that the AEW&C is on line, it is hoped that the troubled Jindalee Operational Radar Network (JORN, an over-the-horizon radar) will be operational. When these two assets are fully integrated into the proposed Australian Air Defence System 2000+, it will, for the first time in Australia's history, adequately safeguard the nation's northern approaches. Historically,

threats to the security of Australia have been from the north, a large and sparsely populated area that has been almost impossible to adequately patrol, let alone defend, on a modest budget. This is the reason behind the construction of the Bare Bases, and the reorganisation of the RAAF to sustain operations from these airfields. In times of tension, the RAAF would form two Contingency Wings, one offensive and one defensive, to operate from one or more of the bases as required. These wings (No. 95 Contingency Strike, and No. 96 Contingency Air Defence) are now regularly raised during exercises, and may even include assets from allied forces (a recent example was Pitch Black '98, in which an RAF Sentry operated under the command of No. 96 Wing, as did Singaporean A-4SUs and an E-2C).

e DHC-4 Caribou has been in RAAF service for nearly 40 ars and is the subject of a soon-to-be-resolved replacement mpetition. People involved in the follow-on tactical airlifter gramme acknowledge, however, that even though the new craft will be more modern and more economical, there will ll be Caribou missions that it cannot fulfil.

stralia is now the last erator of the F-111 – but the g', as it is affectionately own, plays a vital role in F planning and will be the rnerstone of the RAAF strike ce for decades to come. o squadrons, Nos 1 and 6, based at RAAF Amberley d all wear the lightning bolt signia of No. 82 Wing on ir fins (top). The Strike and connaissance Group is ked with overland (right) d maritime strike missions – latter employing AGM-84 rpoons (above). The F-111 ce has an expanding range PGMs available to it and going upgrade programmes ll secure its warfighting abilities for the 21st ntury. RAAF F-111 crews o hone their skills at Green d Red Flag exercises (above ht).

The recently re-elected Liberal/National Party coalition government of Prime Minister John Howard has led a far-reaching restructure of the support elements of the RAAF. In an attempt to spend more defence dollars on the many re-equipment and upgrade programmes, much of the work done previously by RAAF personnel (maintenance and support) is now done by civilian contract labour, and several Air Base Wings have now been redesignated as Combat Support Squadrons (or Wings), reflecting their front-line role in times of conflict. In addition, the maintenance units within each Wing (Nos 481, 482, 492 Sqns, etc.) have been disbanded, and much of the personnel transferred into the flying squadrons, conferring a much larger degree of self-sufficiency. Much of the 'depot' level work previously carried out by the maintenance squadrons will be contracted out to the civilian sector, but there will still be a uniformed maintenance element within each wing. Reorganisation does not come without cost, as the activation of the Bare Bases would have a serious impact on the functions of the southern bases, whose (fewer) service personnel would be required to man any or all of these contingency airfields.

As noted earlier, almost every aircraft type currently operated by the RAAF is to be either upgraded or replaced in the next decade, and though total numbers (of aircraft) will not greatly change, the capability of the service will be vastly improved. Several programmes span more than one type of aircraft and, in some cases, more than one service – the privatisation of Basic Flying Training – and the supply of a common EWSP system for the C-130, F-111, CH-47D, Blackhawk and Sea King being just two examples. Platforms such as the F/A-18A (despite a strong sales push by BAe for the Eurofighter Typhoon), F-111 and P-3C are all in various stages of upgrade programmes, while the C-130E, MB-326H, DHC-4A and (probably) the HS.748 will all leave the inventory over the next five years.

The RAAF is organised into three major Commands, reporting to the Chief of the Air Force (CAF); Air Command (ARDU, Strike and Reconnaissance Group, Maritime Patrol Group, Tactical Fighter Group and Air Lift Group), Training Command (2 FTS, CFS, SAN, RSTT, etc.), and Support Command (really a tri-service command). Of these, Support Command does not operate aircraft, and the flying units supervised by Training Command report directly to that organisation. Air Command, however, is divided into the four major Groups, and controls the operational flying squadrons of the RAAF via these Groups and their subordinate Wings.

Strike and Reconnaissance Group

During normal operation, the Strike and Reconnaissance Group oversees No. 82 Wing and the F-111s of Nos 1 and 6 Squadrons. In times of tension, though, both squadrons would operate as part of No. 95 Contingency Strike Wing. This hostilities-only wing could possibly include other assets, or even other regional Air Forces, reporting directly to the Air or Land Commander depending on the threat.

The F-111 is still considered the ideal aircraft for the task at hand, and it should be noted that, aside from deployed US units, No. 82 Wing is currently the only night-capable strike force in the Southern Asia/Pacific region. No other aircraft type, flying or planned, can provide the same capability as the 'Pig' (the name by which the aircraft is universally and affectionately known).

No. 82 Wing

The last few years have brought much change within the F-111 community: 15 ex-USAF F-111Gs were delivered to Amberley between late 1993 and early 1994, the F-111C/RF-111C fleet is cycling through the Avionics Upgrade Programme, and a re-engining programme is underway to fit the last-mentioned variant with a later model of the TF30, taken from retired USAF F-111E/EF-111As. The AUP programme is well underway, with the 21st and final aircraft due to be delivered in August 1999. In addition, test flying of the more powerful TF30-P-109 engine has now been completed, clearing the way for fitment to the F-111C/RF-111C fleet between August 1998 and the end of 1999. The -P-109 cannot be fitted to the F-111G, as the engine has a 3° 'kink' between the core engine and afterburner unit (the -P-107 of the F-111G is straight), so RAAF technicians (in conjunction with Pratt & Whitney) have developed a TF30-P-107/-P-109 hybrid dubbed the '-P-108'. Test flying of this engine began in August 1998, and completion of the last aircraft is scheduled for the first half of 2000.

An avionics upgrade for the F-111G fleet is in the project definition phase (under Project Air 5404), and will possibly find funding in the 1999/2000 financial year. This upgrade will build on F-111C AUP experience, and will hopefully confer the autonomous laser designation capability currently lacking in this variant. It is not clear how many aircraft will go through this upgrade, as the future fleet strength has not been defined. Six of the 15 delivered are now in service, with the balance held in rotational storage. One F-111G was lost on 18 April 1999.

With the withdrawal of the F-111 from USAF service, the RAAF has had to become even more self-reliant. An example of this is the construction of a cold proof load test hangar at Amberley, as each aircraft has to undergo one more cold proof test of the wing carry-through structure to allow operations to the planned retirement date of 2020 (each test permits another 2,500 flying hours). To aid long-term viability, 10 ex-USAF aircraft have been acquired (one F-111A, two F-111Fs, three F-111Gs and four EF-111As) and will be held in storage at Davis-Monthan as a source of major airframe spares should they be required. This arrangement also includes the purchase of 130 TF30 engines and an unspecified number of ALR-67 RWRs. An 11th F-111 fuselage will be shipped to the DSTO to support fatigue testing.

Surplus USAF AN/AVQ-26 Pave Tack pods have also now been purchased, allowing one pod per aircraft (F-111C); Australia is now the sole operator of this system. Aside from the avionics upgrades, several new weapons have been purchased, or are under consideration, to enhance the big aircraft's already formidable capability.

The AGM-142E Have Nap has been selected as the much needed stand-off weapon, and firing tests are scheduled to begin in the first half of 2000, with full operational capability to be achieved in May 2003. A second tranche of these missiles was ordered in September 1998, allowing both the blast, and the penetrating (semi-hardened target) warhead versions to be introduced. The datalink pod for this missile will be carried on the rear fuselage station, once used for the (now) redundant GBU-15 datalink system.

The current lack of an anti-radiation missile (ARM) and area denial/hardened target weapons is being addressed, with approval being sought to obtain such armaments under the auspices of Project Air 5398 (the above-mentioned penetrating warhead AGM-142Es were also purchased as part of this project). The BAe ALARM had been expected to be trialled in the near future, using missiles loaned from the RAF, though an announcement was made in the latter part of 1998 rejecting the proposal on the grounds that it would take too long to integrate the weapon with the F-111 mission system.

Self-defence capability is also planned to be upgraded under Project Air 5412 which will seek a replacement for the AIM-9M Sidewinder (the MATRA/BAe AIM-132 ASRAAM has been selected as the new within visual range (WVR) missile for the Hornet force, and it is presumed that this missile would also equip the F-111 fleet in the future). The AUP upgrades are now standardising the countermeasures suite on the AN/ALE-40 countermeasures dispensing system (CMDS), the ex-USAF F-111Gs having had this equipment since delivery.

The four 'Recce Jets' (RF-111C) are also slated to have their reconnaissance suite upgraded, and this, too, is in the project definition stage.

The aircrew at Amberley are very enthusiastic about their aircraft (defending it aggressively against criticism), and the post-AUP jets are regarded as a quantum leap forward in operational viability. The 'Achilles heel' of the fleet now is the lack of a self-designation capability for the F-111G. Over the past three years, No. 6 Sqn has developed close air support and medium-altitude dive-bombing procedures, finding the aircraft well suited to the task and extremely accurate.

The lack of a compatible tanker is another area that could hinder the effectiveness of the force, though all crews keep current in AAR procedures by regularly tanking from the USAF tanker fleet. It is hoped that this deficiency will be rectified by the tanker replacement project, which is also in the definition stage.

All aircraft are now being repainted in the overall Gunship Grey worn by the F-111Gs since delivery, as this is deemed highly effective over the haze of northern Australia (the likely area of operations, Amberley being only a peacetime base). The days of colourful squadron insignia also seem to be over, but a high degree of esprit de corps exists within No. 82 Wing and the F-111 will continue to be a (relatively) common sight in Australian skies for some years to come.

Maritime Patrol Group (MPG)

Charged with overseeing No. 92 Wing and the Orion fleet, the Maritime Patrol Group is based at RAAF Edinburgh, north of Adelaide in South Australia, and shares this base with the subordinate units. The MPG is directly responsible to the Air Commander Australia (HQ Air Command, at Glenbrook in NSW) for the surveillance of Australia's maritime approaches, but also provides assistance, when requested, for the Australian Maritime Search and Rescue Co-ordination Centre (AUSSAR) in Canberra. This latter

The spectacular 'dump and burn' technique of igniting jettisoned fuel in the F-111's afterburner plume (above left) has become a RAAF air show standard – and an international crowd-puller. The RAAF's pride in its F-111s is reflected in the special scheme applied to this aircraft (above) for the F-111's 25th anniversary in Australian service, in 1998. The scheme is retained to this day. RAAF Amberley (left) will continue to be home to the recently expanded F-111 force and the search for a replacement strike aircraft is unlikely to take shape until 2010 at the earliest.

Above and above left: A yellow fin-flash marks the Hornets of No. 2 Operational Conversion Unit, part of No. 81 Wing. No. 2 OCU is based at Williamtown, or 'Bill Ville', alongside two of the RAAF's other three Hornet squadrons.

...ove and above right: No. 3 Squadron has a primary air ...fence tasking, along with No. 77 Sqn which shares its ...me at RAAF Williamtown. Forthcoming upgrades will see ...e RAAF's Hornets armed with ASRAAM and AMRAAM ...ssiles, placing them among the very best armed fighter ...craft in service anywhere in the world.

...is No. 75 Sqn F/A-18A (above) wears special marks on its ..., singling it out as the squadron commander's aircraft. The ...ety margin provided by the Hornet's twin engines was an ...portant factor in its selection by the RAAF. This aircraft ...ght) is seen deep in the Outback, over Ayres Rock (Uluru).

143

responsibility prompted the RAAF Orion fleet's participation in the Southern Ocean rescues of Tony Bullimore and Thiery Dubois, and more recently of several missing boats and yachtsmen off the southeast coast of Australia during the course of the Sydney to Hobart yacht race.

The recent manpower drawdown and 'sharp-end first' restructuring of the Air Force has seen some major changes in the operation of the MPG which, when coupled with the current Orion upgrade (Project Air 5276, or Sea Sentinel), will allow the fleet to operate until around 2015 (the current life-of-type projection).

No. 92 Wing

Since the delivery of the final 600-series P-3C (Update II.5 aircraft A9-665) in 1986, No. 92 Wing had operated the Orion fleet as a pool, maintained by No. 492 Sqn (the maintenance and support unit for the wing) and allocated as required to the three flying squadrons (Nos 10, 11 and the training unit, No. 292). It should be noted that the aircraft presently wear 'nominal' squadron markings, No. 10 Sqn for the first series aircraft (serialled in the A9-7xx block) and No. 11 Sqn for the second series (A9-6xx). This changed on 27 April 1998, when each squadron gained its own complement of (a mixture of) 600- and 700-series aircraft and recently-delivered TAP-3s. This allocation paved the way for the dissolution of No. 492 Sqn, and the transfer of maintenance and support personnel into each unit. This change is in keeping with the more flexible posture of the RAAF, and is designed to allow each squadron to be capable of deploying and operating from a forward base with a large degree of autonomy.

During the period of transition, the aircraft and maintenance personnel were divided into two Maintenance Flights (Nos 10 and 11), finally becoming part of Nos 10 and 11 Squadrons, respectively, with the disbandment of No. 492 Sqn on 15 December 1998.

The Orion training unit, No. 292 Squadron, does not have aircraft permanently allocated, though the three training aircraft (TAP-3s) wear the unit's Sea Eagle on their fins. The squadron borrows aircraft as required.

A detachment, managed at wing rather than squadron level, has an aircraft positioned at Butterworth in Malaysia as part of the Five Power Defence Arrangement, and aircraft regularly deploy to airfields in Australia and the neighbouring South Pacific region.

Standard weapons and stores for the fleet are the Mk 46 torpedo, Mks 36 and 41 Destructor mines, AGM-84D Harpoon, SUS, Storpedo and (10-man) Air Sea Rescue Kit. At the time of writing, there has been no announcement regarding the fitment of weapons procured for other assets (AGM-142, Penguin, etc.), but several undisclosed weapons are currently under consideration. The 19 surviving P-3Cs (after losing much of a wing leading edge, one ditched in the Cocos Islands in April 1991) have recently completed an upgrade by Israel's Elta to install ALR-2001 ESM equipment. The visible modifications are a plethora of antennas under the fuselage and redesigned wingtip fairings housing additional antennas.

The P-3C fleet is embarking on a major systems upgrade and will be known as AP-3Cs upon completion. No. 10 Sqn will be the initial recipient of the reworked aircraft, followed in due course by No. 11 Sqn. The three ex-USN P-3Bs procured as part of this project are known as TAP-3s (Training Australian P-3). This upgrade will allow operations until the projected retirement date of 2015, and possibly beyond, by reducing aircraft weight and utilising the TAP-3 to relieve the stresses of circuit flying and support duties.

Project Air 5276

Known also as Project Sea Sentinel, the project definition study was concluded in 1992 and the contract was signed with E-Systems (now Raytheon Systems Co.) in January 1995. The first aircraft (A9-760) was delivered to Greenville, Texas in November 1997 and is undergoing flight test at time of writing. All remaining aircraft will be modified at Raytheon's Avalon facility, sub-contracted to Boeing Australia, where the first aircraft (A9-759) arrived on 18 January 1999 to commence rework. The final aircraft is scheduled to be handed back to the RAAF in March 2002.

The upgrade will completely replace the radar, acoustic, navigation, communication and data management systems, and is touted by Raytheon as one of only two completely integrated ASW upgrades currently being embarked upon in the world (the other being the UK's Nimrod 2000). Incorporated in the upgrade are: a CAE Magnetic Anomaly Detector, Elta ALR-2001 ESM (now fitted), Elta EL/M-2022(V)2 Inverse Synthetic Aperture Radar, Computing Devices Canada UYS-503 Acoustic Processor, Lockheed DDC-060 Data Management System, Honeywell 764 laser-ring embedded GPS and three UHF/VHF, two HF, and SATCOM units. All this will be managed by twin, linked MIL-STD 1553 databuses, one nominally for the navigation systems and one for the data management and sensor systems.

Phase Two of the project oversaw the purchase and modification of the three TAP-3s (and a fourth that was acquired for spares). These aircraft will not have the AP-3C flight deck, though, and funding is being sought to apply at least a 'replica' cockpit upgrade to them in order to provide realistic training value once the fleet modifications have been completed.

It is hoped that future phases of Project Air 5276 will introduce an electronic warfare self-protection (EWSP) system and electro-optic sensors to the aircraft, though these have yet to be approved by the Department of Defence.

Tactical Fighter Group

Headquartered at Williamtown, the Tactical Fighter Group controls the air defence ('fighter') squadrons of No. 81 Wing and, until recently, oversaw the radar units of No. 41 Wing. This latter unit split away on 1 September 1998 to join the RAAF's new Surveillance and Control Group.

No. 81 Wing

Primarily equipped with the dual-role F/A-18A Hornet, No. 81 Wing also operates two squadrons of the elderly CAC-built MB-326H Macchi and three grey-painted FAC-modified PC-9/As, flying from three permanent airfields (Williamtown, Tindal and Pearce). Although each of the Hornet squadrons is nominally tasked to either air defence (Nos 3 and 75 Sqns) or close air support (No. 77 Sqn), all units are proficient in the other role and the demarcation line is now blurred.

No. 75 Sqn is based at Tindal in the Northern Territory, having moved there upon conversion to the F/A-18 in 1988, and is the largest of the four Hornet units in terms of personnel; this is due to the greater level of autonomy required by the remote location of Tindal. The huge Delamere Range Facility is only 100 km (62 miles) away, allowing 75 Squadron to train with a large variety of weapons, and the northern location of Tindal (and therefore the proximity to many air defence exercises) means that pilots have the opportunity to regularly train with American, New Zealand and Singaporean units.

Of the two front-line Hornet squadrons at Williamtown, Nos 3 and 77, the latter has a flight of three forward air control PC-9/As attached, due to its primary CAS tasking. The grey-painted PC-9s replaced CAC Winjeels in the FAC Flight of No. 76 Squadron in mid-1995, transferring to the co-located No. 77 Sqn in April 1997. The final Hornet operator, with the exception of the few aircraft at ARDU, is No. 2 OCU. Also Williamtown-based, this unit is the 'Hornet College' of the RAAF, conducting conversion, training and the Advanced Fighter Combat Instructor courses.

There has been much debate in Australian Defence Force circles in recent times regarding which level (if any) of mid-life upgrade should be applied to the Hornet force. Several alternative plans were studied, including phasing out the aircraft in favour of a new type in the early years of the next decade (hence the aggressive marketing of the Eurofighter Typhoon in Australia), which would dictate only an interim upgrade. It was finally announced in August 1998 (after an initial upgrade decision was made in 1995!), that a $A1.25 billion comprehensive mid-life upgrade would take place, with the aircraft projected to remain in service until 2015. The McDonnell Aircraft and Missile Systems Division of Boeing has been awarded a A$250 million First-Phase contract to upgrade the navigation (EGI INS with embedded GPS), AN/ARC-210 jam-resistant communications, IFF systems, EW software, and mission computers, modification of the first aircraft to commence in 2000. Also announced at the same time was the selection of the Raytheon APG-73 radar to replace the current APG-65.

Currently, RAAF F/A-18s are equipped with the AIM-7M/AIM-9M missile combination for air defence, but the shorter-range weapon is due to be replaced by the MATRA/BAe Dynamics ASRAAM from 2000. The AIM-120 AMRAAM has been selected as the new BVR missile. The latter will enter service in 2001, to coincide with aircraft re-emerging from their mid-life upgrade. Air-to-surface weaponry is diverse and includes the AGM-84D Harpoon, Mk 82/Mk 84 bombs, GBU-12/-10/24 LGBs and CVR-7 rocket pods.

Hornet attrition has been light, with only two of each model (F/A-18A and F/A-18B) having been lost in 13 years of operations, leaving 71 (55/16, respectively) to serve until a replacement arrives in the second decade of the next millennium.

The final two flying squadrons of No. 81 Wing are the Macchi-equipped Nos 76 and 79 Squadrons at Williamtown and Pearce, respectively. These units are based near the two main naval operating bases, Fleet Base East at Garden Island in Sydney, and Fleet Base West at HMAS Stirling in Western Australia, and provide fleet co-operation close air support and introductory fighter training.

Above: Australia takes its defence ties with neighbouring nations seriously and undertakes regular training exchanges around the region. This No. 77 Sqn Hornet is seen alongside a MiG-29 of the Royal Malaysian Air Force at Kuantan air base, during the Churinga 98-2 exercise.

Above and right: No. 77 Squadron is unique among the RAAF Hornet units as it operates both F/A-18s and FAC-dedicated PC-9/As in the close air support role.

The RAAF's 'Macchis', as its MB-326Hs are universally known, are now concentrated with No. 76 Sqn (above and below) and a newly-established No. 79 Sqn (right). They undertake lead-in fighter training and naval co-operation missions, but are soon to be replaced by 33 Hawk Mk 127s.

Above and right: Australia's P-3C Orions are operated by No. 92 Wing which has two component squadrons, No. 10 and No. 11. These Orions wear the badge of No. 10 Sqn, though the pooled organisation of the wing means that aircraft regularly swap between the two squadrons.

No. 79 Squadron was reformed at Pearce on 1 July 1998 (having previously operated the Mirage IIIO from Butterworth between 1986 and 1988), taking over the aircraft and duties of No. 25 Sqn. That squadron was unique within the RAAF, being a Reserve unit with a Permanent Air Force Flight to operate the Macchi, and the number plate change now permits No. 25 Squadron to revert to its Reserve support status.

The Macchis are suffering from serious fatigue problems, causing much shuffling of airframes through storage and rebuild (lately, aircraft have been returned to service after being 'retired' at the RAAF School of Technical Training at Wagga), and the introduction of the first of 33 BAe Hawk Mk 127 aircraft in July 2000 is eagerly anticipated. The order for the Hawk was placed in June 1997, with the first 12 to be manufactured and assembled by BAe, with the remainder being assembled by Hunter Aerospace at Williamtown.

The fighter assets of No. 81 Wing would form the bulk of No. 96 Contingency Air Defence Wing during wartime, alongside aircraft from allied air forces, but the dual-role nature of the Hornet would also conceivably mean them operating in the offensive close air support role with No. 95 Contingency Strike Wing.

Surveillance and Control Group (SCG)

The SCG was formed on 1 September 1998 by removing No. 41 Wing from TFG control and joining it with a new unit, No. 42 Wing, which will operate the JORN and 'Wedgetail' AEW&C systems. Williamtown remains the HQ for the SCG and its component wings. No. 41 Wing was to have transferred responsibility for JORN to No. 42 Wing in mid-1999. No. 42 Wing will also control No. 2 Sqn (disbanded on 31 July 1982 with the retirement of the Canberra), which is being reformed to operate the 'Wedgetail' aircraft.

No. 41 Wing

This wing oversees the RAAF's three Control and Reporting Units (CRUs) and (currently) No. 1 Radar Surveillance Unit. Of the CRUs, Nos 2 and 3 are now at Darwin and Williamtown, respectively, to provide radar surveillance and fighter control for the co-located TFG elements (No. 3 CRU also includes the Software Development Unit). The third, No. 114, is a mobile unit (home-based at Tindal) that provides support at relatively short notice anywhere within the RAAF's area of interest.

No. 1 Radar Surveillance Unit (RSU) was formed on 1 July 1992 near Alice Springs in the Northern Territory to operate the Jindalee OTH radar, but had relocated to Edinburgh by July 1999. Jindalee has had a great deal of introductory problems (and detractors), and at the time of writing is still not operational. It is hoped that the bugs can finally be ironed out, allowing IOC in 2001. In the meantime, No. 1 RSU will transfer to the control of No. 42 Wing.

New tactical air defence radars in the form of Lockheed Martin AN/TPS-117 units were purchased in 1998, and will form an integral part of the ADF's Australian Air Defence System 2000+ when delivered. This integrated Air Defence System will (hopefully) be operational in the early years of the next century, and will see a reshuffle of the Control and Reporting Units. A component of the new system, named Project Vigilare (Project Air 5333), will replace the two

Control and Reporting Units at Darwin and Williamtown with a fully integrated air defence command and control organisation, dubbed an Air Defence Ground Environment. Boeing was selected as the preferred tenderer in 1998, and the contract is expected to be signed by mid-1999. The new system, consisting of display, data processing and communications equipment, will be housed within the Northern Regional Operations Centre (NORTHROC) at Tindal, and the Eastern Regional Operations Centre (EASTROC) at Williamtown. Project Vigilare will thus bring a much enhanced Air Defence and Airspace Control capability to the ADF.

No. 2 CRU will relocate to Tindal and be fully operational by the end of 2001, No. 3 CRU at Williamtown will be operational early the following year, and No. 114 (Mobile) CRU will relocate to Darwin and take up residence at the facilities vacated by No. 2 CRU.

No. 42 Wing

This new unit will be established in mid-1999 to operate the AEW&C aircraft of No. 2 Squadron and the Jindalee ORN of No. 1 RSU. It will be the RAAF's 'strategic' surveillance provider. In April 1999 it was announced that the chosen AEW&C aircraft will be based at Williamtown (either four or five depending on the type selected) with a detachment at Tindal (two).

Air Lift Group (ALG)

Unique in being the only group to control two aircraft-operating wings, the Air Lift Group is looking forward to what appears to be a complete change of equipment over the forthcoming decade. Based at RAAF Richmond, west of Sydney in NSW, the ALG is co-located with No. 84 and No. 86 Wings, and oversees assets at bases as diverse as East Sale (a Training Command base) in Victoria and Townsville in Queensland.

No. 84 Wing

No. 84 Wing provides a range of services, from VIP-configured Falcon 900s to AAR-tasked 707s, allowing the C-130s and (currently) Caribous of No. 86 Wing to concentrate on the 'core' airlift operations. No. 32 Sqn at East Sale in Victoria operates six HS.748s and four civil Beech King Air 200s in the navigation training role for the School of Air Navigation (SAN).

A review of navigation training requirements in 1997 resulted in the decision to nominate navigator training as the sole operational role for both types, so it is uncertain if No. 32 Sqn will remain within the ALG structure.

The first two King Airs were introduced in 1997, leased from Airflite, in an attempt to provide a greater economy of scale, and a more realistic tactical navigation environment (the student sits in the right-hand cockpit seat) for those destined to progress to fast jet (F-111) postings. This, coupled with the projected decrease in annual flying hours, has allowed a reduction in the number of 'Draggies' (as the HS.748 is known): the two ex-VIP aircraft (A10-595/596) were recently sold to Sweden, and two of the navigation trainers have been withdrawn from use.

The six remaining aircraft were to have been upgraded by BAe Australia, under Project Air 5232, that would have seen a new navigation training suite developed, coupled with a

Northrop Grumman ground mapping radar, thereby allowing effective operation up to the planned retirement date of 2015. However, this upgrade was the subject of a further review in late 1998, as the success of the King Air platform coupled with the high operating cost of the HS.748 means that it is deemed more efficient to lease additional examples of the smaller type. It is likely that the navigation suite upgrade will go ahead but be installed in leased civilian aircraft of the King Air class, thereby allowing the HS.748 to be retired and sold off.

The HS.748 fleet has been repainted in the increasingly familiar overall-grey scheme with low-contrast markings, the result of a requirement in the mid-1990s to conduct fishery surveillance patrols from neighbouring South Pacific Islands. This mission is no longer performed, and with the likely withdrawal of the type it would appear that this scheme will be the final one worn by the 'Draggie' in RAAF service.

No. 33 Squadron flies the five surviving Boeing 707s (one was lost in a training accident in 1991) on strategic airlift, VIP transport and air-air refuelling missions from its Richmond base.

The VIP role is now seldom performed, and the largest number of flying hours is now spent on strategic airlift. A replacement – in the medium to large business jet class – has been on hold for some time, however, as it has been seen as something of a political hot potato. Nevertheless, the next decade will bring the type's retirement from all but the AAR roles. The RAAF had stated that it required one type with the capability of a Gulfstream V, Global Express or Citation X together with two larger aircraft in the Boeing 737-BBJ or Airbus A319CJ class – collectively known as the 'Special Purpose' aircraft project. By early 1999, however, it was the Dassault Falcon 2000, Bombardier CL-604 Challenger and Gulfstream IVSP that were under close scrutiny.

Useful in the probe-and-drogue AAR training role, the 707 is not equipped with a boom and therefore cannot provide support for the F-111 force. It is this shortcoming, coupled with the noise problems and rapidly increasing maintenance costs, that could mean the type will no longer be viable in this role in the not-too-distant future. A project definition study is currently underway to determine what (if anything) should be procured in the next decade. This last point has not been lost on industry; Raytheon and Airbus, for example, are keen to point out the benefits of a common (A310) airframe for both AAR/transport and AEW&C roles, and the next few years will be of great interest to manufacturers of military transport aircraft.

In January 1999 the first of the four tankers (A20-624) was painted in the overall-grey scheme, with low-visibility markings and a dragon motif on the fin. This embellishment is derived from the DRAGON radio callsign used when performing AAR sorties (transport missions use WINDSOR callsigns for domestic legs and AUSSIE for overseas flights).

Caught in a similar political situation to the 707, No. 34 Squadron's five leased Falcon 900s had their leases renegotiated in 1998, and extended for up to three years. As 1998 was a federal election year, it was feared in some quarters that an announcement on a further VIP aircraft purchase during (or before) the campaign would be seen as feather-bedding.

ove and right: *No. 11 Squadron will follow No. 10 into the
iject Sea Sentinel AP-3C upgrade programme which will
it Australia's Orions with new advanced mission
nputers, sensor systems and avionics. Additional Orion
apons options are also under study.*

ove: *No. 292 Squadron operates three TAP-3 training
craft, with additional P-3C aircraft detached as required.*

*Australia's hard-working
C-130H fleet is split between
two units. No. 36 Sqn (above
and below) is the tactical
Hercules unit, while No. 37
Sqn (above right) handles
'route' or strategic transport
missions. The C-130H will be
replaced by the C-130J (right).*

e Caribou *is an Australian service legend, but one whose
e is now drawing to a close. Today, a declining number of
craft remain in service with No. 35 Sqn, at Townsville
ove) and No. 38 Sqn, at Amberley (below). Both squadrons
intain small detachments around the country.*

It was eventually announced in December 1998 that a tender for two types of 'Special Purpose', or VIP, aircraft would be released to industry in February 1999. This duly occurred, with the RAAF announcing that it would prefer to lease both types selected from a single source. These aircraft will then replace both the Falcon 900s and the transport-dedicated 707 (A20-261). Under Project Air 5402, Australia is now also exploring the possibility of joining the RAF's privately-funded strategic tanker programme which would provide commercially-sourced, on-demand tanker support in the future. The RAF wants its new tankers in service by 2004/06.

No. 86 Wing

The maintenance and support squadrons within the wing structure are being disbanded, and No. 86 Wing has lost No. 486 Sqn as part of this process. This, coupled with the replacement of the older Hercules and the Caribou fleet, has placed No. 86 Wing under a great deal of pressure in recent times, but the unit is looking forward to the increased levels of capability that these changes to personnel and equipment will bring. Now in the twilight of a long and successful career with the RAAF, the Caribou is due to be withdrawn from service in the early part of the next century. Selection of a replacement has yet to be made, and until then the two squadrons (35 Sqn at Townsville and 38 Sqn at Amberley) continue to operate with a handful of aircraft each.

Project Air 5190 seeks to replace the Caribou with a new type, and a Request For Tender has been issued, with selection due in the second quarter of 1999. Three types have been shortlisted: the Lockheed Martin-Alenia (LMATTS) C-27J Spartan, and CASA with both the CN.235-300M and C.295M. The IPTN CN.235-330 Phoenix had been a contender until the financial woes of the state-run company forced a withdrawal from the running in July 1998.

It is intended that the new type will begin re-equipping No. 35 Sqn, the displaced Caribous being consolidated within 38 Sqn. After 35 Sqn achieves full operational capability, No. 38 Squadron will disband and the Caribou be retired. Despite its age, it will be a hard act to follow. Whichever aircraft is selected, the number of landing sites available (particularly in northern Australia, the main area of operations) will be reduced, as the Caribou has a very low 'footprint'.

For the time being, however, both squadrons operate as normal. In June 1998, 38 Squadron deployed to Wagga for Exercise Dark Moose, the first time that unit had exercised at squadron strength with night vision goggles (though 35 Sqn routinely operate with ANVIS-9 NVGs), and both squadrons have recently participated heavily in drought relief operations in Papua New Guinea and Irian Jaya. The unit markings are being further toned down. This will shortly mean the end of the ochre wallaby and blue enfield (or 'electric cat' to the more irreverent members of rival units), which have adorned the fins of Australia's Caribou fleet for so many years.

The Hercules fleet, too, is feeling its age, and even the relatively young (20-year-old) C-130Hs of No. 36 Sqn are suffering fatigue problems. Although No. 36 is the 'tactical' squadron, the other RAAF Hercules squadron, No. 37, has been operating its elderly E models on stores-dropping sorties in recent times.

Twelve C-130Js should have relieved the C-130Es of No. 37 Sqn in the strategic transport role but, due to well-publicised problems, Lockheed Martin will not be delivering the first RAAF example until at least July 1999. One of the RAAF's aircraft (N4187W, to become A97-450) was brought to the country in February, on a demonstration tour to coincide with the 1999 Avalon air show, and impressed many with its performance and user-friendly cockpit systems. Despite Lockheed Martin's assurances that the first aircraft will in fact arrive at Richmond as planned in July, many industry observers are expecting that date to stretch out until at least November. As with Britain's Royal Air Force, this has put considerable additional strain on the maintenance and logistics organisation, with sub-stantial unplanned maintenance having to be carried out. Australia will not take delivery of their aircraft until full certification has been issued by the RAF so, in the meantime, the older Hercules of No. 86 Wing will continue in operation.

Once the C-130J begins to enter service, the better examples of the C-130E will pass to No. 36 Sqn, to partially relieve the burden on the newer model. Ultimately, seven of the 12 will be traded back to Lockheed Martin, and five retained in Australia for museum and training airframe duties.

Aircraft Research and Development Unit (ARDU)

The only unit within Air Command to report directly to Glenbrook, ARDU is responsible for testing, development and service clearance of new equipment for the ADF. Currently based at RAAF Edinburgh, close to the Defence Science and Technology Organisation (DSTO) facility at Sal-isbury, the unit also maintains and operates a test range within the Woomera facility (Prohibited Area). As with other defence organisations, ARDU has recently undergone a sweeping reorganisation.

ARDU provides the ADF with facilities and personnel for the test and evaluation of RAAF and Army aircraft and associated systems, system design and development, aircraft stores capability engineering (ASCENG, the RAAF Service Design Authority that provides approval for stores carriage and employment), and Electronic Warfare Operational Support (encompassing mission planning, software support, ECM technique development, EW test and evaluation and advice relating to acquisition of such capabilities). To achieve this, the unit has been reorganised into a number of elements, known as Domains, the heads of which report (via the E&D Executive) to Commander ARDU. These Domains are: Advanced Aero Systems, Space and Ranges; Fighter; Strike; Maritime and Surveillance; Transport and Training; and Rotary. Each Domain has its own team of flight-test qualified aircrew, engineers and technicians.

In addition to the Domains, the ARDU Electronic Warfare Squadron provides EW support to the RAAF and Army, reporting (due to the immediate operational relevance) directly to Commander ARDU.

ARDU currently operates two specially instru-mented F/A-18s (one single- and one two-seater) and three PC-9/As (instrumented as required), and has on permanent loan single examples of the Army's Iroquois and Blackhawk (permanently instrumented). In addition to this fleet, aircraft are drawn from all three services as required. As new types come on strength, they will either be operated by ARDU aircrew at another location (e.g., C-130J testing at Marietta), or brought on unit strength at Edinburgh (a single BAe Hawk, taken from either the middle or the end of the production run, will be temporarily attached to the unit).

Until the end of 1998, ARDU also operated the venerable C-47B Dakota (three operational aircraft from a fleet of four) on a range of trials and support duties. The aircraft were deemed to be no longer cost-effective and a replacement capability has been tendered out to a civilian operator, Adelaide-based Australian Flight Test Services Ltd (AFTS). No aircraft has been selected, but the level of capability required has been quoted as approximating the Raytheon (Beechcraft) Super King Air type. It is significant, perhaps, to note that AFTS already operates a Fokker F27-100 on behalf of the Commonwealth Scientific and Industrial Research Organisation (CSIRO).

RAAF Training Command

Headquartered at RAAF Williams in Victoria, RAAF Training Command is responsible (in the aircraft-operating terms) for the training of RAAF pilots, navigators, flight engineers, air electronics operators, fighter controllers and flight stewards. RAAF Williams is presently a 'dual campus' base, combining the assets of the former RAAF Laverton and Point Cook. The airfield at Laverton is now closed, and although Point Cook retains its runways and taxiways, it is in the process of drawdown as an RAAF station. Con-sequently, many of the Point Cook-based units are relocating to Laverton, and HQ Training Command is no exception; it is scheduled to complete the move in the early part of 1999.

In 1999, initial pilot training for all three services will pass to a civilian contractor – British Aerospace Flight Training Australia's Tamworth facility, flying civil-registered CT-4B and CAP-10 aircraft. For RAAF and RAN candidates, this training (since the demise of No. 1 FTS and its CT-4s) had been carried out at No. 2 FTS at Pearce on the PC-9/A. More recently, Army students have already utilised BAeA's facility for their basic flying training. To oversee this training, a new tri-service unit will be formed at Tamworth, reporting to RAAF Training Command, and named the Australian Defence Force Basic Flying Training School (ADFBFTS). Previously, only 15 hours of Initial Flight Screening had been carried out at Tamworth for the RAAF, but the new arrangement is in keeping with the ADF's policy of reallocating resources to the 'core' roles of the three services.

It is anticipated that the facility will provide basic flight training for an average of 136 candi-dates annually, with course No. 1 commencing on 1 January 1999 and comprising solely Army students. The second course will have both Army and Navy students, and the first RAAF candidate is not due until the start of the third course in June. To achieve these goals, 22 CT-4Bs and three CAP 10s will be on strength at Tamworth by the end of February 1999. Upon the successful completion of initial training, the RAAF pilot candidate will then pass to No. 2 FTS for further instruction on the Australian-assembled Pilatus PC-9/A before posting to an operational squadron. Army candidates pass directly to the

Above and below: The Caribou remains an effective tactical airlifter, with LAPES capability and NVG compatibility all maintained by the RAAF. Its elderly airframe and engines are now too expensive to operate, and a modern replacement must be found.

ove: The Boeing 707 has a
al role to play in the RAAF
a tanker/transport. The
r HDU-capable aircraft of
. 33 Sqn are now
nsitioning to this overall
y camouflage scheme.

Below: The RAAF's single VIP-dedicated 707 is increasingly falling foul of noise restrictions at many international airports. As a result, its replacement has become a matter of urgency.

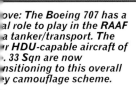

ove: The Falcon 900s of
. 34 Squadron are another
e slated for replacement.
e RAAF is now conducting
otly-contested competition
find a new long-range twin-
gined business jet.

Right: The 707 tankers are hampered by their lack of a refuelling boom, making them incompatible with the F-111s. Their replacement will be a combined boom/HDU-capable aircraft.

ove: The grey paint and sharks-
uth of this Pilatus PC-9/A mark
s one of the FAC-dedicated
raft of No. 77 Sqn.

Right: The RAAF's aerobatic team, the 'Roulettes', is drawn from the Central Flying School, at East Sale. All Training Command PC-9/As now wear the basic red and white scheme of the 'Roulettes'.

Australian Defence Force Helicopter School for rotary-wing training, and the progression of RAN students is currently under review.

Now that the CAC-built MB-326H has been withdrawn from the training role, the PC-9/A is the sole type in Air Force markings used for pilot training, operating with both the No. 2 FTS and the Central Flying School (CFS) at East Sale. The latter provides training for instructors, as well as overseeing the Initial Flying Training at Tamworth, and also provides pilots and aircraft for the RAAF's aerobatic team, the 'Roulettes'.

Initial PC-9/A deliveries to the Central Flying School were in the standard orange and white trainer scheme, but this was soon changed to a red and white scheme in order to provide a better canvas for the application of 'Roulettes' markings (all CFS aircraft carry 'Roulettes' marks to ease maintenance). Aircraft are regularly swapped between 2 FTS and the CFS, so, to avoid expensive painting bills, all aircraft are in the process of being repainted in the red and white scheme.

The School of Air Navigation, also located at East Sale, is responsible for the training of navigators for both the RAAF and RNZAF, and to this end utilises the HS.748 and leased civilian Super King Airs of the co-located No. 32 Sqn. As a result of the operational cost review, the days of the latter type appear to be numbered. The introduction of the King Air in 1997 provided a revolution in navigator training, for it was better able to replicate the fast-jet (F-111) environment, as the pupil sits in the right-hand cockpit seat and not at a console. Initial results also seem to indicate that the pupil becomes more confident at an earlier stage of his training, through being seated beside the pilot.

The RAAF School of Technical Training (RSTT) at Wagga Wagga in NSW trains maintenance personnel, and utilises retired airframes such as the Macchi, CT-4 and Mirage III.

Since the loss of the helicopter fleet to the Army in the late 1980s (and the realisation that the AS 350B was not up to the task, anyway), the RAAF has had to rely on civilian contract helicopters to provide adequate search and rescue

coverage at the fast jet and PC-9 bases. Currently held by Lloyd Helicopters, the contract provides a 50-nm (57-mile; 93-km) radius SAR coverage around East Sale, Tindal and Pearce, and a 120-nm (138-mile; 222-km) radius around Williamtown. The contract, valued at A$7 million, was renewed in 1998 for another five years and provides a total of five Sikorsky S-76A+ helicopters (one at each coastal base and two at Tindal), flying 280 hours per year.

The S-76 is well regarded, having full IFR capability, with a minor avionics upgrade to provide an auto-hover feature, coupled with a reasonably fast (155 kt; 178 mph; 286 km/h) cruise speed.

Royal Australian Air Force (RAAF)

Headquarters Air Command, Glenbrook, NSW

ARDU (Edinburgh, SA) (trials & testing)
F/A-18A, F/A-18B, PC-9/A (plus various types as required)

Strike and Reconnaissance Group, Amberley, Qld
No. 82 Wing Amberley, Qld
| No. 1 Sqn | Amberley | F-111C, RF-111C | strike/reconnaissance |
| No. 6 Sqn | Amberley | F-111C, F-111G | strike/training |

Maritime Patrol Group, Edinburgh, SA
No. 92 Wing Edinburgh SA (Butterworth Det)
No. 10 Sqn	Edinburgh	P-3C*, TAP-3	maritime patrol
No. 11 Sqn	Edinburgh	P-3C*, TAP-3	maritime patrol
No. 292 Sqn	Edinburgh	P-3C, TAP-3 (as required)**	training

*To operate AP-3C upgrade aircraft from 1999
**Operates 10 and 11 Sqn aircraft as required

Tactical Fighter Group, Williamtown, NSW
No. 81 Wing Williamtown, NSW
No. 3 Sqn	Williamtown	F/A-18A, F/A-18B	air defence
No. 75 Sqn	Tindal	F/A-18A, F/A-18B	air defence
No. 76 Sqn	Williamtown	MB-326H*	fleet co-operation, close air support, introductory fighter training
No. 77 Sqn	Williamtown	F/A-18A, F/A-18B, PC-9/A	close air support, FAC
No. 79 Sqn	Pearce	MB-326H*	fleet co-operation, close air support, introductory fighter training
No. 2 OCU	Williamtown	F/A-18A, F/A-18B	Hornet conversion/training

*To be replaced by Hawk Mk 127 commencing 2000

Surveillance and Control Group
No. 41 Wing, Williamtown, NSW (radar units)
No. 1 RSU	Alice Springs*		Jindalee OTHRN
No. 2 CRU	Darwin**		control & reporting unit
No. 3 CRU	Williamtown		control & reporting unit
No. 114 MCRU	Tindal***		mobile control & reporting unit

*Relocating to Edinburgh by July 1999. Will move to No. 42 Wing
**To relocate to Tindal by 2001   ***To relocate to Darwin by 2001

No. 42 Wing, Williamtown
| No. 2 Sqn | Williamtown, Tindal (det) | | 'Wedgetail' |
| No. 1 RSU | Edinburgh | | Jindalee OTHRN |

Air Lift Group, Richmond, NSW
No. 84 Wing Richmond
No. 32 Sqn	East Sale	HS.748, B200 Super King Air	navigator training, transport support
No. 33 Sqn	Richmond	707	strategic and VIP transport, AAR
No. 34 Sqn	Fairbairn	Falcon	special purpose (VIP) ransport

No. 86 Wing Richmond, NSW
No. 35 Sqn	Townsville (Darwin det)	DHC-4A	tactical transport
No. 36 Sqn	Richmond	C-130H*	tactical airlift
No. 37 Sqn	Richmond	C-130H*	strategic airlift
No. 38 Sqn	Amberley (Pearce det)	DHC-4A	tactical transport, training and conversion

Headquarters Training Command, Williams (Laverton), Vic
ADFBFTS	Tamworth	CT-4B, CAP 10*	basic flight training
CFS ('Roulettes')	East Sale	PC-9/A	standards, instructor training
2 FTS	Pearce	PC-9/A	advanced training
SAN	East Sale	HS.748, B200 Super King Air**	navigator training
RSTT	Wagga Wagga	various	technical training

*Operated by BAe Flight Training Australia on behalf of the ADF
**Operated by 32 Sqn on behalf of SAN as required

In addition to the auto-hover capability, the helicopters are modified with a rescue winch on the starboard side, and a Nite-Sun searchlight to port. All five aircraft will be re-engined with the Turboméca Arriel 2S2 engine to improve their 'hot-and-high' performance, becoming known as the S-76A++ in the process.

Although kept at constant readiness during flying operations, the aircraft have also carried out work in support of the Australian Maritime Search and Rescue Co-ordination Centre (AUSSAR), rescuing stranded yachtsmen and fishermen from some of the more treacherous stretches of Australia's immense and varied coastline.

Royal Australian Navy – Fleet Air Arm

The Fleet Air Arm of the RAN has an establishment of three flying squadrons, with various types of helicopters and two fixed-wing HS.748s. Another squadron is due to form at the end of this year to operate the Kaman Super Seasprite and, to maintain the same number of units, two existing squadrons will merge at that time. These squadrons report directly to the Maritime Commander Australia at Naval Headquarters in Sydney.

As with the RAAF, much of the Navy's equipment is in the process of being upgraded, new helicopter-capable ships are entering service, and aviation facilities are undergoing a significant rebuilding programme. A new helicopter servicing facility has been built at HMAS *Stirling* in Western Australia, to provide a shore base for Fleet Base West ships' flights. Although too small to be a naval air station in its own right, this facility is well equipped and is capable of housing either two spread, or four folded, Sea Kings.

HMAS *Albatross*, south of Nowra on the New South Wales coast, remains the main shore base for Fleet Air Arm units, and is due for major

upgrade work in the near future. Among a host of other improvements, this upgrade will provide a new hangar for the Seasprite and Seahawks of 805 and 816 Sqns (20 aircraft), a new control tower and improved airfield lighting, and shelters for the flight line of No. 2 Sqn RNZAF.

Although not an aircraft operating unit in its own right (and not above the squadrons in the FAA order of battle), a significant new organisation was formed in the mid-1990s as the senior aviation operations and policy advisor for Maritime Command. Named Commander Australian Naval Aviation Force (COMAUSNAVAIR), this section currently occupies space in the control tower at Nowra, and is responsible for oversight and management of the Maritime Command elements of the Fleet Air Arm (airworthiness, flying and safety standards). COMAUSNAVAIR also provides strategic aviation policy advice for the Deputy Chief of the Navy, aviation logistics policy advice for the Support Commander – Air Force, and aircrew training requirements advice to the Commander Training Navy.

The arrival of the Super Seasprite/Penguin combination will bring a formidable surface-strike capability. A new Squadron (No. 805) will be formed to operate the type, primarily from the decks of the eight 'Anzac'-class (Meko 200) ships now entering service. The RAN's three DDGs (USN 'Charles F. Adams' class) are due for replacement (under the auspices of Project Sea 1400), and in 1998 the United States Navy offered to transfer the four 'Kidd'-class destroyers to the RAN for a mere A$30 million each. After consideration, and perhaps in light of lessons learned with the second-hand purchase of the two 'Kanimbla'-class (US 'Newport'-class) LPAs (which have required far more work than originally forecast), the offer was declined. It remains to be seen when the Navy will acquire a new class of helicopter-capable ship.

Of the current fleet, the six 'Adelaide'-class FFGs (US 'Perry' class) are to begin a A$1 billion midlife upgrade that will include a new fire-control radar, short-range 3D radar, combat data system, hull-mounted ASW sonar, mine avoidance sonar,

*Right: This PC-9/A wears
the fin badge of No. 2
FTS, the RAAF's
advanced training unit.*

*Below: Leased civil-
registered Super King
Airs operate with the
School of Air Navigation.*

*Above: The SAN HS.748s also provide a useful light transport
capability, a role most often undertaken when acting as a
support aircraft for the 'Roulettes' aerobatic team.*

Two important elements of current RAAF operations are
handled by private contractors. Primary training is conducted
on CT-4Bs (above) and CAP 10s operated by BAe Flight
Training Australia. Base SAR flights are the responsibility of
Lloyd Helicopters and its Sikorsky S-76s (below).

The Aircraft Research and Development Unit is the RAAF's operational test and trials
establishment. It also undertakes the same tasks for the AAAC. Today, it is chiefly equipped
with F/A-18s (above) and PC-9/As, with a few Army helicopters such as this UH-1H (left) on
permanent detachment. ARDU was the last RAAF unit to operate the C-47 (below), which the
unit found impossible to replace. In 1998 this aircraft was decorated with '50 years young'
titles. The ARDU C-47s have now been retired, but not withdrawn, and they await a decision
on their replacement type or types.

*The S-70B-2 Seahawks of the Fleet Air Arm's HS816 are the
most advanced types in the RAN's airborne inventory. They
have a mission fit which is a hybrid of the US Navy SH-60B
and SH-60F. For the squadron's 50th anniversary in 1998 two
Seahawks were painted in this special tiger scheme (right).*

and possibly an eight-cell VLS system for the Evolved Sea Sparrow missile. The first few 'Anzac' frigates will undergo a Warfighting Improvement Programme as they are currently rather austerely equipped, built under the 'for, but without' principle. This programme (Sea 1443) will aim to provide an anti-ship missile defence capability, and air defence enhancements.

In 1998 the final examples of the ASTA (GAF) Jindivik RPV were retired from the Jervis Bay Range Facility (JBRF). This aircraft has now been replaced by the Tracor MQM-107E Kalkara.

Although not part of the Navy's order of battle, two civil companies operate in support of the RAN. The first is Pel-Air Aviation, which took over the fleet support contract from the aptly-named Fleet Support company in 1996. Based at Nowra, Pel-Air operates four Learjet 35A/36/36A and two IAI Westwind I aircraft on target-towing and low-level threat simulation duties. Recently, the majority of flying hours has been in support of the RAAF and Army, engaged in such duties as air defence controller training, threat simulation for the Hornet force, radar weapons system trials and calibration – target-towing is no longer a major role. One of the Learjets has operated with the Aircraft Research and Development Unit (ARDU) at Edinburgh in South Australia, trialling a Generic Airborne Threat Simulation (GTS) pod, produced by Vision Abell of Adelaide. This pod has a radar installed in the nose, and can be used to replicate various types of sea-skimming missiles.

The second company, the LADS Corporation, operates a single example of the DHC-8-202 (in turn leased from National Jet Systems) on laser aerial depth sounding (hydrography) work. The Dash 8 is equipped with what is known as the LADS Mk II system, an earlier standard of equipment (LADS Mk I) also being utilised aboard a Fokker F27-500 based in Cairns.

Prospective naval pilots carry out initial screening and basic flight training at the British Aerospace Australia Flight Training Centre at Tamworth in NSW, then pass to Pearce in Western Australia for advanced flying training with No. 2 FTS RAAF. The candidate then travels to the Australian Defence Force Helicopter School (ADFHS) at RAAF Fairbairn to begin rotary-wing training on the AS 350BA. Once this is completed, the candidate reports to HC723 at Nowra, again flying the AS 350BA, to learn the specifics of naval helicopter operations. This progression is under review, and it is likely that future Navy pilots will pass directly to the ADFHS after completion of their basic flying training, thus bypassing the advanced fixed-wing syllabus at Pearce.

HC723

The only RAN squadron to operate more than one type of aircraft, HC723 is due to merge with HS817 before 2000. This is to maintain the currently budgeted establishment of three flying squadrons once the Super Seasprite enters service and 805 Squadron is raised. HC723 operates the Navy's only fixed-wing aircraft, two Hawker Siddeley HS.748s. They have been modified to perform an electronic warfare training role for the fleet, though only one EW kit has been procured (both aircraft are rotated through the role as flying hours and maintenance requirements dictate, being referred to as either 'clean' or 'dirty'). With

the likely retirement of the HS.748 from RAAF service, and a study underway to determine the suitability of the EW role being contracted to civilian operators, the two Navy aircraft face an uncertain future.

All six examples of the Aérospatiale AS 350B Ecureuil (known as the 'Squirrel' in the ADF) procured in the mid-1980s remain on squadron strength, and all have now been modified to AS 350BA standard. It is this modification that has seen the aircraft withdrawn from sea-going operations, as it was found that the aircraft now has inadequate control authority if hydraulic power is lost or switched off at high operating weights (discovered after the crash of an ADFHS example). The aircraft will be cleared for ship-board operations again if and when a duplex hydraulic system is fitted, though there are no plans to do so.

The withdrawal of the Squirrel from sea-going duties has meant that two more CAC-built Bell Kiowas have had to be procured from the Army, to provide the 'Anzac'-class ships with an interim helicopter until the arrival of the SH-2G(A). Five Kiowas are on squadron strength, including the two ex-Army machines, and there are no plans to retire the aircraft in the foreseeable future.

HC723 provides the continuation training of pilots once they have passed through the BAe Flying College at Tamworth and the ADF Helicopter School (ADFHS) at Fairbairn, as well as the aforementioned duties of providing helicopters for the 'Anzac' ships (as a detachment of the squadron, as opposed to the ship's flight model of HS816). When the unit merges with HS817, it will create what will be (by far) the largest squadron in the Navy, with 20 aircraft of four different types on strength.

HS816

Using the Sikorsky S-70B-2 Seahawk, HS816 has the primary roles of anti-submarine warfare (ASW) and anti-surface surveillance and targeting (ASTT). Secondary roles include SAR, medevac, troop transport and (Seahawk) aircrew and maintainer training. The Seahawk is well liked on the squadron and, despite initial systems integration problems, has matured into a very capable weapons system. It is reported that other navies are only now fielding comparable systems, and an impending mid-life upgrade will ensure that this high level of capability continues.

Under the auspices of Project Sea 1405 (Phases 1 and 2), the aircraft will receive a Hughes AAQ-27 FLIR, and ESM (chaff and flare dispenser), fully integrated into the weapons system. These two phases have been funded and work will commence shortly; Phase 3 (the mid-life upgrade) is now in the capability definition stage.

Another project, Sea 1431 (already approved and funded), will reactivate the four attrition airframes. In the past, only 12 of the 16 helicopters have been used at any one time, the balance held in rotational storage with the Naval Air Logistics Management Section (NALMS, formerly NALO).

Although shore-based at Nowra, the squadron supplies aircraft, aircrew and maintainers to the FFGs. The RAN has six such ships, and the Seahawk cadre operates as the ship's flight during detachment. The RAN has found that this system is better for integration than the USN detachment model, and maintainers tend to remain with the ship, even during the refit cycle.

RAN aircraft are operated with a crew of three: pilot, tactical co-ordinator (TACCO) – front left seat, and sensor operator (SENSO) in the cabin.

The main weapon is the Mk 46 torpedo, though the Mk 11 depth charge (a shallow water weapon) is currently undergoing carriage and release trials. The aircraft is Penguin-capable, and it is anticipated that, post-MLU, the Seahawk will be so-equipped. A GPMG can be fitted in the cabin, and is operated if required by the SENSO, who routinely train to operate this weapon.

With the removal some years ago of the dipping sonar gear from the Sea Kings of HS817, the RAN has been without such a capability, as the Seahawk is not fitted with such a system. The airframes are structurally similar to the USN SH-60F, however, and a dipping sonar could be fitted if necessary. The most likely addition to the helicopter's suite of sensors, though, will be a low frequency sonobuoy. Aircrew are very pleased with the performance of the MEL Super Searcher radar, and were able to cover the entire Gulf of Oman in a single sortie during deployments to that region. It was found that the Seahawk/Ecureuil mix deployed aboard the FFGs sent to the Persian Gulf made a good team: the Seahawk acted almost as a heliborne AWACS, sending the lighter helicopter to investigate contacts.

Planned retirement of the aircraft is due between 2020 and 2025, and the highest-time airframe has only just passed 2,000 hours. The RAN is in the envious position of being able to watch the ageing USN SH-60 fleet to gain prior warning of any developing fatigue problems.

HS817

Despite being replaced in the anti-submarine role by the Seahawk, and the removal of dipping sonar from its Sea Kings in 1993, the squadron is still officially known as HS817. It currently operates seven Westland Sea Kings in the maritime utility role, and provides a ship's flight for HMAS *Success* (the fleet replenishment ship) as well as detachments for HMAS *Tobruk* and the ex-USN LPAs HMAS *Kanimbla* and *Manoora* (soon to enter service). HS817 retains a limited ASW and surface search capability via its original radar and crutches for two Mk 46 torpedoes or depth charges.

All its Sea Kings have now completed the Life Of Type Extension (LOTE) modifications that added new communications (including HF), an RNS252 navigation system (Doppler only), and new signal processor and displays for the existing ARI 5995 radar; the only externally visible components of the LOTE upgrade are the addition of engine air intake filter boxes, and a step beneath the cabin door. The LOTE programme was carried out by GKN Westland, which sub-contracted the work to British Aerospace Australia.

Seven LOTE kits were purchased, with the aim of upgrading the seven surviving Sea King Mk 50/50As, but before work could begin one aircraft was lost in a forced landing near Bamaga in the far north of Queensland. To make good this loss, an ex-RN attrition replacement was purchased, so the original Australian machines are now known as Mk 50A and the ex-British example (N16-918, ex-XZ918) as Mk 50B.

A decision on which service (and which type) will fulfil the ADF's newly created amphibious role is eagerly awaited, and if awarded to HS817 would see the purchase of more second-hand Sea

To provide suppressive fire the Seahawks can carry a 7.62-mm machine-gun in the rear cabin (left). To date, no Seahawks (right) have been lost in 10 years of demanding operations, and 816 Sqn is rightly proud of this accomplishment.

arly 1999 only two **HS817 Sea Kings** remained in the old eme (above) as the rest of the fleet had moved to the new all grey scheme. **RAN Sea Kings** are virtually all Mk 50As ow) with a single **Mk 50B** (right) acquired as an attrition acement. There is no difference between the two variants.

723 operates six **AS 350BA Squirrels** (right) which are now pletely shore-based. They are tasked largely with tinuation training for RAN pilots. In recent times several irrels have been decorated with cartoon mascots, uding **The Simpson's** Barney Gumble (above) – a great model for all aviators.

JetRanger has many names in Australia. The Bell Model B-1 was built under licence as the CA-32. Given the official e Kalkadoon (which is never used) they are always rred to as Kiowas. HC723 has five aircraft (right), uding two bailed back from the Army (above).

Kings. Such a decision is imminent, and the capability (provided by the 'new' LPAs) will either be supplied by the Army with the S-70A-9 Blackhawk, or by the RAN. HS817 is keen to point out that the Sea King is fully 'marine-ised' and has a larger cabin than the Sikorsky product which, along with the radar, would provide a superior troop lift capability.

There is no replacement in sight for the Sea King, the oldest airframe having only some 5,500 hours, or one-quarter that of some RN examples. The virtues of the type which make it well suited to use in conjunction with the Army – 6.5 hours' endurance (with extra tanks), quietness and size of the cabin – should ensure continued use in the foreseeable future.

With the exception of the *Success* Flight, the unit provides detachments to the ships it supports, and does not integrate into a ship's company as is standard in the Seahawk community.

SH-2G(A) Super Seasprite

Stemming from a 1993 requirement for a helicopter to equip both the 'Anzac'-class frigates and the (subsequently abandoned) offshore patrol combatants (OPCs), the Kaman SH-2G(A) Super Seasprite was selected in January 1997 in preference to the GKN Westland Lynx. Contract negotiations took place in the first half of 1997, with the A$662 million contract being finally signed on 26 June of that year.

Eleven ex-USN aircraft are to be delivered as operational airframes, in addition to another four that have been purchased for spares use. The latter will subsequently be repatriated to Australia to serve as training and programme studies airframes. The 11 operational aircraft are all to be rebuilt SH-2Fs, with the exception of the prototype, which is a partially complete SH-2G. As at the end of 1998, all aircraft had been retrieved from

desert storage to Kaman's Bloomfield facility to be inducted into the strip-out/pre-production line. It is planned that the first four helicopters will be wholly built in the USA, with the remaining seven (after conversion to G configuration by Kaman) being completed at Nowra.

Flight trials of the first SH-2G(A) are due to commence in August 1999, the first helicopter to be delivered to Australia in November 2000, and the operational test and evaluation phase to take place throughout 2001. To operate the type in RAN service, No. 805 Squadron will be raised in the middle of 2000, having the prime tasking of surface surveillance, followed by anti-surface warfare (ASuW), ASW, contact investigation and counter-infiltration duties, utility and training.

The Australian SH-2G(A)s will be required to operate, day or night, in weather up to Sea State 5 conditions. They will have the integrated tactical avionics system (ITAS), providing four colour MFDs with all sensor and instrument display requirements. Included in the integrated weapons system (IWS), of which ITAS is the core, are dual LN-100G INS/GPS units, ARN-147 VOR/ILS, DME-442 and ARN-149 LF/ADF and MDF-124 VHF/UHF communications units, and APX-100 IFF. Sensors, once again fully integrated through ITAS, include APS-143B(V)3 radar, AAQ-27 FLIR (optimised for operations in the high-humidity environment encountered off Australia's northern shore), and an ESM fit which includes AAR-54 missile approach warning system, and threat-adaptive Tracor ALE-47 CMDS.

The only major external changes to the airframe will be the fitting of composite main rotor blades (reportedly offering a 15,000-hour life), and a RAST haul-down secure and traverse system. The composite blades began test flying in a leased USN Seasprite in April 1998. As the RAN version is also designed to be utilised for

SAR, utility and vertical replenishment, it will be equipped with a 600-lb (272-kg) capacity rescue hoist, provision in the cabin for either two litters (with crewman) or up to five troops, and a 4,000-lb (1814-kg) capacity cargo hook.

Weapons for the Seasprites will include the Kongsberg Penguin Mk 2 Mod 7 (AGM-114B) air-to-surface missile – the primary weapon for the ASuW role – and the more common Mk 46 torpedo/Mk 11 depth charge combination, and general-purpose machine-gun.

No. 2 Squadron RNZAF

No review of the aviation assets of the RAN would be complete without mention of the A-4K Skyhawks of No. 2 Squadron, Royal New Zealand Air Force. Resident at Nowra since February 1991, the squadron provides air defence support for the both the fleet and the ADF as a whole. In this role it currently flies some 800 hours per year, in addition to providing Skyhawk conversion and operational training. The current agreement with the RAN expires in mid-2001, and it is anticipated that it will be renewed. No. 2 Squadron will transition to the F-16A/B during this period, but it will continue to fulfil its taskings as set out by the Nowra Agreement.

Royal Australian Navy Fleet Air Arm

HC723	Nowra	AS 350BA, B.206B-1 Kiowa, HS.748	
		SAR, medevac, EW training, fleet support,	
		communications, ship's flights	
		Due to be merged with HS817 by 2000	
HS816	Nowra	S-70B-2	ASW, ASTT, ship's flights, SAR,
			medevac, troop transport, training
HS817	Nowra	Sea King Mk 50A/Mk 50B	fleet utility

Note: *805 Sqn will be raised prior to 2000 to operate the SH-2G(A) in the anti-surface warfare role*

Australian Army Aviation Corps – AAAC

Responsible to the Land Commander Australia for the provision of aviation assets, the Army Aviation Corps consists of two aviation regiments and two helicopter training units. The flying arm of the Army has now largely overcome the problems created by the transfer of the battlefield support helicopter role from the RAAF in the late 1980s; the large influx of men and machinery placed the AAAC under a great deal of pressure, and it is really only now, with the Army 21 concept, that Air Corps planners can objectively develop strategies and doctrines that will take the service into the next century. Army 21 is a series of papers, trials and exercises designed to keep the service at the cutting edge of modern battlefield developments. Some of the aviation-related components of the study will experiment with the use of UAVs (a capability that Army aviation is keen to acquire), a multi-mode radar platform and multi-role aviation battalions. The acquisition of an aerial fire support (AFS) capability will bring the biggest change to the flying squadrons.

Another project with the potential for further aircraft (or, at least, air vehicle) purchases is Project JP-129, intended to provide airborne surveillance for land operations (in a similar vein to the UK's ASTOR requirement). So far, an Australian-developed synthetic aperture radar, named

Ingara, has been installed in a leased King Air 350 and is undergoing trials, and UAV capability has been simulated during exercises (most recently during Exercise Phoenix in the Northern Territory, which also saw the Ingara-equipped King Air put through its paces).

The effect of these changes on the current structure of Army aviation is yet to be decided. In the meantime, No. 1 Aviation Regiment at Oakey is to relocate to Darwin to better support the Army units that have already relocated (or are in the process of relocating) to the Northern Territory. This would leave the Army Aviation Centre at Oakey with only the School of Army Aviation (and the Super Pumas of No. 126 Sqn, RSAF) as residents. A logical step, perhaps, would see the Australian Defence Force Helicopter School (currently at Fairbairn) relocate to Oakey to make use of the facilities in place.

1st Aviation Regiment

The task of 1 Avn Regt is to provide reconnaissance and surveillance, and to this end it controls four aircraft operating units – two reconnaissance squadrons, one battlefield support and one surveillance squadron. Only the latter two are based at the regiment's Oakey headquarters,

however, the reconnaissance units being based close to the Army brigades they are required to support. Of the two reconnaissance squadrons within 1 Aviation Regiment, 161 Sqn is based at Darwin operating in support of 1 Brigade (currently in the process of relocating to the Northern Territory from Sydney), and 162 Sqn is based at Townsville's Lavarack Barracks to provide support for the co-located 3 Brigade. Both units are currently equipped with the CAC-built Bell 206B-1 Kiowa (initially to be known as the Kalkadoon, though this name never gained acceptance), and look forward to receiving the new AFS helicopter from 2003.

A Request For Proposals (RFP) for the new AFS helicopter (under the auspices of Project Air 87) was issued in April 1998, with a Request For Tender (RFT) expected in the latter part of 1999. Dedicated attack helicopter proposals such as the Agusta A 129 Scorpion, Bell AH-1Z Viper, Denel Rooivalk (known locally as the Redhawk), Eurocopter 'Aussie Tiger' and Boeing AH-64D Apache were examined. Sikorsky offered the Armed Blackhawk, or 'Battlehawk', basically a UH-60L fitted with the Rafael/Elbit Systems Toplite II Targeting Sensor System, and a Giat 20-mm turreted gun. A short-list of the Apache, Tiger and Scorpion was drawn up in April 1999.

ove: The RAN Historic Flight operates this Bell UH-1C ong with some more exotic types such as a Fairey Firefly d a Grumman Tracker.

Above and right: HC723 operates two HS.748s as EW aggressor aircraft to train air defence crews aboard ship.

Working closely with HC723 are four Learjet 35/36s of Pel-Air (left, below left and below) which undertake target towing and target simulation tasks for the RAN. Pel-Air also operates IAI Westwinds (above left).

e S-70A-9s of the Australian Army Air Corps are divided tween the two squadrons of the 5th Aviation Regiment. re, an A Squadron Blackhawk is seen undergoing a routine shdown (above), to combat the salty air at Townsville. is B Squadron aircraft (above right) is carrying extra fuel nks on the Blackhawk's ESSS pylons.

ove and right: The Blackhawk brought a new dimension in bility to the AAAC. It gave the Army a modern, flexible tical transport helicopter that will soon be complemented the Army's new combat helicopter.

Designated as an Operational Support Squadron, No. 171, flying the UH-1H Iroquois, is in the process of absorbing the gunship Iroquois of the Aerial Fire Support Troop of C Sqn/5 Avn Regt. This unit will then be used to develop the doctrine required for the operation of the new AFS helicopter, although it will not receive the new type itself. In the meantime, the fleet of Iroquois will continue to provide sterling service.

The Army's only fixed-wing squadron, No. 173 Surveillance Squadron operates a mix of Beechcraft Super King Airs and DHC Twin Otters, leased from Hawker Pacific, as a replacement for the Pilatus Turboporter and indigenous ASTA (formerly GAF) Nomad. These aircraft retain their Australian civil registrations (although each has an individual Army callsign), as it has yet to be decided if they are the best types for the job.

The Turboporters were withdrawn from use at the end of 1992 and replaced by a batch of N22/N24 Nomads that had remained, unsold, with ASTA for a decade. The Nomad (in its then form) was not up to the rigours of Army flying, and with the benefit of hindsight it may be said that the loss of the Turboporter left a void in the capabilities of 173 Sqn that was not filled until the arrival of the Twin Otters some three years later. The last of the Nomads left Oakey in the middle of 1997 for the Indonesian navy, having been prematurely retired in August 1995. The only examples remaining are a pair (one of each version) with the Museum of Army Flying, and the refurbished second prototype serving as the base gate guardian.

The pair of Twin Otters (a third example was acquired in mid-1998 as a replacement for one lost in Papua New Guinea) is detached to Darwin to provide support for NORCOM (Army Northern Command). Three Beech 200 Super King Airs provide general transportation, while a King Air 350 has been recently acquired and fitted with an Australian-developed DSTO Ingara Synthetic Aperture Radar and Westcam 16-M FLIR as part of Project JP-129 (more commonly referred to as Project Warrendi). The structural modifications to this aircraft were carried out at Bankstown by Hawker Pacific, the radar and FLIR then being installed at ARDU, RAAF Edinburgh. The first operational test of the system came during Exercise Phoenix at Katherine in September 1998. The aircraft is on a three-year lease to the Army, specifically to test these systems, and will shortly be reconfigured with an ESM system, long-range oblique photographic system and a multi-spectral scanner.

1 Aviation Regiment is due to move to Darwin in the early years of the next century, as much of the Army that it supports is now in the process of moving to the north of the country, reflecting the northern defence posture of the ADF.

5th Aviation Regiment

Formed in November 1987 to provide the Army with an organic battlefield air mobility capability (historically provided by the RAAF), 5 Avn Regt is based at RAAF Townsville and therefore close to 3 Brigade, the operational deployment force of the Australian Army. The regiment consists of a headquarters squadron, technical support squadron, and three aircraft-operating squadrons. A and B Sqns are both equipped with the Sikorsky S-70A-9 Blackhawk, but differ in their roles:

A Sqn is the training and special operations unit (operating with special forces), whereas B Sqn conducts airmobile operations and provides troop and cargo lift capacity. Both squadrons have a headquarters troop (one helicopter) and three troops of three aircraft. The third flying squadron, C Sqn, consists of a headquarters troop, and two troops each operating a different type of helicopter: the Aerial Fire Support Troop operates four gunship-capable UH-1H Iroquois, while the Medium Lift Troop flies four Boeing-Vertol CH-47D Chinooks (two more are on order).

The Iroquois is now nearing the end of its service life with 5 Avn Regt, and will be replaced in the AFS role by the Armed Reconnaissance Helicopter. It is not clear whether the ARH will have a role with 5 Avn Regt, though studies are underway as part of the Army 21 plan for the next century to trial multi-role aviation battalions. In preparation for the introduction of the new type, in December 1998 the Iroquois of C Sqn relocated to Oakey to become the AFS Troop within 171 Sqn (1 Avn Regt). This will assist in the development of the doctrine that will be required upon acceptance of the new type, as well as simplifying logistics by having the fleet at one location.

Known as 'Bushrangers' in Australian service (a term coined during the Vietnam War, when 9 Sqn first gained the capability), the Iroquois are equipped with dual 2.75-in rocket pods and dual GAU-2BA Miniguns. The four CH-47Ds currently operated are ex-RAAF CH-47C aircraft that were brought up to D model standard by Boeing in the USA after a period of storage at Amberley. Funding for the conversion of the quartet came from the sale of the remaining seven to the US Army. Two more aircraft were ordered in July 1998, for delivery in March 2000, allowing greater flexibility in the medium lift tasking.

The Chinooks wear the standard US Army drab scheme, as opposed to the specially-developed disruptive scheme of the Blackhawk, because the aircraft logistic management plan is for the Chinook to remain compatible with the US Army fleet. It is admitted, however, that the Blackhawk scheme is better suited to Australian conditions.

Much work has been done on improving the facilities at Townsville, a good example being the August 1998 commissioning of purpose-designed hangars for the Blackhawk/Chinook fleet, providing dehumidification during periods of inactivity. Due to their impending transfer, however, the Iroquois remain exposed to the salt-laden Townsville environment.

Army Training Command

Two Army helicopter units fall under the jurisdiction of Army Training Command (as opposed to the normal aviation regiment command structure) as they are pure training organisations with no operational role. The first is the (nominally) tri-service Australian Defence Force Helicopter School at RAAF Fairbairn, which introduces Army and Navy students (the RAAF no longer operates helicopters) who have graduated from the BAeA Flying College at Tamworth to helicopter flying. The unit also trains loadmasters for the Army, and both pilots and loadmasters for the Papua New Guinea Defence Force (PNGDF). Equipped with the AS 350BA Ecureuil (Squirrel),

the unit was formed from the remains of No. 5 Sqn, RAAF when the battlefield helicopter role passed to the Army in 1990, and still uses the 'wedgetail eagle' badge of 5 Sqn on its helicopters. As a result of the recent fleet-wide Squirrel grounding (refer to RAN section for details), a brace of Kiowas operated with the ADFHS to provide for the continuation of airmanship skills for the based QFIs. With the lifting of the grounding order, the Kiowas returned to their parent units.

The second unit under the auspices of Army Training Command is the School of Army Aviation (SAA) at the Army Aviation Centre at Oakey. This unit introduces the novice helicopter pilot (and loadmaster) from the ADFHS to Army flying, before a posting to one of the aviation regiments. The stated role of the School of Army Aviation is to "conduct Australian Army Aviation Corps individual training, including the tactical employment of aviation systems and forces, and to contribute to the development of Aviation Corps doctrine". To achieve this, the unit is divided into a number of wings: an Administration Wing; a Corps and Tactics Wing that conducts promotion courses for all ranks and the training of ground crew, loadmasters, observers and pilots; an Operational Flying Training Wing that provides the necessary support to conduct aircrew transition, conversion, refresher and flying instructor standardisation courses; and an Operations Wing that provides refuelling, ground handling, etc. to ensure the availability of aircraft for the tasked operations.

The School of Army Aviation operates the Blackhawk, Iroquois and Kiowa on a permanent basis, but can also make use of No. 173 Sqn's King Air or Twin Otter aircraft as required. It is anticipated that a small number of the Aerial Fire Support helicopters will be operated by the SAA upon that type's introduction into service. With the current trend towards outsourcing of training and support, it may well be that the ADFHS role is tendered for contract in the coming years. However, given the doctrinal aspect of the SAA's role within Army Aviation, this unit's future seems assured.

Australian Army Aviation Corps (AAAC)

1 Aviation Regiment, Oakey, Qld

Regimental Headquarters, Oakey			B.206B-1

RHQ/1 Avn Regt operates a single Kiowa, maintained by 171 Sqn

161 Sqn	Darwin	B.206B	reconnaissance
162 Sqn	Townsville/Lavarack Barracks	B.206B-1	reconnaissance
171 Sqn	Oakey	UH-1H	battlefield support

171 Sqn gained AFS Troop/role from C Sqn/5 Avn Regt by 2/99

173 Sqn	Oakey (Darwin Det)	King Air, Twin Otter	surveillance

5 Aviation Regiment, Townsville

A Squadron	Townsville	S-70A-9	troop lift, airmobile support, training, special forces support
B Squadron	Townsville	S-70A	troop lift, airmobile support
C Squadron	Townsville	CH-47D, UH-1H	medium lift, airmobile support, aerial fire support

C Sqn/5 Avn Regt lost AFS Troop (UH-1H) by 02/99

Army Training Command

ADFHS	Fairbairn	AS 350BA	basic rotary-wing training

May yet move base from Fairbairn but no decision taken

School of Army Aviation	Oakey	B.206B-1, S-70A-9, UH-1H	operational training

King Air and Twin Otter aircraft detached as required

ove: 161 and 162 Squadron ˙the 1st Aviation Regiment ˙erate the Army's Bell Model ˙B-1 Kiowas.

Below: This Beech Super King Air is flown by 173 Sqn, 1st Aviation Regiment, on special reconnaissance tasks.

Above: C Squadron, 5th Avn Regiment is the AAAC's CH-47D operator.

Right: AAAC Hueys are spread among several units. This is another C Squadron aircraft.

Left: The AS 350BAs of the Army's ADFHS undertake basic helicopter training.

e Nomad Searchmasters (above) of the ACS are no longer ˙service. Their place has been taken by FLIR- and search-˙Jar-equipped Dash 8s (right) and Caravan IIs.

Australian Customs Service

˙hough not part of the military, the Australian ˙istoms Service plays an important part in the ˙veillance of the country's coastline, particularly ˙ northern regions, in the war against smuggling, ˙ig running and illegal fishing. As such, it faces ˙ same problems as the ADF, that is: vast areas ˙unpopulated land, numerous remote and ˙controlled airstrips (that can be used covertly by ˙ugglers) and extensive coastline and territorial ˙ters to patrol, and (relatively) meagre resources ˙th which to carry out the job. The aircraft ˙lised by the government for this work have ˙dergone a complete change since 1994, and a ˙matic increase in capability. Like the military, ˙ Customs Service is turning to state-of-the-art ˙uipment to carry out its functions.

˙Only a single example of the GAF Nomad is in ˙, for the visual surveillance role. One Nomad is ˙Darwin, still wearing its Customs markings, but ˙ been sold (along with the others of the type) ˙ a private buyer. Many of the ex-coast watch

Aero Commander aircraft are sitting idle, with-drawn from use, at Darwin.

The airborne surveillance requirements of the Australian Customs Service are currently contracted out to a private company, Surveillance Australia – a subsidiary of the Adelaide-based National Jet Systems. Surveillance Australia provides 13 aircraft, 120 personnel and 15,000 flying hours per year in a complete, integrated service. To fulfil its con-tracted obligations, Surveillance Australia operates three different types of aircraft, with varying levels of capability, from airfields throughout northern Australia. To support these operations, bases and engineering support facilities have been established at Broome, Darwin, Cairns and Horn Island.

A trio of de Havilland Canada DHC-8-202s is flown from Broome in Western Australia, Darwin in the Northern Territory, and Cairns in Queensland in the long-range/offshore role. The aircraft are extensively equipped for the task at hand, including the provision of a Texas Instruments SV1022 sur-

veillance radar and a dual-sensor (FLIR and TV) stabilised turret under the lower forward fuselage. The Dash Eights are supported by three Reims/Cessna F406 Caravan IIs in the inshore surveillance role, also equipped with the SV1022 radar. For visual surveillance, the aforementioned Aero Commander and six examples of the Pilatus-Britten Norman BN-2B-20 Islander can be found throughout the top end of the country, as they go about their business of operating routine patrols. All aircraft are fitted with an extensive avionics and communications suite, lap-top computers and modified interiors that include observation windows.

There are no plans to introduce new aircraft, but new technology is being constantly monitored. Indigenous technology such as the DSTO Ingara synthetic aperture radar, currently undergoing trials with the Australian Army to meet its battle-field surveillance requirements, may find a new application aboard Surveillance Australia's aircraft in the years to come.

INDEX

158

INDEX

Picture acknowledgments

Front cover: Lockheed Martin. **4:** Jos Schoofs (two). **5:** J. Spacek (two). **6:** Frederic Lert (six). **7:** Jack L. Bosma, Ton van Dreumel. **8:** Sgt Jack Pritchard/DPR RAF, Darron Hall, Peter R. Foster. **9:** Peter R. Foster (three), Shlomo Aloni. **10:** Alan Key (two). **11:** Derek Bower, Pushpindar Singh. **12:** Nigel Pittaway (four), Richard Siudak via Nigel Pittaway. **13:** Nigel Pittaway (five), Richard Siudak via Nigel Pittaway. **14:** US Navy, Bill Crimmins. **15:** Lockheed Martin. **16:** KLu, Canadian Forces. **17:** Christian Gerard, USAF, Gert Kromhout. **18:** Tim Ripley, Gert Kromhout, US Navy. **19:** David Donald, Stuart Lewis (two), Dylan Eklund (two). **20:** Gert Kromhout (three). **21:** Luigino Caliaro, Christian Gerard, Dylan Eklund, Aerospace, Gert Kromhout (two). **22:** USAF, E. Strobl (two). **23:** Gert Kromhout (four). **24:** Gert Kromhout (two), Blue Forces, Tim Ripley. **25:** E. Strobl, Cpl John Cassidy/Strike Command (two), Tim Ripley, Chris Ryan. **26:** Canadian Forces, Tom Spencer, Tim Ripley. **27:** AMI, Luigino Caliaro. **28:** USAF (two), Gert Kromhout. **29:** USAF, Gert Kromhout (two). **30-34:** US DoD. **35:** Sgt Jack Pritchard/DPR RAF, David Donald, Kevin Storer via Peter R. March (two). **39-40:** Kawasaki, Yoshitomo Aoki. **42:** Yoshitomo Aoki (two). **43:** Yoshitomo Aoki (two), Peter R. Foster. **44:** Kawasaki, Yoshitomo Aoki. **45:** Kawasaki (two). **46-53:** Gert Kromhout. **54-55:** Boeing. **56-57:** Lockheed Martin. **58:** US DoD, Lockheed Martin, Bill Sweetman. **59:** Lockheed Martin, US DoD. **60-63:** Lockheed Martin. **64:** Northrop (two). **65:** Bill Sweetman, Northrop. **66:** AFFTC via Terry Panopalis, Lockheed Martin. **67:** AFFTC via Terry Panopalis. **68:** AFFTC via Terry Panopalis (two). **69:** Lockheed Martin. **70:** Pratt & Whitney via Bill Sweetman, Pratt & Whitney. **72:** Boeing (two), Bill Crimmins (three). **75-76:** Lockheed Martin. **77:** AFFTC via Terry Panopalis, Lockheed Martin. **78:** Lockheed Martin. **79:** AFFTC via Terry Panopalis. **80:** Lockheed Martin (two). **81:** Lockheed Martin via Terry Panopalis. **82:** AFFTC via Terry Panopalis, Lockheed Martin. **83:** AFFTC via Terry Panopalis. **84-87:** Lockheed Martin. **88:** Luigino Caliaro

(two), José Terol. **89:** Luigino Caliaro. **90:** José Terol, Luigino Caliaro (three). **91:** José Terol, Luigino Caliaro (three). **92:** Luigino Caliaro (three), José Terol. **93:** Luigino Caliaro, José Terol (three). **94:** Luigino Caliaro (four), José Terol. **95:** José Terol (two), Luigino Caliaro. **96:** José Terol (three), Luigino Caliaro (two). **97:** Luigino Caliaro (two), José Terol (three). **98:** Patrick Allen. **99:** Boeing (two), via Terry Panopalis, US Army. **100:** US Army, Boeing (two), Robert Hewson. **101:** Boeing, US Army, Paul Jackson. **102:** Craig Kaston, Australian MoD. **103:** Craig P. Justo/Aero Aspects (two), Australian MoD (two). **104:** Boeing (two). **105:** Ted Carlson/Fotodynamics (two). **106:** Aerospace, Gianandrea Gaiani, Atsushi Tsubota. **107:** Boeing, Patrick Allen, Pacemaker Press. **108:** Boeing, Tim Ripley, GIAT Industries, Patrick Allen. **109:** Patrick Allen. **110:** Patrick Allen, David Donald. **111:** Patrick Allen, David Donald. **112:** Boeing (two), US Army. **113:** Boeing (four), Robert E. Kling. **114:** Boeing (two), Don Logan. **115:** Craig Kaston, Boeing (two), B. MacArthur. **116:** Craig P. Justo/Aero Aspects, Boeing (two), Dick Lohuis, Terry Panopalis (two), Canadian Forces, Craig Kaston, Anthony D. Chong. **117:** Boeing, David Donald, Arnaud Boxman/Kees van der Mark. **118:** Boeing (two), Charles T. Robbins, E.D. Sewell via Robert F. Dorr. **119:** Patrick Allen (two), Alan Key, Craig P. Justo/Aero Aspects, Peter R. Foster. **120:** Boeing (two), Carl L. Richards. **121:** Terry Panopalis, Boeing. **122-123:** Boeing. **124:** Roberto Yañez, Robert F. Dorr, Patrick Allen. **125:** Patrick Allen (two). **1** Patrick Allen (two), Tim Senior. **127:** Patrick Allen (five), Yoshitomo Aoki. **128:** Kawasaki, Yoshitomo Aoki, Satoshi Akatsuka. **129:** Gianandrea Gaiani, Agusta (four), Aldo Ciarini via Paul Jackson. **130-139:** Ted Carlson/Fotodynamics. **141:** RAAF PR via Nigel Pittaway (two), Robert Hewson (two), RA PR. **143:** Nigel Pittaway (six), Robert Hewson, 81 Wing via Nigel Pittaway, RAAF Tindal via Nigel Pittaway. **145:** RAAF PR via Nigel Pittaway, Nigel Pittaway (two), 81 Wing via Nigel Pittaway, Robert Hewson (two) David Donald, 92 Wing via Nigel Pittaway. **147:** Nigel Pittaway (two), 92 Wing via Nigel Pittaway, Robert Hewson, 86 Wing via Nigel Pittaway. **149:** Robert Hewson, RAAF PR via Nigel Pittaway (two), Nigel Pittaway (five). **151:** Nigel Pittaway (six), RAAF PR via Nigel Pittaway (three), Robert Hewson. **153:** Nigel Pittaway (nine). **155:** Nigel Pittaway (five), Robert Hewson (two), David Donald (three), DoD EMU via Nigel Pittaway. **157:** Nigel Pittaway (seven).